This book is dedicated to:
    Richard
    Jessica
    Jonathan

*"The joys and sorrows of parenthood are silent."*

# CONTENTS IN BRIEF

Contents in Detail  v
Preface  xi

Part One

## BACK TO BASICS 1

Chapter One
### UNDERSTANDING WHAT YOU READ: A REVIEW 2

Chapter Two
### GETTING THE MOST OUT OF YOUR TEXTBOOKS: A REVIEW 50

Part Two

## DEALING WITH COMPLEXITY 105

Chapter Three
### CRITICAL THINKING AND CONTEMPORARY ISSUES 106

Chapter Four
### BASIC PROBLEM SOLVING 168

Part Three

## CRITICAL READING: EVALUATING WHAT YOU READ 221

Chapter Five
### USING INFERENCE 222

Chapter Six
### DISTINGUISHING BETWEEN FACTS AND OPINIONS 250

Chapter Seven
### RECOGNIZING PURPOSE AND TONE 274

Chapter Eight
### LOOKING AT ADVERTISEMENTS WITH A CRITICAL EYE 318

Glossary  375
Credits  377
Index  379

# CRITICAL READING, CRITICAL THINKING

## A Contemporary Issues Approach

**RICHARD PIROZZI**

PASSAIC COUNTY COMMUNITY COLLEGE

**LONGMAN**

An imprint of Addison Wesley Longman, Inc.

New York • Reading, Massachusetts • Menlo Park, California • Harlow, England
Don Mills, Ontario • Sydney • Mexico City • Madrid • Amsterdam

Editor in Chief: Richard Wohl
Acquisitions Editor: Steven Rigolosi
Marketing Manager: Melanie Goulet
Supplements Editor: Donna Campion
Project Manager: Ellen MacElree
Design Manager: John Callahan
Cover Designer: Kay Petronio
Art Studio: ElectraGraphics, Inc.
Technical Desktop Manager: Heather A. Peres
Electronic Production Specialist: Sarah Johnson
Electronic Page Makeup: Dorothy Bungert/*EriBen Graphics*
Printer and Binder: Von Hoffman Graphics
Cover Printer: Coral Graphic Services, Inc.

For permission to use copyrighted material, grateful acknowledgment is made to the copyright holders on pp. 377–380, which are hereby made part of the copyright page.

Please visit our website at http://www.awlonline.com

ISBN 0-321-00331-4

12345678910—VH-0302010099

# CONTENTS IN DETAIL

Preface  xi

## Part One
## BACK TO BASICS  1

### Chapter One
### UNDERSTANDING WHAT YOU READ: A REVIEW  2

Think About It!  3

Determining the Meanings of Key Terms in Context  4
  Punctuation  5
  Synonyms  6
  Antonyms  6
  Examples  7
  General Sentence Clues  7

Distinguishing Main Ideas, Major Details, and Minor Details  11
  Unstated Main Ideas  13

Recognizing Patterns of Organization  18
  Simple Listing of Facts  18
  Time Sequence  20
  Comparison and Contrast  21
  Cause and Effect  22

Uncovering the Central Message of a Longer Selection  28

Looking Back  35

Think Again! And Again!  35

Mastery Test 1  38

### Chapter Two
### GETTING THE MOST OUT OF YOUR TEXTBOOKS: A REVIEW  50

Think About It!  51

Overviewing Your Textbooks  52

Previewing Textbook Chapters  73

Reading a Textbook Chapter Critically: Questions and Answers 75

Looking Back 92

Think Again! 92

Mastery Test 2 94

Playing Sherlock Holmes and Dr. Watson 100

## Part Two

# DEALING WITH COMPLEXITY 105

### Chapter Three
# CRITICAL THINKING AND CONTEMPORARY ISSUES 106

Think About It! 107

Critical Thinking Versus Random Thinking 108

Benefits of Critical Thinking 109

Characteristics of Critical Thinking 109

*Flexibility 110*

*Clear Purpose 112*

*Organization 114*

*Time and Effort 114*

*Asking Questions and Finding Answers 114*

*Research 120*

A Word Of Caution When Using the Internet For Research 121

*Coming to Logical Conclusions 136*

What Is a Contemporary Issue? 139

*Determining What Is at Issue 141*

*Distinguishing Among Opposing Viewpoints 142*

*Expressing a Personal Viewpoint 143*

Looking Back 159

Think Again! 159

Mastery Test 3 160

### Chapter Four
# BASIC PROBLEM SOLVING 168

Think About It! 169

Problem-Solving Exercise 170

What Is a Problem? 170

What Is a Solution? 171

How Do You Solve Problems? 172

Problem Solving and Critical Thinking 172

A Basic Method for Personal Problem Solving 172

   *Step 1: Identifying the Problem 173*

   *Step 2: Gathering Information and Determining If the Problem Can Be Broken Down 173*

   *Step 3: Thinking About Possible Solutions and Weighing the Advantages and Disadvantages of Each 174*

   *Step 4: Choosing a Possible Solution 175*

   *Step 5: Checking Back on the Problem and the Possible Solution 176*

Applying the Method to a Typical Problem Situation 176

Looking Back 210

Think Again! 210

Mastery Test 4 211

Playing Holmes and Watson 216

Part Three

# CRITICAL READING: EVALUATING WHAT YOU READ 221

Chapter Five
# USING INFERENCE 222

Think About It! 223

Problem-Solving Exercise 225

What Is Critical Reading? 225

Drawing Inferences 226

   *Using Knowledge to Infer 227*

   *Using Experience to Infer 228*

   *Using Clues to Infer 229*

Looking at the World with a Questioning Mind 231

Using Inferences with Contemporary Issues and Problem Solving 231

Looking Back 244

Think Again! 244

Mastery Test 5 245

Chapter Six

## DISTINGUISHING BETWEEN FACTS AND OPINIONS 250

Think About It!  251

Problem-Solving Exercise  252

Why Distinguish Between Facts and Opinions?  252

What Is a Fact?  254

What Is an Opinion?  255

Facts and Opinions in Combination  256

Relating Facts and Opinions to Problem Solving
and Contemporary Issues  256

Looking Back  267

Think Again!  268

Mastery Test 6  269

Chapter Seven

## RECOGNIZING PURPOSE AND TONE 274

Think About It!  275

Problem-Solving Exercise  276

The Importance of Recognizing Purpose  276

*To Inform 277*

*To Persuade 280*

*To Entertain 282*

*Combination of Purposes 283*

The Importance of Recognizing Tone  293

*Matter-of-Fact Tone 294*

*Humorous Tone 294*

*Angry Tone 295*

*Sad Tone 296*

*Ironic Tone 296*

Looking Back  305

Think Again!  306

Mastery Test 7  307

Chapter Eight

## LOOKING AT ADVERTISEMENTS WITH A CRITICAL EYE 318

Think About It!  319

Problem-Solving Exercise  320

Advertisements and Critical Thinking  321

Evaluating an Advertisement  322

   *How Does It Try to Catch the Interest of Readers?  322*

   *To Whom Is It Designed to Appeal?  322*

   *What Is It Trying to Persuade Readers to Buy, Do, or Think?  323*

   *What Benefit to Readers Is It Stressing?  325*

   *How Convincing Is It?  327*

Looking Back  354

Think Again!  354

Mastery Test 8  357

Playing Holmes and Watson  372

Holmes and Watson to the Rescue One Last Time  372

*Glossary  375*
*Credits  377*
*Index  379*

# PREFACE

From the earliest stages of planning this textbook, my objective has remained the same: to write a critical reading and thinking text that is interesting, relevant, and fun for both instructors and students. To accomplish that goal, I focus on contemporary issues and problem solving to teach critical reading and critical thinking skills. My underlying assumption is that students will enjoy reading, thinking, writing, and talking about hypothetical problems and a wide variety of important issues of the day.

The result is *Critical Reading, Critical Thinking*, which is best described as an advanced developmental textbook-reader for students taking introductory college-level courses. It tries to relate reading, thinking, and writing skills to personal situations and contemporary issues.

## Organization

For reinforcement purposes, *Critical Reading, Critical Thinking* begins with two chapters in Part One, Back to Basics, that provide a condensed review of basic and textbook reading skills for students who need to brush up on them. Part Two, Dealing with Complexity, which is the heart of the text, is composed of two chapters that present the approaches to contemporary issues and basic problem solving that are used throughout the remainder of the book. Finally, the four chapters in Part Three, Critical Reading: Evaluating What You Read, cover some of the more advanced critical reading skills, including using inference, distinguishing between facts and opinions, recognizing purpose and tone, and looking at advertisements with a critical eye.

## Features

Each chapter starts with a "Think About It!" feature, which presents photographs for discussion, and ends with a "Think Again!" feature, which calls for student reactions to puzzles, problems, or quotations. I hope that readers will find these sections stimulating, enjoyable, and thought-provoking, putting them in the mood to think critically.

Chapter outlines and outcomes keep students informed as to where they are going and what they are supposed to accomplish along the way. A "Looking Back" exercise at the end of each chapter asks students to collaborate in order to list the most important points they learned in the chapter and determine how these insights can be put to use in their courses. Finally, every chapter ends with a "Mastery Test" that can be completed by students, removed from the textbook, and handed in to the instructor for grading purposes.

## Book-Specific Ancillaries

An *Instructor's Manual* (0-321-04456-8), with suggestions and answers to the activities, is available and should prove useful to instructors. Many of the suggested answers can serve as guides, because the articles and textbook excerpts used for most of the activities allow for a variety of possible answers. Thus they will encourage different points of view, which should make for very interesting and lively class discussions. A *Test Bank* (0-321-05525-X) of skill questions is also available for additional testing and reinforcement.

## Other Useful Ancillaries

In addition to the book-specific supplements discussed above, a series of other skills-based supplements are available for both instructors and students. All of these supplements are available either free or at greatly reduced prices.

### For Additional Reading and Reference

*The Dictionary Deal.* Two dictionaries can be shrinkwrapped with any Longman Basic Skills title at a nominal fee. *The New American Webster Handy College Dictionary* (0-451-18166-2) is a paperback reference text with more than 100,000 entries. *Merriam Webster's Collegiate Dictionary*, tenth edition (0-87779-709-9), is a hardback reference with a citation file of more than 14.5 million examples of English words drawn from actual use.

*Penguin Quality Paperback Titles.* A series of Penguin paperbacks is available at a significant discount when shrinkwrapped with any Longman Basic Skills title. Some titles available are: Toni Morrison's *Beloved* (0-452-26446-4), Julia Alvarez's *How the Garcia Girls Lost Their Accents* (0-452-26806-0), Mark Twain's *Huckleberry Finn* (0-451-52650-3), *Narrative of the Life of Frederick Douglass* (0-451-52673-2), Harriet Beecher Stowe's *Uncle Tom's Cabin* (0-451-52302-4), Dr. Martin Luther King, Jr.'s *Why We Can't Wait* (0-451-62754-7), and plays by Shakespeare, Miller, and Albee. For a complete list of titles or more information, please contact your Addison Wesley Longman sales consultant.

*The Pocket Reader First Edition.* This inexpensive volume contains 80 brief readings (1–3 pages each) on a variety of themes: writers on writing, nature, women and men, customs and habits, politics, rights and obligations, and coming of age. Also included is an alternate rhetorical table of contents. 0-321-07668-0

*The Longman Textbook Reader.* This supplement, for use in developmental reading courses, offers five complete chapters from AWL textbooks: computer science, biology, psychology, communications, and business. Each chapter includes additional comprehension quizzes, critical thinking questions, and group activities. Available FREE with the adoption of *Critical Reading, Critical Thinking: A Contemporary Issues Approach.* 0-321-04617-X

**Newsweek Alliance.** Instructors may choose to shrinkwrap a 12-week subscription to *Newsweek* with any Longman text. The price of the subscription is 57 cents per issue (a total of $6.84 for the subscription). Available with the subscription is a free "Interactive Guide to Newsweek"—a workbook for students who are using the text. In addition, Newsweek provides a wide variety of instructor supplements free to teachers, including maps, Skills Builders, and weekly quizzes. *Newsweek* subscription card: 0-321-04759-1. Interactive Guide: 0-321-05528-4.

## Electronic and Online Offerings

**Reading Road Trip Multimedia Software.** This innovative and exciting multimedia reading software is included free with this text. The software takes students on a tour of 15 cities and landmarks throughout the United States. Each of the 15 modules corresponds to a reading or study skill (for example, finding the main idea, understanding patterns of organization, and thinking critically). All modules contain a tour of the location, instruction and tutorial, exercises, interactive feedback, and mastery tests.

**The Longman English Pages Web Site.** Both students and instructors can visit our free content-rich Web site for additional reading selections and writing exercises. From the Longman English pages, visitors can conduct a simulated Web search, learn how to write a resume and cover letter, or try their hand at poetry writing. Stop by and visit us at **http://longman.awl.com/englishpages.**

**The Longman Electronic Newsletter.** Twice a month during the spring and fall, instructors who have subscribed receive a free copy of the Longman Basic Skills Newsletter in their e-mailbox. Written by experienced classroom instructors, the newsletter offers teaching tips, classroom activities, book reviews, and more. To subscribe, visit the Longman Basic Skills Web site at http://longman.awl.com/basicskills, or send an e-mail to **Basic Skills@ awl.com.**

**Teaching Online: Internet Research, Conversation, and Composition, *Second Edition*.** Ideal for instructors who have never surfed the Net, this easy-to-follow guide offers basic definitions, numerous examples, and step-by-step information about finding and using Internet sources. Free to adopters. 0-321-01957-1

**Researching Online, *Third Edition*.** A perfect companion for a new age, this indispensable new supplement helps students navigate the Internet. Adapted from *Teaching Online*, the instructor's Internet guide, *Researching Online* speaks directly to students, giving them detailed, step-by-step instructions for performing electronic searches. Available free when shrinkwrapped with any Longman Basic Skills text. 0-321-05802-X

### Test Preparation Guides

**CLAST Test Package, Fourth Edition.** These two 40-item objective tests evaluate students' readiness for the CLAST exams. Strategies for teaching CLAST preparedness are included. Free with any Longman English title. Reproducible sheets: 0-321-01950-4 Computerized IBM version: 0-321-01982-2 Computerized Mac version: 0-321-01983-0

**TASP Test Package, Third Edition.** These 12 practice pretests and posttests assess the same reading and writing skills covered in the TASP examination. Free with any Longman English title. Reproducible sheets: 0-321-01959-8 Computerized IBM version: 0-321-02623-3 Computerized Mac version: 0-321-02622-5

## Acknowledgments

I am indebted to many people who were instrumental in making this textbook a reality. Janice Peters of Passaic County Community College pushed me in the direction of critical thinking, for which I will be eternally grateful, and the rest of the English Department has also been very supportive. The board of trustees and administration of the college were generous in giving me the time to get the project off the ground. My students were more than willing to use and comment on the worth of various aspects of the manuscript. Arlene Trzcinski of the copy center helped make that possible by providing last-minute copies quickly, efficiently, and always pleasantly. Alice Ferrer, our graphic artist, came up with some very creative designs that were used in the "Think About It!" and "Think Again!" sections of the book.

I owe a special debt of gratitude to the people who work at Addison Wesley Longman. Ellen Schatz, although no longer at Longman, was the editor who initially saw the worth of the project, and Sharon Balbos made useful suggestions during the early stages of the project. Steven Rigolosi, who in effect became my developmental editor, was extremely helpful with suggestions on improving the manuscript and making this a much better book. Ellen MacElree, my project manager, was conscientious and caring during the final stages of production. Gail Kehler went way out of her way to chase down the permissions. Donna Campion, because of her flexibility, made completion of the *Instructor's Manual* much easier for me. The high quality of the *Test Bank* was the result of the efficiency and efforts of Betty Cassidy of Adirondack Community College. I apologize to anyone else at Longman whom I have not mentioned, but I am acutely aware of the quality work done by many others.

The following reviewers made valuable suggestions during the development of the manuscript, for which I am very appreciative: Robert Brunner, Northern Virginia Community College; Elizabeth Cassidy, Adirondack Community College; Kathleen Engstrom, Fullerton College; Michael Kamil, Stanford University; Peter Kyper, West Chester University; Dr. Sharona A. Levy, Borough of Manhattan Community College; Alice Mackey, Missouri Western State College; Jane Melendez, East Tennessee State University; Jane Rhoads, Wichita State University; Susan Riley, DeVry Institute of Technology, Columbus; Victoria Sarkisian, Marist College; Bonnie M. Smith, St Mary's University of Minnesota; and Suzanne Weisar, San Jacinto College South.

Finally, on the home front, my wife, Susan, should get an award for putting up with my physical and mental absences and always supporting my efforts, even when they had a negative effect on our lives. Also, on many occasions, she graciously found the sources I was so desperately seeking. And of course there was Quincy, who spent the last years of his life in quiet dignity, and Lucas, who gave up his puppyhood willingly to lie silently for hours at a time while I labored at the computer.

*Richard Pirozzi*

# Part One

# Back to Basics

# Chapter One

# Understanding What You Read: A Review

## Chapter Outline

Determining the Meanings of Key Terms in Context
- Punctuation
- Synonyms
- Antonyms
- Examples
- General Sentence Clues

Distinguishing Main Ideas, Major Details, and Minor Details
- Unstated Main Idea

Recognizing Patterns of Organization
- Simple Listing of Facts
- Time Sequence
- Comparison and Contrast
- Cause and Effect

Uncovering the Central Message of a Longer Selection

# THINK ABOUT IT!

*Every chapter in this textbook begins with "Think About It!" and ends with "Think Again!" sections. They are fun and are designed to get you into the mood and keep you in the mood to think critically. Enjoy them.*

Critical thinkers are very careful about observing their surroundings. As a critical thinker, look carefully at photograph 1 below. There is something unusual in the scene. Do you know what it is? Discuss the photograph with your classmates.

Is there anything strange about the scenes in photographs 2, 3, and 4 below? Discuss them with your classmates.

(1)

(2)

(3)

(4)

## Chapter Outcomes

After completing Chapter 1, you should be able to:

- Use the context to determine the meanings of words
- Distinguish main ideas, major details, and minor details
- Recognize patterns of organization (simple listing of facts, time sequence, comparison and contrast, and cause and effect)
- Uncover the central message of a longer selection

When you looked at the outcomes and outline for this chapter, you probably said to yourself, "I already had this stuff!" or "I already know this stuff!" In fact, you may react the same way to the next chapter, which also deals with developmental reading skills. At this point in your education, it is understandable that you are not very enthusiastic about covering material that you may consider basic and familiar. Keep in mind, however, that this review will help you make better sense of the kind of reading you are asked to do in college and serve as a foundation on which to build the advanced critical reading and thinking skills presented in the other chapters.

Throughout this book, you will encounter some very interesting topics that should add to and enrich your educational experience as a college student. In addition, you will confront issues and problems that are both controversial and thought-provoking. Therefore, try to be patient as you make your way through the first two chapters even if you feel that they are too elementary. Remember that the skills reviewed in them will help you deal more effectively with the "good stuff" that comes later.

## Determining the Meanings of Key Terms in Context

Which of the following is the correct definition of the word *bar?*

1. The legal profession
2. A room or counter where alcohol is served
3. A piece of solid material longer than it is wide
4. Anything that impedes or prevents
5. All of the above

The answer to the question is "All of the above" because the meaning of *bar* depends on how it is used in a sentence. For example, the following sentences all use the word correctly:

1. Jessica was admitted to the *bar* two years after she graduated from law school.
2. After class, the students went to a *bar* to relax and have a few drinks.

3. Hold on to the *bar* so you don't fall if the subway comes to a sudden stop.

4. The police set up a roadblock to *bar* his escape.

The **context** refers to the surrounding words in a sentence that give a word its specific meaning. Like the word *bar*, many other words have multiple meanings, and you can determine which meaning applies by the way those words are used in a sentence. Thus you can often use the context to help you figure out the meanings of unfamiliar words, saving you the time and trouble of consulting a dictionary.

Various aspects of the context can be used to reveal word meanings, including punctuation, synonyms, antonyms, examples, and general sentence clues, individually or in combination.

## Punctuation

After mentioning a word, writers sometimes provide its meaning and set it off through the use of punctuation marks, making the definition easy for readers to recognize. For example, a definition can be introduced with a colon:

Pedro's general condition deteriorated after the physician discovered that he was suffering from **edema**: the accumulation of fluid in various organs of the body.

➤**edema** = the accumulation of fluid in various organs of the body

It can be set off between commas (or just one comma if it falls at the end of a sentence):

Lovelock's theory is intricately tied to **cybernetics**, the study and analysis of how information flows in electronic, mechanical, and biological systems.

F. Kurt Cylke Jr., *The Environment,* p. 78

➤**cybernetics** = the study and analysis of how information flows in electronic, mechanical, and biological systems

For greater emphasis, dashes can be used instead of commas:

Regulation increased substantially during the 1970s. By the end of that decade, numerous proposals for **deregulation**—the removal of old regulations—had been made.

Roger LeRoy Miller, *Economics Today,* p. 591

➤**deregulation** = the removal of old regulations

Definitions can also be enclosed in parentheses:

Music consists of three basic elements: **pitch** (melody); **rhythm** (sounds grouped according to a prescribed system); and **timbre** (the qualities of a tone that make a C-sharp sound different, say, on a tuba than on a guitar). From these building blocks, human beings have created rock and roll, rap, sonatas, blues, folk songs, chants, symphonies, jazz, opera, . . . the variations are endless. Where there are human beings, there is music.

Carol Tavris and Carole Wade, *Psychology in Perspective,* p. 575

© 2000 Addison-Wesley Educational Publishers, Inc.

➤**pitch** = melody

➤**rhythm** = sounds grouped according to a prescribed system

➤**timbre** = the qualities of a tone that make a C-sharp sound different, say, on a tuba than on a guitar

The definition of a term in a foreign language is usually placed in quotation marks:

> **The *Ceteris Paribus* Assumption: All Other Things Being Equal.** Everything in the world seems to relate in some way to everything else in the world. It would be impossible to isolate the effects of changes in one variable on another variable if we always had to worry about the many other variables that might also enter the analysis. As in other sciences, economics uses the ***ceteris paribus*** assumption. *Ceteris paribus* means "other things constant" or "other things equal."
>
> Roger LeRoy Miller, *Economics Today,* p. 10

➤***ceteris paribus*** = "other things constant" or "other things equal"

The same is true of a definition taken from an outside source:

> **Affirmative action**—"programs instituted by private and public institutions to overcome the effects of and to compensate for past discrimination" (Greenberg and Page, 1997, p. 576)—has recently come under attack in many parts of the United States.

➤**affirmative action** = programs instituted by private and public institutions to overcome the effects of and to compensate for past discrimination

## Synonyms

Writers sometimes use **synonyms**, or words that mean the same, to provide you with the meanings of unfamiliar words, as in the following sentence:

> First, **psychotropic** or **mood-altering** drugs became increasingly popular among health practitioners, made patients easier to handle and increased their chances of being released.
>
> Richard Sweeney, *Out of Place: Homelessness in America,* p. 69

➤**Psychotropic** and **mood-altering** are synonyms. Therefore, psychotropic drugs are drugs that alter or change our mood.

## Antonyms

Writers also use **antonyms**, or words that mean the opposite, to help you to figure out the meanings of unfamiliar words, as in the following sentence:

> **Whereas** Princess Diana was rather **tall**, Mother Teresa was **diminutive**.

➤**Whereas** indicates that a contrast is being drawn between Princess Diana and Mother Teresa. **Tall** and **diminutive** must be antonyms; therefore, *diminutive* means "short" or "small."

## Examples

Sometimes writers use familiar examples that *may* be helpful in determining word meanings, as in the following sentence:

> The United States, Canada, England, and France are all examples of **autonomous** nations, because they are not controlled by any other governments.

> ➤If you have knowledge about some or all of these countries and are aware of what they have in common, perhaps you can figure out that **autonomous** means "independent" or "self-governing."

## General Sentence Clues

You may be able to figure out the meaning of an unfamiliar word by studying the general sense of the sentence and focusing on the key words used in it, as in the following example:

> The **driver's eyes** were **bloodshot** and his **speech** was **slurred**; the **police officer** quickly concluded that he was **inebriated**.

> ➤The sense of the sentence—with the use of the key words **driver**, **bloodshot** with reference to **eyes**, **slurred** with reference to **speech**, and **police officer**—is that this is a scene involving a drunken driver and hence that **inebriated** must mean "intoxicated" or "drunk."

## ACTIVITY 1

Using the context, try to determine the meanings of the words that appear after the sentences. In each case, be prepared to discuss what clues are present to help you. Many of the sentences are taken from college textbooks.

1. She arrived at the party wearing a sari: the garment worn by Hindu women.

   **sari:** _____

2. Judy does not talk very much at the staff meetings, but James is quite loquacious.

   **loquacious:** _____

3. Would you like ketchup on your hamburger, or do you prefer some other condiment?

   **condiment:** _____

4. For years, cigarette manufacturers denied that cigarette smoke was carcinogenic even though millions of smokers were dying from lung cancer.

   **carcinogenic:** _____

5. Adolf Hitler, Fidel Castro, and Saddam Hussein are good examples of authoritarian leaders.

   **authoritarian:** _____

6. The rainstorm is expected to mitigate the extremely high temperature.

**mitigate:** _____

7. Although the movie character James Bond is always involved in "clandestine" or "secret" activities, some intelligence work today is actually accomplished out in the open.

**clandestine:** _____

8. Whereas the center is very slow, the quarterback is extremely nimble.

**nimble:** _____

9. Because of his attitude and harsh treatment of women in general, the captain has been called a misogynist by the female officers.

**misogynist:** _____

10. There are examples in the Koran, the Muslim Bible, of female saints and intellectuals, and powerful women often held strong informal powers over their husbands and male children.

Janell L. Carroll and Paul Root Wolpe, *Sexuality and Gender in Society*, p. 19

**Koran:** _____

11. We define inflation as an upward movement in the average level of prices. The opposite of inflation is deflation, defined as a downward movement in the average level of prices.

Roger LeRoy Miller, *Economics Today*, p. 149

**inflation:** _____

**deflation:** _____

12. From the larynx, inhaled air passes toward the lungs through the trachea, or windpipe.

Neil A. Campbell, Lawrence G. Mitchell, and Jane B. Reece, *Biology*, p. 444

**trachea:** _____

13. Welfare reform has often been couched in terms of workfare—the requirement that welfare recipients perform public service jobs in exchange for benefits.

Roger LeRoy Miller, *Economics Today*, p. 689

**workfare:** _____

14. Morals, or personal standards of right and wrong, are central to dealing with sexual matters.

George Zgourides, *Human Sexuality*, p. 382

**morals:** _____

15. Then the orgy started. During 1928, the market rose to 331. Many investors and speculators began to buy on margin (borrowing in order to invest).

Gary B. Nash and Julie Roy Jeffrey, The American People, p. 832

**buy on margin:** _____

16. Having briefly discussed sexual laws, morals, and ethics, let's now turn our attention to a particularly important area of legal concern, that of sexual coercion, or the forcing of sexual remarks, pressure, or behavior on another person.

George Zgourides, Human Sexuality, p. 384

**sexual coercion:** _____

17. For example, studies of twins and adopted children suggest that there may be a genetic component in bipolar disorder ("manic depression"), a mood disorder involving alternating episodes of extreme depression and abnormal states of exhilaration.

Carol Tavris and Carole Wade, Psychology in Perspective, p. 176

**bipolar disorder:** _____

18. The reliance on empirical evidence—evidence gathered by careful observation, experimentation, and measurement—is the hallmark of the psychological method.

Carol Tavris and Carole Wade, Psychology in Perspective, p. 13

**empirical evidence:** _____

19. The distinction between problematic and unproblematic drug use is not just a distinction between legal and illegal substances. In terms of avoidable and thus unnecessary morbidity (illness) and mortality (death), all of the illegally abused drugs *combined* take nowhere near the annual toll that alcohol and nicotine take.

James D. Wright and Joel A. Devine, Drugs as a Social Problem, pp. 2–3

**morbidity:** _____

**mortality:** _____

20. During the 1920s and 1930s, they were accused of being part of an international conspiracy to take over U.S. business and government, and anti-Semitism—prejudice or discrimination against Jews—became more widespread and overt.

Alex Thio, Sociology, p. 177

**anti-Semitism:** _____

21. We can gain further insight into ourselves and our society by going beyond our national boundaries to study other societies. Today, the whole world has become a **g**lobal village, a closely knit community of all the world's societies. Whatever happens in a faraway land can affect our lives here.

   Consider the various ways in which economic globalization—the interrelationship of the world's economies—can influence economic life in the United States.

Alex Thio, Sociology, p. 5

**global village:** _____

**economic globalization:** _____

22. Terrorism, which involves "the use of violence to express extreme discontent with a particular government" (Johnson, 1992, p. 5), is all too common today.

**terrorism:** _____

23. Childbirth, or parturition, begins with labor—contractions of the uterine muscles and opening of the cervix—and concludes with delivery—expelling the child and placenta from the vagina.

George Zgourides, *Human Sexuality,* p. 249

**parturition:** _____

**labor:** _____

**delivery:** _____

24. Scientists usually start out with a hypothesis, a statement that attempts to describe or explain behavior. Initially, the hypothesis may be stated quite generally, as in "Misery loves company." But before any research can be done, the hypothesis must be put into more specific terms. For example, "Misery loves company" might be rephrased as "People who are anxious about a threatening situation tend to seek out others who face the same threat."

Some hypotheses are suggested by previous findings or casual observation. Others are derived from a general theory, an organized system of assumptions and principles that purports to explain certain phenomena and how they are related.

Carol Tavris and Carole Wade, *Psychology in Perspective,* p. 41

**hypothesis:** _____

**theory:** _____

25. Antidepressant drugs are used primarily in treating mood disorders such as depression, anxiety, and phobias (irrational fears), and symptoms of obsessive-compulsive disorder, such as endless hand washing and hair pulling.

Carol Tavris and Carole Wade, *Psychology in Perspective,* p. 191

**antidepressant drugs:** _____

**phobias:** _____

**obsessive-compulsive disorder:** _____

## ACTIVITY 2

Bring to class ten examples of context clues taken from your other textbooks, and include the word meanings you were able to figure out using those clues. If you do not have other textbooks at this time, ask your classmates who are using other books to share their examples with you.

# Distinguishing Main Ideas, Major Details, and Minor Details

In addition to using context to determine word meanings, being able to differentiate among main ideas, major details, and minor details is an extremely important skill because it contributes to a much better understanding of what you are reading. Read the following paragraph; then answer the question "What is this about?"

> One way to recover the past is through music. Popular songs not only provide insight into attitudes and beliefs but also quickly convey the mood and feelings of an era. Through their lyrics, songwriters express the hopes and fears of a people and the emotional tone of an age. Consider, for example, the powerful message conveyed in the Democratic party adoption of "Happy Days Are Here Again" as a campaign theme during the Great Depression. The decline of pop music and the rise of rock and roll in the 1950s tells historians a great deal about the mood of that period. Similarly, the popularity of both folk music and rock in the 1960s provides another way of following social change in that turbulent decade.

> Gary B. Nash and Julie Roy Jeffrey, *The American People*, p. 1058

If your answer to the question was "music," you are correct: Virtually all of the sentences in the paragraph deal with that particular topic. The **topic** is the subject of a given paragraph, and it can usually be expressed in a word or phrase that can serve as a title.

Now reread the same paragraph, and try to answer the following question: "What is the overall message the writer is communicating about the topic?" The answer to that question can be found in the first sentence, which states: "One way to recover the past is through music." That sentence is the **main idea** of the paragraph because it lets you know in a general sense exactly what the writer wants to say about the topic, and it sums up all or most of the remaining sentences. In fact, the main idea always mentions the topic, which explains why the main idea—when it is stated—is also referred to as the **topic sentence.** The rest of the paragraph then consists of **details** that provide more information in order to make the main idea clearer.

Not all details, however, are of equal importance. Some lend direct support to the main idea and are called **major details.** Others, called **minor details,** lend direct support to the major details but only indirect support to the main idea. In other words, major details explain main ideas more specifically, and minor details explain the major details more specifically. For instance, the second and third sentences in the paragraph on music are the major details because they support the main idea directly by telling you specifically how or why the past can be recovered through music. In short, they supply more information to help make the main idea clearer. The remaining sentences are minor details that explain the major details further by providing very specific examples. Look again at the paragraph, reprinted here, and take note of the main idea, major details, and minor details.

Main idea          <u>One way to recover the past is through music.</u> Popular songs    ⎤ Major
                   not only provide insight into attitudes and beliefs but also    ⎥ details
                   quickly convey the mood and feelings of an era. Through their    ⎦
                   lyrics, songwriters express the hopes and fears of a people    ⎤
                   and the emotional tone of an age. Consider, for example, the
                   powerful message conveyed in the Democratic party adoption
                   of "Happy Days Are Here Again" as a campaign theme during
                   the Great Depression. The decline of pop music and the rise of    ⎥ Minor
                   rock and roll in the 1950s tells historians a great deal about      details
                   the mood of that period. Similarly, the popularity of both folk
                   music and rock in the 1960s provides another way of follow-
                   ing social change in that turbulent decade.    ⎦

As a reader, it is very important for you to be aware of the main idea of
every paragraph that you encounter, because it sums up the other sentences
and focuses on the overall message that the writer is trying to convey about a
given topic. Details give you additional information that make it easier for you
to understand the main idea.

When the main idea is stated, as in the example on music, it can be found
anywhere in a paragraph—at the beginning, at the end, or somewhere in between. In addition, sometimes a paragraph will have a main idea expressed in
more than one sentence. Look at the following examples illustrating each of
these, and pay particular attention to the main ideas, major details, and minor
details, which have been labeled for you.

**Main idea**       <u>The total number of insect species is greater than the total</u>    ⎤ Main idea
**at the**          <u>of all other species combined.</u> About a million insect species    ⎦
**beginning**       are known today, and researchers estimate that at least twice    ⎤ Major
                    this many exist (mostly in tropical forests) but have not yet    ⎦ detail
                    been discovered. Insects have been prominent on land for    ⎤
                    the last 400 million years. They have been much less success-    ⎥ Minor
                    ful in aquatic environments; there are only about 20,000    ⎥ details
                    species in freshwater habitats and far fewer in the sea.    ⎦

Neil A. Campbell, Lawrence G. Mitchell, and Jane B. Reece, Biology, p. 384

**Main idea**       Throughout U.S. history, various groups that believed the    ⎤ Minor
**at the end**      government would not respond to their needs have resorted    ⎦ detail
                    to one form of violence or another. Analyzing 53 U.S.    ⎤
                    protest movements, William Gamson (1975) found that 75    ⎥ Major
                    percent of those groups that used violence got what they    ⎥ detail
                    wanted, compared with only 53 percent of those that were    ⎦
                    nonviolent. <u>Violence, it seems, can pay off.</u>    ⎤ Main idea

Alex Thio, Sociology: A Brief Introduction, p. 275

**Main idea**       Children usually experience strong short-term reactions to    ⎤
**somewhere in**    being sexually abused but are often too confused or fright-    ⎥ Minor
**between**         ened to tell. They feel upset, helpless, frightened, and    ⎥ details
                    guilty; if physically injured, the pain experienced makes    ⎦

them particularly fearful of future contacts. <u>The child's experience of abuse can be minimized or exacerbated by a nonabusing significant adult's management of the event.</u> Parents (nonabusers) who handle the event as an unfortunate but not devastating experience and who can reassure the child that he or she is in no way to blame reduce the impact on the child significantly. On the other hand, the impact of the event may be very much intensified by the parents' negating, angry, and hostile responses. Parents often react so strongly and negatively out of their own feelings of anger, powerlessness, and (too often) denial that they cannot focus constructively on the child, thus isolating the child and providing inadequate help to prevent long-term consequences.

> Main idea
>
> Major details
>
> Minor detail

Kay Johnston Starks and Eleanor S. Morrison, Growing Up Sexual, p. 183

**Main idea expressed in more than one sentence**

Twenty or thirty years ago, high school health and safety courses may have mentioned some of the hazards of sustained alcohol abuse but with that exception, drug education would not have been found in the high school curriculum. <u>Today, one would be hard-pressed to find a single school in America that does not offer anti-drug education as part of its basic curriculum.</u> Usually, anti-drug programming begins in the elementary grades and intensifies in junior high and high school. <u>In addition to school-based programs, the Partnership for a Drug-Free America and other advocacy groups have sponsored national anti-drug media campaigns targeted mainly at youth</u> ("This is your brain. This is your brain on drugs"). Contemporary youth are bombarded with messages about the evils of drugs and exhortations to avoid their use. If American children watch as much television as alleged, the average teenager is exposed to anti-drug messages several times each day.

> Minor detail
>
> Main idea
>
> Major detail
>
> Main idea
>
> Major details

James D. Wright and Joel A. Devine, Drugs as a Social Problem, p. 51

## Unstated Main Ideas

On occasion, a paragraph will consist of just details with no topic sentence or stated main idea. However, that does not mean that there is no overall message regarding the topic. It is simply unstated and therefore cannot be found in the paragraph. When that occurs, the details should point you in the direction of the message, which you can then put into your own words. Look at this example:

> The average major-league baseball player today earns about $1.2 million a year. The average professional football player earns about $68,000 a year. The average professional basketball player earns about $2 million a year. At the same time, professional sports team owners continue to buy and sell professional franchises for tens and hundreds of millions of dollars.

Roger LeRoy Miller, Economics Today, p. 628

The topic of the paragraph has to do with the salaries paid to professional athletes and the money involved when owners buy and sell professional sports franchises. Although there is no sentence that expresses the overall message regarding the topic, three of the four major details provide examples of the high salaries paid to professional athletes, and the last one talks about the large sums of money involved in the buying and selling of professional franchises. Therefore, the **unstated main idea** of the paragraph could be expressed as "Professional athletes get paid very high salaries, and the teams they play for are worth huge amounts of money."

Every paragraph has a topic or subject and an overall message about the topic that is expressed as the main idea. When there is no stated main idea, remember to consider carefully what most or all of the major details in a paragraph have in common, which should then help you figure out the unstated main idea. Remember that major details explain main ideas further while minor details provide more information about major details. Whether the main idea is stated or not, be sure to come away from each paragraph that you read with the overall message clearly in mind.

## ACTIVITY 3

For each of the paragraphs that follow, find and label the topic, the main idea, and the major details. If the main idea is unstated, write it out in your own words after the passage. Remember that the topic is the answer to the question "What is this about?" and the main idea answers the question "What is the overall message the writer is communicating about the topic?" Also keep in mind that the major details are *major* because they lend direct support to the main idea.

### 1

One major difference between arithmetic and algebra is the use of *variables* in algebra. When a letter can represent a variety of different numbers, that letter is called a **variable.** For example, if $n$ represents the number of students enrolled in a college's 8 A.M. section of Elementary Algebra, the number $n$ will vary, depending on how many students drop or add the class. Thus the number $n$ is a variable. If each student pays \$600 for the course, the college collects a total of $600 \cdot n$ dollars from the students. Since the cost to each student is consistently \$600, the number 600 is called a **constant.**

Marvin L. Bittinger and David J. Ellenbogen, *Elementary Algebra*, p. 2

### 2

Have you ever found yourself sitting at the breakfast table reading the label on a box of cereal or loaf of bread? It can be interesting to compare the way a product is advertised on the front of the package with the actual nutritional information on the side or back. For instance, so-called fiber-enriched white bread may have less fiber than an unenriched whole-grain product. Similarly, products like cheese and chips are often labeled "low fat" or "lite." This merely means that they have less fat than the same products without these labels. In fact, their actual fat content may be surprisingly high, and by eating just a few more "lite" chips than regular ones, you may consume just as much fat.

Neil A. Campbell, Lawrence G. Mitchell, and Jane B. Reece, *Biology*, p. 435

## 3

One of the greatest benefits of studying psychology is that you learn not only how the brain works in general but also how to use yours in particular—by thinking critically. **Critical thinking** is the ability and willingness to assess claims and to make objective judgments on the basis of well-supported reasons. It is the ability to look for flaws in arguments and to resist claims that have no supporting evidence. Critical thinking, however, is not merely negative thinking. It also fosters the ability to be *creative and constructive*—to come up with various possible explanations for events, think of implications of research findings, and apply new knowledge to a broad range of social and personal problems. You can't separate critical thinking from creative thinking, for it is only when you question *what is* that you can begin to imagine *what can be*.

Carol Tavris and Carole Wade, *Psychology in Perspective*, p. 10

## 4

During the past few years, diversity has become one of the most urgent concerns of business, education, and government. Many of the nation's largest companies have hired executives who are responsible for corporate diversity. There are videos available on the topic, consultants specializing in the subject who have more business than they can handle, and nationally prominent diversity institutes. One educational publisher has begun to market a game called "Diversity Bingo." The management training programs of many of the nation's most successful companies include a module on diversity. Newsletters devoted to the topic have thousands of readers.

B. Eugene Griessman, *Diversity*, p. 1

## 5

Sex was taboo at our house, you couldn't say that "dirty" three letter word without somebody blushing, trying to hush it up, or giggling. If you'll pardon the pun, you could say that sex was kept under the blankets at our house. My parents never really told me about the "facts of life"—my mother made a vain attempt by asking my older brother to read a book about sex, but that's as far as it went with us kids. Just recently I got into a bit of an argument with my mom when she expressed her negative feelings about sex education in the public school system. I got angry and told her she was being hypocritical because neither she nor my Dad had educated any of us kids about sex. It is important that kids learn about sex in school because some parents don't do it at all.

Kay Johnston Starks and Eleanor S. Morrison, *Growing Up Sexual*, p. 83

## 6

It would be nice if everything we said was understood exactly as intended. Unfortunately, this is not the case. Messages are filtered by listeners' attitudes, values, and beliefs; consequently, changes in their meaning may occur. Someone who distrusts others and is skeptical of what people say, for example, will interpret the words "I like you a lot" differently from someone who is more trusting. A skeptic might think, "He doesn't really mean that, he's only saying it to get on my good side." A more trusting person will accept the message and treat it as a genuine expression of affection. The difference in interpretation between what the "speaker said" and what the "receiver heard" is called the interpersonal gap. Other examples include:

> Lisa: "I'm really feeling angry. That's the last time I want to see you do that."
> Manuel's interpretation: She is always blaming me for things. I wish she would stop.
> Jasmine's interpretation: It was my fault. She is right. I'll try to do things differently in the future.
> Courtney's interpretation: She's got to be kidding. What I did could not be that important.

Anthony F. Grasha, *Practical Applications of Psychology,* p. 259

## 7

Americans have a history of disapproving of relationships that take place between blacks and whites. After all, we must remember that such relationships were actually illegal in many states until the Supreme Court overturned these laws in 1967. In many other countries, interracial couples are not unusual. Latino-white relationships, as well as Asian-white, Native American–white, Latino-black, and other combinations—while still often looked upon negatively—are more acceptable in the United States than black-white. Unfortunately, these negative feelings can lead to discrimination against such couples and their children.

Janell L. Carroll and Paul Root Wolpe, *Sexuality and Gender in Society,* p. 287

## 8

The preferred drug among youth is alcohol and has been for as long as we have gathered data. Alcohol use among the young is a serious social problem. A fairly large minority of the young will also experiment with marijuana. The proportion of young people who have used marijuana in the last year (about a quarter) is in the same range as the proportion of the adult population who have used marijuana (about a third). There are some young people, a few percent at most, who will also experiment with hard drugs, and an even smaller number who will become regular users or even addicts. The usual pattern of drug use is relatively high rates of use in the early adult years and fairly sharp declines as people mature into adulthood.

James D. Wright and Joel A. Devine, *Drugs as a Social Problem,* p. 58

## 9

Perhaps the most important business trend of the decade was the emergence of a new kind of manager. No longer did family entrepreneurs make decisions relating to prices, wages, or output. Alfred P. Sloan, Jr., an engineer who reorganized General Motors, was a prototype of the new kind of manager. He divided the company into components, freeing the top managers to concentrate on planning new products, controlling inventory, and integrating the whole operation. Marketing and advertising became as important as production, and many businesses began to spend more money on research. The new manager often had a large staff, but owned no part of the company. He was usually an expert at cost accounting and analyzing data. Increasingly, he was a graduate of one of the new business colleges.

Gary B. Nash and Julie Roy Jeffrey, *The American People*, pp. 803–804

## 10

Over the past two decades, most Americans have become familiar with such terms as environmental disaster, acid rain, ozone depletion, deforestation, and global warming. Many of these environmental issues, like acid rain and ozone depletion, are global in nature and appear remote and only vaguely threatening. Other issues, such as air pollution and pesticide residues on our foods, confront us in our homes on a daily basis. However, both the seemingly remote global issues and the more immediately threatening environmental problems are intricately intertwined. Like a pebble thrown into a pond, changes in a local ecosystem cause ripple effects. They have the potential to initiate or contribute to changes in the global ecosystem.

F. Kurt Cylke Jr., *The Environment*, p. 1

## 11

Who discovered America? This is not an easy question to answer. The first human beings to set foot on the continents of North and South America were the ancestors of the modern Indians. These people came from Asia; they entered the North American continent tens of thousands of years ago during the Ice Age, when a land bridge connected northeastern Asia with Alaska. Being hunters and herders, they were looking for game and green grass. Almost certainly the settlers were unaware that they were entering "new" territory. So we must look elsewhere (and much later in time) for the "discoverer" of America as we use that word.

John A. Garraty, *A Short History of the American Nation*, p. 1

## 12

It is referred to as "underground," "gray," "subterranean," "informal," "off-the-books," or "unofficial." Whatever it is called, the underground economy exists in a big way in the United States and in an even bigger way in Latin America, Europe, and elsewhere. Have you ever bought a cheap umbrella or a pair of earrings from a street vendor? If so, both you and the vendor were partaking in the off-the-books underground economy. If you have ever done odd jobs and been paid in cash or paid someone else in cash to do odd jobs for you, you have participated in the underground economy.

Roger LeRoy Miller, *Economics Today*, p. 163

Using your other textbooks, find examples of paragraphs with the types of main ideas that we have discussed. Find a variety with topic sentences in the beginning, at the end, and somewhere in between. Also look for examples of paragraphs with a main idea expressed in more than one sentence and ones that have unstated main ideas. If you do not have other textbooks at this time, ask your classmates who are using other books to share their examples with you.

## Recognizing Patterns of Organization

Look carefully at this sequence of numbers:

16-1-20-20-5-18-14-19      1-18-5      8-5-12-16-6-21-12

Does this mean anything to you? Can you see a message? Probably not. What if you were told that each number corresponds to a letter in the alphabet, numbered in order from 1 to 26? Is that better? After a few minutes, you should be able to figure out that the message is "Patterns are helpful"!

Once you determine the arrangement or pattern of something, it is much easier to understand. Have you ever heard someone say, "I am starting to see a pattern here." That comment usually means that several pieces of similar information are enabling the person to come to a particular conclusion. For example, if Jonathan has consistently arrived late for psychology class during the first three weeks of the semester, his instructor would see a pattern and might conclude that Jonathan is not a very responsible student. Again, patterns can be useful by adding meaning to given situations.

Writers often help readers recognize important details by arranging them in a certain way. These arrangements of details are called **patterns of organization,** and there are four major ones: **simple listing of facts, time sequence, comparison and contrast,** and **cause and effect.** When reading material is organized using one or more of these patterns, it should help you see not only details but also the main idea. Or the main idea may tip you off to the presence of a specific pattern of organization. So it is a two-way process. Let us take a look at each of the patterns.

### Simple Listing of Facts

This pattern involves a list of details that could include the causes, characteristics, examples, or types of something. Writers will often use **transition words** such as the following to help you to recognize this pattern:

*also, another, examples, factors, finally, following, in addition, last, list, many,* numbers (*first, second,* etc.), *other, part, several,* and *types*

Determining the main idea can also be of help, because it will let you know exactly what is being listed. Look at the following example.

1    At least three factors contributed to the steady increase in concern about environmental issues during the 1980s. First, there was a great deal of highly publicized political controversy surrounding environmental issues. The Reagan administration's pro-business and anti-environmental regulation position, as well as a series of scandals involving conflicts of interest by key officials in the Environmental Protection Agency (EPA), were criticized by many of the nation's leading environmental organizations. Controversy and media coverage increased significantly when the Reagan administration slashed EPA funding dramatically. During President Ronald Reagan's first year in office, the EPA budget was cut by 29 percent, resulting in a 30 percent reduction in staff.

2    A second factor which contributed to the rise of public concern was the increased coverage of specific environmental problems. Global issues such as climate change and ozone depletion received substantial attention. Also, a series of specific environmental disasters captured the nation's attention, not the least of which was a 1989 oil spill which occurred after the Exxon corporation's supertanker *Valdez* ran aground in Prince Edward Sound, Alaska.

3    A third contributing factor was increased media coverage of the activities of environmental activists. This included not only protest marches, but also video images of Greenpeace activists in small inflatable rafts risking their lives by placing themselves between the harpoons of whale hunters and the whales they were trying to save. Environmentalists were aware of the necessity for media coverage, and during the 1980s, many dedicated and hard-working activists capitalized on strategies designed to attract the attention of the mass media.

F. Kurt Cylke Jr., *The Environment,* pp. 26 and 28

Notice how the main idea—"At least three factors contributed to the steady increase in concern about environmental issues during the 1980s"—covers three paragraphs and lets you know that the list involves three factors. In fact, in most instances, the main idea will be found right before the beginning of a list. The transition words *three factors*, *first*, *second*, and *third* also help you recognize the presence of the list, which includes the following major details:

➤ "First, there was a great deal of highly publicized political controversy surrounding environmental issues."

➤ "A second factor which contributed to the rise of public concern was the increased coverage of specific environmental problems."

➤ "A third contributing factor was increased media coverage of the activities of environmental activists."

The rest of the passage includes minor details that provide more specific examples of the major details.

A simple listing of facts does not always involve numbered details, as illustrated by the following example:

America can be fairly called a "drug culture" in the sense that nearly everyone uses drugs of one sort or another. When we are ailing, we expect to be given some drug that will make us feel better. If we have trouble sleeping, we take sleeping medica-

tions, whether over-the-counter or prescribed. If we feel anxious, we want anti-anxi-
ety drugs and if we feel depressed we seek antidepressants. If we want sex without
the risk of pregnancy, we take "the pill." Millions of us get "up" with caffeine and
come "down" with alcohol. It has even been argued that mood-altering drugs satisfy
an *innate* human need to suspend ordinary awareness, a need much like sexual tension
that "arises spontaneously from within, builds to a peak, finds relief, and dissipates"
(Weil, 1972: 22). The use of drugs to make one feel better or to solve one's problems,
whatever they might be, is deeply entrenched in our culture and our expectations.

James D. Wright and Joel A. Devine, *Drugs as a Social Problem*, p. 2

In this example, the main idea is stated in both the first and last sentences,
which convey just about the same overall message. Writers will sometimes repeat the same—or close to the same—main idea in the first and last sentences
of a paragraph, which makes it easier to spot. All the rest of the sentences in
the paragraph are major details that list the kinds of drugs people take and
their reasons for taking them. Although there is no numbering, you are
helped to recognize the presence of the list by the repetition of the words
*when we* and *if we*.

## Time Sequence

This pattern involves details placed in the order in which they occur in time.
Transition words often found in time sequence include these:

*after, before, beginning,* dates, *finally, first, last, later, next, once, prior, repeat, steps, then, thereafter, times of day, when,* and *year*

Historical and other material with dated events or times of the day are the
most obvious place to find this pattern, as in the following example:

American cities grew rapidly in the last part of the nineteenth and the first part of
the twentieth centuries. New York, which had a population of 1.2 million in 1880,
grew to 3.4 million by 1900 and 5.6 million in 1920. Chicago expanded even more
dramatically, from 500,000 in 1880 to 1.7 million in 1900 and 2.7 million in 1920.
Los Angeles was a town of 11,000 in 1880, but multiplied ten times by 1900, and
then increased another five times, to more than a half million, by 1920.

Gary B. Nash and Julie Roy Jeffrey, *The American People*, p. 744

Once again, the main idea is stated in the first sentence, which informs
you that the time sequence organizes details that illustrate how "American
cities grew rapidly in the last part of the nineteenth and the first part of the
twentieth centuries." The dates throughout the paragraph make it easy to
identify the major details that directly support the overall message.

This pattern can also include the steps in a process, directions, or anything
else that is accomplished in a definite time order, as in the example below.

In courtship, a male and female loon swim side by side while performing a series of
displays. ① The courting birds frequently turn their heads away from each other. (In
sharp contrast, a male loon defending his territory often charges at an intruder with

his beak pointed straight ahead.) ② The birds then dip their beaks in the water, and ③ submerge their heads and necks. Prior to copulation, the male invites the female onto land by ④ turning his head backward with his beak held downward. There, ⑤ they copulate.

Neil A. Campbell, Lawrence G. Mitchell, and Jane B. Reece, *Biology*, p. 741

The main idea is stated in the first sentence, which tells you that "In courtship, a male and female loon swim side by side while performing a series of displays." That sentence, along with the transition words *series*, *then*, and *prior*, lets you know that a behavior process is being traced that must be accomplished in a definite sequence. The rest of the sentences, with the exception of the one in parentheses, are major details that trace the steps in the process. Although the major details are numbered, the pattern of organization here is time sequence rather than a simple listing of facts because the steps in the process must be done in that order. In other words, step 1 must be accomplished before step 2, step 2 must be accomplished before step 3, step 3 must be accomplished before step 4, and step 4 must be accomplished before step 5. With a simple listing, the items on a given list are not in any specific time order. This is the key difference between those two patterns.

## Comparison and Contrast

This pattern organizes details that deal with the similarities (comparison) and differences (contrast) between persons, events, ideas, or things. Transition words that are often found with comparison and contrast include these:

*alike, between, common, commonalities, compare, contrast, debate, difference, disagree, distinction, distinguish, like, likeness, on the other hand, same, similarity, unlike,* and *whereas*

Also, the main idea usually tells you exactly what is being compared or contrasted. Read the following example:

1   Think of all the ways that human beings are alike. Everywhere, no matter what their backgrounds or where they live, people love, work, argue, dance, sing, complain, and gossip. They rear families, celebrate marriages, and mourn losses. They reminisce about the past and plan for the future. They help their friends and fight with their enemies. They smile with amusement, frown with displeasure, and glare in anger. Where do all these commonalities come from?

2   Think of all the ways that human beings differ. Some of us are extroverts, always ready to throw a party, make a new friend, or speak up in a crowd; others are shy and introverted, preferring the safe and familiar. Some are trailblazers, ambitious and enterprising; others are placid, content with the way things are. Some take to book learning like a cat to catnip; others don't do so well in school but have lots of street smarts and practical know-how. Some are overwhelmed by even the most petty of problems; others, faced with severe difficulties, remain calm and resilient. Where do all these differences come from?

Carol Tavris and Carole Wade, *Psychology in Perspective*, p. 83

The first paragraph deals with how human beings are similar as stated by the main idea: "Think of all the ways that human beings are alike." The transition words *alike* and *commonalities* help you recognize the pattern. All of the remaining sentences, with the exception of the last one, are major details that directly support the overall message by giving examples of similarities. The main idea of the second paragraph—"Think of all the ways that human beings differ"—tells you that it is concerned with how human beings are different, and the transition words *differ* and *differences* are also revealing. Again, the rest of the sentences in the paragraph, except the last one, are major details that directly support the overall message by providing examples of differences.

Do you notice that there is an additional pattern of organization in both paragraphs? A simple listing of facts. The repetition of the word *they* in the first paragraph and *some* and *others* in the second one give strong indication that lists are present. As you can see, writers sometimes use a *combination of patterns*, which is very helpful to you, because it gives you more than one opportunity to recognize important details and thus better understand what you are reading.

## Cause and Effect

This pattern organizes details that present causes or reasons along with their effects or results. In other words, it explains why something has happened. For example, if one of your classmates asked you how you got an A+ on the last history test *(effect)*, you might proceed to explain that you attended all classes *(cause)*, took down every word the professor said *(cause)*, read all the assignments *(cause)*, and studied on a daily basis *(cause)*. In essence, you would be using the cause-and-effect pattern to give the reasons why you earned such a high grade.

Transition words to look for when this pattern is present include these:

*affects, because, brings out, cause, consequences, contributed, create, effect, leads to, reaction, reason, result, therefore,* and *whereas*

Sometimes the causes are stated first, as in the following example:

> During the late 1980s, news articles, TV shows, and radio commentaries proclaimed that the nation was facing a shortage of scientists. The growth in high-tech industries was going to create demands for scientists and engineers that would not be met. The government even suggested that this shortage would endanger national security. The result was an increase in the number of students seeking postgraduate education, especially doctoral degrees in engineering, the sciences, mathematics, and computer science. For example, in 1981–1982, a total of 2,621 Ph.D.s were granted in engineering; by 1991–1992, the number had more than doubled, to 5,488. Similar, though less dramatic, increases were seen in the number of doctorates awarded in the sciences and mathematics.

Roger LeRoy Miller, *Economics Today*, p. 77

The first three sentences in the paragraph provide causes:

➤ "During the late 1980s, news articles, TV shows, and radio commentaries proclaimed that the nation was facing a shortage of scientists."

➤ "The growth in high-tech industries was going to create demands for scientists and engineers that would not be met."

➤ "The government even suggested that this shortage would endanger national security."

The fourth sentence states the effect:

➤ "The result was an increase in the number of students seeking postgraduate education, especially doctoral degrees in engineering, the sciences, mathematics, and computer science."

More specific information, which directly supports the effect, is found in the remaining sentences, preceded by the words *for example*. Notice the two transition words *create* and *result*, which help you recognize the pattern. The main idea, which for the most part is unstated, would read something like this: "There was an increase in the number of students seeking postgraduate education in engineering, sciences, mathematics, and computer science as a result of national concern in the late 1980s that there was a serious shortage of scientists and engineers."

This pattern sometimes presents effects first, followed by causes, as in the following example:

> People became homeless for a variety of reasons. Some started life in seriously disturbed families. Others fell prey to alcohol and drugs. Still others had health or learning problems that eroded the possibility of a stable life. For millions of working Americans, homelessness was just a serious and unaffordable illness away. Though many Americans initially regarded the homeless as "bag ladies, winos, and junkies," they gradually came to realize that the underclass category included others as well.
>
> Gary B. Nash and Julie Roy Jeffrey, *The American People,* p. 1101

The first sentence—"People became homeless for a variety of reasons"—has the transition word *reasons* and also lets you know that *homelessness* is the effect. Causes are presented in the second, third, and fourth sentences, which are the major details:

➤ "Some started life in seriously disturbed families."

➤ "Others fell prey to alcohol and drugs."

➤ "Still others had health or learning problems that eroded the possibility of a stable life."

Did you notice a second pattern of organization? Right again! The words *some, others,* and *still others* indicate that the causes are also organized in a simple listing of facts. When you read, recognizing one or more than one pattern of organization enables you to focus on important information and thus helps you comprehend better.

# ACTIVITY 5

In the following passages, find the main ideas, patterns of organization, and the most important details organized by the patterns. Write your answers in your notebook. Be prepared to discuss the transition words that help you identify the patterns.

## 1

1   If you follow tennis, you know that John McEnroe was famous for his on-court antics and spectacular temper tantrums; he was the bad boy of the tennis circuit. Once, when McEnroe noticed a small microphone that could pick up what the players were saying, he walked over and hit it with his racquet, breaking a string. Then he strolled to the sidelines and got a new racquet. There was no penalty for this little episode. In fact, it seemed to work to his advantage: He got all charged up for the game, while his opponent's performance suffered from the interruption. McEnroe also received plenty of attention from fans and the media, who loved him or loved to hate him.

2   In contrast, Bjorn Borg, another tennis champion, was controlled and civilized on the court. "Once I was like John [McEnroe]," he told a reporter. "Worse. Swearing and throwing rackets. Real bad temper. Ask anyone who knew me in Sweden then, 10 or 11 years ago. Then, when I was 13, my club suspended me for six months. My parents locked my racket in a cupboard for six months. Half a year I could not play. It was terrible. But it was a very good lesson. I never opened my mouth on the court again. I still get really mad, but I keep my emotions inside" (quoted in Collins, 1981).

Carol Tavris and Carole Wade, *Psychology in Perspective,* p. 211

## 2

Victims of rape often suffer battered faces with cut lips and broken noses, bruises, abrasions, broken ribs, bites, and internal damage and bleeding. These immediate effects can bring on emotional symptoms characteristic of a severe anxiety reaction, a condition termed *rape trauma syndrome* (Burgess & Holmstrom, 1988; Rynd, 1988). Some women react with uncontrolled crying, anxiety, restlessness, depression, and feelings of self-blame. In addition to the pain and discomfort from the physical abuse suffered during the rape, they may have other physical complaints, including gastrointestinal upsets, headaches, insomnia, and loss of appetite. Other women encase themselves behind a smiling, cool, and relaxed exterior, masking the trauma and emotional turmoil held inside.

George Zgourides, *Human Sexuality,* pp. 389–390

## 3

John Rempel (1986) and John Holmes (1989) suggest that answers to three questions can help us make decisions about whether to trust someone. Each is based on an important element of trust.

1.   *How predictable is that individual?* A predictable person is someone whose behavior is consistent—consistently good or bad. An unpredictable person keeps us

guessing about what might happen next. Such volatile people may make life interesting, but they don't inspire much in the way of confidence.

2. *Can I depend upon him or her?* A dependable person can be relied upon when it counts. One way to tell is to see how a partner behaves in situations where it is possible to care or not to care.

3. *Do I have faith in that person?* Are you able to go beyond the available evidence and feel secure that your friend or partner will continue to be responsible and caring? We have faith in another person when our doubts are put aside and we feel safe in a relationship.

Anthony F. Grasha, *Practical Applications of Psychology*, p. 295

## 4

A view from the window of a plane on a transcontinental flight from Boston to California is revealing to an ecology-minded passenger. Below, the pattern of vegetation changes from the mixed coniferous-hardwood forests of the northeast to the oak forests of the central Appalachians with patches of high-elevation spruce forests. Then the forest cover merges with midwestern croplands of corn, soybean, and wheat, land that once was the domain of tallgrass prairie. Wheat fields yield to high-elevation shortgrass plains, and then the plains give way to the coniferous forest of the Rocky Mountains, capped by tundra and snowfields. Beyond the mountains to the southwest lie the tan-colored desert regions.

Robert Leo Smith and Thomas M. Smith, *Elements of Ecology*, p. 378

## 5

A lecture hall, for example, provides lots of opportunity to listen but very few opportunities to respond. Research shows that such settings promote a **one-way communication** pattern in which the teacher talks and students, for the most part, listen. For example, 70 percent of the time in a typical college classroom is spent with the teacher talking. Of the remaining time in a class period, students spend about 15 percent of it either responding to questions or asking questions and 15 percent remaining silent (Bonwell and Eison, 1991). When snuggling close to someone you care about, you and your partner have opportunities to talk and to listen. Thus, a **two-way communication** pattern is established.

Anthony F. Grasha, *Practical Applications of Psychology*, p. 262

## 6

Virtually every discussion of the history of American environmental concern identifies two major events, both occurring after World War II, as having helped popularize environmental issues. One notable event was the 1962 publication of *Silent Spring,* Rachel Carson's shocking exposé of the harmful environmental effects of pesticides. Carson's book quickly became a best-seller, eventually winning eight literary awards. Perhaps even more influential than Carson's book was the celebration of the first Earth Day on April 22, 1970. Millions of Americans participated in celebrations across the nation.

F. Kurt Cylke Jr., *The Environment*, p. 17

## 7

The person most responsible for the growth of the automobile industry was Henry Ford, a self-taught mechanic from Greenfield, Michigan. In 1908 he designed the Model T Ford, a simple, tough box on wheels. In a year he sold 11,000 Model Ts. Thereafter, relentlessly cutting costs and increasing efficiency by installing the assembly-line system, he expanded production at an unbelievable rate. By 1925 he was turning out more than 9,000 cars a day, one approximately every ten seconds, and the price of the Model T had been reduced to below $300.

John A. Garraty, *A Short History of the American Nation*, p. 431

## 8

American blacks were deeply involved in the Revolution. In fact, the conflict provoked the largest slave rebellion in American history prior to the Civil War. Once the war was under way, blacks found a variety of ways to turn events to their own advantage. For some, this meant applying revolutionary principles to their own lives and calling for their personal freedom. For others, it meant seeking liberty behind English lines or in the continent's interior.

Gary B. Nash and Julie Roy Jeffrey, *The American People*, p. 201

## 9

1    The extraordinary popularity of sports in the postwar period can be explained in a number of ways. People had more money to spend and more free time to fill. Radio was bringing suspenseful, play-by-play accounts of sports contests into millions of homes, thus encouraging tens of thousands to want to see similar events with their own eyes.

2        There had been great athletes before, such as Jim Thorpe, a Sac and Fox Indian, who won both the pentathalon and the decathalon at the 1912 Olympic Games, made Walter Camp's All-America football team in 1912 and 1913, then played major league baseball for several years before becoming a pioneer founder and player in the National Football League. But what truly made the 1920s a Golden Age was the emergence of a remarkable collection of what today would be called "superstars."

John A. Garraty, *A Short History of the American Nation*, p. 423

## 10

If the 1920s was the age of the bathroom, the 1930s was the era of the modern kitchen. The sale of electrical appliances increased throughout the decade, with refrigerators leading the way. In 1930, the number of refrigerators produced exceeded the number of iceboxes for the first time. Refrigerator production continued to rise throughout the decade, reaching a peak of 2.3 million in 1937. At first, the refrigerator was boxy and looked very much like an icebox with a motor sitting on top. In 1935, however, the refrigerator, like most other appliances, became streamlined. Sears, Roebuck advertised "The New 1935 Super Six Coldspot . . . Stunning in Its Streamlined Beauty." The Coldspot, which quickly influenced the look of all other models, was designed by Raymond Loewy, one of a group of industrial designers who emphasized sweeping horizontal lines, rounded corners, and a slick modern look. They hoped modern design would stimulate an optimistic attitude and, of course, increase sales.

Gary B. Nash and Julie Roy Jeffrey, *The American People,* p. 865

## 11

1   Sexual freedom also contributed to the revival of the women's rights movement. For one thing, freedom involved a more drastic revolution for women than for men. Effective methods of contraception obviously affected women more directly than men, and the new attitudes heightened women's awareness of the way the old sexual standards had restricted their entire existence. In fact, the two movements interacted with each other. Concern for better job opportunities and for equal pay for equal work, for example, fed the demand for day-care centers for children.

2       Still another cause of the new drive for women's rights was concern for improving the treatment of minorities. Participation in the civil rights movement encouraged women to speak out more forcefully for their own rights. Feminists argued that they were being demeaned and dominated by a male-dominated society and must fight back.

John A. Garraty, *A Short History of the American Nation,* p. 540

## 12

No one disputes the worldwide influence of Sigmund Freud (1856–1939). But there is plenty of dispute about the lasting significance of his work, reflected in three current attitudes toward Freud and his ideas. The first, held by Freud himself and by his most devoted followers to this day, is that Freud was one of the geniuses of history, an intellectual revolutionary like Copernicus, Darwin, and Newton; with minor exceptions, his theory is correct, universal, and timeless. The second view, probably the most common among psychiatrists and clinical psychologists today, is that Freud was a great thinker and that many of his ideas have lasting value, but some are dated, and others are plain wrong. The third view, held by many scientists and by psychologists in other perspectives, is that Freud was a fraud—a poor scientist and even an unethical therapist (Crews, 1995). The British scientist and Nobel laureate Peter Medawar (1982) called psychoanalysis a dinosaur in the history of ideas, doomed to extinction. For good measure, he added that it is "the most stupendous intellectual confidence trick of the twentieth century."

Carol Tavris and Carole Wade, *Psychology in Perspective,* p. 509

## ACTIVITY 6

Using your other textbooks, find examples of passages that illustrate the four patterns of organization that we have discussed. If you do not have other textbooks at this time, ask your classmates who are using other books to share their examples with you.

## Uncovering the Central Message of a Longer Selection

To this point, we have been discussing using context to find word meanings; distinguishing main ideas, major details, and minor details; and recognizing patterns of organization in paragraphs. All of these skills, of course, can be applied to selections or passages containing several paragraphs. Examples are articles, essays, textbook sections, and chapters.

Just as every paragraph has a main idea, every longer selection also has a main idea that gives the central message of all of the paragraphs within that selection. The **central message** represents the specific aspect of the topic that the writer wishes to discuss, and it is supported by the information in the selection, including the main ideas of the individual paragraphs and most, if not all, of the details. Patterns of organization can help you uncover the central message by directing you to the most important details.

Once again, it is important to determine first what the topic is by answering the question "What is this about?" Most longer selections will have a title or a heading to help you determine the topic. If there is no title or heading, you can usually figure out the topic by reading the selection carefully, concentrating particularly on sentences near the beginning, which will often mention the subject matter. Once you have determined the topic, you identify the central message by answering the question "What is the central message that the writer is communicating about the topic?"

The main idea of a longer selection can be stated or unstated, as is the case with main ideas in paragraphs. When it is stated, it can usually be found somewhere within the first few paragraphs or the last few paragraphs. When it is unstated, a very careful reading of the selection will usually enable you to figure out the overall main idea. Read the following example, determine the topic, and see if you can identify the main idea by answering the question "What is the central message that the writer is communicating about the topic?"

## Homeless Advocates

1   Robert Hayes and Mitch Snyder, although differing in many respects, were both catalysts for change during the dreary days of homelessness in the early 1980s. Both helped to awaken Americans to the appalling conditions of homelessness and convinced them that something could be done.

2   Robert Hayes saw firsthand the plight of New York City's homeless and decided to do something about it. In 1979, the recent law school graduate sued the city and the state seeking adequate shelter for his six clients, including one whose residence was a cardboard box on Park Avenue. Even though it was his first court appearance and he was scared to death, he claimed that the state had a constitutional responsibility to provide shelter for anyone who requested it. The judge agreed and New York began to turn armories and other public buildings into shelters with cots, showers, and simple meals. Requests from other states led Hayes to quit his job with a top corporate law firm and to form the National Coalition for the Homeless. Over

the years, dozens of cities have learned from Hayes and the Coalition and have persuaded municipal officials and private organizations to pool their resources to help
the homeless.

3      Mitch Snyder also left a well-paying job to take up the cause of the homeless.
As passionate and zealous as Hayes was studious and methodical, Snyder typified
the label of "activist" by being bothersome to many, particularly the Reagan administration. Losing sixty pounds during a fifty-one-day hunger strike, Snyder prodded
President Reagan in 1984 to agree to fund an emergency shelter in Washington,
D.C. But one accomplishment simply led to another goal in Snyder's ongoing battle
to "kick in doors where necessary" to help the homeless. Although a laudatory
movie about him starring Martin Sheen made him famous, he continued to live in a
shelter, and persistently challenged reluctant authorities to act on his recommendations. He persuaded members of Congress to hold hearings at his Community for Creative Non-Violence shelter, and was instrumental in the creation of the McKinney
Homeless Assistance Act of 1988.

Richard Sweeney, *Out of Place: Homelessness in America,* pp. 98–100

The heading of the textbook passage lets you know that the subject matter
deals with "homeless advocates," and the first paragraph gives their names.
Thus the topic of the selection is "Homeless advocates Robert Hayes and
Mitch Snyder." The two sentences in the first paragraph, which express the
main idea of the entire selection, provide the central message: "Robert Hayes
and Mitch Snyder, although differing in many respects, were both catalysts
for change during the dreary days of homelessness in the early 1980s. Both
helped to awaken Americans to the appalling conditions of homelessness and
convinced them that something could be done." The first sentences of the remaining two paragraphs are main ideas that support the central message:

Paragraph 1:   "Robert Hayes saw firsthand the plight of New York
               City's homeless and decided to do something about it."

Paragraph 2:   "Mitch Snyder also left a well-paying job to take up the
               cause of the homeless"

The rest of the selection, which consists of details organized by the compari-
son-and-contrast pattern of organization, also lends support to the central
message.

Let's look at another example, which was also taken from a textbook. As
you read the selection, take note of how the information is structured differently than it was in our first example, and think carefully about the topic and
central message.

## Tragedy of Sea

1   During the height of tensions during the Iran-Iraq war, a number of United States
Navy warships were in the Persian Gulf protecting the shipment of oil and other
commodities. On July 3, 1988, the *USS Vincennes,* a high-tech warship, was on rou-

tine patrol when one of its helicopters was attacked by Iranian gunboats. The *Vincennes* moved into Iranian territorial waters to help and opened fire with superior weapons on the gunboats.

2    To some observers, this was like shooting at rabbits with a radar guided-missile. However, to Captain Will Rogers and the crew of the *USS Vincennes,* this was the combat for which they had trained for years. As the shooting at the gunboats continued, tension aboard the *Vincennes* remained high. They were still positioned inside Iranian waters, and uncertainty about possible attacks by Iranian missiles and F-14 fighter planes lurked in the back of their minds.

3    Besides the threat of Iranian attack, stress was higher than usual under such circumstances. Neither Captain Rogers nor the crew were combat veterans. This was their first hostile encounter outside of wargames and other naval simulations where the ship's captain had developed a reputation as a risky decision maker.

4    At 9:47 A.M. an Iran Air 655 airbus took off from Bandar Abbas, Iran, with 290 civilian passengers aboard on a commercial air route over the Persian Gulf. Almost immediately, the radar on the *Vincennes* picked up the airliner and fed information about the aircraft into a sophisticated computer system designed to identify airplanes as "friendly," "hostile," or "unidentified."

5    The computer initially labeled the aircraft as a commercial flight. Unfortunately, in the tension and semidarkness of the ship's command center, a crew member checking commercial flight schedules for the Persian Gulf missed the listing for the airbus. Direct radio contact with the plane was initiated; but the aircraft's radio channels were busy with air traffic control information and the plane did not receive the initial messages or later warning from the *Vincennes.*

6    By this time, Captain Rogers had taken complete control of the situation. He was directing the fight with the gunboats and was trying to monitor information provided by the computer and his staff about the unidentified airplane. There were simply too many things to think about.

7    Then something happened that psychologists call scenario fulfillment—you see what you expect. In the tension of the moment, anxious crew members tagged the unidentified aircraft as an F-14 fighter and reported that it was descending, picking up speed, and closing in on the *Vincennes.* A later review of the tapes from the warship would reveal that no such thing occurred. In reality the passenger plane was slowing down and climbing to 12,000 feet.

8    Captain Rogers was confronted with incomplete and inaccurate information. He had seconds to make a decision and accepted his crew's conclusion that the aircraft was hostile. He gave the command to fire, and two SM-2 surface-to-air missiles were launched. Within seconds, the airbus, with its crew and 290 passengers, was destroyed.

Anthony F. Grasha, *Practical Applications of Psychology,* pp. 82–83

The heading, "Tragedy at Sea," gives a general idea of the topic, but you have to read the entire passage to find out exactly what happened. Although there is no stated main idea, a careful look at all of the information presented helps you uncover the central message. Notice how many of the sentences in the selection are organized in the time-sequence pattern of organization, which makes it easier to focus on the most important details and thus follow the events described. As a result, you are in a better position to piece together the facts and come up with the central message, which should read something like:

> In 1988, the United States Navy warship *USS Vincennes* shot down an Iran Air 655 airbus in the Persian Gulf, resulting in the deaths of the crew and 290 civilian passengers. Due to the stress involved in a conflict situation and the combat inexperience of Captain Will Rogers and his crew, the airbus was mistaken for an F-14 fighter plane that was about to attack the warship.

As you can see, uncovering the topic and central message of a selection is very useful, because it requires that you focus on the most important information. That should help you derive more meaning from textbook material and other kinds of reading. It will also help you master the approach to contemporary issues discussed in Chapter 3 by enabling you to determine what is at issue, distinguish among opposing viewpoints, and arrive at an informed personal viewpoint.

## ACTIVITY 7

Find the topic and central message for each of the selections that follow by answering the questions "What is this about?" and "What is the central message that the writer is communicating about the topic?" Remember to look carefully at main ideas within the paragraphs and any patterns of organization that may be present, because they will help you focus on the most important information.

### 1

## Problem Solving and Decision Making: Two Sides of the Same Coin

1    Each of us needs to solve problems and make decisions under a variety of circumstances. Some of them, like the situation faced by the captain of the *Vincennes,* are tension arousing. Incomplete information exists; there is little room for error; and quick decisions are needed. Other circumstances, while not life threatening, are just as important and demand our best efforts to manage them. Included here are such things as where to invest money, what career path to choose, whether or not to marry, how to resolve a personal problem, choosing what car to purchase, and deciding how to decorate a room or repair a small appliance.

2    Problem solving and decision making are sometimes treated in the literature as if they were separate topics. In reality, they are very much interrelated. To solve **problems** we have to make a number of important **decisions.** We must decide, among other things: how to adequately define our problem; what information is most important; which alternative **solutions** are possible and which one would be the "best" choice; and how to implement a particular solution or course of action. Having to deal with problems forces us to make decisions.

3    Similarly, whenever we say to ourselves, "I have got to make a decision. What should I do?" we are responding to a problem in our lives. That is, we are reacting to something for which we do not have a readily available response. The need to make a decision reflects the fact that we have a problem. *Consequently, suggestions for improving one process ultimately help us to do the other more effectively.*

Anthony F. Grasha, *Practical Applications of Psychology,* p. 83

## 2

1    It was Michael's first day at the university. Besides feeling a little overwhelmed, he was concerned about obtaining the right signatures from the right advisors, dealing with the financial aid office, locating the right buildings, and finding his class-rooms. During orientation week, Michael had also found registering for classes to be a nightmare. Long lines. Short tempers. And he couldn't get into all the classes he wanted, at least not at convenient times. Michael certainly didn't relish the thought of being in class at 8:00 every weekday morning.

2    Michael had signed up for some of the usual courses: Math, History, Art Appreciation, English, and Human Sexuality. These classes sounded interesting, but the idea of also taking Human Sexuality really appealed to him: "Taking a sex class is going to be a breeze! I'm already an expert. I probably won't even have to open the book. I can look for dates. X-rated videos. Sexy stories. Way to go, Mike! At least I'll have one 'easy A' this semester!"

3    If you're like Michael, your initial expectation of a course in human sexuality might be to watch sex education films, listen to people talk about their sex lives, and follow the instructor's discussion of sexual activities you've already experienced. You may see the class as a way of meeting potential sexual partners or maintaining a good grade point average. If you already think of yourself as a sexual expert, you may even consider this course a less than valuable way to spend your time.

4    You'll soon realize, however, that studying human sexuality involves much more than just reading stimulating sexual case studies and watching videos. You'll encounter a great deal of new material. You'll spend time rethinking your values and attitudes about sexuality. The differing viewpoints of your classmates will at times challenge your beliefs about what is acceptable. You'll come to view human sexuality for what it is—a beautiful and integral, but complex, part of life.

George Zgourides, *Human Sexuality,* pp. 2–3

## 3

## Are Car Phones Too Dangerous?

1    On January 13, 1996, Kayla Segerstron was driving in a minivan along a winding country road in Texas when her cellular phone rang. Reaching down to answer it, she missed a sharp turn and plowed into a car carrying the Colvin family.

2    Three-year-old Cole Colvin died; two-year-old Briana broke her neck. Their father suffered brain damage, rendering his left side virtually useless; their mother sustained minor injuries. Segerstron, 17, emerged virtually unhurt.

3    "This accident was directly attributable to the cell phone," says Steven DeWolf, the Colvins' attorney. "They're dangerous as hell." Last May, a jury awarded the

Colvins $7 million in damages, to be paid by the insurance company of the Segerstron's family business.

4     Cell phones are becoming almost as common as VCRs in the United States—an estimated 50 million are in use today. Yet society may be paying a high price for this convenience. A widely publicized 1997 study by the University of Toronto indicates that using a cell phone while driving quadruples the risk of having an accident—about the same risk as driving after having had two to three alcoholic drinks.

5     Even hands-free cell phones (which utilize speakers) didn't cut the risk factor in the study. "It's losing your concentration that's dangerous, much more than losing your grip on the steering wheel," says study author Donald A. Redelmeier, M.D. Other research reveals that even the most careful, experienced drivers increase their risk of accident if they talk on the phone and drive.

6     A number of countries, including Great Britain, Sweden, Italy, Brazil and Singapore, have passed or are considering legislation to limit the use of cell phones by drivers. Similar laws are under consideration in several states—yet cell phones also have determined advocates, from police officers to working mothers.

7     Many law enforcement officials defend the use of car phones because they turn drivers into emergency spotters. Approximately 60,000 calls are placed daily to 911 centers by motorists reporting accidents, fires or crimes. And alerts to radio stations about delays have helped improve traffic conditions.

8     Those opposed to banning cell phones also view the proposed legislation as drastic. The increased risk of accident, they point out, appears to be related to intense conversation coupled with driving maneuvers that require caution. But many who dial and drive limit themselves to quick check-ins or fast exchanges of information.

9     "Some argue that cell phones pose no more risk than other distractions, like fiddling with the radio or putting on makeup," notes Michael Goodman, Ph.D., an engineering research psychologist with the National Highway Traffic Safety Administration. "Of course, it's not possible to outlaw all those things. The bottom line is, *all* distractions at inopportune times can cause crashes."

10    Millions of commuters would be loath to give up calls, particularly parents eager to stay in touch with their kids and baby-sitters, and to be reachable in case of an emergency. On-the-go workers also find that talking in transit boosts productivity. Yet for women, having a cell phone is often an issue of safety—and peace of mind. "I work late and I'd be afraid to leave my car if there was a problem," says Cathy Barker, a nurse living in Birmingham, Alabama. "My cell phone makes me feel secure."

*Glamour*, September 1997, p. 232

# 4

## Close Your Eyes. Hold Your Nose. It's Dinner Time.

ERIC ASIMOV

1     Got a hankering for some calf testicles?

2     Wait, don't gag just yet. In the Rocky Mountain states, calf testicles—sliced, lightly battered and fried—are considered a delicacy by people who themselves might turn vivid shades of green at the thought of devouring a clam. And if neither

calf resticles nor clams repulse you, something in humanity's vast pantry will surely turn your stomach.

3      Humans eat just about anything that can be speared, hooked, shot or reared, from rooster coxcombs (the red things on their heads) to ox tails to grasshoppers to, yes, puppies and kittens. The species' wide-ranging tastes, which so easily arouse disgust among those who do not partake, are reflected in recent reports about two prized regional delicacies: squirrel brains, considered a treat in rural western Kentucky, and geoducks, freakishly large clams that thrive in the saltwater tidelands of the Pacific Northwest.

4      It seems that consuming squirrel brains can transmit to humans a fatal variant of mad cow disease, which essentially shreds human brain tissue. Scientists last month warned devotees to lay off the gray matter of the gray rodents, though those outside the Squirrel Brain Belt might argue that consuming the delicacy in the first place suggests that the damage has already been done.

5      And then there is the geoduck (oddly enough, pronounced GOO-ee-duck), a clam that can weigh as much as 16 pounds, with a neck like a flexible fire hydrant. Why a geoduck? Organized crime has apparently gotten into the business, smuggling this especially homely bivalve to Asia, where a single clam can sell for $50.

6      The mind may say "Yuck" to such formidable meals, but somewhere, sometime, a mouth first watered at the prospect. Who, after all, would have thought to eat an animal as hideous as a lobster?

7      "What's a lobster other than an insect, but slightly larger?" asked Andrew F. Smith, author of *The Tomato in America* (North Carolina University Press, 1994). Mr. Smith, who teaches culinary history at the New School for Social Research in New York, noted that crickets and grasshoppers were commonly eaten in the United States through the 19th century. "If you're hungry, you tend to eat things," he said, simply enough.

8      That logic might explain the cannibalistic Donner Party, settlers trapped in the Sierra Nevada a century and a half ago—but squirrel brains? "I'm sure that people who lived on the frontier, if they shot a squirrel—what's wrong with eating the brains?" Mr. Smith asked. "What's wrong with eating eyeballs? In Asian societies, eyeballs are considered common foods. If I were hungry, would I eat eyeballs? You bet I would!"

9      You may as well ask who was brave enough to taste a tomato. Mr. Smith said northern Europeans considered tomatoes too revolting to eat when Spanish conquistadors first brought them back from the New World. "Squeamishness depends on cultural background," he said, noting that slime from the surfaces of rivers and lakes was a prized food of the Aztecs.

10      While Mr. Smith's personal diet has occasionally included calf testicles, he does draw the line at the durian, a spiked, football-shaped fruit popular in Southeast Asia that is so famously stinky that Singapore, for one, prohibits slicing them open in public places.

11      It's a shame people can't do a better job of adapting to foods they consider gross, argued Calvin W. Schwabe in his 1979 book *Unmentionable Cuisine* (University Press of Virginia); he asserted that the world, and Americans in particular, may face dire long-term consequences by irrationally rejecting such foods, which can help

sustain the food supply and are often cheap, nutritious and tasty. He has collected recipes for foods that are actually eaten, somewhere in the world, including Samoan baked bat, Turkish lamb tongues and Hawaiian broiled puppy.

12      "How strange that we think it natural to eat *some* arthropods—even crabs, which are notorious scavengers of the deep—but just the idea of eating any of our really beautiful bugs and caterpillars, which feed on clean vegetation, makes us shudder," he lamented.

13      Paul Rozin, a professor of psychology at the University of Pennsylvania who studies human choices, says foods that disgust are almost all animal products. Asking why humans find a few scattered animal foods disgusting is the wrong question, he said. "We eat so few animal products that the real question is, why aren't all animal products revolting?" he said.

14      In the United States, which he termed "basically a muscle-eating country," viscosity—that state between solid and liquid that characterizes, say, squirrel brains—generally repulses, as does the odor of decay. But he pointed out that every culture has its exceptions.

15      "We prize cheese, which is rotted milk and smells that way," he said. "Fish sauce, which is rotted fish, is prized in Southeast Asia."

16      Clearly, people's tastes in food depend on what they grew up eating. Those who vow that rodent entrails will never pass between their lips think nothing of eating strips of pig flesh. But maybe if people were more familiar with the smells, squeals and butchery required to turn the pig into bacon, they would be less likely to shrink back from the innards and oddities of other cultures. Or maybe they would give up bacon.

17      Perhaps examining the food on the plate too closely is something we should all avoid. Have you ever looked closely at a Cheez Doodle? Now you can gag.

*The New York Times*, September 14, 1997, p. 2

## LOOKING BACK

With two of your classmates, come up with a list of the most important points you learned from this chapter and determine how they can be put to use in other classes. Be prepared to discuss both the list and the uses.

## THINK AGAIN!

How can you prove that 3 is half of 8?

## AND AGAIN!

For each of the signs that follow, write a paragraph in your notebook in which you discuss your interpretation of the message.

(1)

AS YOU
GO DOWN
THE BANISTER
OF LIFE

HERE'S
HOPING
THAT ALL THE
SPLINTERS GO
IN YOUR DIRECTION

(2)

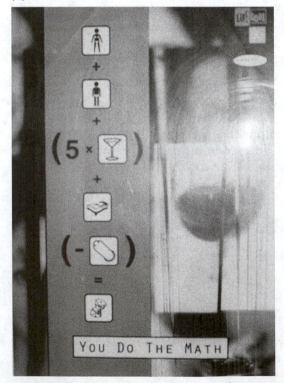

YOU DO THE MATH

(3)

A. Using the context, write the meanings next to the words that appear after the sentences.

1. Finally, the concept of **social engineering** was born—the belief that *strong governmental leaders, advised by social scientists, could use social science to design a preferred social order.* This notion remains a central ingredient in modern sociological thought.

Richard P. Appelbaum and William J. Chambliss, Sociology, pp. 18–19

**social engineering:** _____

_____

2. Your readers will expect an essay you write to be focused on a central idea, or **thesis,** to which all the essay's paragraphs, all its general statements and specific information, relate. The thesis is the controlling idea, the main point, the conclusion you have drawn about the evidence you have accumulated. (Even if you create a hypertext document, such as a site on the World Wide Web, you'll have a core idea that governs the links among pages and sites.)

H. Ramsey Fowler and Jane E. Aaron, The Little, Brown Handbook, p. 47

**thesis:** _____

3. Communicating via electronic devices, especially facsimile (fax) machines and computerized electronic mail (e-mail), speeds up correspondence but also creates new challenges. For both fax transmissions and e-mail, the standards are the same as for other business correspondence: state your purpose at the outset and write straightforwardly, clearly, concisely, objectively, courteously, and correctly.

H. Ramsey Fowler and Jane E. Aaron, The Little, Brown Handbook, p. 757

**fax:** _____

**e-mail:** _____

4. When the press secretary announced that the president had "passed away" instead of saying that he had died, he was using a euphemism.

**euphemism:** _____

_____

5. **Antipsychotic drugs,** or *major tranquilizers,* include chlorpromazine (Thorazine), haloperidol (Haldol), clozapine (Clozaril), and risperidone. These drugs have transformed the treatment of schizophrenia and other **psychoses** (extreme mental disorders that involve distorted perceptions and irrational behavior).

Carol Tavris and Carole Wade, Psychology in Perspective, p. 190

**antipsychotic drugs:** _____

_____

**psychoses:** _____

_____

6. You will often have multiple audiences, some *primary* (the people for whom your document is specifically intended) and some *secondary* (other people who may have reason to read all or part of the document). For example, your engineering report may be read by people who need to analyze the details of what you've written and by those who need to know only the conclusions and recommendations. If you know this in advance, you can make decisions about the document that can accommodate both types of readers. For example, you can decide whether it would be better to "frontload" the document . . . by putting the recommendations first or to begin with the background discussion.

Kristin R. Woolever, Writing for the Technical Professions, pp. 12–13

**primary audience:** _____

_____

**secondary audience:** _____

_____

**frontload:** _____

7. In the autumn, groves of quaking aspen trees turn Colorado mountainsides a rich gold. Up close you can hear the soft rustling of the leaves. It's almost constant, and in a gust of wind, whole trees seem to tremble, or quake. The trembling is an unusual property of aspen leaves, one that results from the unique combination of the parts of the leaves. . . . The stalk of each aspen leaf is flattened and acts like a hinge, letting the small, light leaf blade flutter back and forth in the slightest breeze. The fluttering seems to help the leaves breathe— that is, take up carbon dioxide and give off oxygen gas to the air. Plants use carbon dioxide and solar energy to make food (sugar molecules) by photosynthesis. They give off oxygen as a by-product of photosynthesis.

Neil A. Campbell, Lawrence G. Mitchell, and Jane B. Reece, Biology, p. 17

**photosynthesis:** _____

_____

8. Many people in the United States are still very much opposed to miscegenation, marriage between whites and blacks.

**miscegenation:** _____

9. Abortion will remain a contentious issue for many years to come.

   **contentious:** _____

10. Whereas the professor's lecture last night was very clear, her remarks today were ambiguous.

    **ambiguous:** _____

11. Those who oppose capital punishment offer incarceration for life with no chance for parole as an acceptable alternative.

    **incarceration:** _____

B. Write out the main idea for each of the following passages.

12. Many people report that speaking in front of an audience is their number-one fear. Even many experienced and polished speakers have some anxiety about delivering an oral presentation, but they use this nervous energy to their advantage, letting it propel them into working hard on each presentation, preparing well in advance, and rehearsing until they're satisfied with their delivery. They know that once they begin speaking and concentrate on their ideas, enthusiasm will quell anxiety. They know, too, that the symptoms of anxiety are usually imperceptible to listeners, who cannot see or hear a racing heart, upset stomach, cold hands, and worried thoughts. Even speakers who describe themselves as nervous usually appear confident and calm to their audiences.

H. Ramsey Fowler and Jane E. Aaron, *The Little, Brown Handbook*, p. 791

Main idea: _____

_____

_____

13. The term "technical profession" applies to a broad spectrum of careers in today's changing workplace where technology is making astonishingly rapid advances and boundaries between companies, countries, and continents are blurring and jobs are being redefined. In the past, the term "technical" conjured up an image of a male engineer with his T-square and slide rule, who made his living by his prowess at mathematical calculations. Today the computer has replaced the slide rule, and the technical professionals include an expanding cast of characters: women as well as men, engineers and scientists of all types, computer programmers, MIS professionals, technicians, laboratory personnel, biotechnical workers—anyone whose job entails working with specialized skills and knowledge in the hands-on fields of science, engineering, and technology.

Kristin R. Woolever, *Writing for the Technical Professions*, p. 1

Main idea: _____

_____

_____

14. For most people, choosing a spouse has never been an inexpensive or easy activity. Not long ago, some people were arguing that the institution of marriage was dying. Yet recent statistics show that the opposite is true: The percentage of Americans getting married has increased. Spouse selection is clearly an activity that most people eventually choose to engage in. A variety of considerations are involved. For example, the ease or difficulty of obtaining a divorce may have an effect on how spouses are chosen; so may the factor called love. Is there a rational, economic reason why individuals prefer a marriage in which there is mutual love? To answer this question, you need to know about the nature of economics.

Roger LeRoy Miller, *Economics Today*, p. 3

Main idea: _____

_____

_____

15. John, age 10, accompanies his mother on a shopping trip to some department stores. He notices the numerous sales and discounts across each of the stores. He asks his mother, "Why do stores offer all these discounts? Wouldn't they be better off keeping the same high price?" Mary, age 10, frequently accompanies her dad on grocery shopping trips. She notices how prices change regularly on hundreds of products. She asks, "Why do retailers change the prices on hundreds of items each week? Wouldn't they be better off finding one price for each item and sticking to it?" Indeed, wouldn't everyday high prices make for higher profit, greater efficiency and easier management?

Gerard J. Tellis, *Advertising and Sales Promotion Strategy*, p. 217

Main idea: _____

_____

_____

16. Currently, 25 nations suffer from chronic water shortages. The number of countries affected by such shortages is expected to increase to at least 90 within ten years. International tension over water availability is increasing rapidly. Currently there are 155 rivers and lakes shared by two or more countries. More than 30 are shared by three countries and 20 are shared by dozens of countries. United Nations estimates suggest that there is a real danger of war erupting in at least 10 areas around the world as a direct result of international competition over water resources. Shortages do not stem from the disappearance of water.

The nature of the planet's hydrologic cycle is such that, for the most part, the total supply of freshwater never increases or diminishes. Shortages stem from population growth, misuse and waste, the latter two frequently making water unfit for human consumption.

F. Kurt Cylke Jr., *The Environment*, p. 58

Main idea: _____

_____

_____

17. For a time after World War II, the nation seemed on the verge of a literary outburst comparable to that which followed World War I. A number of excellent novels based on the military experiences of young writers appeared, the most notable being Norman Mailer's *The Naked and the Dead* (1948) and James Jones's *From Here to Eternity* (1951). Unfortunately, a new renaissance did not develop. The most talented younger writers rejected materialist values but preferred to bewail their fate rather than rebel against it. Jack Kerouac, founder of the "beat" (for beatific) school, reveled in the chaotic description of violence, perversion, and madness. At the other extreme, J. D. Salinger, perhaps the most popular writer of the 1950s and the particular favorite of college students—*The Catcher in the Rye* (1951) sold nearly 2 million copies in hardcover and paperback editions—was an impeccable stylist, witty, contemptuous of all pretense; but he too wrote about people entirely wrapped up in themselves.

John A. Garraty, *A Short History of the American Nation*, p. 530

Main idea: _____

_____

_____

18. Imagine you are standing before an enormous clock on which the hands tick away the years of the earth's history. The clock is set so that 24 hours represent the nearly 5-billion-year history of our planet. On this cosmic scale, a single second equals nearly 60,000 years; a single minute, 3.5 million years. The first life on earth—the simple one-celled organisms that emerged in the oceans some 2.5 to 3.5 billion years ago—do not make their appearance until at least 7 hours on the clock have passed by. The dinosaurs appear at about the twenty-third hour; they walk the planet for less than 42 minutes, then disappear forever. On this 24-hour clock, the first humanlike creatures appear during the last 2 minutes (4.5 million years ago), and *Homo sapiens* emerges in the last 4 seconds, some 250,000 years ago. What we call human history has barely appeared at all. Written languages, cities, and agriculture, which date back some 12,000 years, emerge only in the last quarter second, representing not even a tick.

2    On a planetary scale, human beings are very recent arrivals indeed, and what we proudly refer to as human history barely registers. Yet, although we arrived only an instant ago, we have certainly made our presence known. Our

population has exploded a thousandfold during the last 17 seconds on the planetary clock, from five million people before written language heralded the dawn of human history to nearly six billion people today. Within 40 years, another five billion people will be added to our crowded planet. Human beings already occupy every corner of the earth, crowding out other forms of plant and animal life. Thanks to modern science, technology, and industry, each of us today is capable of consuming a vastly greater amount of the planet's limited resources than were our prehistoric ancestors. The damage to our planet caused by this explosion in the population is one of the major global issues facing the world today.

P. Appelbaum and William J. Chambliss, *Sociology*, p. 4

Main idea: _____

_____

_____

19. "Among the nations of the earth today America stands for one idea: *Business*," a popular writer announced in 1921. "Through business, properly conceived, managed and conducted, the human race is finally to be redeemed." Bruce Barton, the head of the largest advertising firm in the country, was the author of one of the most popular nonfiction books of the decade. In *The Man Nobody Knows* (1925), he depicted Christ as "the founder of modern business." He took 12 men from the bottom ranks of society and forged them into a successful organization. "All work is worship; all useful service prayer," Barton argued. If the businessman would just copy Christ, he could become a supersalesman.

2    Business, especially big business, prospered in the 1920s, and the image of businessmen, enhanced by their important role in World War I, rose further. The government reduced regulation, lowered taxes, and cooperated to aid business expansion at home and abroad. Business and politics, always intertwined, were especially allied during the decade. Wealthy financiers such as Andrew Mellon and Charles Dawes played important roles in formulating both domestic and foreign policy. Even more significant, a new kind of businessman was elected president in 1928. Herbert Hoover, international engineer and efficiency expert, was the very symbol of the modern techniques and practices that many people confidently expected to transform the United States and the world.

Gary B. Nash and Julie Roy Jeffrey, *The American People*, p. 823

Main idea: _____

_____

_____

20. A friend of ours attended a conference in which psychologists were discussing the case of a troubled girl. The girl was disruptive and belligerent, and this behavior made her mother angry. The father, who worked long hours, came home tired most nights and didn't want to deal with the situation.

2      The first psychologist thought the problem was that the child was temperamentally difficult from birth—a biological matter that could be treated with drugs. The second psychologist thought the problem was that the child had learned to behave inappropriately and aggressively in order to get the attention of her father; this pattern could be treated with behavior therapy. The third psychologist thought the problem was the mother, who was misinterpreting her daughter's behavior as an intentional effort to provoke her; the mother could be helped with cognitive therapy. The fourth psychologist saw the situation as stemming from traditional gender roles within this family's culture (the "absent" father, the "overprotective" mother) and the role of each individual in a family network; all of them would benefit from family therapy. The fifth psychologist thought that the problem was the child's unresolved Oedipal feelings, the mother's displacement of affectional needs for her husband onto the child, and the father's unconscious anxieties about being a father; the child and the parents could be helped with psychodynamic therapy.

Carol Tavris and Carole Wade, *Psychology in Perspective*, p. 573

Main idea: _____

_____

_____

C. Identify the pattern of organization for each of the following passages.

21. Managing stress is not unlike training to participate in any sport. Those who are healthy are in good physical condition, get proper amounts of rest, and eat a healthy diet typically perform well. Such individuals have the physical endurance and strength to handle the stresses of the event. In much the same way, we need "to be in shape" to handle the demands and challenges of daily living. People who are physically fit become fatigued less easily; they remain alert to cope with the demands placed upon them; their immune systems are stronger; they possess more energy for handling events in their lives; and they are less susceptible to illnesses.

Anthony F. Grasha, *Practical Applications of Psychology*, p. 413

Pattern of organization: _____

22. The overhead door installation has caused delays and cost overruns for the HOTCELL chamber operation. The door motor terminal strip was not labeled, and the terminals were not consistent. This required significant time for the electrical contractor to troubleshoot and complete accurate terminations. The overhead door installer was not able to provide assistance, since he had no way of knowing how they were factory wired. In addition, at least one motor was factory wired incorrectly, which was corrected by the electrical contractor. The door limit switch and safety edges have had to be periodically reset on frequent failures of operation.

The door seals have also been a problem. In addition, the wall panels have had to be returned because of a lack of fit at the joints.

Kristin R. Woolever, *Writing for the Technical Professions,* p. 316

Pattern of organization: _____

23. Although it was easy to romanticize the West, that region lent itself better to the realistic approach. Almost of necessity, novelists writing about the West described coarse characters from the lower levels of society, and dealt with crime and violence. It would have been difficult indeed to write a genteel romance about a mining camp. The outstanding figure of western literature, the first great American realist, was Mark Twain.

2       Twain, whose real name was Samuel L. Clemens, was born in 1835. He grew up in Hannibal, Missouri, on the banks of the Mississippi. After having mastered the printer's trade and worked as a riverboat pilot, he went west to Nevada in 1861. Soon he was publishing humorous stories about the local life under the *nom de plume* Mark Twain. In 1865, while working in California, he wrote "The Celebrated Jumping Frog of Calaveras County," a story that brought him national recognition. A tour of Europe and the Holy Land in 1867–1868 led to the writing of *The Innocents Abroad* (1869), which made him famous.

John A. Garraty, *A Short History of the American Nation,* p. 342

Pattern of organization: _____

24. **Rebates** are a guarantee by firms to reimburse consumers directly for the purchase of a product, subject to certain conditions. Technically, the term has the same meaning as **refund,** except that *rebate* is used for durables and *refund* for nondurables. The typical conditions for a rebate are the mailing in of (1) the refund voucher, (2) a proof of purchase from the product container or package and (3) the sales receipt. The rebate is similar to the coupon. Thus much of our discussion about coupons would apply to rebates. However, rebates differ from coupons in one important way: they require much greater effort to redeem.

Gerard F. Tellis, *Advertising and Sales Promotion Strategy,* p. 282

Pattern of organization: _____

D. Write out the central message for each of the following selections.

25. **Life in a Nursing Home**

1   *Life in a nursing home is almost never the idyll pictured in brochures. Inside, residents are sometimes neglected by the staff, often abandoned by family, and almost always diminished physically and mentally by advancing age. Men and women in wheelchairs are lined up in day rooms and hallways, dozing in and out of reality; others are curled up in their beds, tubes dangling from their bodies. Diminished though they may be, residents still cling to their dignity.*

2    "Don't tie me in, please," a lady named Anna cries out. She sees an aide approach with a tan waist belt that will bind her to the wheelchair. "I don't care if I fall out. Don't tie me up. That's terrible." Her bony fingers reach out to push away the hated restraint. "I'm not going to be tied." Her hands tremble as she grasps the hand rail along the corridor. "No, that's cruel. Don't tie me, don't tie me. Thoughtless. That's what they are," she shouts, her voice firm and determined. Anna is lucky that day. A visitor questions a nurse at the Beverly Hills Nursing Center, in Royal Oak, Mich. Is there a doctor's order for the restraint, as there must be? The nurse backs off. For a while, Anna is free.

3    Helga, dressed in pink with a bandage on her leg, sobs uncontrollably. She misses Roy, her special friend. She doesn't remember Roy has just come to see her. The admissions director, whose name is Nancy, stops a tour to reassure her. Roy has been here and will come again. "I know you miss him," Nancy says gently. Down the hall, Theresa, another resident, misses Archie, her husband of many years. Archie and Theresa both lived at the Moroun Nursing Home, on the east side of Detroit—Theresa on one floor for residents with dementia and Archie on another. Archie died a week ago, and Theresa, 87, is working through her initial grief. She is better dressed than most nursing-home residents and her hair is carefully set. Theresa cries and caresses Archie's picture. She says she had five sons—or was it four? The admissions director again stops, looks at the picture, and listens. "He was a good husband," Theresa says. "Part of loving is letting go," Nancy tells her.

4    Boris, in a purple jogging suit with no place to run, struggles to stand up. Catheter tubes tangle around his legs. He tries to walk, but a waist belt traps him in his wheelchair. His fingers tug at the belt. He tries to loosen it. Unable to free himself, he calls out to the nurse working at the station a few feet in front of him. "What is it, Boris?" she snaps. "Don't get excited. Your daughter's coming." Boris yanks at the belt again, but it is stubborn. He remains tethered to his chair. "You can't take it off," the nurse tells him. "It's to keep you safe." She makes no effort to release Boris even for a moment, or hold his hand, or give him a hug, or otherwise comfort him in his isolated world at the Hillhaven nursing facility, in San Francisco, Calif.

5    The plump woman, her white hair fashioned in a knot at the back of her head, sits whimpering. She looks like everyone's grandmother, a woman who once might have whipped up oatmeal cookies and dished out love. On this day she is helpless in her home—the Charlestown Care Center, in Catonsville, Md. Blood leaks from the bridge of her nose. It drips from her nostrils; her hands are bruised. Perhaps she has fallen. An attendant with a stethoscope removes a small bandage from the woman's nose, then goes away, but the blood keeps oozing. The woman tries to wipe it. An hour and a quarter passes. There's more blood but no help, even though she is positioned right in front of a densely populated nurses' station. The whimpering continues as bloody tissues pile around her feet.

6    A lady wearing a blue sock and a red sock has wheeled herself to the nurses' station. A yellow lap blanket is on the floor beside her. Her skirt is hiked

up to her groin, revealing bloody, raw sores on her legs. She pulls at her diaper, struggling to take it off. Undoubtedly, she is wet. But the nurses pay no attention. An admissions official giving a tour of The Arbor, in Austin, Tex., spots the woman and whisks her down the nearest hall—even though a nurse calls out that the woman's room is in another direction.

7   "Ninety-five percent of the people here you can't communicate with," says Harry. "This is where I stay. I have no one to talk to. The staff doesn't talk too much—only if I ask them questions." So Harry, age 72, sits in his wheelchair and paints in his "studio," an art room at the end of a long, drab hall at the Heartland Community Care Center, in Detroit. He squirts colors out of a tube—orange, yellow, red, purple, white—and matches them to the notes of Beethoven's Fifth Symphony piped through his earphones. Yellows and whites are high notes; deeper colors, the lower tones. "If I didn't do this I would go bananas," he says. "I wouldn't exist. This is a prison without gates. You can't go far." Harry is a big man with a head of curly hair. "I'm supposed to be walked every day. But they don't do it. I'm supposed to get range of motion everyday. There's no plan. It's whatever some aide feels like doing. I need therapy. I have two daughters. They never come. They don't understand that one day they might have to come here."

8   One by one residents are wheeled into a large room, clutching a wedding photograph, a stuffed cat with white fur, a statue of Jesus. One woman carries an engagement ring given to her 60 years ago. It's shared treasure time at Kensington Gardens, in Kensington, Md. The staff member leading the activity holds up each treasure and walks it around so every resident can see it closely, and with great sensitivity describes the souvenirs of life long ago. One man has lugged in a cello. He has no medical need to be at Kensington Gardens, a visitor is told, but he has no other place to live. He came for a short time after an illness and stayed on. He saved his money and one day rode a bus to a music store and rented a cello. He is the rare resident who still has his freedom.

9   A 94-year-old woman summons a visitor passing by her door. An aide has mistakenly placed her roommate's pillow on her bed. The roommate, sitting in the corner, is annoyed, her face hardened in silence. The woman needs someone to put the pillow back in its right spot. "I'm so worried," she says. "My son-in-law had a bypass today." She has yet to hear from her daughter, who lives around the corner from the Randolph Hills Nursing Center, in Wheaton, Md. The woman begins to cry. "My hands and legs hurt. I want to die." Visitors tell her they are glad they could come and talk to her today. "Why?" she asks.

Consumer Reports, August 1995, p. 521

Central message: _____

_____

_____

## 26. The Cost of Being Different: Effects of Lesbian and Gay Prejudices

### JODY:

1   Jody is a junior in the honors program, majoring in women's studies. She is energetic, outgoing, affectionate, and an animated speaker. She has very short hair and wears no make up. She says that people attribute her appearance to her feminism and do not recognize her lesbian identity until told.

2   In class, she feels very comfortable talking about lesbian issues as well as the issues facing other oppressed groups. She is aware that there is some negative reaction to her. Sometimes she sees other students rolling their eyes and hissing while she talks; other times, she feels that instructors are trying to placate her and move on to safer topics very hastily. She must also bear hearing teachers say things that are false such as, "There were no gay or lesbian people in colonial times. We can't dwell on irrelevant issues."

3   Her activism sometimes brings her close to burnout. She gets tired of answering questions such as, "In lesbian couples, who is the man and who is the woman?" The burden of educating others at times seems unreasonable to her. Jody also chooses her courses carefully, based on advice she hears within her community on which instructors are receptive.

### GREGG:

4   Gregg is a sophomore with a major in mechanical engineering. He comes across as a serious, intelligent, and likeable college student. Although his friends and family now know of his identity, he is still reluctant to come out publicly, fearing violence or verbal attacks that he does not feel strong enough to handle. Gregg views his mental agony as "hellish," and he has difficulty concentrating on his coursework. He once told a friend, "I'm one step short of a nervous breakdown." The worst part was that he felt so alone.

5   He hadn't anticipated the overt and subtle ways fellow students and teachers show their disapproval of gay men. When he hears students snickering about "faggots" and "fruitcakes," he cringes. When teachers tolerate homophobic remarks by ignoring them, he feels furious but not empowered to take the initiative. He is hoping that one day he will feel strong enough to confront such negative stereotypes and hatreds. For now, he is silent. He is reluctant to write about gay topics, fearing there will be grade retaliation or that his papers will be considered too "personal" rather than scholarly. Gregg also recognizes he is majoring in a field where there is discrimination against gay men, so he has to be very cautious about his identity—something he will have to do for the rest of his life.

Anthony F. Grasha, *Practical Applications of Psychology*, p. 307

Central message: _____

_____

_____

## GO ELECTRONIC!

For additional readings, exercises, and Internet activities, visit our Website at:

### http://longman.awl.com/englishpages

If you need a user name and password, see your instructor.

**Take a Road Trip to** the Library of Congress, the Maine Woods, the St. Louis Arch, and Ellis Island. Be sure to visit the Vocabulary, Main Idea, Supporting Details, and Patterns of Organization modules in your Reading Road Trip CD-ROM for multimedia tutorials, exercises, and tests.

## Chapter Two

# Getting the Most out of Your Textbooks: A Review

**Chapter Outline**

Overviewing Your Textbooks

Previewing Textbook Chapters

Reading a Textbook Chapter Critically:
Questions and Answers

The store in the photograph below has an unusual way of advertising. What is it doing that is out of the ordinary? Discuss your answer with your classmates.

(1)

Look carefully at the signs in the following photographs. Why are they examples of clever advertising strategies? Discuss your answers with your classmates.

(2)

(3)

## Overviewing Your Textbooks

If you were to move to a new town, one of your chief concerns would be getting to know your way around as quickly and efficiently as possible. You would want to become familiar with your neighborhood in order to locate the nearest bank, the best store for food shopping, the movie theaters, the hospital, the post office, and any other establishments that are important or helpful to you. By accomplishing this task at the very beginning, you would feel more secure and comfortable with your new surroundings, and it would save you time by enabling you to get places faster.

As a college student, at the beginning of every semester, you should get to know your way around your new textbooks as quickly and efficiently as possible. Other than instructors, textbooks are the most important sources of information that you use in most of your courses. Thus you want to become very familiar with them in order to save time and feel secure and comfortable when reading them. You accomplish this through the use of **overviewing,** which is a quick method of getting acquainted with textbooks.

Overviewing involves **skimming,** or quickly glancing over, the front and back parts of a textbook in order to find out what it is about, how it is organized, and what aids to understanding are offered to help you comprehend it better. **Aids to understanding,** or **learning aids**—which make it easier to use your textbooks—could include appendixes, bibliographies, glossaries, graphic aids, indexes, objectives, outlines, prefaces, previews, questions, reference sources, summaries, tables of contents, and vocabulary lists.

At the very least, the front pages of a textbook usually include a title page, table of contents, and preface. As you know, the **title page** tells you what the book is about in addition to providing the name of the author, the publishing company, and the edition. The back of the title page gives the copyright date or the date of publication of that particular edition of the book so you know if you are dealing with material that is current. After the title page, you will most often find the **table of contents,** which is a blueprint of the entire book's organization. It lists not only the section and chapter titles but also all the main headings in each chapter. In short, it tells you more specifically what the textbook is about and helps you understand how the chapter headings are related to one another. For example, if in a chapter, headings such as "Anxiety Disorders," "Schizophrenia," "Anger," and "Depression" are listed under a larger heading like "Understanding Emotional Disorders," you would recognize immediately that the four subheadings are all examples of emotional disorders. Recognizing these kinds of connections or relationships would help make it easier to understand the chapter when you read it later on.

The **preface,** which generally comes after the table of contents, is also referred to as an introduction. Sometimes it is divided into "To the Instructor" and "To the Student" sections, or it may be a combination of both. Regardless of how it is structured or for whom it is written, the preface is valuable because it usually gives the author's purpose for writing the textbook, lists the features that make the book noteworthy, tells how the book is organized to help the reader, and lists and explains the aids to understanding. All of this information lets you know what you should accomplish as a result of reading the book and what is provided by the writer to help you to use it more efficiently. Although the table of contents shows what is included in the back part of a textbook, you should take a quick look for yourself.

The back pages of a textbook almost always include an alphabetically arranged **index,** which gives page locations for very specific information. Sometimes the index is divided into name and subject sections, which makes it faster to use. An alphabetically arranged **glossary** is also often found in the back, and it provides definitions of either individual words or combinations of words that fit the context of a given text. Many of those combinations of words will not even be found in a dictionary. For example, the glossary in a biology textbook defines *neutral variation* as "genetic variation that provides no apparent selective advantage for some individuals over others." Although the dictionary provides separate definitions for *neutral* and *variation*, it does not define them in combination. Thus glossaries give the meanings for specialized terms. They are also quicker to use than a dictionary because you do not have to search through a long list of definitions to find the specific one that fits the subject matter.

A **bibliography** containing sources used by the author to write the book, often supplemented by a list of **reference sources** or **suggested readings,** may be located at the back of a textbook or at the end of each chapter. **Credits** and **notes** are sometimes listed as well. They are all useful if research is necessary in order to read further on a given topic or perhaps to write a paper. On occasion, you can also find an **appendix** that includes supplementary or additional information such as definitions, experiments, maps, or diagrams that can prove helpful in understanding the subject matter of the textbook.

Overviewing takes only a short time, but it is well worth the effort. The sooner you become familiar with a textbook, the better your chances of reading it faster and with much more understanding. Furthermore, your awareness of all the aids to understanding included in the book by the writer should make the whole experience easier and more rewarding—and these elements come in very handy when studying for exams.

## ACTIVITY 1

Overview the following pages (pp. 55–72) taken from the front and back of a college textbook. Then, in your notebook, answer the overview questions. Be prepared to discuss where you found your answers to the questions.

### Overview Questions

1. What is the textbook about?
2. Who is the author?
3. What is the edition?
4. What is the name of the publishing company?
5. What is the date of publication?
6. How many chapters are in the book?
7. Name four "Agents of Socialization" and five "Examples of Deviance."
8. What can be found in the back of the book?
9. What is the author's purpose for writing the book?
10. What are the major features?
11. Is there anything new in this edition of the book?
12. What aids to understanding are included?
13. What is a "vignette"?
14. What is the "glass ceiling"?
15. What is a "budget deficit"?
16. What book did Paul Bohannan write?
17. What is the name of the article written by David C. Anderson?
18. What is the first credit listed for Chapter 7?
19. On what pages can you find information on Confucius?
20. On what page can you find information on "battered women"?

**Front Pages**

# SOCIOLOGY

## A Brief Introduction

### THIRD EDITION

# ALEX THIO
## OHIO UNIVERSITY

 LONGMAN

An imprint of Addison Wesley Longman, Inc.

New York • Reading, Massachusetts • Menlo Park, California • Harlow, England
Don Mills, Ontario • Sydney • Mexico City • Madrid • Amsterdam

Sociology: A Brief Introduction, Third Edition

Acquisitions Editor: Alan McClare
Developmental Editor: Ann Torbert
Supplements Editor: Tom Kulesa
Project Coordination and Text Design: Thompson Steele Production Services
Cover Design: Kay Petronio
Photo Researcher: Julie Tesser
Electronic Production Manager: Eric Jorgensen
Manufacturing Manager: Hilda Koparanian
Electronic Page Makeup: Thompson Steele Production Services
Printer and Binder: RR Donnelley & Sons Company
Cover Printer: Phoenix Color Corp.

For permission to use copyrighted material, grateful acknowledgment is made to the
copyright holders on pages 381–382, which are hereby made part of this copyright page.

Library of Congress Cataloging-in-Publication Data

Thio, Alex.
    Sociology : a brief introduction / Alex Thio. — 3rd ed.
        p.    cm.
    Includes bibliographical references (p.  ) and index.
    ISBN 0-673-98111-8
    1. Sociology.      I. Title.
    HM24.T495   1997
    301—dc20                                     96-16015
                                                 CIP

ISBN 0-673-98111-8

12345678910—DOW—99989796

# Detailed Contents

Preface   xiii
About the Author   xix

## 1  The Essence of Sociology   2

**The Study of Social Life   4**
More Than Common Sense   4
Analyzing Social Diversity   5
Exploring the Global Village   5
Sociology as a Science   5
The Sociological Imagination   6
**The Development of Sociology   8**
The Pioneers of Sociology   8
Sociology in the United States   10
**Major Perspectives in Sociology   11**
Functionalist Perspective   11
Conflict Perspective   12
Symbolic Interactionist Perspective   14
A Multiple View   14
**Sports: Illustrating the Three
Perspectives   15**
Sports as Beneficial to Society   16
Sports as Harmful to Society   16
Sports as Symbolic Interaction   18
**Major Research Methods   19**
Survey   19
Observation   20
Experiment   22
Analysis of Existing Data   22
**How Sociology Can Enrich Our Lives   24**

## 2  Society and Culture   28

**Components of Society   30**
Statuses   30
Roles   31
Groups   32
Institutions   32
**Societies in Sociocultural Evolution   33**
Hunting-Gathering Societies   34
Pastoral Societies   35
Horticultural Societies   35
Agricultural Societies   36
Industrial Societies   37

Postindustrial Societies   37
**Components of Culture   39**
Knowledge and Beliefs   41
Norms and Values   41
Language   42
**U.S. Culture   44**
Basic Values   44
Multiculturalism   44
Pop Culture   46
**A Global Analysis of Culture   47**
Cultural Universals   47
Culture Clash   49
Ethnocentrism   49
Cultural Relativism   49
**Perspectives on Culture   50**
Functionalist Perspective   51
Conflict Perspective   51
Symbolic Interactionist Perspective   51

## 3  Socialization   56

**The Significance of Heredity   58**
**The Significance of Socialization   59**
Impairing Development   59
Creating Geniuses   60
**Theories of Personality Development   60**
Freud: Psychosexual Development   60
Piaget: Cognitive Development   61
Kohlberg: Moral Development   63
Sociology of Emotions: Affective
Development   63
Feminist Theory: Gender Development   64
**Perspectives on Socialization   65**
Functionalist Perspective   65
Conflict Perspective   65
Symbolic Interactionist Perspective   66
**Agents of Socialization   68**
The Family   68
The School   68
The Peer Group   69
The Mass Media   70
**Adult Socialization   70**
Learning New Roles   70
Continuing Development   71

© 2000 Addison-Wesley Educational Publishers, Inc.

viii    Detailed Contents

Aging and Dying  72
A Global Analysis of Socialization  73
Are We Puppets of Society?  75

## 4  Social Interaction in Everyday Life  78

Functionalist Perspective  81
Exchange  81
Cooperation  81
Conflict Perspective  81
Competition  82
Conflict  82
Symbolic Interactionist Perspective  83
Interpreting Supportive Interaction  83
Interpreting Oppositional Interaction  83
Interaction as Symbolic Communication  83
The Nature of Human Communication  84
A Global Analysis of Communication  85
U.S. Diversity in Communication  86
Communication Between Women and Men  87
Speaking Different Genderlects  87
Playing the Gendered Game of Proxemics  88
Dramaturgy: Interaction as Drama  89
Behaving Like Actors  89
Presenting the Self  90
Performing Interaction Rituals  91
The Art of Managing Impressions  92
Defensive Measures by Performers  92
Protective Measures by Audience  92
The Social Construction of Reality  93
Thomas Theorem: Creating Reality with Definition  93
Ethnomethodology: Exposing Hidden Reality  94
Humorology: Subverting Reality with Humor  95

## 5  Groups and Organizations  98

Social Groups  100
In-Groups and Out-Groups  100
Reference Groups  101
Primary and Secondary Groups  101
Group Leadership  103
Group Conformity  103
Group Size  104
Social Networks  105

Characteristics  105
Effects  106
Formal Organizations  106
Goals and Means  106
Power and Involvement  107
Classifying Organizational Theories  109
Functionalist Perspective  109
Scientific Management  109
Human Relations  110
Conflict Perspective  111
Collectivist Model  111
Feminist Model  112
Symbolic Interactionist Perspective  112
Organizational Culture: Shared Definitions  112
Bureaucracy: Embodiment of "Rational" Worldview  113
The Realities of Bureaucracy  114
Bureaucratic Benefits  114
Bureaucratic Problems  115
The Future of Bureaucracy  116
A Global Analysis of Organizations  116

## 6  Deviance and Control  120

What Is Deviance?  123
Examples of Deviance  123
Homicide  123
Drug Abuse  124
Rape  125
Corporate Crime  127
Mental Disorder  128
Functionalist Perspective  129
Durkheim: Functionalist Theory  129
Merton: Strain Theory  129
Hirschi: Control Theory  130
Braithwaite: Shaming Theory  131
Conflict Perspective  132
Conflict Theory  132
Power Theory  133
Feminist Theory  133
Symbolic Interactionist Perspective  134
Differential Association Theory  134
Labeling Theory  134
Phenomenological Theory  135
Controlling Deviance  136
Social Control  136
Criminal Justice  137
The War on Drugs  138
A Global Analysis of Deviance  139

*7*   **U.S. and Global Stratification   142**

**The Bases of Stratification   144**
Wealth   144
Power   145
Prestige   146
**The U.S. Class Structure   146**
Identifying Classes   146
Class Profiles   148
The Influence of Class   148
**Poverty in the United States   150**
What Is Poverty?   150
Feminist Perspective on Poverty   151
Causes of Poverty   153
**Homelessness in the United States   154**
Who Are the Homeless?   154
Causes of Homelessness   154
**Welfare in the United States   155**
Beliefs About Welfare   155
Reforming Welfare   155
**Social Mobility in U.S. Society   156**
Patterns   156
Sources   157
**Global Stratification   158**
Global Classes   158
Interclass Relations   159
International Inequality   160
Mobility in Global Society   161
**Perspectives on Stratification   162**
Functionalist Perspective   162
Conflict Perspective   162
Symbolic Interactionist Perspective   163
**Toward Social Equality   163**

*8*   **Race and Ethnicity   166**

**Sociological Definitions   168**
Race   168
Ethnicity   169
Minority   170
**Race and Ethnicity in the United States   170**
Native Americans   171
African Americans   172
Hispanic Americans   173
Asian Americans   175
Jewish Americans   177
European Americans   178
Putting It All Together   179
**Racial and Ethnic Relations   180**
Functionalist Perspective   180

Conflict Perspective   181
Symbolic Interactionist Perspective   182
**Prejudice and Discrimination   182**
Characteristics   182
Causes   183
Consequences   184
Attempted Solutions   185
**A Global Analysis of Race and Ethnicity   185**

*9*   **Gender and Age   188**

**Gender Roles   190**
Gender Roles in the United States   190
Gender Roles in Other Societies   191
Biological Constraints   192
The Role of Culture   192
**Gender Socialization   193**
The Family   193
The Peer Group   194
The School   194
The Mass Media   195
The Learning Process   195
**Gender Inequality   196**
Sexism   197
Education   197
Employment   198
Politics   199
Religion   200
Sexual Harassment   201
**Perspectives on Gender Inequality   202**
Functionalist Perspective   202
Conflict Perspective   202
Symbolic Interactionist Perspective   203
**A Global Analysis of Gender Inequality   204**
**The Aging Process   204**
Biological Consequences of Aging   204
Psychological Consequences of Aging   205
Social Effects on Aging   205
**Perspectives on Aging   206**
Functionalist Perspective   206
Conflict Perspective   207
Symbolic Interactionist Perspective   207
**A Global Analysis of Aging   208**

*10*   **Families   212**

**Families: A Global Analysis   214**
Family Composition   214
Mate Selection   214
Residence and Descent   215

**x**   Detailed Contents

Authority   216
**Perspectives on the Family   216**
Functionalist Perspective   216
Conflict Perspective   217
Symbolic Interactionist Perspective   217
**Patterns of U.S. Marriages   218**
Preparing for Marriage   218
Marriage Choices   219
Marital Happiness   220
**Family Problems   221**
Violence   221
Divorce   221
**Changes in the U.S. Family   224**
Historical Background   224
Two-Career Families   225
Single-Parent Families   226
Stepfamilies   226
**Alternative Lifestyles   227**
Staying Single   227
Living Together   228
Gay and Lesbian Marriages   228
**Ethnic Diversity of U.S. Families   229**
Native American Families   229
Hispanic American Families   230
African American Families   230
Asian American Families   230
**The Future of the Family   231**

*11*   **Education and Religion   234**

**Sociological Perspectives on Education   236**
Functionalist Perspective   236
Conflict Perspective   237
Symbolic Interactionist Perspective   239
**Education in the United States   240**
Problems in Perspective   240
Head Start   241
School Choice   242
Lifelong Learning   242
**A Global Analysis of Education   243**
Schools in Belgium   243
Schools in Finland   244
Schools in France   244
Schools in Japan   244
**Sociological Perspectives on Religion   245**
Functionalist Perspective   245
Conflict Perspective   247
Symbolic Interactionist Perspective   248
**Religion in the United States   249**
Religious Affiliation   249
The Class Factor   249

The Age Factor   249
The Fundamentalist Revival   250
The Rise of Islam   251
**A Global Analysis of Religion   252**
Theism   252
Ethicalism   253
Animism   254

*12*   **Economy and Politics   258**

**The Economy in Perspective   260**
The Industrial Revolution   260
Sociological Perspectives on Capitalism   262
**The World's Economic Systems   264**
The Economic Continuum   264
The U.S. Economy Today   264
The Economies in Other Countries   265
**Work in the United States   267**
Occupations   267
The Workers   267
Job Satisfaction   268
The Changing Workplace   269
**Power and Authority   270**
The Nature of Power   270
Types of Authority   270
Citizens' Attitudes Toward Government   271
**Who Really Governs in U.S. Society?   272**
The Pluralist View   272
The "Elitist" View   273
The Marxist View   274
**Political Violence: A Global Analysis   275**
Causes of Revolution   275
Revolution in Eastern Europe   276
The Collapse of the Soviet Union   276
The Nature of Terrorism   277
Responses to Terrorism   277
**Sociological Perspectives on War   278**
Functionalist Perspective   278
Conflict Perspective   278
Symbolic Interactionist Perspective   279

*13*   **Health and Population   282**

**Health and Society   284**
Social Factors   284
Epidemiology   285
AIDS   286
A Global Analysis of Health   287
**Medical Care   288**
The Changing Medical Profession   288
Sexism in Medical Research   289

Social Diversity in Using Health Care  289
Health Care Delivery  291
The Right to Die  291
**Perspectives on Health and
    Medical Care  292**
Functionalist Perspective  292
Conflict Perspective  292
Symbolic Interactionist Perspective  293
**The Study of Population  294**
How the Census Is Taken  294
Population Growth  296
Birth Rates  296
Death Rates  297
International Migration  298
Age, Gender, and Marriage  298
**Patterns of Population Change  299**
Malthusian Theory  299
The Demographic Transition  299
Demographic "Fallout"  300
**Combating Population Growth  300**
Voluntary Family Planning  300
Compulsory Population Control  301
U.S. Population Policy  302

**14  Environment and
        Urbanization  306**

**Environment  308**
Elements of Ecology  308
Diminishing Resources  308
Environmental Pollution  309
A Primary Cause  309
Saving the Environment  310
**A Global Analysis of Urbanization  312**
The Preindustrial City  312
The Industrial City  312
Metropolis and Megalopolis  313
The World's Megacities  314
**Cities in the United States  315**
A Demographic Profile  315
Edge Cities  316
Recent Trends  316
**The Urban Environment  317**
Spatial Patterns  317
Ecological Processes  318

**The Nature of City Life  319**
Urban Anomie Theory  319
Compositional Theory  320
Subcultural Theory  320
**Causes of Urban Problems  321**
Population Decline  321
Fiscal Squeeze  322
Political Dilemma  322
Housing Segregation  322
**Perspectives on Urbanization  323**
Functionalist Perspective  323
Conflict Perspective  324
Symbolic Interactionist Perspective  324
**The Future of U.S. Cities  324**

**15  Collective Behavior
        and Social Change  328**

**The Study of Collective Behavior  330**
General Characteristics  330
Social Factors  331
**Forms of Collective Behavior  332**
Panics  332
Crowds  334
Fashions  335
Rumor  336
Public Opinion  337
Social Movements  338
**A Global Analysis of Social Change  340**
Tradition and Modernization  340
Convergence and Divergence  340
Is the United States in Decline?  341
**Functionalist Perspective  342**
Evolutionary Theory  342
Cyclical Theory  342
Equilibrium Theory  343
**Conflict Perspective  344**
**Symbolic Interactionist Perspective  344**
**Major Changes in Our Future  345**

**Glossary  351**
**References  359**
**Credits  381**
**Name Index  383**
**Subject Index  388**

# *Preface*

Like its previous editions, this book is designed to help students have fun learning sociology. We live in a period of rapid social change, and it is an exciting time to be studying sociology. We will explore many of the ongoing social changes in this new edition of *Sociology: A Brief Introduction*. It is a major revision packed with current information and new ideas from sociological research. I have, however, continued to present the essentials of sociology without a loss of substance or concreteness. In pruning away those topics that are not central to learning about sociological issues, I have concentrated on major areas in depth, with enough lively details to maintain student interest. Although this text is relatively short, it provides instructors and students with the full range of sociological analyses and issues. To ensure that students learn a great deal from this brief text, I have retained the more successful features of my full-length book. I have also tried to convey the excitement I feel about sociology.

## FEATURES

A unique blend of style and substance makes this text stand out from the rest. This distinguishing feature and others make the book easier for students to learn sociology.

### Solid Scholarship

There is a great deal of substance to the text. All analyses are based on empirical studies or data-informed theories, or both. In addition, no attempt has been made to gloss over or water down complex sociological issues, such as the phenomenological theory of deviance or the causes of upward and downward mobility in global society. Such issues are confronted head-on but explained in a clear and interesting fashion.

### Current Research

Special care has been taken to present the most recent findings from the sociological literature. Sociology is a fast-growing field, reflecting the significant changes that have recently taken place all over the world. Thus, many studies cited in this text are as recent as the mid-1990s. Many current events reported in the nation's first-rate newspapers and newsmagazines are also dis-

cussed to demonstrate the relevancy of sociology to today's world.

### Social Diversity

The diversity of U.S. society, including various racial and ethnic groups as well as women and men of various social classes, is presented in a balanced way. In regard to minorities and women, the text does not focus only on their problems; their strengths and achievements are also revealed, as in Chapter 10 (Families), where Native American, African American, Hispanic American, and Asian American families are discussed.

### Global Analyses

All chapters contain analyses of how peoples around the world live or how their lives affect ours in the United States. Such global analyses enhance and deepen our understanding of other cultures. The analyses also help us gain special insight into our own society by looking at it more objectively—from the outsider's point of view.

### Critical Thinking

In every chapter a list of myths and realities about social behavior is offered to promote truly critical thinking. Many students tend to assume that sociology is merely common sense—that there is nothing new in sociology or that whatever is there they have known all along. In this text students will find some of their firmest assumptions challenged and will start to look at the familiar world around them with a critical, fresh eye.

### Theoretically Illuminating

The three major sociological perspectives are introduced in the first chapter and then consistently applied in *all* the other chapters, which is unique to this text. The application of these theoretical approaches to a specific subject in each chapter is balanced, substantive, and interesting. One can learn more about society from the three perspectives than from one or two only. Together, the three illuminate different facets of society, providing a broader and more realistic view of each subject. Other theoretical views, especially feminist theory, are also presented where appropriate.

**xiii**

xiv        Preface

## Lively Writing

The writing style is second to none. It is simple, direct, and vibrant, making sociology come alive. Many professors have described the writing as clear and engaging. Numerous students have commented that they enjoyed reading the book.

## NEW TO THIS EDITION

A great number of substantive changes have been made, as follows:
- The book has been extensively revised and updated.
- There is a new chapter on social interaction in everyday life.
- A global analysis is provided in *all* chapters.
- The three major sociological perspectives—functionalism, conflict perspective, and symbolic interactionism—are presented in *every* chapter.
- The number of tables and figures has been increased, with some U.S. and global maps added, to reinforce the points made in the text.
- Many new topics have been introduced throughout the text. The most significant are listed below.

### Chapter 1  The Essence of Sociology
New sections on:
- The importance of studying social diversity in the United States.
- The significance of analyzing the global diversity of today.
- The nature of sports as seen through the functionalist, conflict, and symbolic interactionist perspectives.
- How sociology can enrich our lives.

### Chapter 2  Society and Culture
New sections on:
- The nature of institutions.
- Postindustrial societies.
- The global influence of the U.S. pop culture.
- Multiculturalism in the United States.
- Culture clash around the globe.
- A global analysis of culture.
- The three sociological perspectives on culture.

### Chapter 3  Socialization
New sections on:
- Freud's theory of psychosexual development.
- Kohlberg's theory of moral development.
- The feminist theory of gender development.
- The three sociological perspectives on socialization.

- A global analysis of socialization.
- Are we puppets of society?

### Chapter 4  Social Interaction in Everyday Life
This is a new chapter. Some of the subjects covered are unique to this text, such as:
- The functionalist perspective on interaction.
- The conflict perspective on interaction.
- A global analysis of communication.
- U.S. diversity in communication.
- How women and men tend to speak different "genderlects."
- How men and women play the gendered game of proxemics.
- The art of managing impressions.
- Humorology: subverting reality with humor.

### Chapter 5  Groups and Organizations
New sections on:
- How to classify organizational theories.
- The nature of organizations as seen through the three sociological perspectives.
- The feminist model of organizations.
- A global analysis of organizations.

### Chapter 6  Deviance and Control
New sections on:
- Drug abuse.
- Power theory.
- Phenomenological theory.
- Classifying deviance theories into functionalist, conflict, and symbolic interactionist perspectives.
- An analysis of deviance around the world.

### Chapter 7  U.S. and Global Stratification
New sections on:
- Feminist perspective on poverty.
- Popular beliefs about welfare.
- Reforming welfare programs.
- Social classes in global society.
- Social mobility in global society.
- The symbolic interactionist perspective on stratification and class.

### Chapter 8  Race and Ethnicity
New sections on:
- Northern and Western European Americans.
- Using the three sociological perspectives to analyze race and ethnicity.
- A global analysis of racial and ethnic relations.

### Chapter 9  Gender and Age
New sections on:
- Sexual harassment.
- The three sociological perspectives on gender inequality.

◆ A global analysis of gender inequality.
◆ The three sociological perspectives on age and aging.
◆ A global analysis of aging.

**Chapter 10   Families**
New sections on:
◆ A global analysis of families.
◆ The symbolic interactionist perspective on the family.
◆ Gay and lesbian marriages.
◆ Native American families.
◆ African American families.
◆ Hispanic American families.
◆ Asian American families.

**Chapter 11   Education and Religion**
New sections on:
◆ The conflict theory about education as inequality reinforcer and cultural imperialism.
◆ The symbolic interactionist perspective on education.
◆ Schools in Belgium, Finland, France, and Japan.
◆ The three sociological perspectives on the nature of religion.
◆ New trends in U.S. religion.

**Chapter 12   Economy and Politics**
New sections on:
◆ The nature of capitalism as seen through the three sociological perspectives.
◆ The economies of Canada, Latin America, Western Europe, Eastern Europe, Russia, China, and Southeast Asia.
◆ A global analysis of political violence.
◆ Government responses to international and domestic terrorism.
◆ The three sociological perspectives on war.

**Chapter 13   Health and Population**
New sections on:
◆ A global analysis of health.
◆ Sexism in medical research.

**Chapter 14   Environment and Urbanization**
New sections on:
◆ A primary cause of environmental problems.
◆ The megacities of the world.
◆ The three sociological perspectives on urbanization.
◆ Causes of urban problems.
◆ The future of U.S. cities.

**Chapter 15   Collective Behavior and Social Change**
New sections on:
◆ A global analysis of social change.

◆ How the theories of social change are related to the three sociological perspectives.

## LEARNING AIDS

An effective system of learning aids is incorporated into the text to motivate students and facilitate learning. Students are encouraged to think about the materials by themselves or by discussing important issues in class. It is frequently through such active involvement, as opposed to passive acceptance of what one reads, that students begin to sharpen their thinking skills. Then the understanding and absorption of ideas presented in the text will come easily.

### Chapter-Opening Vignettes

Along with a chapter outline and a myths and realities box, each chapter opens with a thought-provoking story. This will stimulate students' interest as well as fix their attention on the main themes of the chapter.

### Stimulating Graphics

Colorful figures, tables, maps, and beautiful photos are interspersed throughout the book. They are designed not only to spark student interest but, more importantly, to reinforce comprehension and retention of the points made in the text.

### Discussion-and-Review Questions

In every chapter there are questions at the end of each main section. Instructors can use them as a springboard for lively discussion in class. Students can use them to review the main ideas that have just been discussed, before moving on to the next topic. However the questions are used, students will learn more as active thinkers than as passive recipients of ideas and facts.

### Chapter Summaries

Each chapter ends with a full summary in a question-and-answer format. The standard form of summary in an introductory text tends to turn students into passive consumers of knowledge. In contrast, the question-and-answer format encourages students to become actively involved, by inviting them to join the author in thinking about important issues. Students who have actively thought about what they have read will more easily understand and remember it later.

**xvi**    Preface

## Key Terms

The most important words are boldfaced and defined when introduced. They are listed and defined again at the end of each chapter, with a page cross-reference to facilitate study. All key terms with their definitions are also presented in the Glossary at the end of the book.

## Suggested Readings

In line with the currency of the material in the text, up-to-date books and articles for further reading are listed at the end of each chapter. These sources enable students to seek additional knowledge about the subject matter of each chapter. Most readings are readily available in school libraries.

## Back Pages

# *Glossary*

**Absolute poverty** The lack of minimum food and shelter necessary for maintaining life.

**Achieved status** A status that is attained through an individual's own actions.

**Activity theory** The theory that most elders maintain a great deal of interaction with others, even when it requires vigorous physical activities.

**Affirmative action** A policy that requires employers and colleges to make special efforts to recruit qualified minorities for jobs, promotions, and educational opportunities.

**Afrocentrism** The view of the world from the standpoint of African culture.

**Age structure** The pattern of the proportions of different age groups within a population.

**Ageism** Prejudice and discrimination against the aged.

**Agricultural society** A society that produces food primarily by using plows and draft animals on the farm.

**Alienation of labor** Marx's term for laborers' loss of control over their work process.

**Amalgamation** The process by which the subcultures of various groups are blended together, forming a new culture.

**Animism** The belief in spirits capable of helping or harming people.

**Anticipatory socialization** The process by which people learn to assume a role in the future.

**Anti-Semitism** Prejudice or discrimination against Jews.

**Aptitude** The capacity for developing physical or social skills.

**Arranged marriage** A marriage in which partners are selected by the couple's parents.

**Ascribed status** A status that one has no control over, such as status based on race, gender, or age.

**Assimilation** The process by which a minority adopts the dominant group's culture as the culture of the larger society.

**Authority** Legitimate power institutionalized in organizations.

**Behavioral assimilation** The social situation in which the minority adopts the dominant group's language, values, and behavioral patterns.

**Belief** An idea that is relatively subjective, unreliable, or unverifiable.

**Bilateral descent** The norm that recognizes both parents' families as the child's close relatives.

**Biosphere** A thin layer of air, water, and soil surrounding the earth.

**Birth rate** The number of babies born in a year for every 1000 members of a given population.

**Budget deficit** Spending more than we take in.

**Bureaucracy** A modern Western organization defined by Max Weber as being rational in achieving its goal efficiently.

**Capitalism** An economic system based on private ownership of property and competition in producing and selling goods and services.

**Census** A periodic head count of the entire population of a country.

**Charisma** An exceptional personal quality popularly attributed to certain individuals.

**Chromosomes** The materials in a cell that transmit hereditary traits to the carrier from the carrier's parents.

**Class conflict** Marx's term for the struggle between capitalists, who own the means of production, and the proletariat, who do not.

**Coercion** The illegitimate use of force or threat of force to compel obedience.

**Collective behavior** Relatively spontaneous, unorganized, and unpredictable social behavior.

**Communism** A classless society that operates on the principle of "from each according to his ability, to each according to his needs."

**Compensatory education** A school program intended to improve the academic performance of socially and educationally disadvantaged children.

**Competition** An interaction in which two individuals follow mutually accepted rules in trying to achieve the same goal before the other does.

**Compositional theory** The theory that city dwellers are as involved with small groups of friends, relatives, and neighbors as are noncity people.

**Concentric-zone theory** The model of land use in which the city spreads out from the center in a series of concentric zones, each used for a particular kind of activity.

**Conflict** An interaction in which two individuals disregard any rules in trying to achieve their own goal by defeating each other.

**Emotional intelligence**  The ability to identify and manage one's own *affect* (feelings).

**Endogamy**  Literally, "marrying within," the act of marrying someone from one's own group.

**Enterprise zone**  The economically depressed urban area that businesses, with the help of generous tax credits, try to revive by creating jobs.

**Epidemiology**  The study of the origin and spread of disease within a population.

**Equilibrium theory**  The theory that all the parts of society serve some function and are interdependent.

**Ethicalism**  The type of religion that emphasizes moral principles as guides for living a righteous life.

**Ethnic group**  A collection of people who share a distinctive cultural heritage.

**Ethnocentrism**  The attitude that one's own culture is superior to those of others.

**Ethnomethodology**  The analysis of how people define the world in which they live.

**Eurocentrism**  The view of the world from the standpoint of European culture.

**Evolutionary theory**  The theory that societies change gradually from simple to complex forms.

**Exchange**  An interaction in which two individuals offer each other something in order to obtain a reward in return.

**Exogamy**  Literally, "marrying outward," the act of marrying someone from outside one's group—such as the clan, tribe, or village.

**Experiment**  A research operation in which the researcher manipulates variables so that their influence can be determined.

**Experimental group**  The subjects in an experiment who are exposed to the independent variable.

**Expressive leaders**  Leaders who achieve group harmony by making others feel good.

**Expressive role**  A role that requires taking care of personal relationships.

**Extended family**  The family that consists of two parents, their unmarried children, and other relatives.

**Fad**  A temporary enthusiasm for an innovation less respectable than a fashion.

**Family of orientation**  The family in which one grows up, made up of oneself and one's parents and siblings.

**Family of procreation**  The family that one establishes through marriage, consisting of oneself and one's spouse and children.

**Fashion**  A great though brief enthusiasm among a relatively large number of people for a particular innovation.

**Feminist theory**  A form of conflict theory that explains human life from the experiences of women.

**Feminization of poverty**  A huge number of women bearing the burden of poverty, mostly as single mothers or heads of families.

**Fluid intelligence**  The ability to grasp abstract relationships, as in mathematics, physics, or some other science.

**Folkways**  Weak norms that specify expectations about proper behavior.

**Formal organization**  A group whose activities are rationally designed to achieve specific goals.

**Functionalist perspective**  A theoretical perspective that focuses on social order.

**Gender identity**  People's image of what they are socially expected to be and do on the basis of their sex.

**Gender role**  The pattern of attitudes and behaviors that a society expects of its members because of their being female or male.

**Genderlects**  Linguistic styles that reflect the different worlds of women and men.

**Generalized others**  Mead's term for people who do not have close ties to a child but do influence the child's internalization of the values of society.

**Genocide**  Wholesale killing of a racial or ethnic group.

**Gentrification**  The movement of affluent people into poor urban neighborhoods.

**Glass ceiling**  The prejudiced belief that keeps minority professionals from holding high, leadership positions in organizations.

**Global village**  A closely knit community of all the societies in the world.

**Groupthink**  The tendency for members of a cohesive group to maintain consensus to the extent of ignoring the truth.

**Healing role**  A set of social expectations regarding how a doctor should behave.

**Homogamy**  Marrying someone with social characteristics similar to one's own.

**Horizontal mobility**  Movement from one job to another within the same status category.

**Hormones**  Chemical substances that stimulate or inhibit vital biological processes.

**Horticultural society**  A society that produces food primarily by growing plants in small gardens.

**Humorology**  The study or practice of humor.

**Hunting-gathering society**  A society that hunts animals and gathers plants as its primary means for survival.

**Hypothesis**  A tentative statement about how various events are related to one another.

**Id**  Freud's term for the part of personality that is irrational, concerned only with seeking pleasure.

# *References*

Abbott, Pamela, and Claire Wallace. 1990. *An Introduction to Sociology: Feminist Perspectives*. London: Routledge.

Abramovitz, Mimi, and Frances Fox Piven. 1994. "Scapegoating women on welfare." *New York Times*, September 2, p. A13.

Acton, H. B. 1967. *What Marx Really Said*. New York: Schocken.

Alba, Richard D. 1990. *Ethnic Identity: The Transformation of White America*. New Haven, Conn.: Yale University Press.

Aldrich, Howard E. 1992. "Incommensurable paradigms? Vital signs from three perspectives." In Michael Reed and Michael Hughes (eds.), *Rethinking Organization: New Directions in Organization Theory and Analysis*. Newbury Park, Calif.: Sage.

Alexander, Karl L., and Martha A. Cook. 1982. "Curricula and coursework: A surprise ending to a familiar story." *American Sociological Review*, 47, pp. 626–40.

Alonso, William. 1964. "The historic and the structural theories of urban form: Their implications for urban renewal." *Journal of Land Economics*, 40, pp. 227–31.

Alter, Jonathan. 1995. "Decoding the contract." *Newsweek*, January 9, pp. 26–27.

Altman, Lawrence K. 1990. "Changes in medicine bring pain to healing profession." *New York Times*, February 18, pp. 1, 20–21.

Ames, Katrine. 1990. "Our bodies, their selves." *Newsweek*, December 17, p. 60.

Andersen, Margaret L. 1993. *Thinking About Women*, 3rd ed. New York: Macmillan.

Anderson, David C. 1994. "The crime funnel." *New York Times Magazine*, June 12, pp. 57 –58.

Archer, Margaret S. 1985. "The myth of cultural integration." *British Journal of Sociology*, 36, pp. 333–53.

Aronoff, Joel, and William D. Crano. 1975. "A reexamination of the cross-cultural principles of task segregation and sex role differentiation in the family." *American Sociological Review*, 40, pp. 12–20.

Asch, Solomon E. 1955. "Opinions and social pressure." *Scientific American*, 193, pp. 31–35.

Ashe, Arthur. 1977. "An open letter to black parents: Send your children to the libraries." *New York Times*, February 6, section 5, p. 2.

———. 1992. "A zero-sum game that hurts blacks." *New York Times*, February 27, p. A10.

Atchley, Robert C. 1988. *Social Forces and Aging*, 5th ed. Belmont, Calif.: Wadsworth.

Azmitia, Margarita. 1988. "Peer interaction and problem solving: When are two hands better than one?" *Child Development*, 59, pp. 87–96.

Babbie, Earl R. 1995. *The Practice of Social Research*, 7th ed. Belmont, Calif.: Wadsworth.

Bailey, J. Michael, and Richard C. Pillard. 1991. "A genetic study of male sexual orientation." *Archives of General Psychiatry*, 48, pp. 1089–96.

Bailey, Kenneth D. 1994. *Methods of Social Research*, 4th ed. New York: Free Press.

Balkan, Sheila, Ronald J. Berger, and Janet Schmidt. 1980. *Crime and Deviance in America: A Critical Approach*. Belmont, Calif.: Wadsworth.

Baltzell, E. Digby. 1991. *The Protestant Establishment Revisited*. New Brunswick, N.J.: Transaction.

———. 1994. *Judgment and Sensibility: Religion and Stratification*. New Brunswick, N.J.: Transaction.

Bane, Mary Jo, and David T. Ellwood. 1994. *Welfare Realities: From Rhetoric to Reform*. Cambridge, Mass.: Harvard University Press.

Banfield, Edward C. 1974. *The Unheavenly City Revisited*. Boston: Little, Brown.

Barlett, Donald L., and James B. Steele. 1992. *America: What Went Wrong?* Kansas City: Andrews and McMeel.

Barringer, Felicity. 1989. "Doubt on 'trial marriage' raised by divorce rates." *New York Times*, June 9, pp. 1, 23.

———. 1991. "Population grows in state capitals." *New York Times*, January 26, pp. 1, 10.

Bart, Pauline B. 1991. "Feminist theories." In Henry Etzkowitz and Ronald M. Glassman (eds.), *The Renascence of Sociological Theory*, pp. 249–65. Itasca, Ill.: Peacock.

**360**     References

Bartley, Robert L. 1991. "Beyond the recession." *Wall Street Journal,* January 2, p. A6.

Basow, Susan A. 1986. *Sex-Role Stereotypes.* Monterey, Calif.: Brooks/Cole.

Baum, Alice S., and Donald W. Burnes. 1993. *A Nation in Denial: The Truth About Homelessness.* Boulder, Colo.: Westview.

Becerra, Rosina. 1988. "The Mexican American family." In Charles Mindel et al. (eds.), *Ethnic Families in America: Patterns and Variations,* 3rd ed. New York: Elsevier.

Beck, E. M., and Stewart E. Tolnay. 1990. "The killing fields of the deep South: The market for cotton and the lynching of blacks, 1882–1930." *American Sociological Review,* 55, pp. 526–39.

Beck, Melinda. 1990a. "The politics of cancer." *Newsweek,* December 10, pp. 62–65.

———. 1990b. "Trading places." *Newsweek,* July 16, pp. 48–54.

Becker, Howard S. 1963. *Outsiders: Studies in the Sociology of Deviance.* New York: Free Press.

———. 1982. "Culture: A sociological view." *The Yale Review,* 71, pp. 513–27.

Begley, Sharon. 1990. "The search for the fountain of youth." *Newsweek,* March 5, pp. 44–48.

Beirne, Piers, and James Messerschmidt. 1995. *Criminology,* 2nd ed. San Diego: Harcourt Brace Jovanovich.

Belkin, Lisa. 1990. "Many in medicine are calling rules a professional malaise." *New York Times,* February 19, pp. A1, A9.

Bellah, Robert N., et al. 1986. *Habits of the Heart: Individualism and Commitment in American Life.* New York: Harper & Row.

Benderly, Beryl Lieff. 1989. "Don't believe everything you read . . . " *Psychology Today,* November, pp. 67–69.

Bendix, Reinhard. 1962. *Max Weber: An Intellectual Portrait.* Garden City, N.Y.: Anchor.

Bennett, William J. 1989. "A response to Milton Friedman." *Wall Street Journal,* September 19, p. A32.

Bennis, Warren. 1989. "The dilemma at the top." *New York Times,* December 31, p. F3.

Benson, Michael L. 1985. "Denying the guilty mind: Accounting for involvement in a white-collar crime." *Criminology,* 23, p. 594.

Berger, Peter L. 1992. "Sociology: A disinvitation?" *Society,* November/December, pp. 12–18.

Bernstein, Richard. 1990. "In U.S. schools a war of words." *New York Times Magazine,* October 14, pp. 34, 48–52.

Berreby, David. 1995. "Unabsolute truths: Clifford Geertz." *New York Times Magazine,* April 9, pp.44–47.

Beyer, Lisa. 1990. "Lifting the veil." *Time,* September 24, pp. 38–44.

Biggart, Nicole Woolsey. 1994. "Labor and leisure." In Neil J. Smelser and Richard Swedberg (eds.), *The Handbook of Economic Sociology.* Princeton, N.J.: Princeton University Press.

Bilheimer, Robert S. 1983. *Faith and Ferment: An Interdisciplinary Study of Christian Beliefs and Practices.* Minneapolis, Minn.: Augsburg.

Billingsley, Andrew. 1993. *Climbing Jacob's Ladder: The Enduring Legacy of African-American Families.* New York: Simon & Schuster.

Black, Donald. 1983. "Crime as social control." *American Sociological Review,* 48, pp. 34–45.

Blakeslee, Sandra. 1989. "Race and sex are found to affect access to kidney transplants." *New York Times,* January 24, pp. 19, 23.

Blalock, Hubert M., Jr. 1984. *Basic Dilemmas in the Social Sciences.* Beverly Hills, Calif.: Sage.

Blau, Peter M., and Otis Dudley Duncan. 1967. *The American Occupational Structure.* New York: Wiley.

Blumer, Herbert. 1978. "Elementary collective groupings." In Louis E. Genevie (ed.), *Collective Behavior and Social Movements.* Itasca, Ill.: Peacock.

Blumstein, Alfred. 1995. "Violence by young people: Why the deadly nexus?" *National Institute of Justice Journal,* August, pp. 2–9.

Blundell, William E. 1986. "Gripe session." *Wall Street Journal,* May 9, pp. 1, 9.

———. 1987. "When the patient takes charge." *Wall Street Journal,* April 24, pp. D5–D6.

Bohannan, Paul. 1995. *How Culture Works.* New York: Free Press.

Bornstein, Marc H. et al. 1991. "Parenting in cross-cultural perspective: The United States, France, and Japan." In Marc H. Bornstein (ed.), *Cultural Approaches to Parenting,* pp. 69–90. Hillsdale, N.J.: Lawrence Erlbaum Associates.

Bossard, James. 1932. "Residential propinquity as a factor in marriage selection." *American Journal of Sociology,* 38, pp. 219–44.

Boudon, Raymond. 1983a. "Individual action and social change: A no-theory of social change." *British Journal of Sociology,* 34, pp. 1–18.

# *Credits*

## Chapter 1

Page 2 © David Madison/Tony Stone Images; p. 6 © Lee Snider/The Image Works; p. 8 © The Bettmann Archive; p. 9 © The Bettmann Archive; p. 10 © The University Library/University of Illinois at Chicago/ Jane Addams Memorial Collection at Hull House; p. 13 © Rouchon/Explorer/Photo Researchers; p. 16 © Bob Daemmrich/Stock Boston; p. 17 © Monica Almeida/NYT Pictures; p. 20 © Schwadron; p. 21 © R. Scott/The Image Works.

## Chapter 2

Page 28 © Will & Deni McIntyre; p. 31 © Jesse Nemerofsky/Photoreporters; p. 33 © Bachmann/ Photo Researchers; p. 34 © DeVore/Anthro-Photo; p. 36 © Holland/Stock Boston; p. 38 © Alan Levenson/Tony Stone Images; p. 39 © Nicholas DeVore/Tony Stone Images; p. 43 © Superstock; p. 45 © The Bettmann Archive; p. 48T © Joe Carini/The Image Works; p. 48C © Richard Dean/The Image Works; p. 48B © Bob Daemmrich/The Image Works.

## Chapter 3

Page 56 © Robert Frerck/Odyssey/Chicago; p. 59 © Sam Abell; p. 61 © Kerry Hayes/The Kobal Collection; p. 66 © Freeman/Photo Edit; p. 67 © Brent Jones; p. 69 © Eiler/Stock Boston; p. 70 © Brenda Tharp/ Photo Researchers, Inc.; p. 73 © Oddie/Photo Edit; p. 74 © Penny Tweedie/Tony Stone Worldwide.

## Chapter 4

Page 78 © Frank Siteman/The Picture Cube; p. 82 © Jerry Irwin/Photo Researchers, Inc.; p. 84 © Stephen Dunn/Allsport; p. 85 CATHY: © 1995 Cathy Guisewite. Reprinted with permission of UNIVERSAL PRESS SYNDICATE. Reprinted with permission. All rights reserved.; p. 86 © Azzi/ Woodfin Camp & Associates; p. 89 © B. Daemmrich/The Image Works;

p. 90 © Milt & Joan Mann/Camermann International, Ltd.; p. 93 © Tom McCarthy/Unicorn Stock Photos.

## Chapter 5

Page 98 © Dick Luria/Science Source/Photo Researchers, Inc.; p.101 Drawing by Hamilton; © 1991/The New Yorker Magazine, Inc.; p. 102 © Will & Deni McIntyre/Photo Researchers, Inc.; p. 103 © Laima Druskis/Photo Researchers, Inc.; p. 107 © Ron Sherman/Stock Boston; p. 108 © Crandall/The Image Works; p. 110 © Rick Browne/Stock Boston; p. 115 © Lawrence Migdale/Stock Boston; p. 117 © Paolo Koch/ Photo Researchers, Inc.

## Chapter 6

Page 120 © Campbell/Sygma; p. 123 © Reuters/ Bettmann; p. 126 © D. Wells/The Image Works; p. 127 "From The Wall Street Journal-Permission, Cartoon Features Syndicate"; p. 128 © David Young-Wolff/Photo Edit; p. 131 © Rodger Kingston Vintage/ The Picture Collection; p. 135 © Martin R. Jones/Unicorn Stock Photos.

## Chapter 7

Page 142 © Reinstein/The Image Works; p. 145 © Lewis Hine Photo/Library of Congress; p. 149T © Jeff Dunn/The Picture Cube; p. 149B © Granitsas/ The Image Works; b © S. Katz/Black Star; p. 152B © Andrew Hollbrooke/ Black Star; p. 153 © M. Siluk/The Image Works; p. 155 © Joel Gordon; p. 158 © Paul Conklin/ Photo Edit; p. 159 © Bob Daemmrich/Stock Boston; p. 161 © Stephanie Maze/Woodfin Camp & Associates.

## Chapter 8

Page 166 © Johnny Crawford/The Image Works; p. 169 © I. Berry/Magnum Photos; p. 171 © John Running/Black Star; p. 173 © UPI/ Bettmann; p. 175 © M. Granitsas/The Image Works; p. 176 © Hires/Gamma-Liaison; p. 178 © California Institute of Technology; p. 179 © Robert Frerck/Odyssey/Chicago; p. 181 © Superstock; p. 184 © Paul Dagys.

# *Name Index*

Abbott, Pamela, 13
Abramovitz, Mimi, 156
Aburdene, Patricia, 38, 39, 250, 262
Acton, H.B., 247
Addams, Jane, 10-11
Adler, Stephen J., 122
Alba, Richard D., 179
Aldrich, Howard E., 112
Alexander, Karl L., 239
Alonso, William, 317
Alter, Jonathan, 265
Altman, Lawrence K., 288, 289
Ames, Katrine, 289
Andersen, Margaret L., 201
Anderson, David C., 138
Anderson, Leon, 155
Appleby, R. Scott, 251
Archer, Margaret S., 44
Aristotle, 310
Aronoff, Joel, 202
Asch, Solomon E., 103
Ashe, Arthur, 18
Atchley, Robert C., 207
Aviad, Janet O'Dea, 246
Avnet, Jon, 46
Azmitia, Margarita, 82

Bailey, Kenneth D., 23
Bales, Robert F., 202
Balkan, Sheila, 132
Baltzell, E. Digby, 178
Bane, Mary Jo, 155
Banfield, Edward C., 153
Barlett, Donald L., 274
Barringer, Felicity, 228, 317
Bart, Pauline B., 13
Bartley, Robert L., 262
Basow, Susan A., 196
Baum, Alice S., 155
Beall, Cynthia M., 208
Becerra, Rosina, 230
Beck, E.M., 184
Beck, Melinda, 207, 289
Becker, Howard S., 52, 135
Begley, Sharon, 205
Beirne, Piers, 133
Belkin, Lisa, 288
Bellah, Robert N., 44
Benderly, Beryl Lieff, 193
Bendix, Reinhard, 115
Bengston, K.L., 207
Bennett, William J., 139
Bennis, Warren, 104
Benson, Michael L., 127
Berger, Peter L., 5
Berger, Ronald J., 132
Berger, Seymour M., 335

Berkman, Lisa F., 285
Bernstein, Richard, 174
Berreby, David, 49
Berscheid, Ellen, 219
Beyer, Lisa, 341
Biggart, Nicole Woolsey, 263
Biggs, Mae A., 89
Bilheimer, Robert S., 249
Billingsley, Andrew, 230
Black, Donald, 136
Blakeslee, Sandra, 290
Blalock, Hubert M., Jr., 11
Blau, Peter M., 157
Blumer, Herbert, 334
Blumstein, Alfred, 124
Blundell, William E., 288, 321
Bohannan, Paul, 44
Bornstein, Marc H., 74
Bossard, James, 220
Boudon, Raymond, 343
Bowles, Samuel, 238
Box, Steven, 133
Bradburd, Daniel, 35
Bradford, Calvin P., 260
Bradsher, Keith, 145
Braithwaite, John, 131
Brawer, Florence B., 243
Brewer, Robert E., 22
Bridges, William P., 103
Brinkley, Joel, 330
Brinson, Susan L., 126
Brock, Fred, 243
Brody, Jane E., 221
Brooke, James, 266
Brookhiser, Richard, 178
Brown, A. Theodore, 313
Brown, Nicole, 4
Brown, Roger, 333
Bryant, Barbara, 295
Buford, Bill, 16
Buller, David B., 293
Buller, Mary Klein, 293
Bumpass, Larry, 228
Burgess, Ernest W., 317
Burke, Ronald J., 225
Burnes, Donald W., 155
Burtless, Gary, 268
Bush, George, 154, 279, 302
Butler, Robert, 204, 205

Campbell, Anne, 191
Campbell, Bruce, 219
Campbell, Richard T., 157
Canning, Claire, 320
Cantril, Hadley, 333-334
Capron, Alexander Morgan, 291
Carlson, Eugene, 322

Carmody, Deirdre, 195
Carney, James, 185
Carnoy, Martin, 238
Carpenter, Betsy, 309
Carroll, David, 228
Carter, Jimmy, 337
Casper, Lynn M., 151, 152
Castelli, Jim, 249, 250
Castro, Janice, 268
Celis, William, 3rd, 242
Chalfant, H. Paul, 246
Chaliand, Gerard, 253
Chambliss, William J., 132
Charon, Joel M., 182
Cherlin, Andrew J., 223, 224, 226, 227
Chesney-Lind, Meda, 134
Chideya, Faria, 230
Childe, Gordon, 312
Chilman, Catherine Street, 230
Chomsky, Noam, 162
Christopher, Robert C., 240
Church, George J., 116
Clark, Charles S., 70
Clark, Kenneth, 184
Clark, Mamie, 184
Clinton, Bill, 50, 155, 185, 278, 302
Close, Ellis, 173
Cockerham, William C., 285, 286, 290, 291
Cohen, Albert K., 129
Cohen, Arthur M., 243
Cohn, Steven F., 83
Coleman, James William, 184
Collins, Randall, 11, 203
Columbus, Christopher, 45, 171
Commoner, Barry, 312
Comte, Auguste, 8-9
Confucius, 253-254
Conrad, Peter, 292
Cook, Martha A., 239
Cook, Philip J., 156
Cooley, Charles Horton, 66, 102
Cooper, Kristina, 226
Corliss, Richard, 46
Cornell, Claire Pedrick, 217, 221
Corsaro, William A., 69
Cory, Christopher T., 203
Cose, Ellis, 4
Coverman, Shelley, 32
Cowell, Alan, 201
Cowgill, Donald W., 208
Cowley, Geoffrey, 84
Cox, Harvey, 321
Cramer, Jerome, 269
Crano, William D., 202
Cressey, Donald R., 184

# *Subject Index*

Abortion, 302
Absolute poverty, 150, 152
Accents, 86
Acceptance stage of dying, 73
Achieved characteristics, 158
Achieved statuses, 30
Acid rain, 309
Acting crowds, 334
Activity theory of aging, 207
Acute illnesses, 284
Adult socialization, 70-73
Affective development, 63-64
Affiliations, religious, 249-252
Affirmative action, 185
African Americans, 172-173
    discrimination against, 172-173, 183
    families, 230
    movement into cities, 315-316
    racial inequality in sports and, 17-18
Afrocentrism, 45
Age. *See also* Aging
    religious participation and, 249-250
    use of health care and, 290
Ageism, 207
Age structure, 298
Aggregates, social, 32, 100
Aggression, 13, 125-127
Aging, 72-73, 204-209
    biological consequences of, 204-205
    global analysis of, 208-209
    perspectives on, 206-208
    prejudice/discrimination and, 207
    psychological consequences of, 205
    social effects of, 205-206
Agricultural productivity, 267
Agricultural societies, 36-37, 40
AIDS (acquired immune deficiency syndrome), 286-287
Air pollution, 309
Alienation of labor, 263
Alienative involvement, 107
All-weather liberals/illiberals, 182, 183
Alternative lifestyles, 227-229
Amalgamation, 180, 181
Anal stage, 62, 71
Anger stage of dying, 73
Animal communication, 84
Animism, 252, 254
Anomie, urban, 319-320, 321
Anticipatory socialization, 71
Antipollution laws, 310-311
Anti-Semitism, 177
Anxiety, rumor and, 336-337

*Apartheid*, 181
Applied sciences, 11
Aptitude, 58-59
Arranged marriage, 214-215
Ascribed characteristics, 158
Ascribed statuses, 30
Asian-Americans, 175-177
    families, 230-231
    use of health care, 290
Assimilation, 180, 181
Association, differential, 134, 137
Associative effects of reference group, 101
Audience, protective measures by, 92
Authority, 216, 270-271
Autonomy vs. doubt, 71, 72

Backstage behavior, 91
Bandwagon, 337
Bargaining stage of dying, 73
Basic sciences, 11
Battered women, 221
Behavioral assimilation, 180
Belgium, schools in, 243
Beliefs, 32-33, 41, 331
Bias, gender, 18
Bilateral descent, 216
Biological classification of races, 168-169
Biological consequences of age, 204-205
Biological constraints on gender, 192
Biosphere, 308
Biotechnology, 38
Birth control, 300-302
Birth rates, 296-297, 299-300
Black English, 86
"Blame the poor" theories of poverty, 153
Blended families, 226-227
Body language, 85, 87
Bonds, social, 130-131
*Bourgeoisie*, 144
Brain structure, sex differences in, 192
Buddhism, 248, 253
Budget deficit, 265
Bureaucracies, 113-116
Busing programs, 185
Calculative involvement, 107
Calvinist sect, 248
Canada, economy of, 265
Capitalism, 260
    conflict theory of deviance and, 132
    Marx on, 144-145, 344
    perspectives on, 262-263
    Protestant ethic and emergence of, 248

social equality and, 163
    socialist feminism on, 13
Capitalist class, 274
Card stacking, 337
Career mobility, 156
Careers, gender inequality and, 198-199
Carrying capacity of ecosystem, 308
Casual crowds, 334
Categories, social, 100
Caucasoids, 168, 169
Causes, social movements and, 339-340
CDCs (community development corporations), 322
Censuses, 294-296
Change, social. *See* Social change
Charisma, 270
Charismatic authority, 270-271
Chicago School, 10
Child abuse, 65
Childcare, 74
Children. *See* Family(ies)
China, economy of, 266
Christianity, 249-251, 252
Chromosomes, 192
Chronic illnesses, 284
Circumspection, dramaturgical, 92
Cities. *See also* Urban environment
    edge, 316
    industrial, 312-313
    megacities, 314-315
    metropolises/megalopolises, 313-314
    preindustrial, 312
    in U.S., 315-317, 324-325
Citizens' attitudes toward government, 271-272
Civil inattention, 324
Civil Rights Act of 1964, 172, 173, 201
Civil rights movement, 185
Class. *See* Social class
Class conflict, 9
Coercion, 270
Coercive organizations, 107-108
Coercive power, 107
Cognitive abilities, 196
Cognitive component of culture, 41
Cognitive development, 61-63, 196, 236
Cohabitation, 228
Cold War, end of, 346
Collective behavior, 330-340
    defined, 330
    forms of, 332-340
    general characteristics of, 330-331
    social factors in, 331-332

## ACTIVITY 2

Do an overview of one of the textbooks you are using in another course, and write a few paragraphs in which you discuss what you learned from your overview. If you do not have other textbooks at this time, ask your classmates who are using other books to share their paragraphs with you.

## Previewing Textbook Chapters

Suppose you are invited to a party this Saturday night in an unfamiliar part of your state, and you are very excited about going because all your friends will be there. Unfortunately, you are working until 9 P.M. that night, which means that you have to travel alone and arrive late for the affair. When Saturday night comes around, you certainly would not get into your car and drive around aimlessly trying to find the party. Not only would you waste time and gas, but there is a real chance you would never arrive! Instead, you would have found out specifically where the party is, the best way to get there, and approximately how long the trip is going to take you. Furthermore, when getting directions, you would have asked for landmarks like traffic lights, service stations, and other structures to help guide your way. In short, you would have tried to become familiar with the route so that you could get to your destination as quickly and efficiently as possible.

We can apply the same principle to reading textbook chapters. Before starting an assignment, you should find out where you are going by familiarizing yourself with the material as much as possible. Not only will it ultimately save time and effort to do this, but it will result in much better comprehension because you know where you are going and what to look for along the way. The process by which you become acquainted with a textbook chapter is called **previewing**. Like overviewing, it involves skimming or quickly glancing over the material to determine what you will be reading about, how it is organized, and what aids to understanding are provided to help you with the task.

When previewing a textbook chapter, proceed through the following steps:

1. Take note of the title, which tells you the topic of the chapter. Once again, it is the answer to the question "What is this about?"

2. Check the length of the chapter so that you can gauge how long it will take you to read. While you are at it, try to get an idea how difficult the material is, because that also affects the time it will take you to get through it. The purpose here is for you to prepare yourself psychologically for the task and come up with a schedule for its completion, which could involve dividing up the assignment.

3. Check to see if there are objectives, goals, or outcomes at the beginning of the chapter. They tell you exactly what you are expected to know when you finish reading it, so they can serve as your personal study goals.

4. Skim the first several paragraphs, which are often an introduction to the main points to be covered and sometimes present the central message of the entire chapter.

5. Skim the last several paragraphs, which could serve as a summary of the most important information including, once again, the central message of the chapter. Keep in mind that writers sometimes provide a more formal summary or review in a separate section at the end of a chapter, which makes it easy to recognize.

6. Skim the major and minor chapter headings so that you become aware of the topics covered and how they are related to one another. As noted earlier, it is important to note connections between major and minor headings.

7. Look carefully at the **graphic aids**, which include charts, graphs, maps, pictures, and tables. They illustrate important information mentioned in the context of the textbook and often sum up major points made by the writer. Pay particular attention to the **captions** or **titles** and any explanations that appear over, under, or alongside the graphic aids, because you want to find out what they are about and be aware of the information that they stress. In short, no matter what graphic aid you encounter, you should always be able to answer the following two questions: "What is this graphic aid about?" and "What are the major points stressed?"

8. Check if there are questions within or at the end of the chapter. Because they also focus on the major points, you should keep any questions in mind and try to answer them as you read. At the very least, they can serve as guides to direct your reading to the most valuable information.

9. Take note of any other aids to understanding offered in the chapter, such as exercises, outlines, previews, vocabulary lists, or boldfaced and italicized vocabulary defined in context or in the margins. All of these aids can help make your reading more meaningful.

After you have completed your preview of a chapter, take a few moments to think carefully about what you have learned. As you read the chapter, remember what you have discovered from your preview so that you can focus on the most important information. Although it only takes a short time, previewing is an excellent way to get acquainted with textbook material. That familiarity will pay off later on by enabling you to read quicker and with much more understanding.

## ACTIVITY 3

Chapter 3 in this textbook contains very important information that will be used throughout the rest of the book. Familiarize yourself with that chapter by previewing it, and then answer the preview questions in your notebook.

**Preview Questions**

1. What is the chapter about?
2. How long will it take you to read it?
3. Are there objectives, goals, or outcomes at the beginning of the chapter that can serve as your personal study goals?
4. Is an introduction or a summary provided?
5. What is the central message of the entire chapter?
6. How many major and minor headings are there? Name them.
7. How many characteristics of critical thinking are there?
8. Are any graphic aids provided? If so, what are they about? What major points do they stress?
9. Are there questions within or at the end of the chapter?
10. What other aids to understanding are offered in the chapter that can help make your reading more meaningful?

**Essay**

Write a few paragraphs in which you discuss what you learned from your preview of the chapter and how it will help you read it more quickly and with greater understanding.

## ACTIVITY 4

Preview a chapter from one of the textbooks you are using in another course, and write a few paragraphs in which you discuss what you learned from your preview. If you are not using any other textbooks at this time, preview Chapter 4 in this textbook.

# Reading a Textbook Chapter Critically: Questions and Answers

When police officers investigate a crime, they ask such questions as "When did the criminal activity occur?" "Are there any clues?" "Who was involved?" "Are there any witnesses?" "What were the possible motives?" Answers to these and questions like them enable the police to piece together information so that they can solve the crime.

As a student, before you go into a test situation, you always ask your instructor questions to find out what the test will cover, what kind of test it will be, how many questions will be on it, and how many points each will be worth.

The information gathered from the answers to those questions helps you to prepare more efficiently for the test and receive a higher grade for your efforts.

The importance of asking questions also applies to reading, as you saw in Chapter 1, when we discussed how to find the topic, main idea, details, and central message. Furthermore, in this chapter, questions were used to gather information for overviewing and previewing purposes. In the remaining chapters, you will be answering questions that help focus and improve your understanding and require that you evaluate or read critically material from various sources. Thus questioning has a very important role to play when it comes to dealing with textbooks and other kinds of reading as well.

How, then, do you actually apply **critical reading** to a textbook chapter? As you may have guessed, it involves the use of questions. When we discussed overviewing and previewing, we emphasized the importance of major and minor chapter headings because they make you aware of the topics covered and how the topics are related. Headings are generally highlighted in boldface or in colored type to stress their importance to the reader. *By simply turning those headings into questions, you are focusing your attention on the most important information in a textbook chapter and evaluating that information to answer your questions.* Sometimes writers actually provide headings that are already in question form, which makes your job even easier. Nevertheless, when you have to make headings into questions yourself, you can do so through the use of words often found in questions, such as *who, when, what, where, how,* and *why.* For example, look at the following headings and their corresponding questions.

| HEADING | QUESTION |
|---|---|
| Booker T. Washington | Who was Booker T. Washington? |
| The Best Time to Study | When is the best time to study? |
| Physical Needs | What are physical needs? |
| The Cradle of Civilization | Where was the cradle of civilization? |
| Preventing Accidents | How do you prevent accidents? |
| The Need for Love | Why do we need love? |

Sometimes it is very important to develop a question that relates a minor heading to a major one in order to understand how they are connected or related to each other. For instance, if the minor heading "Genetic Factors" is found under the major heading "The Development of Emotions" in a given chapter, then an appropriate question would read something like "What are genetic factors, and how do they contribute to the development of emotions?" By asking a question like this, you are focusing not only on the meaning of genetic factors but also on their relationship to the development of emotions. Certainly, that is what the textbook writer wants you to do.

When answering the questions that you have developed, you should always look for the central message of each chapter section and be aware of main ideas, patterns of organization, and context definitions. Although we have already discussed them at length in Chapter 1, it should be stressed again here that they are all extremely important because they provide the information with which to answer your questions. Furthermore, it is a very good idea to underline or highlight with a marker the information contained in main ideas, patterns of organization, and context definitions to separate it from the other material.

Underlining or highlighting is a useful technique that contributes to better comprehension because it requires that you evaluate carefully when deciding what information needs to be separated from the rest. That makes you into a more active, attentive reader, which is also an aid to concentration. Finally, this skill makes it easier to review the important information that you have separated in each section of a chapter without having to go back to reread everything. In short, underlining, highlighting, marking up, and even writing in your textbooks will help you master them by making you into a much more involved reader.

Take a careful look at the chapter section that follows. Think about how you would make the heading into a question, and then answer it. Pay particular attention to the sentences that have been underlined.

1    ***Isolate and Locate the Source of the Problem*** <u>This means finding the part of the environment that is most likely responsible for the issue. A source can be one of three things.</u> *<u>First, the source of a problem might be other people in your life.</u>* An organization I once consulted with was having trouble keeping its staff washrooms clean. They were used by staff and visitors. Management issued washroom keys to its staff and had visitors use a public washroom in the building. Unfortunately, the washrooms remained as messy as ever. The problem was incorrectly linked with visitors and not members of the organization. Once this was called to the staff's attention and washroom rules were discussed with people, the appearance of the washrooms improved.

2    *<u>Second, the source of a problem might be some object in your environment.</u>* A neighbor's car radio went out whenever he approached a local radio station. He complained to the station manager that its equipment was causing his radio to malfunction. As far as the radio station manager knew, my neighbor was the only person with this problem. Thus, it seemed unlikely that the radio station's equipment was in some way responsible. He had one of his technicians check my neighbor's radio. The technician found a loose wire that apparently turned the radio off when it was jarred by potholes in the street near the station. Those same potholes jarred the radio back into operation. Properly locating the problem led to a solution.

3    *<u>The third source of a problem might be a relationship.</u>* Whenever we have an interpersonal problem, a natural tendency is to blame the other person. "It couldn't be my fault," we might think to ourselves. Interpersonal problems are much easier to resolve when the relationship is viewed as the source.

4    A former neighbor and his wife, for example, used to argue over who would take the garbage out to their garbage cans, located in their backyard. One would think this would be a simple problem to solve. At the very least, the chore could be rotated. Unfortunately, whatever strategy they chose, one of them would inevitably break the deal. Each blamed the other for being absentminded, stubborn, and purposely irritating. They eventually entered counseling for other problems in their marriage and discovered that the techniques they employed to manipulate and control each other in-

terfered with their relationship. Their therapist pointed out that the garbage became a symbol for "who is the garbage person in this relationship" and, by implication, the low-status person in the marriage. The source of the issue was not the garbage per se, but unresolved control and authority issues in their relationship.

Anthony F. Grasha, *Practical Applications of Psychology*, p. 91

If the question you developed from the heading reads something like "How or where do you isolate and locate the source of the problem?" you are correct. You never know for sure whether you have asked the right question until you have at least skimmed the material. However, just the process of thinking about possible appropriate questions forces you from the very beginning to consider the information in front of you carefully. For example, you might have been tempted to make up questions using the words *who, when,* or *why,* but a quick look at the section indicates that the information provides a better answer to a *how* or *where* question. Hence by trying to decide the best question to ask, you have already begun evaluating the section, which makes for much better comprehension in the long run.

You probably noticed that the first two sentences present the central message, and the major details—which are italicized—are organized into a simple listing-of-facts pattern. Together, they provide the answer to our question:

Finding the part of the environment that is most likely responsible for the issue involves one of three things: other people in your life, some object in your environment, or a relationship.

Once again, we see the importance of recognizing central messages and patterns of organization, because they contain the most valuable information. You should always be on the lookout for them. The rest of the section consists of minor details that relate various examples designed to make the material clearer.

Reading a textbook chapter with a questioning mind helps focus your attention on the most important information. Furthermore, it makes you into a more active reader, who is thinking carefully about the chapter material in order to find answers. That in turn leads to greater concentration, improved comprehension, and a much better chance of remembering what you have read. In fact, all of the skills that we have discussed in this chapter and Chapter 1 are designed to help you deal more effectively with textbooks. As a result, the experience with your textbooks should be more meaningful and worthwhile. Take the time to use and improve on these skills as you continue with your education. Your efforts should enable you to increase your learning and achieve higher grades. That is a very good return for your hard work.

## ACTIVITY 5

The following passages are taken from various textbook chapters. For each of them, turn the heading into a question and answer it by using the central message and any main ideas, context definitions, and patterns of organization that may be present. Underline or highlight the most important information before writing out the answers in your notebook.

# 1

## Defining Health and Wellness

1   To be responsible for your well-being, you must understand what health and wellness are. Health is defined differently among experts, but all definitions have a common theme: self-responsibility and life-style.

> Health is a state of complete physical, mental, and social well-being and not merely the absence of disease or infirmity.
>
> —World Health Organization, 1947

> (Health is) an integrated method of functioning which is oriented toward maximizing the potential of which the individual is capable. It requires that the individual maintain a continuum of balance and purposeful direction with the environment where he/she is functioning.
>
> —Dunn, 1967

Wellness has been defined as

> an approach to personal health that emphasizes individual responsibility for well-being through the practice of health-promoting lifestyle behaviors.
>
> —Hurley and Schlaadt, 1992

2   Wellness is many times referred to in a broader context than health, which sometimes means only physical health. For the purposes of this book, we consider health multidimensional, involving the whole person's relation to the total environment. We refer to wellness as a process of moving toward optimal health.

Gordon Edlin, Eric Golanty, and Kelli McCormack Brown, *Health and Wellness*, p. 4

# 2

## 16.7 Predators Have Evolved Efficient Hunting Tactics

1   As prey have evolved ways of avoiding predators, predators have evolved better ways of hunting. Predators have three general methods of hunting: ambush, stalking, and pursuit. Ambush hunting means lying in wait for prey to come along. This method is typical among some frogs, alligators and crocodiles, lizards, and certain insects. Although ambush hunting has a low frequency of success, it requires minimal energy. Stalking, typical of herons and some cats, is a deliberate form of hunting with a quick attack. The predator's search time may be great, but pursuit time is

minimal. Pursuit hunting, typical of many hawks, lions, and wolves, involves minimal search time, because the predator usually knows the location of the prey, but pursuit time is usually great. Stalkers spend more time and energy encountering prey. Pursuers spend more time capturing and handling prey.

2     Predators, like their prey, may use cryptic coloration to blend into the background or break up their outlines. Predators use deception by resembling the prey. Robber flies *(Mallophora bomboides)* mimic bumblebees, their prey. The female of certain species of fireflies imitates the mating flashes of other species, attracting males of those species, which she promptly kills and eats. Predators may also employ chemical poisons, as shrews and rattlesnakes do. They may form a group to attack large prey, as lions and wolves do.

Robert Leo Smith and Thomas M. Smith, *Elements of Ecology,* p. 199

# 3

## Microeconomics Versus Macroeconomics

**Microeconomics**
The study of decision making undertaken by individuals (or households) and by firms.

**Macroeconomics**
The study of the behavior of the economy as a whole, including such economywide phenomena as changes in unemployment, the general price level, and national income.

1     Economics is typically divided into two types of analysis: **microeconomics** and **macroeconomics.**

> Microeconomics is the part of economic analysis that studies decision making undertaken by individuals (or households) and by firms. It is like looking through a microscope to focus on the small parts of our economy.

> Macroeconomics is the part of economic analysis that studies the behavior of the economy as a whole. It deals with economywide phenomena such as changes in unemployment, the general price level, and national income.

Microeconomic analysis, for example, is concerned with the effects of changes in the price of gasoline relative to that of other energy sources. It examines the effects of new taxes on a specific product or industry. If price controls were reinstituted in the United States, how individual firms and consumers would react to them would be in the realm of microeconomics. The raising of wages by an effective union strike would also be analyzed using the tools of microeconomics.

2     By contrast, issues such as the rate of inflation, the amount of economywide unemployment, and the yearly growth in the output of goods and services in the nation all fall into the realm of macroeconomic analysis. In other words, macroeconomics deals with **aggregates,** or totals—such as total output in an economy.

**Aggregates**
Total amounts or quantities; aggregate demand, for example, is total planned expenditures throughout a nation.

3     Be aware, however, of the blending of microeconomics and macroeconomics in modern economic theory. Modern economists are increasingly using microeconomic analysis—the study of decision making by individuals and by firms—as the basis of macroeconomic analysis. They do this because even though in macroeconomic analysis aggregates are being examined, those aggregates are made up of individuals and firms.

Roger LeRoy Miller, *Economics Today,* p. 5

# 4

## Sports as Beneficial to Society

1   According to the functionalist perspective, sports contribute to the welfare of society by performing at least three major functions.

2   First, sports are conducive to success in other areas of life. Being competitive, sports inspire athletes to do their utmost to win, thereby helping them to develop such qualities as skill and ability, diligence and self-discipline, mental alertness, and physical fitness. These qualities can ensure success in the larger society. In the words of General Douglas MacArthur: "Upon the fields of friendly strife are sown the seeds that, upon other fields, on other days, will bear the fruits of victory." By watching athletes perform, spectators also learn the importance of hard work, playing by the rules, and working as a team player, characteristics that help ensure success in a career and other aspects of life.

3   Second, sports enhance health and happiness. Participants can enjoy a healthy and long life. The health benefit is more than physical. It is also psychological. Runners and joggers, for example, often find that their activity releases tension and anger as well as relieving anxiety and depression. Moreover, many people derive much pleasure from looking upon their participation as a form of beauty, an artistic expression, or a way of having a good time with friends. Similarly, sports improve the quality of life for the spectators. Fans can escape their humdrum daily routines, or find pleasure in filling their leisure time. They can savor the aesthetic pleasure of watching the excellence, beauty, and creativity in an athlete's performance. The fans can therefore attain greater happiness, life satisfaction, or psychological well-being (Smith, 1993).

4   Third, sports contribute to social order and stability. This is because sports serve as an integrating force for society as a whole. Sports are in effect a social mechanism for uniting potentially disunited members of society. Through their common interest in a famous athlete or team, people of diverse racial, social, and cultural backgrounds can feel a sense of homogeneity, community, or intimacy that they can acquire in no other way. Athletes, too, can identify with their fans, their community, and their country.

Alex Thio, *Sociology*, p. 16

# 5

## Why We Sleep

1   One likely function of sleep is to provide a "time out" period, so that the body can restore depleted reserves of energy, eliminate waste products from muscles, repair cells, strengthen the immune system, or recover physical abilities lost during the day. The idea that sleep is for physical rest and recuperation accords with the unde-

niable fact that at the end of the day we feel tired and crave sleep. Though most people can function fairly normally after a day or two of sleeplessness, sleep deprivation that lasts for four days or longer is quite uncomfortable. In animals, forced sleeplessness leads to infections and eventually death (Rechtschaffen et al., 1983), and the same may be true for people. There is a case on record of a man who, at the age of 52, abruptly began to lose sleep. After sinking deeper and deeper into an exhausted stupor, he developed a lung infection and died. An autopsy showed he had lost almost all of the large neurons in two areas of the thalamus that have been linked to sleep and hormonal circadian rhythms (Lugaresi et al., 1986).

2　　Nonetheless, when people go many days without any sleep, they do not then require an equal period of time to catch up; one night's rest usually eliminates all symptoms of fatigue (Dement, 1978). Moreover, the amount of time we sleep does not necessarily correspond to how active we have been; even after a relaxing day on the beach, we usually go to sleep at night as quickly as usual. For these reasons, simple rest or energy restoration cannot be the sole purpose of sleep.

3　　Many researchers believe that sleep must have as much to do with brain function as with bodily restoration. Even though most people still function pretty well after losing a single night's sleep, mental flexibility, originality, and other aspects of creative thinking may suffer (Horne, 1988). Chronic sleepiness can impair performance on tasks requiring vigilance or divided attention, and it can lead to automotive and industrial accidents (Dement, 1992; Roehrs et al., 1990). Laboratory studies and observations of people participating in "wake-athons" have shown that after several days of sleep loss, people become irritable and begin to have hallucinations and delusions (Dement, 1978; Luce & Segal, 1966).

4　　The brain, then, needs periodic rest. Researchers are trying to find out how sleep may contribute to the regulation of brain metabolism, the maintenance of normal nerve-cell activity, and the replenishment of neurotransmitters. It is clear, however, that during sleep, the brain is not simply resting. On the contrary, most of the brain remains quite active, as we are about to see.

Carol Tavris and Carole Wade, *Psychology in Perspective*, pp. 162–163

# 6

## What Is Deviance?

1　Deviance is generally defined as any act that violates a social norm. But the phenomenon is more complex than that. How do we know whether an act violates a social norm? Is homosexuality deviant—a violation of a social norm? Some people think so, but others do not. There are at least three factors involved in determining what deviance is: time, place, and public consensus or power.

2　　First, what constitutes deviance varies from one historical period to another. In the last century in the United States, opium and cocaine were legal and easily available common drugs; today their use is a criminal offense. Nowadays in most countries cigarette smoking is legal, but in the seventeenth century it was illegal. In fact, in some countries at that time, smokers were punished harshly: in Russia their noses were cut off and in Hindustan their lips sliced off (Goode, 1989).

3    Second, the definition of deviance varies from one place to another. A polyga-mist (a person with more than one spouse) is a criminal in the United States but not in Saudi Arabia and other Muslim countries. Prostitution is illegal in the United States (except in some counties in Nevada), but legal in Denmark, Germany, France, and many other countries.

4    Third, whether a given act is deviant depends on public consensus. Murder is un-questionably deviant because nearly all societies agree that it is. In contrast, long hair on men is not generally considered deviant. Public consensus, however, usually reflects the vested interests of the rich and powerful. As Marx would have said, the ideas of the ruling class tend to become the ruling ideas of society. Like the power-ful, the general public tends, for example, to consider bank robbery to be a serious crime but not fraudulent advertising, which serves the interests of the powerful.

5    In view of those three determinants of deviant behavior, we may more precisely define **deviance** as an act considered by public consensus or by the powerful at a given time and place to be a violation of some social rule.

Alex Thio, *Sociology: A Brief Introduction*, p. 123

## ACTIVITY 6

The three textbook selections that follow are longer than those in Activity 5. In addition, two of them contain both major and minor headings and have graphic aids. Turn the headings into questions, taking into consideration the relationship or connection between the major and minor ones in Selections 2 and 3. Answer your questions by using the central message and any main ideas, context definitions, and patterns of organization that may be present. Underline or highlight the most important information before writing out the answers in your notebook. With regard to the graphic aids, answer the follow-ing two questions for each of them: "What is this graphic aid about?" and "What are the major points stressed?"

# 1

## 33.4 Value of Wetlands

1    Just as we like to dam rivers, so we are motivated to drain wetlands and convert them into dry land. The Romans drained the great marshes about the Tiber to make room for the city of Rome. In spite of the enormous amount of vacant dry land about him, George Washington proposed draining the Great Dismal Swamp (most of which has been done since his time). Many of us consider wetlands to be wastelands, areas to be drained for more productive uses by human standards: agricultural land, solid waste dumps, housing, industrial developments, and roads. We also look on wetlands as forbidding mysterious places, sources of pestilence, the home of dangerous and pestiferous insects, the abode of slimy sinister creatures that rise out of swamp wa-ters. We are blind to the ecological, hydrological, and economic values of wetlands.

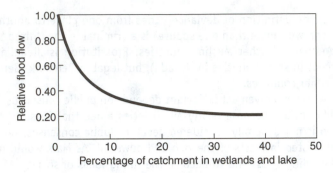

**Figure 33.9** The influence of different percentages of wetlands in a watershed on relative flood flows in Wisconsin.

2      Wetlands assume an importance, ecologically and economically, out of proportion to their size. Their major contribution is to the hydrology of a region. Basin
wetlands, in particular, are groundwater recharge points. They hold rainwater,
snowmelt, and surface runoff in their basins and discharge the water slowly into the
aquifers. These same basins also function as natural flood-control reservoirs. As little as 5 percent of the watershed or catchment area in wetlands can reduce flood
flows by as much as 50 percent (Figure 33.9).

3      Wetlands act as water-filtration systems. Wetland vegetation takes up excessive
nitrogen, phosphorus, sulfates, copper, iron, and other heavy metals brought by
surface runoff and inflow, incorporates them into plant biomass, and deposits much
of them in anaerobic bottom muds. Because of their ability to filter out heavy metals and to reduce pH, we are beginning to treat urban wastewater and drainage from
surface mines by diverting these flows into natural or specially created wetlands.

4      Wetlands contribute to the human economy in other ways. They provide places
of recreation, sources of horticultural peat and timber—notably baldcypress and
bottomland hardwoods in the southern United States—and sites for growing cran-
berries in the northeastern United States. These uses, however, tend to interfere
with the natural function and integrity of the wetland ecosystems.

5      Wetlands are vitally important as wildlife nesting and wintering habitat. Many
species of wildlife, some of them endangered, are dependent on wetlands. Worldwide, wetlands are home to numerous species of amphibians and reptiles, including
alligators and crocodiles. Many species of fish of the Amazon and other tropical rivers
depend on seasonal flooding of riverine swamps and floodplains to forage for terrestrial foods and to spawn. Waterfowl, wading birds, gulls and terns, herons, and storks
depend on marshes and wooded swamps for nesting and foraging. In fact, the prairie
pothole region of the north central United States and Canada is used by two-thirds of
the continent's 10 to 12 million waterfowl as a nesting area. Waterfowl in concentrated numbers use southern marshes and swamps as wintering habitat. Moose, hip-
popotamus, waterbuck, otters, and muskrat are mammalian inhabitants of wetlands.

6      In addition to wetland dwellers, wetlands support animal life in other ecosystems. A mosaic of wetlands in an upland terrestrial environment increases the abundance and diversity of wildlife populations.

Robert Leo Smith and Thomas M. Smith, *Elements of Ecology*, pp. 459–460

# 2

## Styles of Conflict

1   There are four ways in which people can act when their needs aren't met. Each one has very different characteristics, as we can show by describing a common problem. At one time or another almost everyone has been bothered by a neighbor's barking dog. You know the story: every passing car, distant siren, pedestrian, and falling leaf seems to set off a fit of barking that leaves you unable to sleep, socialize, or study. By describing the possible ways of handling this kind of situation, the differences between nonassertive, directly aggressive, indirectly aggressive, and assertive behavior should become clear.

### Nonassertive Behavior

2   There are two ways in which nonasserters manage a conflict. Sometimes they ignore their needs. Faced with the dog, for instance, a nonassertive person would try to forget the barking by closing the windows and trying to concentrate even harder. Another form of denial would be to claim that no problem exists—that a little barking never bothered anyone. To the degree that it's possible to make problems disappear by ignoring them, such an approach is probably advisable. In many cases, however, it simply isn't realistic to claim that nothing is wrong. For instance, if your health is being jeopardized by the cigarette smoke from someone nearby, you are clearly punishing yourself by remaining silent. If you need to learn more information from a supervisor before undertaking a project, you reduce the quality of your work by pretending that you understand it at all. If you claim that an unsatisfactory repair job is acceptable, you are paying good money for nothing. In all these and many more cases simply pretending that nothing is the matter when your needs continue to go unmet is clearly not the answer.

3   A second nonassertive course of action is to acknowledge your needs are not being met but simply to accept the situation, hoping that it might clear up without any action on your part. You could, for instance, wait for the neighbor who owns the barking dog to move. You could wait for the dog to be run over by a passing car or to die of old age. You could hope that your neighbor will realize how noisy the dog is and do something to keep it quiet. Each of these occurrences is a possibility, of course, but it would be unrealistic to count on one of them to solve your problem. And even if by chance you were lucky enough for the dog problem to be solved without taking action, you couldn't expect to be so fortunate in other parts of your life.

4   In addition, while waiting for one of these eventualities, you would undoubtedly grow more and more angry at your neighbor, making a friendly relationship between the two of you impossible. You would also lose a degree of self-respect, since you would see yourself as the kind of person who can't cope with even a common everyday irritation. Clearly, nonassertion is not a very satisfying course of action—either in this case or in other instances.

### Direct Aggression

5   Where the nonasserter underreacts, a directly aggressive person overreacts. The usual consequences of aggressive behaviors are anger and defensiveness or hurt and

humiliation. In either case aggressive communicators build themselves up at the expense of others.

6    You could handle the dog problem with direct aggression by abusively confronting your neighbors, calling them names and threatening to call the dogcatcher the next time you see their hound running loose. If the town in which you live has a leash law, you would be within your legal rights to do so, and thus you would gain your goal of bringing peace and quiet to the neighborhood. Unfortunately, your direct aggression would have other, less productive consequences. Your neighbors and you would probably cease to be on speaking terms, and you could expect a complaint from them the first time you violated even the most inconsequential of city ordinances. If you live in the neighborhood for any time at all, this state of hostilities isn't very appealing.

### Indirect Aggression

7    In several of his works psychologist George Bach describes behavior that he terms "crazymaking." Crazymaking occurs when people have feelings of resentment, anger,

## Crazymakers: Indirect Aggression

1  What's your conflict style? To give you a better idea of some unproductive ways you may be handling your conflicts, we'll describe some typical conflict behaviors that can weaken relationships. In our survey we'll follow the fascinating work of George Bach, a leading authority on conflict and communication.

2    Bach explains that there are two types of aggression—clean fighting and dirty fighting. Either because they can't or won't express their feelings openly and constructively, dirty fighters sometimes resort to "crazymaking" techniques to vent their resentments. Instead of openly and caringly expressing their emotions, crazymakers (often unconsciously) use a variety of indirect tricks to get at their opponent. Because these "sneak attacks" don't usually get to the root of the problem, and because of their power to create a great deal of hurt, crazymakers can destroy communication. Let's take a look at some of them.

3  **The Avoider**   The avoider refuses to fight. When a conflict arises, he'll leave, fall asleep, pretend to be busy at work, or keep from facing the problem in some other way. This behavior makes it very difficult for the partner to express his feelings of anger, hurt, etc., because the avoider won't fight back.

Arguing with an avoider is like trying to box with a person who won't even put up his gloves.

4  **The Pseudoaccommodator**   The pseudoaccommodator refuses to face up to a conflict either by giving in or by pretending that there's nothing at all wrong. This really drives the partner, who definitely feels there's a problem, crazy and causes him to feel both guilt and resentment toward the accommodator.

5  **The Guiltmaker**   Instead of saying straight out that she doesn't want or approve of something, the guiltmaker tries to change her partner's behavior by making him feel responsible for causing pain. The guiltmaker's favorite line is "It's O.K., don't worry about me . . . ." accompanied by a big sigh.

6  **The Subject Changer**   Really a type of avoider, the subject changer escapes facing up to aggression by shifting the conversation whenever it approaches an area of conflict. Because of his tactics, the subject changer and his partner never have the chance to explore their problem and do something about it.

7  **The Distracter**   Rather than come out and express his feelings about the object of his dissatisfaction, the distracter

attacks other parts of his partner's life. Thus he never has to share what's really on his mind and can avoid dealing with painful parts of his relationships.

8 **The Mind Reader**   Instead of allowing her partner to express her feelings honestly, the mind reader goes into character analysis, explaining what the other person really means or what's wrong with the other person. By behaving this way the mind reader refuses to handle her own feelings and leaves no room for her partner to express himself.

9 **The Trapper**   The trapper plays an especially dirty trick by setting up a desired behavior for her partner, and then when it's met, attacking the very thing she requested. An example of this technique is for the trapper to say, "Let's be totally honest with each other," and then when the partner shares his feelings, he finds himself attacked for having feelings that the trapper doesn't want to accept.

10 **The Crisis Tickler**   This person almost brings what's bothering him to the surface, but he never quite comes out and expresses himself. Instead of admitting his concern about the finances he innocently asks, "Gee, how much did that cost?" dropping a rather obvious hint but never really dealing with the crisis.

11 **The Gunnysacker**   This person doesn't respond immediately when she's angry. Instead, she puts her resentment into her gunnysack, which after a while begins to bulge with large and small gripes. Then, when the sack is about to burst, the gunnysacker pours out all her pent-up aggressions on the overwhelmed and unsuspecting victim.

12 **The Trivial Tyrannizer**   Instead of honestly sharing his resentments, the trivial tyrannizer does things he knows will get his partner's goat—leaving dirty dishes in the sink, clipping his fingernails in bed, belching out loud, turning up the television too loud, and so on.

13 **The Joker**   Because she's afraid to face conflicts squarely, the joker kids around when her partner wants to be serious, thus blocking the expression of important feelings.

14 **The Beltliner**   Everyone has a psychological "beltline," and below it are subjects too sensitive to be approached without damaging the relationship. Beltlines may have to do with physical characteristics, intelligence, past behavior, or deeply ingrained personality traits a person is trying to overcome. In an attempt to "get even" or hurt his partner the beltliner will use his intimate knowledge to hit below the belt, where he knows it will hurt.

15 **The Blamer**   The blamer is more interested in finding fault than in solving a conflict. Needless to say, she usually doesn't blame herself. Blaming behavior almost never solves a conflict and is an almost surefire way to make the receiver defensive.

16 **The Contract Tyrannizer**   This person will not allow his relationship to change from the way it once was. Whatever the agreements the partners had as to roles and responsibilities at one time, they'll remain unchanged. "It's your job to . . . feed the baby, wash the dishes, discipline the kids . . . ."

17 **The Kitchen Sink Fighter**   This person is so named because in an argument he brings up things that are totally off the subject ("everything but the kitchen sink"): the way his partner behaved last New Year's eve, the unbalanced checkbook, bad breath—anything.

18 **The Withholder**   Instead of expressing her anger honestly and directly, the withholder punishes her partner by keeping back something—courtesy, affection, good cooking, humor, sex. As you can imagine, this is likely to build up even greater resentments in the relationship.

19 **The Benedict Arnold**   This character gets back at his partner by sabotage, by failing to defend him from attackers, and even by encouraging ridicule or disregard from outside the relationship.

or rage that they are unable or unwilling to express directly. Instead of keeping these feelings to themselves, the crazymakers send these aggressive messages in subtle, indirect ways, thus maintaining the front of kindness. This amiable façade eventually crumbles, however, leaving the crazymaker's victim confused and angry at having been fooled. The targets of the crazymaker can either react with aggressive behavior of their own or retreat to nurse their hurt feelings. In either case indirect aggression seldom has anything but harmful effects on a relationship.

8   You could respond to your neighbors and their dog in several crazymaking, indirectly aggressive ways. One strategy would be to complain anonymously to the city pound and then, after the dog has been hauled away, express your sympathy. Or you could complain to everyone else in the neighborhood, hoping that their hostility would force the offending neighbors to quiet the dog or face being a social outcast. A third possibility would be to strike up a friendly conversation with one of the owners and casually remark about the terrible neighborhood you had just left, in which noisy dogs roamed the streets, uncontrolled by their thoughtless owners. (Or perhaps you could be more subtle and talk about noisy children instead!)

9   There are a number of shortcomings to such approaches as these, each of which illustrate the risks of indirect aggression. First, there is the chance that the crazymaking won't work: the neighbors might simply miss the point of your veiled attacks and continue to ignore the barking. On the other hand, they might get your message clearly, but either because of your lack of sincerity or out of sheer stubbornness they might simply refuse to do anything about the complaining. In either case it's likely that in this and other instances indirect aggression won't satisfy your unmet need.

10   Even when indirect aggression proves successful in the short run, a second shortcoming lies in its consequences over the longer range. You might manage to intimidate your neighbors into shutting up their mutt, for instance, but in winning that battle you could lose what would become a war. As a means of revenge, it's possible that they would wage their own campaign of crazymaking by such tactics as badmouthing things like your sloppy gardening to other neighbors or by phoning in false complaints about your allegedly loud parties. It's obvious that feuds such as this one are counterproductive and outweigh the apparent advantages of indirect aggression.

11   In addition to these unpleasant possibilities, a third shortcoming of indirect aggression is that it denies the people involved a chance of building any kind of honest relationship with each other. As long as you treat your neighbors as if they were an obstacle to be removed from your path, there's little likelihood that you'll get to know them as people. While this thought may not bother you, the principle that indirect aggression prevents intimacy holds true in other important areas of life. To the degree that you try to manipulate friends, they won't know the real you. The fewer of your needs you share directly with your coworkers, the less chance you have of becoming true friends and colleagues. The same principle holds for those people you hope to meet in the future. Indirect aggression denies closeness.

### Assertion

12   Assertive people handle conflicts skillfully by expressing their needs, thoughts, and feelings clearly and directly, but without judging others or dictating to them. They have the attitude that most of the time it is possible to resolve problems to everyone's satisfaction. Possessing this attitude and the skills to bring it about doesn't

## Styles of Conflict

|  | Nonassertive | Directly Aggressive | Indirectly Aggressive | Assertive |
|---|---|---|---|---|
| Approach to Others | I'm not O.K., You're O.K. | I'm O.K., You're not O.K. | I'm O.K., You're not O.K. (But I'll let you think you are.) | I'm O.K. You're O.K. |
| Decision Making | Let others choose | Choose for others. They know it. | Chooses for others They don't know it. | Chooses for self |
| Self-Sufficiency | Low | High or low | Looks high but usually low | Usually high |
| Behavior in Problem Situations | Flees, gives in | Outright attack | Concealed attack | Direct confrontation |
| Response of Others | Disrespect, guilt, anger, frustration | Hurt, defensiveness, humiliation | Confusion, frustration, feelings of manipulation | Mutual respect |
| Success Pattern | Succeeds by luck or charity of others | Beats out others | Wins by manipulation | Attempts "no lose" solutions |

Adapted with permission from S. Phelps and N. Austin, *The Assertive Woman*. San Luis Obispo, CA: Impact, 1974 p. 11, and Gerald Piaget, American Orthopsychiatric Association, 1974.

guarantee that assertive communicators will always get what they want, but it does give them the best chance of doing so. An additional benefit of such an approach is that whether or not it satisfies a particular need, it maintains the self-respect of both the asserters and those with whom they interact. As a result, people who manage their conflicts assertively may experience feelings of discomfort while they are working through the problem. They usually feel better about themselves and each other afterward—quite a change from the outcomes of no assertiveness and aggression.

13    An assertive course of action in the case of the barking dog would be to wait a few days to make sure that the noise is not just a fluke. If things continue in the present way, you could introduce yourself to your neighbors and explain your problem. You could tell them that although they might not notice it, the dog often plays in the street and keeps barking at passing cars. You could tell them why this behavior bothers you. It keeps you awake at night and makes it hard for you to do your work. You could point out that you don't want to be a grouch and call the pound. Rather than behaving in these ways, you could tell them that you've come to see what kind of solution you can find that will satisfy both of you. This approach may not work, and you might then have to decide whether it is more important to avoid bad feelings or to have peace and quiet. But the chances for a happy ending are best with this assertive approach. And no matter what happens, you can keep your self-respect by behaving directly and honestly.

Ronald B. Adler and Neil Towne, *Looking Out/Looking In*, pp. 198–204

## 3

## Causes of Urban Problems

1   Almost every problem in U.S. society—drug abuse and crime, racism and poverty, poor education and environmental pollution—seems more severe in the cities, particularly in the older and more congested ones. Even as newer cities grow and age, their problems will probably become more severe. The difficulties that cities face and their ability to deal with them are shaped to a great extent by the intertwining effects of various social forces. We discuss some of them here.

### POPULATION DECLINE

2   In the last ten years Detroit, Cleveland, Pittsburgh, St. Louis, and other big cities have lost more than 10 percent of their populations. In fact, most of the cities that have more than 200,000 people have suffered population declines (U.S. Census Bureau, 1994). On the face of it, this may look like good news for the cities' finances: Fewer people should mean less demand for, and less spending on, police protection, fire protection, education, and other public services. In reality, however, population decreases have created serious problems.

3       As the years go by, a city must spend more on maintaining its road, sewer, and water networks, even if it has fewer residents to pay for those services. Similarly, when families abandon the central city, the need for police and fire protection increases, because abandoned homes can become magnets for vandalism and crime. They become fire hazards and finally must be torn down at the city's expense. Furthermore, behind the statistics of declining populations lies the fact that those who move out of the cities are largely middle-class whites, and with them go many businesses. Thus, the cities have fewer private-sector jobs and declining revenues. Those left behind in the city are typically less educated, poorer, and older—the people most in need of government spending for education, housing, health services, and welfare.

### FISCAL SQUEEZE

4   In large part, urban problems stem from the city government's inability to generate sufficient income to provide various kinds of service to the public. Cities get most of their revenues from taxes on property, income, sales, and corporations. Some money can come from charging fees for services. But all these revenues have shrunk over the last decade: the suburbs have drained off much of the cities' tax base by attracting industries and stores and middle-class and upper-class people.

5       There are other potential sources of revenue, but cities generally cannot tap these sources. In many states, cities are prohibited from raising as much in taxes as they wish. Cities are also deprived of other revenue-producing opportunities: When federal and state governments use city property, they are exempted from paying city taxes worth billions of dollars. Suburbanites come into town, adding to traffic congestion, garbage, and wear and tear on roads and parks, while benefiting from police protection and other urban resources, but they pay no taxes to the city for these services. Consequently, since the 1960s cities have come to depend increas-

ingly on the state and federal governments to help pay their bills. Since the late 1980s, however, the federal government has been forced by its huge budget deficit to end its revenue-sharing program.

## POLITICAL DILEMMA

6   Part of the cities' fiscal problem originates with elected officials' unwillingness to raise taxes even if they have the power to do so and their citizens have the ability to pay. Given the unpopularity of tax increases, politicians tend to avoid risking taxpayers' anger even when taxes are low and necessary. But this political dilemma seems to have forced the cities to rely increasingly on private enterprise to tackle urban problems.

7   With their eyes on economic development, cities compete with one another to keep or attract businesses and industries. Low taxes and tax exemptions are used as lures. Although this may undermine the current tax base, the cities hope to build a larger tax base, through an increase in jobs, for the future.

8   Cities also set up **enterprise zones,** economically depressed urban areas that businesses, with the help of generous tax credits, try to revive by creating jobs. In the late 1980s the U.S. Congress voted against a bill designed to create 75 enterprise zones around the country. A majority of states have nonetheless proceeded on their own, creating thousands of jobs for the poor residents of the special zones (Carlson, 1991). A similar effort to solve public ills with private cures has appeared. Grass-roots entrepreneurs known as CDCs—community development corporations—have rehabilitated abandoned homes, created commercial enterprises, and organized social services in various large cities. Their objective is to succeed where governments have failed—by reclaiming city streets from crime and economic decline (*New York Times,* 1991).

## HOUSING SEGREGATION

9   Every year billions of dollars are spent on housing in the United States. The government helps out by granting billions in tax deductions to landlords and homeowners. As a result, we are among the best-housed people in the world, with most of the nation's families owning their own homes. But it has become more difficult financially to own or rent a home. Housing problems are most severe for the nation's minorities. For one thing, minorities, especially African Americans, make up a high percentage of the population of the inner cities, where good housing at reasonable prices is increasingly scarce. While most blacks living in metropolitan areas are concentrated in the inner cities, most of the metropolitan whites are spread out in the surrounding suburbs. In both the inner cities and in the suburbs, blacks are frequently segregated from whites, with the housing of blacks being inferior to that of whites.

10   Economics may be a factor in the segregation. Because African Americans tend to have lower incomes, they often cannot afford to move into more expensive white neighborhoods. But racial discrimination is an even bigger factor. Real estate agents tend to steer potential black buyers and renters away from white neighborhoods, perpetuating segregation. Banks are often more cautious in granting loans to blacks than to whites, making it difficult for blacks to own or rehabilitate homes

and thus encouraging the deterioration of black neighborhoods. Many blacks will not move into white neighborhoods because they wish to avoid rejection by whites (Hayes, 1990).

QUESTIONS FOR DISCUSSION AND REVIEW

1. What impact does population decline have on a city?
2. Why do many cities have serious financial problems?
3. How have cities dealt with the political dilemma of raising taxes?
4. What factors contribute to housing segregation?

Alex Thio, *Sociology: A Brief Introduction*, pp. 321–323

## ACTIVITY 7

For Activity 3, you previewed Chapter 3 from this textbook. Now turn all of the headings in that chapter into questions, and answer them in your notebook. Once again, use central messages, main ideas, context definitions, and patterns of organization to help you identify the most important information, and do not hesitate to underline or highlight it.

## ACTIVITY 8

Using the same chapter that you previewed for Activity 4, turn all of the headings into questions, and answer them in your notebook.

## LOOKING BACK

With two of your classmates, come up with a list of the most important points you learned from this chapter, and determine how they can be put to use in other classes. Be prepared to discuss both the list and the uses.

## THINK AGAIN!

The following paragraphs are part of a graphic aid taken from a textbook chapter. Can you figure out the point or central message of **all** three stories?

## Picture These Scenes

1    A little league batter leaves the on-deck circle and enters the batter's box. The kid looks kind of scrawny, so you don't expect much, until you notice the gaze of determination and concentration in the batter's eyes and the coach's confident stance.

The pitcher winds up, throws—and the kid swings, the bat cracks, and the ball sails sharply over the left-fielder's head. The kid rounds second to third, stares down the third baseman, and executes a perfect slide. Then the batter turns, takes off her cap and lets her long hair fall free, and flashes her winning smile at her third-base coach.

2    The nurse wipes the sweat from the surgeon's brow. The hip replacement surgery is going well, and the saw buzzes in the hand of the skillful surgeon as it is carefully moved through the pelvic bone. The work is demanding and physical. The nurse is adept at handing the surgeon each instrument at exactly the right moment; they have worked together before and make a good team. Now it is time to close, and as the nurse prepares the sutures for the surgeon, a brief smile breaks out. "I am good at what I do," the nurse thinks to himself as he once again reaches over to wipe the surgeon's brow. The surgeon smiles in gratitude, grateful that she has such dedicated and able professionals working with her.

3    Robin undresses, feeling nervous and apprehensive, and then feels silly. After all, the photographer is a professional and has probably seen a thousand naked bodies, so what is one more? All that work in the weight room, the aerobics—why not show off, after all the work it took to get a such a tight body? "I should be proud," Robin thinks, slipping into the robe thoughtfully provided by the photographer. Once exposed to the lights of the studio, Robin gets another pang of doubt but dismisses it and drops the robe. The photographer suggests a seated pose, and Robin strikes it, but he drops his hands to cover his genitals. "Move your hands to your knees, please," the photographer says gently. After all, she is a professional and knows how to put her models at ease.

Janell L. Carroll and Paul Root Wolpe, *Sexuality and Gender in Society,* p. 162

## MASTERY TEST 2

A. Fill in the blanks and answer the questions.

1. The method used to get acquainted with a new textbook is called

   _____.

2. The method used to familiarize yourself with a textbook chapter is

   called _____.

3. Questions, reference sources, and summaries are examples of
   _____ aids.

4. A textbook's organization can be seen in the
   a. index
   b. bibliography
   c. glossary
   d. all of the above
   e. none of the above

5. The preface is important because
   a. it gives the author's purpose
   b. lists features
   c. explains the aids to understanding
   d. all of the above
   e. none of the above

6. Page locations for very specific information can be found in the
   a. index
   b. preface
   c. table of contents
   d. appendix
   e. none of the above

7. A _____ provides definitions of words or combinations of
   words that fit the context of a given textbook.

8. Supplementary or additional information, such as maps and diagrams,
   can be found in the
   a. table of contents
   b. preface
   c. appendix
   d. index
   e. none of the above

9. For research purposes, it is useful to consult
   a. the bibliography
   b. a list of general reference sources
   c. footnotes
   d. a list of suggested readings
   e. all of the above

10. A _____ contains sources used by the author to write the textbook.

11. The _____ states the topic of a given textbook chapter.

12. You can determine exactly what you are expected to know in a chapter and also set personal study goals by looking at the
    a. objectives
    b. goals
    c. outcomes
    d. all of the above
    e. none of the above

13. _____ aids include charts, graphs, maps, pictures, and tables.

14. _____ or titles let you know what a graphic aid is about.

15. The _____ message of a chapter can sometimes be found in the first or last paragraph.

16. You can plan how to tackle a reading assignment by checking the length and difficulty of a chapter. True or False

17. "Questions at the end of a chapter can help direct your reading to the most valuable information." Is this statement true or false?

18. Turning _____ into questions helps you focus your attention and evaluate the most important information in a chapter.

19. Underlining or highlighting textbook information is a useful technique that enables you to
    a. comprehend better
    b. review more quickly
    c. concentrate better
    d. all of the above
    e. none of the above

20. The words _____, _____, _____, _____, _____, and _____ should be used to make questions out of chapter headings.

B. For the two textbook selections that follow, turn the headings into questions, underline or highlight the most important information, and then write out the answers in the spaces provided. Also, indicate what two questions should be asked and answered concerning the graphic aid in the second selection.

21. ## Causes of Revolution

1    If a protest movement turns to violence, it may produce a **revolution**—the movement aimed at the violent overthrow of the existing government. Numerous studies on revolutions in many different societies differ in explaining the

causes of revolution, but they all suggest in one way or another that a revolution is likely to occur if the following conditions are met (Goldstone, 1982):

2    1. *A group of rather well-off and well-educated individuals is extremely dissatisfied with the society.* They may be intellectuals or opinion leaders such as journalists, poets, playwrights, teachers, clergy, and lawyers. These people would withdraw support from the government, criticize it, and demand reforms. Discontent may also exist within such elites as wealthy landowners, industrialists, leading bureaucrats, and military officials. It is from among all these people that most revolutionary leaders emerge.

3    2. *Revolutionary leaders rely on the masses' rising expectation to convince them that they can end their oppression by bringing down the existing government.* By itself, poverty does not produce revolution. Most of the world, after all, is poor. When people have long lived with misery, they may become fatalists, resigned to their suffering. They may starve without raising a fist or even uttering a whimper against the government. But, if their living conditions improve, then fatalism may give way to hope. They may expect a better life. It is in times of such a *rising expectation* that revolutionary leaders may succeed in attracting mass support.

4    3. *A deepening economic crisis triggers peasant revolts and urban uprisings.* In a social climate of rising expectations, large masses of peasants and workers tend to respond explosively to serious economic problems. When the state raises taxes too high, and landlords, in turn, jack up the dues of tenant farmers or take over their lands, the peasants are likely to revolt. When the cost of food and the rate of unemployment soar, food riots and large-scale antigovernment protests tend to erupt in the cities.

5    4. *The existing government is weak.* Usually, before a government is overthrown, it has failed to resolve one problem after another and has gradually lost legitimacy. As the crisis mounts, the government often tries to initiate reforms, but usually too little or too late. This only reinforces people's conviction that the regime is flawed, and encourages demands for even bigger reforms. All this can quicken the government's downfall. As Machiavelli (1469–1527) said in his warning to rulers, "If the necessity for [reforms] comes in troubled times, you are too late for harsh measures. Mild ones will not help you, for they will be considered as forced from you, and no one will be under obligation to you" (Goldstone, 1982).

Alex Thio, *Sociology: A Brief Introduction*, pp. 275–276

## Question and Answer

_____

_____

_____

_____

_____

_____

_____

_____

_____

_____

## 22. Evaluating Electronic Sources

Most books and periodical articles are reviewed before publication, so you can have some confidence in the information they contain. But many Internet sources are self-published by their authors with no preliminary review by others, so you must be the sole judge of reliability. To a great extent, the same critical reading that serves you with books and periodical articles will help you evaluate Internet sources (see the box). . . . But you should do some digging as well:

- *Check electronic addresses.* Look for an abbreviation that tells you where the source originates: *edu* (educational institution), *gov* (government body), *org* (nonprofit organization), or *com* (commercial organization). (Two-letter codes indicate origin outside the United States—for example, *uk* is United Kingdom.) Immediately before this abbreviation, the address will indicate the particular institution, government, or organization: for instance, *ed.gov* is the US Department of Education, *ca.gov* is the government of California, *greenpeace.org* is the environmental group Greenpeace, and *ibm.com* is the computer company IBM.
- *Check authorship.* Many sites list the author(s) or group(s) responsible for the site. You can research an author or group through a biographical dictionary, through a work such as the *National Directory of Addresses and Telephone Numbers,* or through a keyword search of the World Wide Web. . . . A site on the Web may provide links to information about, or other work by, an author or group. The author or group may also show up in your other sources.
- *Communicate directly with the author.* For a posting on a Listserv or a Usenet newsgroup, try to reach the author directly to ask about publications and background or to seek further information about your subject. . . . Listservs usually publish subscribers' names and e-mail addresses, so it should be easy to reach an author. Newsgroups . . . are generally more anonymous: you may have to address a posting to the author requesting his or her name and e-mail address. Drop the source from your list if you can't trace the author or the author fails to respond to your requests for information.
- *Check for references or links to reliable sources.* The source may offer as support the titles of sources that you can trace and evaluate—articles in periodicals, other Internet sources, and so on. A Web site may include links to these other sources.
- *Evaluate the source as a whole.* For Web sites, especially, consider the links to other sites. What is the purpose of the site in establishing and organizing links?

Are the links worthwhile, or mere window dressing? Is the site trying to sell a particular product, service, or idea? Do some links raise questions about the intentions of the source—because the links are frivolous, say, or indecent?

- *Back up Internet sources.* Always consider Internet sources in the context of other sources so that you can distinguish singular, untested views from more mainstream views that have been subjected to verification. . . . Only a range of sources will give you a broad and reliable picture of your topic.

## Guidelines for Evaluating Sources

Determine relevance:

- Does the source devote some attention to your topic?
- Where in the source are you likely to find relevant information or ideas?
- Is the source appropriately specialized for your needs? Check the source's treatment of a topic you know something about, to ensure that it is neither too superficial nor too technical.
- How important is the source likely to be for your writing?

Judge reliability:

- How up to date is the source? Check the publication date.

- Is the author an expert in the field? Look for an author biography, look up the author in a biographical reference . . . , or try to trace the author over the Internet.
- What is the author's bias? Check biographical information or the author's own preface or introduction. Consider what others have written about the author or the source.
- Whatever his or her bias, does the author reason soundly, provide adequate evidence, and consider opposing views?

H. Ramsey Fowler and Jane E. Aaron,
*The Little, Brown Handbook*, pp. 565–567

## *Questions and Answers*

_____

_____

_____

_____

_____

_____

_____

_____

_____

_____

_____

_____
_____
_____
_____
_____
_____
_____
_____
_____
_____
_____
_____
_____
_____
_____
_____
_____
_____
_____
_____
_____

## Graphic Aid Questions

_____
_____
_____
_____

## PLAYING SHERLOCK HOLMES AND DR. WATSON

Arthur Conan Doyle's fictional detective, Sherlock Holmes, is probably the greatest critical thinker of all time. This semester, you and a classmate will be given the opportunity to play Sherlock Holmes and his loyal companion, Dr. Watson. By putting your minds together, you will attempt to solve the case in "The Adventure of the Three Students."

At the end of each part of this textbook, the two of you will answer questions concerning the case, which ideally will lead you to the identity of the "culprit." As a start, you and your partner should read the first part of the short story and then answer the questions that follow it in your notebooks. Have fun!!

## The Return of Sherlock Holmes
### *The Adventure of the Three Students: Part One*

A. Conan Doyle

It was in the year '95 that a combination of events, into which I need not enter, caused Mr. Sherlock Holmes and myself to spend some weeks in one of our great University towns, and it was during this time that the small but instructive adventure which I am about to relate befell us. It will be obvious that any details which would help the reader to exactly identify the college or the criminal would be injudicious and offensive. So painful a scandal may well be allowed to die out. With due discretion the incident itself may, however, be described, since it serves to illustrate some of those qualities for which my friend was remarkable. I will endeavour in my statement to avoid such terms as would serve to limit the events to any particular place, or give a clue as to the people concerned.

We were residing at the time in furnished lodgings close to a library where Sherlock Holmes was pursuing some laborious researches in early English charters—researches which led to results so striking that they may be the subject of one of my future narratives. Here it was that one evening we received a visit from an acquaintance, Mr. Hilton Soames, tutor and lecturer at the College of St. Luke's. Mr. Soames was a tall, spare man, of a nervous and excitable temperament. I had always known him to be restless in his manner, but on this particular occasion he was in such a state of uncontrollable agitation that it was clear something very unusual had occurred.

"I trust, Mr. Holmes, that you can spare me a few hours of your valuable time. We have had a very painful incident at St. Luke's, and really, but for the happy chance of your being in the town, I should have been at a loss what to do."

"I am very busy just now, and I desire no distractions," my friend answered. "I should much prefer that you called in the aid of the police."

"No, no, my dear sir; such a course is utterly impossible. When once the law is evoked it cannot be stayed again, and this is just one of those cases where, for the credit of the college, it is most essential to avoid scandal. Your discretion is as well known as your powers, and you are the one man in the world who can help me. I beg you, Mr. Holmes, to do what you can."

My friend's temper had not improved since he had been deprived of the congenial surroundings of Baker Street. Without his scrap-books, his chemicals, and his homely untidiness, he was an uncomfortable man. He shrugged his shoulders in ungracious acquiescence, while our visitor in hurried words and with much excitable gesticulation poured forth his story.

"I must explain to you, Mr. Holmes, that to-morrow is the first day of the examination for the Fortescue Scholarship. I am one of the examiners. My subject is Greek, and the first of the papers consists of a large passage of Greek translation which the candidate has not seen. This passage is printed on the examination paper, and it would naturally be an immense advantage if the candidate could prepare it in advance. For this reason great care is taken to keep the paper secret.

"To-day about three o'clock the proofs of this paper arrived from the printers. The exercise consists of half a chapter of Thucydides. I had to read it over carefully, as the text must be absolutely correct. At four-thirty my task was not yet completed. I had, however, promised to take tea in a friend's rooms, so I left the proof upon my desk. I was absent rather more than an hour.

"You are aware, Mr. Holmes, that our college doors are double—a green baize one within and a heavy oak one without. As I approached my outer door I was amazed to see a key in it. For an instant I imagined that I had left my own there, but on feeling in my pocket I found that it was all right. The only duplicate which existed, so far as I knew, was that which belonged to my servant, Bannister, a man who has looked after my room for ten years, and whose honesty is absolutely above suspicion. I found that the key was indeed his, that he had entered my room to know if I wanted tea, and that he had very carelessly left the key in the door when he came out. His visit to my room must have been within a very few minutes of my leaving it. His forgetfulness about the key would have mattered little upon any other occasion, but on this one day it has produced the most deplorable consequences.

"The moment I looked at my table I was aware that someone had rummaged among my papers. The proof was in three long slips. I had left them all together. Now I found that one of them was lying on the floor, one was on the side table near the window, and the third was where I had left it."

Holmes stirred for the first time.

"The first page on the floor, the second in the window, the third where you left it," said he.

"Exactly, Mr. Holmes. You amaze me. How could you possibly know that?"

"Pray continue your very interesting statement."

"For an instant I imagined that Bannister had taken the unpardonable liberty of examining my papers. He denied it, however, with the utmost earnestness, and I am convinced that he was speaking the truth. The alternative was that someone passing had observed the key in the door, had known that I was out, and had entered to look at the papers. A large sum of money is at stake, for the scholarship is a very valuable one, and an unscrupulous man might very well run a risk in order to gain an advantage over his fellows.

"Bannister was very much upset by the incident. He had nearly fainted when we found that the papers had undoubtedly been tampered with. I gave him a little brandy and left him collapsed in a chair while I made a most careful examination of the room. I soon saw that the intruder had left other traces of his presence besides the rumpled papers. On the table in the window were several shreds from a pencil which had been sharpened. A broken tip of lead was lying there also. Evidently the rascal had copied the paper in a great hurry, had broken his pencil, and had been compelled to put a fresh point to it."

"Excellent!" said Holmes, who was recovering his good-humour as his attention became more engrossed by the case. "Fortune has been your friend."

"This was not all. I have a new writing-table with a fine surface of red leather. I am prepared to swear, and so is Bannister, that it was smooth and unstained. Now I found a clean cut in it about three inches long—not a mere scratch, but a positive cut. Not only this, but on the table I found a small ball of black dough, or clay, with specks of some- thing which looks like sawdust in it. I am convinced that these marks were left by the man who rifled the papers. There were no footmarks and no other evidence as to his identity. I was at my wits' ends, when suddenly the happy thought occurred to me that you were in the town, and I came straight round to put the matter into your hands. Do help me, Mr. Holmes! You see my dilemma. Either I must find the man or else the examination must be postponed until fresh papers are prepared, and since this cannot be done without explana- tion there will ensue a hideous scandal, which will throw a cloud not only on the college, but on the University. Above all things I desire to settle the matter quietly and discreetly."

"I shall be happy to look into it and to give you such advice as I can," said Holmes, rising and putting on his overcoat. "The case is not entirely devoid of interest. Had any- one visited you in your room after the papers came to you?"

"Yes; young Daulat Ras, an Indian student who lives on the same stair, came in to ask me some particulars about the examination."

"For which he was entered?"

"Yes."

"And the papers were on your table?"

"To the best of my belief they were rolled up."

"But might be recognised as proofs?"

"Possibly."

"No one else in your room?"

"No."

"Did anyone know that these proofs would be there?"

"No one save the printer."

"Did this man Bannister know?"

"No, certainly not. No one knew."

"Where is Bannister now?"

"He was very ill, poor fellow. I left him collapsed in the chair. I was in such a hurry to come to you."

"You left your door open?"

"I locked up the papers first."

"Then it amounts to this, Mr. Soames, that unless the Indian student recognised the roll as being proofs, the man who tampered with them came upon them accidentally without knowing that they were there."

"So it seems to me."

Holmes gave an enigmatic smile.

"Well," said he, "let us go round. Not one of your cases, Watson—mental, not phys- ical. All right; come if you want to. Now, Mr. Soames—at your disposal!"

The sitting-room of our client opened by a long, low, latticed window on to the ancient lichen-tinted court of the old college. A Gothic arched door led to a worn stone stair- case. On the ground floor was the tutor's room. Above were three students, one on each story. It was already twilight when we reached the scene of our problem. Holmes halted and looked earnestly at the window. Then he approached it, and, standing on tiptoe with his neck craned, he looked into the room.

"He must have entered through the door. There is no opening except the one pane," said our learned guide.

"Dear me!" said Holmes, and he smiled in a singular way as he glanced at our companion. "Well, if there is nothing to be learned here we had best go inside."

The lecturer unlocked the outer door and ushered us into his room. We stood at the entrance while Holmes made an examination of the carpet.

"I am afraid there are no signs here," said he. "One could hardly hope for any upon so dry a day. Your servant seems to have quite recovered. You left him in a chair, you say; which chair?"

"By the window there."

"I see. Near this little table. You can come in now. I have finished with the carpet. Let us take the little table first. Of course, what has happened is very clear. The man entered and took the papers, sheet by sheet, from the central table. He carried them over to the window table, because from there he could see if you came across the courtyard, and so could effect an escape."

As a matter of fact he could not," said Soames, "for I entered by the side door."

"Ah, that's good! Well, anyhow, that was in his mind. Let me see the three strips. No finger impressions—no! Well, he carried over this one first and he copied it. How long would it take him to do that, using every possible contraction? A quarter of an hour, not less. Then he tossed it down and seized the next. He was in the midst of that when your return caused him to make a very hurried retreat—*very* hurried, since he had not time to replace the papers which would tell you that he had been there. You were not aware of any hurrying feet on the stair as you entered the outer door?"

"No, I can't say I was."

"Well, he wrote so furiously that he broke his pencil, and had, as you observe, to sharpen it again. This is of interest, Watson. The pencil was not an ordinary one. It was above the usual size, with a soft lead; the outer colour was dark blue, the maker's name was printed in silver lettering, and the piece remaining is only about an inch and a half long. Look for such a pencil, Mr. Soames, and you have got your man. When I add that he possesses a large and very blunt knife, you have an additional aid."

Mr. Soames was somewhat overwhelmed by this flood of information. "I can follow the other points," said he, "but really in this matter of the length—"

Holmes held out a small chip with the letters NN and a space of clear wood after them. "You see?"

"No, I fear that even now—"

"Watson, I have always done you an injustice. There are others. What could this NN be? It is at the end of a word. You are aware that Johann Faber is the most common maker's name. Is it not clear that there is just as much of the pencil left as usually follows the Johann?" He held the small table sideways to the electric light. "I was hoping that if the paper on which he wrote was thin some trace of it might come through upon this polished surface. No, I see nothing. I don't think there is anything more to be learned here. Now for the central table. This small pellet is, I presume, the black, doughy mass you spoke of. Roughly pyramidal in shape and hollowed out, I perceive. As you say, there appear to be grains of sawdust in it. Dear me, this is very interesting. And the cut—a positive tear, I see. It began with a thin scratch and ended in a jagged hole. I am much indebted to you for directing my attention to this case, Mr. Soames. Where does that door lead to?"

"To my bedroom."

"Have you been in it since your adventure?"

"No; I came straight away for you."

"I should like to have a glance round. What a charming, old-fashioned room! Perhaps you will kindly wait a minute until I have examined the floor. No, I see nothing. What about this curtain? You hang your clothes behind it. If anyone were forced to conceal himself in this room he must do it there, since the bed is too low and the wardrobe too shallow. No one there, I suppose?"

As Holmes drew the curtain I was aware, from some little rigidity and alertness of his attitude, that he was prepared for an emergency. As a matter of fact the drawn curtain disclosed nothing but three or four suits of clothes hanging from a line of pegs. Holmes turned away and stooped suddenly to the floor.

"Halloa! What's this?" said he.

It was a small pyramid of black, putty-like stuff, exactly like the one upon the table of the study. Holmes held it out on his open palm in the glare of the electric light.

"Your visitor seems to have left traces in your bedroom as well as in your sitting-room, Mr. Soames."

"What could he have wanted there?"

"I think it is clear enough. You came back by an unexpected way, and so he had no warning until you were at the very door. What could he do? He caught up everything which would betray him and he rushed into your bedroom to conceal himself."

"Good gracious, Mr. Holmes, do you mean to tell me that all the time I was talking to Bannister in this room we had the man prisoner if we had only known it?"

"So I read it."

"Surely there is another alternative, Mr. Holmes. I don't know whether you observed my bedroom window?"

"Lattice-paned, lead framework, three separate windows, one swinging on hinge and large enough to admit a man."

"Exactly. And it looks out on an angle of the courtyard so as to be partly invisible. The man might have effected his entrance there, left traces as he passed through the bedroom, and, finally, finding the door open have escaped that way."

*The Complete Original Illustrated Sherlock Holmes,* pp. 566–570

## Questions

1. What is the problem that confronts Holmes and Watson?
2. What are the clues?
3. At this point in the mystery, are there any suspects? If so, who are they, and why do you consider them suspects?

## GO ELECTRONIC!

For additional readings, exercises, and Internet activities, visit our Web site at:

### http://longman.awl.com/englishpages

If you need a user name and password, see your instructor.

**Take a Road Trip to** the Grand Canyon! Be sure to visit the Reading Textbooks module in your Reading Road Trip CD-ROM for multimedia tutorials, exercises, and tests.

# Part Two

# Dealing with Complexity

# Chapter Three

# CRITICAL THINKING AND CONTEMPORARY ISSUES

## Chapter Outline

Critical Thinking Versus Random Thinking

Benefits of Critical Thinking

Characteristics of Critical Thinking
*Flexibility*
*Clear Purpose*
*Organization*
*Time and Effort*
*Asking Questions and Finding Answers*
*Research*
*Coming to Logical Conclusions*

What Is a Contemporary Issue?
*Determining What Is at Issue*
*Distinguishing Among Opposing Viewpoints*
*Expressing a Personal Viewpoint*

# THINK ABOUT IT!

What is the central message of each of the signs in the photographs?
Discuss your answers with your classmates.

(1)

(2)

(3)

(4)

---

**Chapter Outcomes**

After completing Chapter 3, you should be able to:
- Distinguish between critical thinking and random thinking
- Discuss the benefits of critical thinking
- List, explain, and demonstrate the characteristics of critical thinking
- Define a "contemporary issue"
- Find topics and central messages in contemporary issue passages in order to determine what is at issue, distinguish among opposing viewpoints, and express personal viewpoints

---

## Critical Thinking Versus Random Thinking

Take a few moments just to let some thoughts pass through your mind. What are you thinking about? Are you reflecting on what you did last night or what you intend to do this weekend? Are you worried about an assignment that is due or a test that is coming up? Maybe you are focusing on an important person in your life. Perhaps you are just thinking about how hungry or tired you are. The possibilities are endless.

What you just did was an example of **random thinking,** which is thinking without a clear purpose or objective in mind. We all do this kind of thinking countless times each day, often without even realizing it. Sometimes we are simply daydreaming, thinking about past experiences, or wondering or worrying about some future activity. Thoughts pop into mind and just as quickly out; they just come and go without much effort on our part. Nothing is really accomplished as a result, except perhaps a rest or escape from whatever we may be doing at that particular time.

Random thinking is not critical thinking. How do they differ? Let's look at an example.

Suppose that you and a friend are considering whether to take a particular course next semester. The two of you approach another student who enrolled for that course last year, and she informs you that she dropped it after two weeks because it was so boring. On the basis of that conversation, your friend decides not to take the course. Although you are tempted to do the same thing, you decide instead to give the matter some more thought because you do not think it wise to base your decision solely on the opinion of one student, who might have had a personal reason for not appreciating the course. For example, she could have had a problem at the time that interfered with her ability to fulfill the course requirements, or she could have been uncomfortable with the instructor's personality and teaching style. These may have been good reasons at the time for her not to stay in the course, but that does not mean that they should have an effect on your decision. Consequently, rather than automatically accepting one person's opinion, you decide to spend more time and effort getting additional information before coming to a final decision.

You organize your efforts by first getting a class schedule for next semester in order to find out the days and times that the course is offered and which faculty teach it. You want to determine if you can fit the course into your schedule and whether or not you have a choice of instructor. Second, you check the college catalog so that you can read the course description to see what it is about in a general sense and whether it can be used as part of your program of study. Third, you obtain a copy of a recent course syllabus from the department, a counselor, the instructor, or a student so that you can get additional information on assignments and grading. Fourth, you ask around so that you can find and talk to more students who have taken the course. Fifth, you discuss the course with a faculty member and your counselor or academic adviser.

After considering carefully all the information you gathered, you now feel confident about coming to a conclusion regarding whether or not to enroll in the course. You know that it fits into your program of study and your schedule, and you have a better understanding of its content. Furthermore, you are aware of who teaches the course and can determine if you are comfortable with his teaching style, grading policies, and personality. No matter what you ultimately decide to do, you have placed yourself in a much stronger position to make the right decision *for you.* However, you do continue to reconsider that decision right up until the time of registration, just in case you find out some additional information that changes your mind.

The process that you used in the example above involved **critical thinking,** which is best described as a very careful and thoughtful way of dealing with events, issues, problems, decisions, or situations. As you can see, it can be very helpful to you. Let's take a brief look at its many benefits.

## Benefits of Critical Thinking

Critical thinking is important because it makes you a much more careful decision maker who has the best chance of assessing situations accurately, making sense of issues and events, and coming up with solutions to problems. Because critical thinkers do not accept blindly everything they see, hear, or read, they place themselves in a better position to understand what is going on around them, to avoid costly mistakes, and to accomplish whatever they set out to do.

There are no limits to the uses of critical thinking. It can help you evaluate textbook material and other types of reading; uncover motivations and assess arguments; consider options, products, advertisements, and commercials; and judge policies and programs such as those offered by the various levels of government. The benefits of critical thinking for you are very real and substantial no matter what roles you play in life now and in the future, including those of student, professional, parent, and citizen. Make it a habit to think critically about everything!

## Characteristics of Critical Thinking

How do you know for sure when you are thinking critically? The answer to that question involves a discussion of its characteristics. Critical thinking requires flexibility, a clear purpose, organization, time and effort, asking questions and finding answers, research, and coming to logical conclusions. Let's consider each of these characteristics in more detail.

### Flexibility

Critical thinking is **flexible thinking** because it involves a willingness to consider various possibilities before coming to a conclusion. Critical thinkers do not jump to conclusions or automatically accept what they first see, hear, or read. They are willing to gather and consider additional information, even if it does not support what they initially think or want to do. In the course selection example, it would have been easy for you simply to accept the first student's opinion and your friend's decision regarding the course. Even though you may have been tempted to take the quick and easy way out, you delayed your decision until you had a chance to gather more information. Realizing that your first reaction to the course was negative, you still managed to keep an open mind and were willing to consider carefully other viewpoints.

Critical thinkers, then, are aware of their initial feelings about decisions, issues, problems, or situations yet willing to look at other possibilities before taking action. They are also willing to allow others the opportunity to voice their opinions, and they give careful consideration to those opinions before coming to their own conclusions. In the end, critical thinkers may stick with their initial feelings, but only after much investigation and thought.

## ACTIVITY 1

Think about an instance in your life in which you showed flexibility and an instance in your life in which you did not. Be prepared to discuss your two examples.

## ACTIVITY 2

Read and think carefully about the following passage. Decide which side of the argument you *disagree* with and why, and show flexibility by writing a paragraph *in support* of that position. You will be asked to provide the reasons why you disagree with the argument and also discuss the paragraph you wrote in support of it.

### Pro & Con: Should Poor Immigrants Be Denied Free Medical Care?

*The 1996 welfare reform law cuts off most health care benefits for new immigrants. It also permits states to end subsidized medical care for those already living in the United States. Families that sponsor immigrants will now be required to pay their bills. If sponsors refuse, immigrants could go without care or turn to hospital emergency rooms, which cannot deny treatment in life-threatening situations.*

## YES

1 Since this nation began, our policy has been to deport any noncitizen who becomes a public burden. The idea of immigration has always been to allow a limited number of people to come here for the opportunity to work, become self-sufficient, and contribute to the economy. To ensure self-reliance, all legal immigrants must have sponsors here who promise to support them if necessary. But those obligations have not been honored.

2 Instead, increasing numbers of legal immigrants are older people brought here by their children to go on Medicaid and supplemental security income. These elderly immigrants are our fastest growing welfare population. If the number of immigrants on Medicaid or ssi continues to increase at the present rate, the cost to taxpayers will be about $320 billion over the next ten years. This nation never intended to open its doors to people who would retire on welfare at the taxpayers' expense.

3 Denying nonemergency medical care to immigrants carries little health risk. We already screen immigrants for tuberculosis, and free vaccinations against contagious diseases are available to all at public health clinics. Some immigrants might turn to hospital emergency rooms for care, but in the long run most will stop coming to the United States once the free ride ends.

4 In a nation that spends 5 percent of its money on welfare benefits for the poor, we need to encourage skilled immigrants who will contribute to our economic strength. Ending free health care is the first step.

ROBERT RECTOR *is a senior policy analyst on welfare at the Heritage Foundation in Washington, D.C.*

## NO

1 Historically Congress has exempted sponsors' income when determining immigrants' eligibility for Medicaid. Our leaders recognized that medical care is too important—both to individuals in need and to public health—for anyone to go without. Subsidized treatment for the poor helps us control communicable diseases such as tuberculosis. And, just as important, it supports our system of hospitals, clinics, and doctors, which could otherwise be placed in financial jeopardy.

2 There is no evidence that immigrants bring their elderly parents here to get free medical care. They want to reunite with their mothers and fathers, and help care for them as they age. There's nothing wrong with that. That's family values.

3 The new policy is both inhumane and fiscally foolish. Arriving immigrants virtually always work and pay taxes, but they often don't earn enough to buy health insurance. The longer they go without basic care, the more likely they are to develop disabling conditions that could prevent them from paying taxes in the future. Further, all babies born here are U.S. citizens; they can't be deported. Providing prenatal care to immigrant mothers is much less expensive than caring for children born with severe and preventable health problems.

4 Besides, forcing immigrants to seek treatment in emergency rooms imperils the health of all Americans. When the ERs are clogged with uninsured people, even the millionaire who gets in a car accident may not receive timely care.

LUCY QUACINELLA *is an attorney at the Western Center on Law and Poverty in California.*

*Health*, January-February 1997, p. 28

### Clear Purpose

Critical thinking is deliberate thinking because it always involves a **clear purpose**. When you think critically, you are looking for reasons or explanations for events, considering various sides of an issue, attempting to solve a problem, coming to a decision, or making sense of a situation. For example, you may be trying to figure out how an event like an automobile accident occurred, distinguish among the arguments on both sides of an issue such as abortion, come up with a solution to a problem like a low grade in a course, decide where to go on vacation, or understand the reasons behind a political event such as a war or revolution. In the course example, the decision whether to register for the course was the purpose you, as a critical thinker, had in mind.

## ACTIVITY 3

Think about an experience from your past in which you demonstrated critical thinking by having a clear purpose. It could involve your looking for reasons or explanations for events, considering various sides of an issue, attempting to solve a problem, coming to a decision, or making sense of a situation.

## ACTIVITY 4

Read the following article; then discuss it with a classmate for the purpose of asking questions and trying to come up with possible reasons or explanations for the actions of Joseph Chavis.

## As a Lawyer, He's Exemplary; as a Robber, an Enigma

CHRISTINE BIEDERMAN

1   DALLAS, Jan. 19—Sitting beside his lawyer in Federal District Court today, a diminutive man in a conservative gray suit, starched, striped cotton shirt and conservative tie massaged his temples as if trying to banish a migraine.

2       When his case was called, he stepped before the bench and, in response to the judge's request to state his name and age, he cleared his throat and answered nearly inaudibly. Then, when the judge asked how much education he had, his wavering voice failed him; looking down at the podium, he began to cry.

3       Moments later, Joseph E. Chavis Jr., a 30-year-old lawyer known by colleagues and opponents alike as a quiet, studious and sincere man, would plead guilty to charges of bank robbery in a case that left many in disbelief.

4       A holder of a business degree from Texas A&M University and a law degree from Southern Methodist University, Mr. Chavis is recalled by his law professors as a model student and a caring mentor for other young black men and women making their way through the mostly white world of Dallas law firms.

5    After his arrest, just before Christmas, partners at Clark, West, Keller & Butler—the 100-year-old Dallas labor firm that has employed Mr. Chavis since he graduated from law school in 1990—stood by him and described him as a "terrific advocate and a first-rate lawyer." Friends say both Mr. Chavis and his wife, Debra Ann Lockhart, a fellow lawyer and law school classmate, devoted their spare time to Roman Catholic Church activities.

6    At first the charges against Mr. Chavis seemed a Kafkaesque nightmare of mistaken identity. After his arrest, members of his law firm, as well friends, relatives, former professors and even the dean of S.M.U.'s law school, said that the police had the wrong man, that the Joseph Chavis they knew could not have done this.

7    "So, on his way to work, he robs a bank," said Prof. William Bridge of the S.M.U. Law School. "It's just inconsistent with everything in his background and character, and therefore it's easier for me to believe that it's a mistake."

8    But the authorities continued to insist that there had been no mistake, and on Jan. 5, a Federal grand jury indicted Mr. Chavis.

9    In the course of robbing Bank United, a small bank in the exclusive University Park neighborhood, the authorities say, Mr. Chavis did everything but hold up a sign with his name and Social Security number.

10    The police and the Federal Bureau of Investigation say that about 9 A.M. on Dec. 18, Mr. Chavis left his condominium on the edge of the University Park area and drove two miles to the bank, which is within sight of S.M.U.'s law school in University Park. Once there, they say, Mr. Chavis walked in without a disguise and asked for two rolls of quarters in exchange for $20.

11    Mr. Chavis then left, only to return a few minutes later. This time, prosecutors say, he walked up to a teller and said: "Good morning. I have a gun in my pocket. Please give me your money." He received exactly $1,340 and fled on foot, the authorities said.

12    An F.B.I. spokeswoman, Marge Poche, said that the bank's camera had yielded "a great picture of the suspect" and that within minutes, the "police spotted someone they believed could fit the description of the bank robber in the vicinity of Renaissance Tower," the downtown high-rise where Mr. Chavis worked.

13    "They searched the area, and some units found some discarded money in a bathroom of the parking garage that had a lock," Ms. Poche said.

14    The Federal prosecutors said security cameras showed Mr. Chavis putting something in a trash can. A search of the trash can, they said, turned up white quarter wrappers as well as the dark-brimmed baseball cap that the robber had been seen wearing. The baseball cap, which bore the logo of one of Mr. Chavis's clients, had been a gift for a legal job well done, his lawyer said.

15    About the same time, the police received a call saying banded bundles of money had been found under a water fountain in the hallway near a back entrance to the Clark, West law firm. An officer went to the firm and noticed that Mr. Chavis looked like the robber on the bank video; he was arrested that afternoon.

16    "All but about $10" of the bank's money was recovered, Ms. Poche said.

17    No one involved in the case has a satisfactory answer for the vexing questions it raises.

*The New York Times*, January 20, 1996, p. 7

## Organization

Students often complain that lack of time makes it difficult for them to accomplish everything that they have to do. There is no doubt that their lives are very busy, with classes to attend, assignments to be completed, studying to be done, and tests to be taken. As a typical college student, there are occasions when you must feel under a great deal of time pressure. For that reason, you probably schedule your daily activities very carefully so that you are able to get everything done. You have certain hours that you devote to going to and preparing for classes, and you work your other personal responsibilities around them. In other words, you use **organization** to make the most productive use of your limited time.

Critical thinkers also depend on organization to help them deal effectively with events, issues, problems, decisions, and situations. In the example, you certainly used an organized approach to help you to make a decision regarding whether you should take the course. You went through a series of specific steps in order to gather more information, which placed you in a much stronger position when deciding what to do. Critical thinking always involves that kind of organization.

## Time and Effort

At this point, it is probably obvious to you that critical thinking requires much **time and effort**. The examples you have read about and the activities that you have been asked to complete all involve not only setting aside time but also putting in extra effort. In the example, the easy road would have been for you to follow your first reaction, which was not to register for the course. You opted instead to take some additional time to gather information, because you felt that it would help you make the right decision. In short, you were taking the time and making the effort that critical thinking requires.

### ACTIVITY 5

Pretend that you want to purchase or lease a new automobile. What steps would you follow to help organize your time and efforts? List them in your notebook. To help you decide whether to lease or buy, feel free to play the Lease-or-Buy game presented on the next page.

## Asking Questions and Finding Answers

Critical thinkers are aware of what is going on around them and are willing to take time away from other activities so that they can concentrate on a specific event, issue, problem, decision, or situation. They observe their surroundings carefully and put substantial effort into looking for causes, explanations, or reasons. In other words, critical thinkers **ask questions** continuously and are very patient and persistent when trying to **find answers**. They often use words that are found in questions, such as *who*, *when*, *what*, *where*, *how*, and *why*. For example, critical thinkers would wonder, Who is responsible for determining the price

**The lease-or-buy game**

Answer each question by
following the road marked
"yes" or "no." The route you
follow will show you whether
leasing is a good, indifferent,
or poor choice for you.

 I typically get a new car
every three or four years.

2  I am unable to come up
with a down payment of at
least 20 percent, or I prefer
to put as little of my own money
into a car as possible.

3  I treat my vehicle gently
and maintain it faithfully.
It rarely gets dents and
scratches; small children and
pets are infrequent passengers.

4  I drive less than 15,000
miles per year; I foresee
no change in the next few
years that would significantly alter
the amount of driving I do.

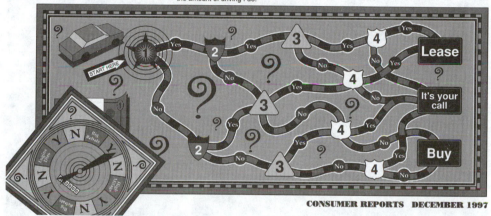

CONSUMER REPORTS   DECEMBER 1997

Illustration by Jeffrey Pelo

of an automobile? When is the best time to study for a test? What provides the pressure that forces water through a faucet? Where does electricity originate from? How is sewage carried through underground pipes without clogging them? Why do leaves turn different colors in many areas of the United States? Have you thought about answers to these questions and others like them? If you have, you have experience at being a critical thinker.

When considering whether to take the course in our example, you asked questions like "Will the course fit into my program of study?" "How will it affect my schedule?" "Do I have a choice of instructor?" "What is the course about?" and "How hard is it?" Furthermore, you were very persistent in trying to find answers *before* making a decision. In other words, you were being a critical thinker.

## ACTIVITY 6

During the next few days, take some time away from other activities to observe and think about your surroundings. Spend a few moments *looking* carefully at your neighborhood or school, *listening* to what is going on, *questioning* what you see and hear, and *finding answers* by being *patient* and *persistent*. Then write an essay describing everything that you saw and heard, including possible answers to your questions. You will be asked to share your essay with your classmates.

## ACTIVITY 7

Look carefully at the scenes in the following photographs, and try to notice little things that seem interesting. Ask questions about what you see, and think about possible explanations. Discuss your questions and possible explanations with your classmates.

(1)

(2)

(3)

(4)

(5)

(6)

## ACTIVITY 8

During the next few days, be patient and persistent when trying to find answers to the questions posed in the discussion in the text:

1. Who is responsible for determining the price of an automobile?
2. When is the best time to study for a test?
3. What provides the pressure that forces water through a faucet?
4. Where does electricity originate from?
5. How is sewage carried through underground pipes without clogging them?
6. Why do leaves turn different colors in many areas of the United States?

Be prepared to discuss your answers and how you found them.

## ACTIVITY 9

Read the following article, and develop questions that will perhaps help you make sense of the atrocious crime described in it. Think about possible answers to your questions, and discuss both your questions and answers with your classmates.

## Witnesses Recall Beaten Woman's Fatal Leap

1   DETROIT, Sept. 1 (AP)—A city bus driver testified today that he and 40 to 50 other people watched as a woman, stripped of most of her clothing, was beaten for nearly half an hour last month before finally jumping off a bridge to her death to escape her attacker.

2   The witness, Harvey Mayberry, said the 19-year-old man charged with the attack, Martell Welch, had apparently been angry over a traffic accident involving his car and the woman's.

3   Mr. Mayberry said he saw Mr. Welch slam the woman's head five or six times against the hood of her car during the attack, which occurred on Aug. 19. The witness said Mr. Welch had then carried the woman toward the crowd, asking: "Does anybody want some of this bitch? Because she has to pay for my car."

4   Eventually, the woman, Deletha Word, 33, jumped off the side of the Belle Isle bridge, falling about 30 feet into the Detroit River. The authorities have said that two men who jumped in to help her only caused her to swim to deeper waters, apparently in the fear that they, too, meant her harm. She drowned, and her body was recovered several hours later.

5   "I just felt bad," Mr. Mayberry said. "There was nothing I could do about it."

6   Mr. Mayberry was one of three witnesses who testified today at a preliminary hearing where Mr. Welch was ordered to stand trial on an open murder charge in Ms. Word's death. The charge means that the defendant could be convicted of either

first- or second-degree murder. First-degree murder carries a mandatory sentence of life in prison; second-degree murder is punishable by up to life in prison.

7     Although the police initially said bystanders had cheered and egged on the attack, they later backed away from that account, and Mr. Mayberry testified that some people had yelled for Mr. Welch not to toss Ms. Word off the bridge.

8     Another witness, Tiffany Alexander, 23, said she and three companions came upon the attack when they drove onto the bridge and their way was blocked. Ms. Alexander testified that a cellular telephone was in their car but that no one used it to call the police. She did not say why.

9     Mr. Mayberry said he came upon the attack after it had begun. He testified that Mr. Welch had carried Ms. Word to a barrier separating the bridge's roadway from its sidewalk, had thrown her over it and had then gone after her with a car jack, saying he was going to "bust your brains out."

10     Ms. Word then climbed onto the railing at the very edge of the bridge, and Mr. Welch said, "You can't go out that way," Mr. Mayberry testified. As Mr. Welch got closer, the witness said, Ms. Word jumped.

11     Tyrone Gribble, 19, testified that Mr. Welch had yelled at Ms. Word not to jump but that after she did, he said, "Good for the bitch!"

*The New York Times,* September 2, 1995

## Research

Critical thinking is a way of dealing with events, issues, problems, decisions, or situations in a very thoughtful, careful manner. For that reason, it often requires **research**, the process of looking for and gathering information to increase your knowledge and understanding of a given topic. In the example that we have been using, you did research to place yourself in a stronger position in deciding whether to take the course. You studied the class schedule, the catalog, and a syllabus and talked with students, faculty, and your counselor to gather as much information as possible concerning the course. In other words, all of the research that you did provided you with more information to help you make a decision.

The kind of research that critical thinkers do and the sources of information that they use will vary with the matter at hand. In other words, research can involve using the Internet, going to libraries, reading official reports or documents, interviewing people, visiting various agencies and organizations, or some combination of these. For example, if a young man wants to find out more about the issue of gun control, he might go to the library or use the Internet to read about the topic in newspapers, magazines, books, or reports. In addition, he might talk with individuals who know something about the issue—perhaps police officials, gun owners, and members of various organizations that support and oppose gun control. By contrast, if he wants to investigate a traffic accident, he might study the police report, read newspaper accounts, talk with persons actually involved, and interview any witnesses who were present.

As these examples illustrate, critical thinkers are careful about using the sources that are most relevant, applicable, or appropriate and therefore most likely to provide useful information. Thus our young researcher would probably not seek information about gun control from a mechanic, a physician, or an accountant unless they were somehow involved with the issue, nor would he read general magazines or books to find out about a particular traffic accident. You certainly used appropriate sources when doing research for the course decision. Each of the individuals you talked with was in a good position to provide useful information, and the written sources were all relevant to the matter under consideration.

Critical thinkers are not only aware of their own feelings and opinions but also try to be aware of any **prejudice** or **bias** on the part of a given source. In other words, our researcher would determine if the source is providing information that supports a particular point of view instead of being impartial or evenhanded. For example, if he is discussing gun control with a representative of an organization that does not support it, like the National Rifle Association, he would keep in mind that the information he is getting is probably slanted in one direction. Similarly, if he is reading literature put out by that same organization, he realizes that it is likely to include only information supporting its viewpoint regarding the issue. Once again, in the example we have been using, you were using critical thinking when you realized that the student who had dropped the course was only giving her personal point of view, which was not unbiased. That is precisely why you turned to additional sources of information before making a decision.

**A Word of Caution When Using the Internet for Research**    As you know, the Internet consists of an enormous number of desktop and much larger computers that are linked through a worldwide network. It is a very rapid means of sharing information, *some* of which is excellent and *some* of which is not very worthwhile. This results from the fact that unlike books and articles in periodicals and newspapers, there is no review by others before publication on the Internet. Thus anyone can publish personal views on a variety of topics without having the information evaluated first by editors, experts, or others who are knowledgeable about the subject matter. Therefore, in those instances, you as the researcher must determine not only the relevance and impartiality of the information presented but its reliability as well. How should you go about doing that?

First, as with all sources, use common sense to make sure that the information offered is useful or appropriate for your research needs. Ask yourself if a particular source focuses on the subject matter that is of interest to you and if it does so in a fair and thorough manner. For instance, if you are investigating the issue of capital punishment, a source that devotes several pages to a discussion of the opposing viewpoints would probably be more useful than one that devotes a few paragraphs to life on death row.

Second, try to use material published by educational institutions like Harvard (with Web addresses that end in *.edu*) or posted on governmental (*.gov*) and military (*.mil*) sites. The information they provide is quite likely to be reliable. Sites maintained by professional organizations (*.org*), such as the American Medical Association, can usually be relied on for accurate information, but keep in mind that some organizations simply want to persuade you to accept their point of view. Commercial sources (sites that end in *.com*), like Philip Morris USA, are more questionable because they are often trying to sell you their products or influence your thinking so that they can continue to make profits. Thus if you were looking into the effects of cigarette advertising on young people, Philip Morris would probably not be a good source of information to use because of its obvious bias, whereas a report put out by the U.S. Office of the Surgeon General would be much more reliable.

Third, when possible, try to find the professional affiliation of the author in the credits or e-mail address so that you can determine his or her expertise on a given topic. For example, if you were investigating an issue involving medical ethics, a medical doctor who is also on the faculty of the University of Pennsylvania Medical School would probably be a more reliable source than an individual complaining about the high cost of medical treatment on a personal home page.

Fourth, see if the author lists a bibliography of the sources used so that you can gauge if they are reputable and scholarly. Publications like the *New York Times*, *Newsweek*, the *New England Journal of Medicine*, and textbooks in general are usually recognized by most people as providers of accurate, well-researched, and well-documented information. Thus if sources like those are listed, you can feel a bit more secure about using the author's material.

As you recall, the reading in Question 22 in Mastery Test 2 provides some additional hints on evaluating sources, particularly electronic ones. If necessary, refer to it to refresh your memory. Remember that the Internet can be a very helpful source of information, but you must exercise great care when using it for research purposes.

## ACTIVITY 10

Assume you wanted to do research to answer the question "Does violence on television contribute to real violence in the United States?" Discuss this question with two of your classmates, and together come up with a list of possible sources that are appropriate to use. Be sure to include a variety of specific sources, and be ready to provide the reasons why you feel they are relevant to the issue. Also try to determine if you think they are likely to be reliable and impartial.

## ACTIVITY 11

With the same two classmates, look carefully at the following sources taken from the Internet in order to determine if they are relevant, reliable, and impartial for the purpose of answering the question posed in Activity 10.

(1)

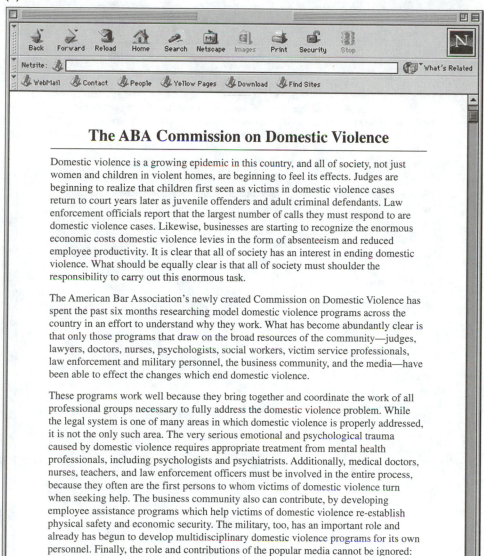

# The ABA Commission on Domestic Violence

Domestic violence is a growing epidemic in this country, and all of society, not just women and children in violent homes, are beginning to feel its effects. Judges are beginning to realize that children first seen as victims in domestic violence cases return to court years later as juvenile offenders and adult criminal defendants. Law enforcement officials report that the largest number of calls they must respond to are domestic violence cases. Likewise, businesses are starting to recognize the enormous economic costs domestic violence levies in the form of absenteeism and reduced employee productivity. It is clear that all of society has an interest in ending domestic violence. What should be equally clear is that all of society must shoulder the responsibility to carry out this enormous task.

The American Bar Association's newly created Commission on Domestic Violence has spent the past six months researching model domestic violence programs across the country in an effort to understand why they work. What has become abundantly clear is that only those programs that draw on the broad resources of the community—judges, lawyers, doctors, nurses, psychologists, social workers, victim service professionals, law enforcement and military personnel, the business community, and the media—have been able to effect the changes which end domestic violence.

These programs work well because they bring together and coordinate the work of all professional groups necessary to fully address the domestic violence problem. While the legal system is one of many areas in which domestic violence is properly addressed, it is not the only such area. The very serious emotional and psychological trauma caused by domestic violence requires appropriate treatment from mental health professionals, including psychologists and psychiatrists. Additionally, medical doctors, nurses, teachers, and law enforcement officers must be involved in the entire process, because they often are the first persons to whom victims of domestic violence turn when seeking help. The business community also can contribute, by developing employee assistance programs which help victims of domestic violence re-establish physical safety and economic security. The military, too, has an important role and already has begun to develop multidisciplinary domestic violence programs for its own personnel. Finally, the role and contributions of the popular media cannot be ignored: television, newspapers, and radio now provide highly effective outreach, teaching thousands of Americans about the causes of domestic violence and the currently available solutions.

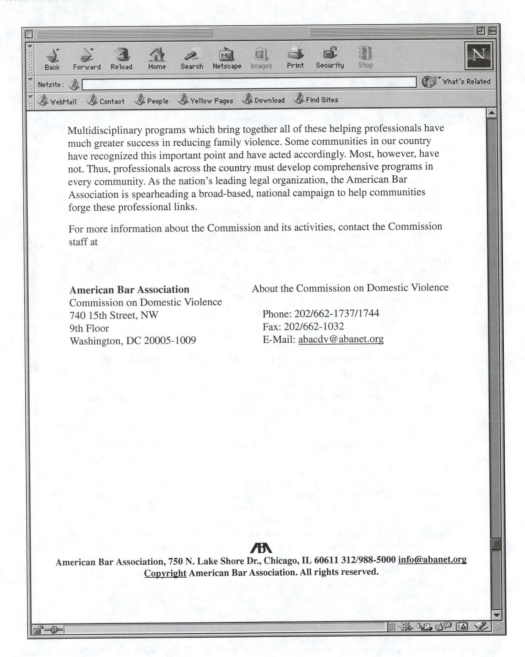

Multidisciplinary programs which bring together all of these helping professionals have much greater success in reducing family violence. Some communities in our country have recognized this important point and have acted accordingly. Most, however, have not. Thus, professionals across the country must develop comprehensive programs in every community. As the nation's leading legal organization, the American Bar Association is spearheading a broad-based, national campaign to help communities forge these professional links.

For more information about the Commission and its activities, contact the Commission staff at

**American Bar Association**
Commission on Domestic Violence
740 15th Street, NW
9th Floor
Washington, DC 20005-1009

About the Commission on Domestic Violence

    Phone: 202/662-1737/1744
    Fax: 202/662-1032
    E-Mail: abacdv@abanet.org

(2)

---

Back    Forward    Reload    Home    Search    Netscape    Images    Print    Security    Stop

Netsite:                                                                              What's Related

WebMail    Contact    People    Yellow Pages    Download    Find Sites

---

## Two New Studies on Television Violence and Their Significance for the Kids' TV Debate

- **The UCLA Television Violence Monitoring Report** (September 1995) UCLA Center for Communication Policy
- **National Violence Study** (February 1996) Mediascope Inc.

**Introduction:** These two reports are the television industry's response to Congressional pressure (primarily from Senator Paul Simon in 1993) that resulted in both the broadcasting and cable industry agreeing in January 1994 to performing self-monitoring studies on television violence. The broadcasting industry chose the Center for Communication Policy at UCLA while the cable industry chose MediaScope Inc. Below is a summary of each.

## The UCLA Television Violence Monitoring Report

(September 1995)

PURPOSE: The primary purpose of this study is to examine the violent content of broadcasting network television during the hours of prime time and Saturday mornings. Because not all violence is created equal, the monitors of the study looked at violence in context focusing on those shows that raise serious concerns among viewers.

- They broke the shows into four different categories.
- Shows that raise serious concerns such as slasher movies or films such as *Faces of Death,* which is a collection of real people being killed on camera.
- Shows that contain scenes of violence but raise few concerns such as accidents on *Home Improvement*.
- Shows that **do not have high levels** of violence but due to the context they raise serious concerns, such as *American Comedy Awards* and other shows that take blood splattering and general violence as a joke.
- Shows that do contain high levels of violence but, due to the context, do not raise serious levels of concern, such as *Schindler's List*.

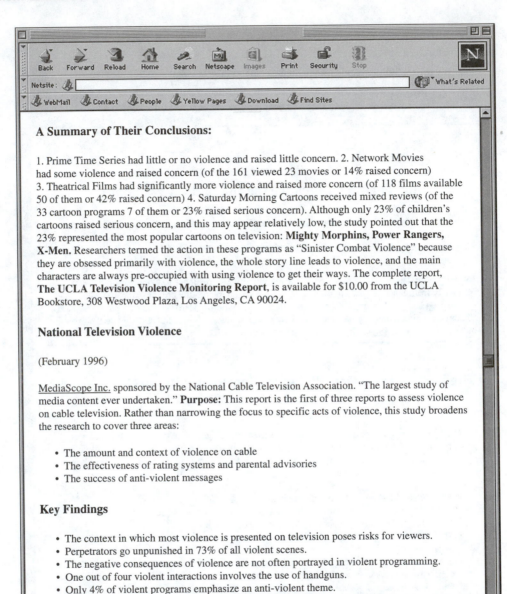

### A Summary of Their Conclusions:

1. Prime Time Series had little or no violence and raised little concern. 2. Network Movies had some violence and raised concern (of the 161 viewed 23 movies or 14% raised concern) 3. Theatrical Films had significantly more violence and raised more concern (of 118 films available 50 of them or 42% raised concern) 4. Saturday Morning Cartoons received mixed reviews (of the 33 cartoon programs 7 of them or 23% raised serious concern). Although only 23% of children's cartoons raised serious concern, and this may appear relatively low, the study pointed out that the 23% represented the most popular cartoons on television: **Mighty Morphins, Power Rangers, X-Men.** Researchers termed the action in these programs as "Sinister Combat Violence" because they are obsessed primarily with violence, the whole story line leads to violence, and the main characters are always pre-occupied with using violence to get their ways. The complete report, **The UCLA Television Violence Monitoring Report**, is available for $10.00 from the UCLA Bookstore, 308 Westwood Plaza, Los Angeles, CA 90024.

### National Television Violence

(February 1996)

MediaScope Inc. sponsored by the National Cable Television Association. "The largest study of media content ever undertaken." **Purpose:** This report is the first of three reports to assess violence on cable television. Rather than narrowing the focus to specific acts of violence, this study broadens the research to cover three areas:

- The amount and context of violence on cable
- The effectiveness of rating systems and parental advisories
- The success of anti-violent messages

### Key Findings

- The context in which most violence is presented on television poses risks for viewers.
- Perpetrators go unpunished in 73% of all violent scenes.
- The negative consequences of violence are not often portrayed in violent programming.
- One out of four violent interactions involves the use of handguns.
- Only 4% of violent programs emphasize an anti-violent theme.
- On the positive side, television violence is usually not explicit or graphic.

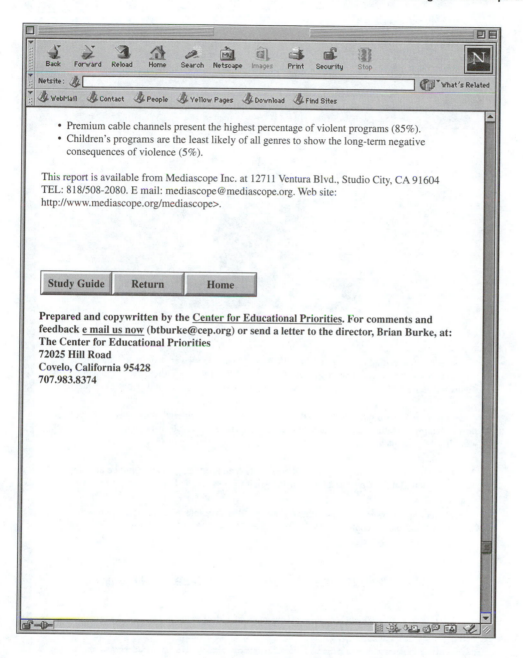

- Premium cable channels present the highest percentage of violent programs (85%).
- Children's programs are the least likely of all genres to show the long-term negative consequences of violence (5%).

This report is available from Mediascope Inc. at 12711 Ventura Blvd., Studio City, CA 91604 TEL: 818/508-2080. E mail: mediascope@mediascope.org. Web site: http://www.mediascope.org/mediascope>.

| Study Guide | Return | Home |
|---|---|---|

**Prepared and copywritten by the <u>Center for Educational Priorities</u>. For comments and feedback <u>e mail us now</u> (btburke@cep.org) or send a letter to the director, Brian Burke, at: The Center for Educational Priorities**
**72025 Hill Road**
**Covelo, California 95428**
**707.983.8374**

(3)

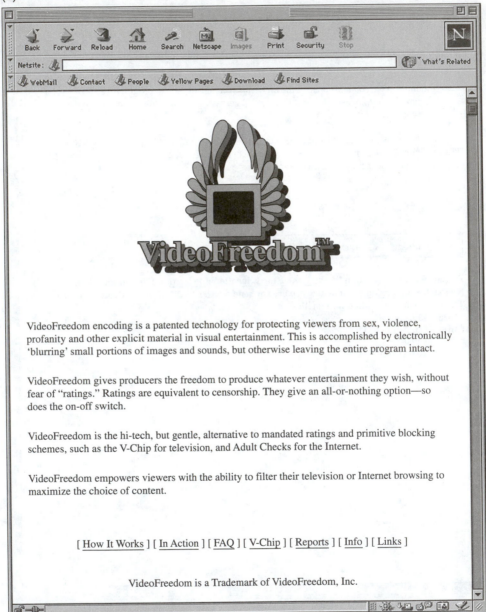

VideoFreedom encoding is a patented technology for protecting viewers from sex, violence, profanity and other explicit material in visual entertainment. This is accomplished by electronically 'blurring' small portions of images and sounds, but otherwise leaving the entire program intact.

VideoFreedom gives producers the freedom to produce whatever entertainment they wish, without fear of "ratings." Ratings are equivalent to censorship. They give an all-or-nothing option—so does the on-off switch.

VideoFreedom is the hi-tech, but gentle, alternative to mandated ratings and primitive blocking schemes, such as the V-Chip for television, and Adult Checks for the Internet.

VideoFreedom empowers viewers with the ability to filter their television or Internet browsing to maximize the choice of content.

[ How It Works ] [ In Action ] [ FAQ ] [ V-Chip ] [ Reports ] [ Info ] [ Links ]

VideoFreedom is a Trademark of VideoFreedom, Inc.

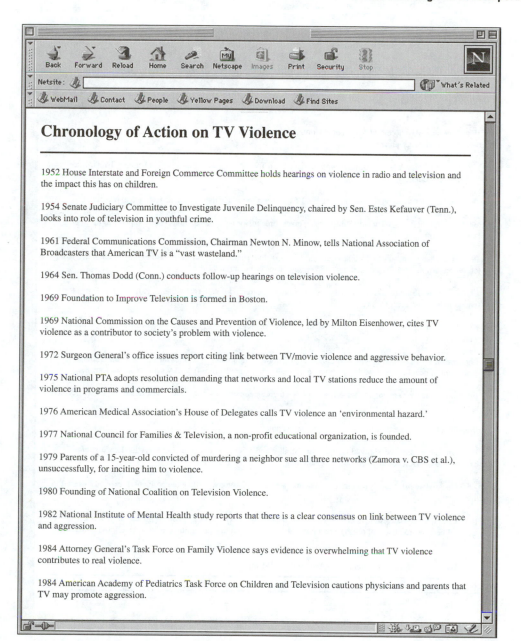

# Chronology of Action on TV Violence

1952 House Interstate and Foreign Commerce Committee holds hearings on violence in radio and television and the impact this has on children.

1954 Senate Judiciary Committee to Investigate Juvenile Delinquency, chaired by Sen. Estes Kefauver (Tenn.), looks into role of television in youthful crime.

1961 Federal Communications Commission, Chairman Newton N. Minow, tells National Association of Broadcasters that American TV is a "vast wasteland."

1964 Sen. Thomas Dodd (Conn.) conducts follow-up hearings on television violence.

1969 Foundation to Improve Television is formed in Boston.

1969 National Commission on the Causes and Prevention of Violence, led by Milton Eisenhower, cites TV violence as a contributor to society's problem with violence.

1972 Surgeon General's office issues report citing link between TV/movie violence and aggressive behavior.

1975 National PTA adopts resolution demanding that networks and local TV stations reduce the amount of violence in programs and commercials.

1976 American Medical Association's House of Delegates calls TV violence an 'environmental hazard.'

1977 National Council for Families & Television, a non-profit educational organization, is founded.

1979 Parents of a 15-year-old convicted of murdering a neighbor sue all three networks (Zamora v. CBS et al.), unsuccessfully, for inciting him to violence.

1980 Founding of National Coalition on Television Violence.

1982 National Institute of Mental Health study reports that there is a clear consensus on link between TV violence and aggression.

1984 Attorney General's Task Force on Family Violence says evidence is overwhelming that TV violence contributes to real violence.

1984 American Academy of Pediatrics Task Force on Children and Television cautions physicians and parents that TV may promote aggression.

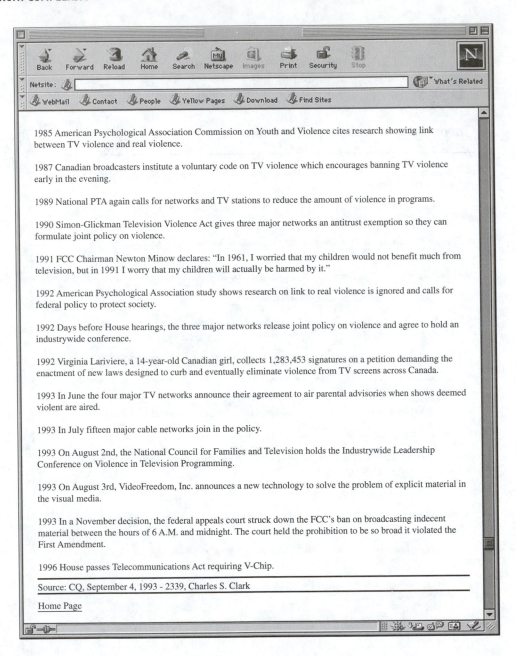

1985 American Psychological Association Commission on Youth and Violence cites research showing link between TV violence and real violence.

1987 Canadian broadcasters institute a voluntary code on TV violence which encourages banning TV violence early in the evening.

1989 National PTA again calls for networks and TV stations to reduce the amount of violence in programs.

1990 Simon-Glickman Television Violence Act gives three major networks an antitrust exemption so they can formulate joint policy on violence.

1991 FCC Chairman Newton Minow declares: "In 1961, I worried that my children would not benefit much from television, but in 1991 I worry that my children will actually be harmed by it."

1992 American Psychological Association study shows research on link to real violence is ignored and calls for federal policy to protect society.

1992 Days before House hearings, the three major networks release joint policy on violence and agree to hold an industrywide conference.

1992 Virginia Lariviere, a 14-year-old Canadian girl, collects 1,283,453 signatures on a petition demanding the enactment of new laws designed to curb and eventually eliminate violence from TV screens across Canada.

1993 In June the four major TV networks announce their agreement to air parental advisories when shows deemed violent are aired.

1993 In July fifteen major cable networks join in the policy.

1993 On August 2nd, the National Council for Families and Television holds the Industrywide Leadership Conference on Violence in Television Programming.

1993 On August 3rd, VideoFreedom, Inc. announces a new technology to solve the problem of explicit material in the visual media.

1993 In a November decision, the federal appeals court struck down the FCC's ban on broadcasting indecent material between the hours of 6 A.M. and midnight. The court held the prohibition to be so broad it violated the First Amendment.

1996 House passes Telecommunications Act requiring V-Chip.

Source: CQ, September 4, 1993 - 2339, Charles S. Clark

Home Page

(4)

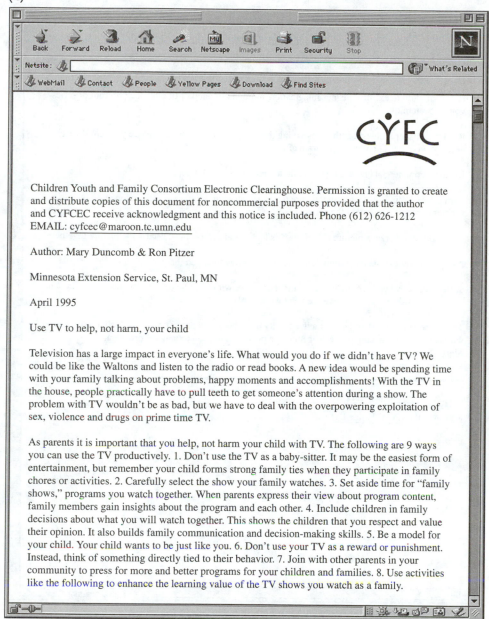

CYFC

Children Youth and Family Consortium Electronic Clearinghouse. Permission is granted to create and distribute copies of this document for noncommercial purposes provided that the author and CYFCEC receive acknowledgment and this notice is included. Phone (612) 626-1212 EMAIL: cyfcec@maroon.tc.umn.edu

Author: Mary Duncomb & Ron Pitzer

Minnesota Extension Service, St. Paul, MN

April 1995

Use TV to help, not harm, your child

Television has a large impact in everyone's life. What would you do if we didn't have TV? We could be like the Waltons and listen to the radio or read books. A new idea would be spending time with your family talking about problems, happy moments and accomplishments! With the TV in the house, people practically have to pull teeth to get someone's attention during a show. The problem with TV wouldn't be as bad, but we have to deal with the overpowering exploitation of sex, violence and drugs on prime time TV.

As parents it is important that you help, not harm your child with TV. The following are 9 ways you can use the TV productively. 1. Don't use the TV as a baby-sitter. It may be the easiest form of entertainment, but remember your child forms strong family ties when they participate in family chores or activities. 2. Carefully select the show your family watches. 3. Set aside time for "family shows," programs you watch together. When parents express their view about program content, family members gain insights about the program and each other. 4. Include children in family decisions about what you will watch together. This shows the children that you respect and value their opinion. It also builds family communication and decision-making skills. 5. Be a model for your child. Your child wants to be just like you. 6. Don't use your TV as a reward or punishment. Instead, think of something directly tied to their behavior. 7. Join with other parents in your community to press for more and better programs for your children and families. 8. Use activities like the following to enhance the learning value of the TV shows you watch as a family.

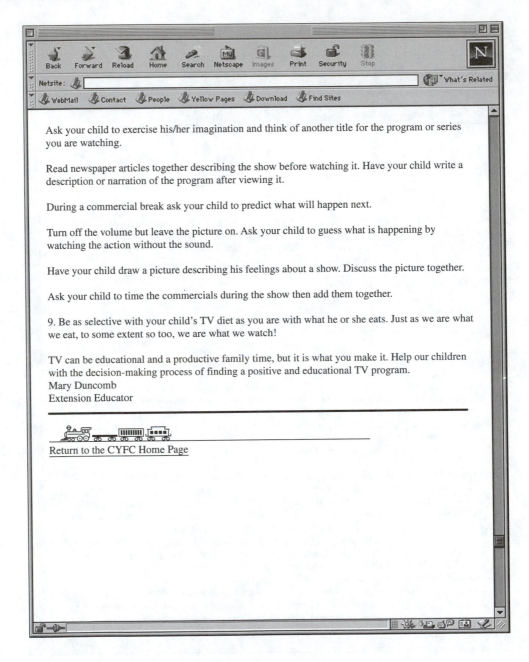

Ask your child to exercise his/her imagination and think of another title for the program or series you are watching.

Read newspaper articles together describing the show before watching it. Have your child write a description or narration of the program after viewing it.

During a commercial break ask your child to predict what will happen next.

Turn off the volume but leave the picture on. Ask your child to guess what is happening by watching the action without the sound.

Have your child draw a picture describing his feelings about a show. Discuss the picture together.

Ask your child to time the commercials during the show then add them together.

9. Be as selective with your child's TV diet as you are with what he or she eats. Just as we are what we eat, to some extent so too, we are what we watch!

TV can be educational and a productive family time, but it is what you make it. Help our children with the decision-making process of finding a positive and educational TV program.
Mary Duncomb
Extension Educator

Return to the CYFC Home Page

(5)

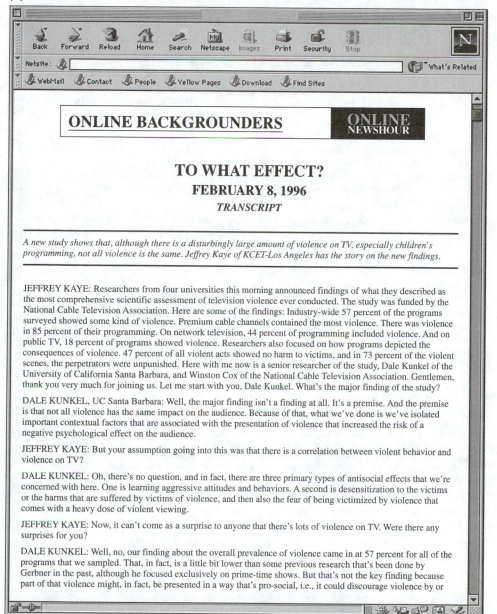

# ONLINE BACKGROUNDERS

ONLINE
NEWSHOUR

## TO WHAT EFFECT?
### FEBRUARY 8, 1996
*TRANSCRIPT*

*A new study shows that, although there is a disturbingly large amount of violence on TV, especially children's programming, not all violence is the same. Jeffrey Kaye of KCET-Los Angeles has the story on the new findings.*

JEFFREY KAYE: Researchers from four universities this morning announced findings of what they described as the most comprehensive scientific assessment of television violence ever conducted. The study was funded by the National Cable Television Association. Here are some of the findings: Industry-wide 57 percent of the programs surveyed showed some kind of violence. Premium cable channels contained the most violence. There was violence in 85 percent of their programming. On network television, 44 percent of programming included violence. And on public TV, 18 percent of programs showed violence. Researchers also focused on how programs depicted the consequences of violence. 47 percent of all violent acts showed no harm to victims, and in 73 percent of the violent scenes, the perpetrators were unpunished. Here with me now is a senior researcher of the study, Dale Kunkel of the University of California Santa Barbara, and Winston Cox of the National Cable Television Association. Gentlemen, thank you very much for joining us. Let me start with you, Dale Kunkel. What's the major finding of the study?

DALE KUNKEL, UC Santa Barbara: Well, the major finding isn't a finding at all. It's a premise. And the premise is that not all violence has the same impact on the audience. Because of that, what we've done is we've isolated important contextual factors that are associated with the presentation of violence that increased the risk of a negative psychological effect on the audience.

JEFFREY KAYE: But your assumption going into this was that there is a correlation between violent behavior and violence on TV?

DALE KUNKEL: Oh, there's no question, and in fact, there are three primary types of antisocial effects that we're concerned with here. One is learning aggressive attitudes and behaviors. A second is desensitization to the victims or the harms that are suffered by victims of violence, and then also the fear of being victimized by violence that comes with a heavy dose of violent viewing.

JEFFREY KAYE: Now, it can't come as a surprise to anyone that there's lots of violence on TV. Were there any surprises for you?

DALE KUNKEL: Well, no, our finding about the overall prevalence of violence came in at 57 percent for all of the programs that we sampled. That, in fact, is a little bit lower than some previous research that's been done by Gerbner in the past, although he focused exclusively on prime-time shows. But that's not the key finding because part of that violence might, in fact, be presented in a way that's pro-social, i.e., it could discourage violence by or

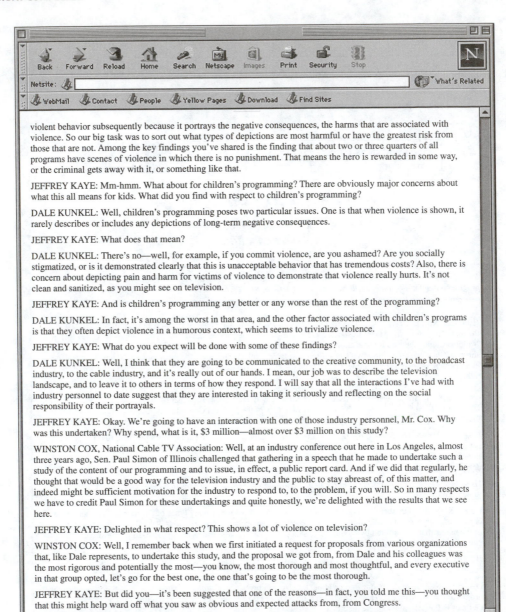

violent behavior subsequently because it portrays the negative consequences, the harms that are associated with violence. So our big task was to sort out what types of depictions are most harmful or have the greatest risk from those that are not. Among the key findings you've shared is the finding that about two or three quarters of all programs have scenes of violence in which there is no punishment. That means the hero is rewarded in some way, or the criminal gets away with it, or something like that.

JEFFREY KAYE: Mm-hmm. What about for children's programming? There are obviously major concerns about what this all means for kids. What did you find with respect to children's programming?

DALE KUNKEL: Well, children's programming poses two particular issues. One is that when violence is shown, it rarely describes or includes any depictions of long-term negative consequences.

JEFFREY KAYE: What does that mean?

DALE KUNKEL: There's no—well, for example, if you commit violence, are you ashamed? Are you socially stigmatized, or is it demonstrated clearly that this is unacceptable behavior that has tremendous costs? Also, there is concern about depicting pain and harm for victims of violence to demonstrate that violence really hurts. It's not clean and sanitized, as you might see on television.

JEFFREY KAYE: And is children's programming any better or any worse than the rest of the programming?

DALE KUNKEL: In fact, it's among the worst in that area, and the other factor associated with children's programs is that they often depict violence in a humorous context, which seems to trivialize violence.

JEFFREY KAYE: What do you expect will be done with some of these findings?

DALE KUNKEL: Well, I think that they are going to be communicated to the creative community, to the broadcast industry, to the cable industry, and it's really out of our hands. I mean, our job was to describe the television landscape, and to leave it to others in terms of how they respond. I will say that all the interactions I've had with industry personnel to date suggest that they are interested in taking it seriously and reflecting on the social responsibility of their portrayals.

JEFFREY KAYE: Okay. We're going to have an interaction with one of those industry personnel, Mr. Cox. Why was this undertaken? Why spend, what is it, $3 million—almost over $3 million on this study?

WINSTON COX, National Cable TV Association: Well, at an industry conference out here in Los Angeles, almost three years ago, Sen. Paul Simon of Illinois challenged that gathering in a speech that he made to undertake such a study of the content of our programming and to issue, in effect, a public report card. And if we did that regularly, he thought that would be a good way for the television industry and the public to stay abreast of, of this matter, and indeed might be sufficient motivation for the industry to respond to, to the problem, if you will. So in many respects we have to credit Paul Simon for these undertakings and quite honestly, we're delighted with the results that we see here.

JEFFREY KAYE: Delighted in what respect? This shows a lot of violence on television?

WINSTON COX: Well, I remember back when we first initiated a request for proposals from various organizations that, like Dale represents, to undertake this study, and the proposal we got from, from Dale and his colleagues was the most rigorous and potentially the most—you know, the most thorough and most thoughtful, and every executive in that group opted, let's go for the best one, the one that's going to be the most thorough.

JEFFREY KAYE: But did you—it's been suggested that one of the reasons—in fact, you told me this—you thought that this might help ward off what you saw as obvious and expected attacks from, from Congress.

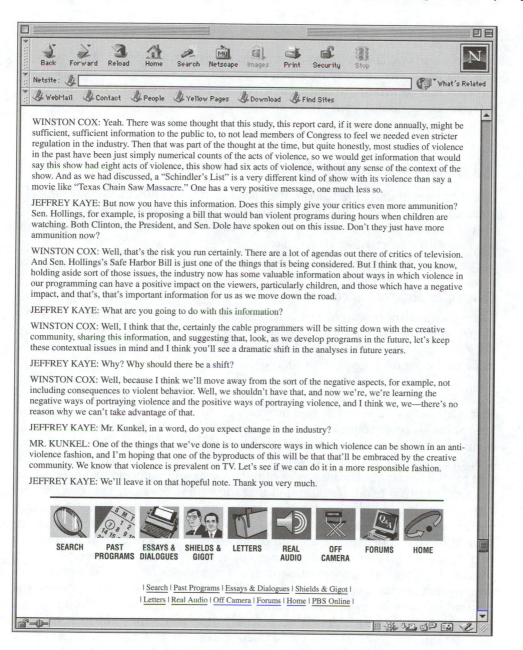

WINSTON COX: Yeah. There was some thought that this study, this report card, if it were done annually, might be sufficient, sufficient information to the public to, to not lead members of Congress to feel we needed even stricter regulation in the industry. Then that was part of the thought at the time, but quite honestly, most studies of violence in the past have been just simply numerical counts of the acts of violence, so we would get information that would say this show had eight acts of violence, this show had six acts of violence, without any sense of the context of the show. And as we had discussed, a "Schindler's List" is a very different kind of show with its violence than say a movie like "Texas Chain Saw Massacre." One has a very positive message, one much less so.

JEFFREY KAYE: But now you have this information. Does this give your critics even more ammunition? Sen. Hollings, for example, is proposing a bill that would ban violent programs during hours when children are watching. Both Clinton, the President, and Sen. Dole have spoken out on this issue. Don't they just have more ammunition now?

WINSTON COX: Well, that's the risk you run certainly. There are a lot of agendas out there of critics of television. And Sen. Hollings's Safe Harbor Bill is just one of the things that is being considered. But I think that, you know, holding aside sort of those issues, the industry now has some valuable information about ways in which violence in our programming can have a positive impact on the viewers, particularly children, and those which have a negative impact, and that's, that's important information for us as we move down the road.

JEFFREY KAYE: What are you going to do with this information?

WINSTON COX: Well, I think that the, certainly the cable programmers will be sitting down with the creative community, sharing this information, and suggesting that, look, as we develop programs in the future, let's keep these contextual issues in mind and I think you'll see a dramatic shift in the analyses in future years.

JEFFREY KAYE: Why? Why should there be a shift?

WINSTON COX: Well, because I think we'll move away from the sort of the negative aspects, for example, not including consequences to violent behavior. Well, we shouldn't have that, and now we're, we're learning the negative ways of portraying violence and the positive ways of portraying violence, and I think we, we—there's no reason why we can't take advantage of that.

JEFFREY KAYE: Mr. Kunkel, in a word, do you expect change in the industry?

MR. KUNKEL: One of the things that we've done is to underscore ways in which violence can be shown in an anti-violence fashion, and I'm hoping that one of the byproducts of this will be that that'll be embraced by the creative community. We know that violence is prevalent on TV. Let's see if we can do it in a more responsible fashion.

JEFFREY KAYE: We'll leave it on that hopeful note. Thank you very much.

SEARCH | PAST PROGRAMS | ESSAYS & DIALOGUES | SHIELDS & GIGOT | LETTERS | REAL AUDIO | OFF CAMERA | FORUMS | HOME

| Search | Past Programs | Essays & Dialogues | Shields & Gigot |
| Letters | Real Audio | Off Camera | Forums | Home | PBS Online |

## ACTIVITY 12

Now that you and your two classmates have considered and evaluated various sources, write an essay in which you answer the question "Does violence on television contribute to real violence in the United States?" Your instructor will ask you to discuss your viewpoint in class.

## ACTIVITY 13

If a computer is available to you, use the Internet to find three relevant, reliable, and impartial sources in order to answer the question "Should there be prayer in our public schools?" Feel free to consult with the two classmates you worked with on Activities 10 and 11.

### Coming to Logical Conclusions

After completing research, critical thinkers try to come to **logical conclusions** about the events, issues, problems, decisions, or situations they are considering. Conclusions are logical or reasonable if they are based solidly on the information or evidence gathered.

Let us look one last time at the example we have been using about whether you should enroll for the course. Suppose while doing the research you found that it fits both your schedule and program of study; that you are interested in at least some of its content; that you are comfortable with the instructor, assignments, and grading; and that most of the people you talk with like the course. Under those circumstances, it would be logical to conclude that it is good for you to take the course because most of the information supports that conclusion.

On the other hand, if you found that the course does not seem very interesting, that it is taught by only one instructor whom you are not too crazy about, and that only half the students you talked with liked it, a logical conclusion is that the course is not for you because most of the information points in that direction. Of course, the evidence could be approximately evenly divided, making it logical to conclude that it may or may not be the right course for you. In that instance, you would have to determine which factors—perhaps the content of the course, the instructor, or the requirements—are the most important to you and then decide accordingly. It is also important to emphasize that the information gathered could change in the future, thereby altering any one of those three possible conclusions. For instance, there could be a change of instructor, which could in turn affect course content, assignments, grading, and opinions regarding the course. That is why critical thinkers always reconsider their conclusions to make sure that the evidence on which they are based has not changed or that no new information has been uncovered.

To return to another example mentioned earlier, suppose that in your investigation of the traffic accident, the police report, newspaper accounts, and several witnesses all state that one person went through a red light. A logical conclusion would be that this driver was responsible for the accident—certainly, most of the information points in that direction. But if none of the evidence is clear as to who actually caused the collision, then the only reasonable conclusion is that no one person can be held responsible, at least at this particular time. However, that conclusion could change if additional evidence comes to light that points to one person as the culprit. Again, it is always necessary for critical thinkers to reconsider their conclusions from time to time.

## ACTIVITY 14

Pretend that there is an imaginary country with the following characteristics:

Rich and corrupt leaders
Crime on the increase
Extreme poverty among the masses
Many natural resources

What logical conclusions could you draw concerning the conditions in the country and what caused them, and what prediction can you make regarding its future? Discuss your conclusions with your classmates.

## ACTIVITY 15

With two of your classmates, look carefully at the four graphic aids that follow, paying particular attention to the captions and organization. For each, remember to answer the two questions we used in Chapter 2: "What is this graphic aid about?" and "What are the major points stressed?" Based on the information presented, draw as many logical conclusions as possible for each of the graphic aids.

(1)

**TABLE 20.1**
*Health Among Industrial Countries*

| Country | Life Expectancy | Country | Infant Mortality Rate |
|---|---|---|---|
| Japan | 79.3 | Japan | 4.3 |
| Sweden | 78.3 | Sweden | 5.7 |
| France | 78.2 | Netherlands | 6.1 |
| Canada | 78.1 | Germany | 6.5 |
| Netherlands | 77.8 | France | 6.6 |
| Australia | 77.6 | Canada | 6.9 |
| Italy | 77.6 | Britian | 7.2 |
| Britain | 76.8 | Australia | 7.3 |
| Germany | 76.3 | Italy | 7.6 |
| U.S. | 75.9 | U.S. | 8.1 |

SOURCE: Data from U.S. Census Bureau, 1994.

Alex Thio, *Sociology*, 4th ed., p. 468

(2) **Use of Tax Dollars.** The following pie chart shows how federal income tax dollars are spent.

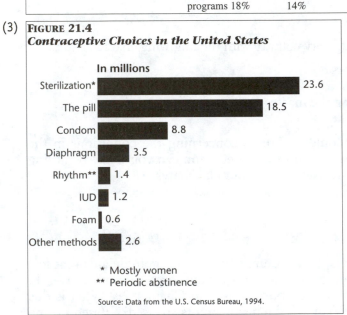

**Where Your Tax Dollars Are Spent**

Social Security/Medicare 35%

Community development 9%

Defense 22%

Law enforcement 2%

Social programs 18%

Debt/Interest 14%

(3)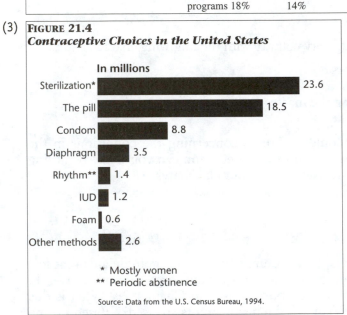

**FIGURE 21.4**
*Contraceptive Choices in the United States*

**In millions**

|  |  |
|---|---|
| Sterilization* | 23.6 |
| The pill | 18.5 |
| Condom | 8.8 |
| Diaphragm | 3.5 |
| Rhythm** | 1.4 |
| IUD | 1.2 |
| Foam | 0.6 |
| Other methods | 2.6 |

\* Mostly women
\*\* Periodic abstinence

Source: Data from the U.S. Census Bureau, 1994.

Marvin L. Bittinger and David J. Ellenbogen, *Elementary Algebra*, p. 121

Alex Thio, *Sociology*, 4th ed., p. 493

(4)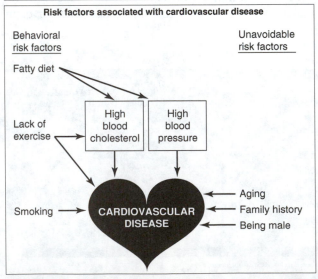

**Risk factors associated with cardiovascular disease**

Behavioral risk factors

Unavoidable risk factors

Fatty diet

Lack of exercise

High blood cholesterol

High blood pressure

Smoking

CARDIOVASCULAR DISEASE

Aging

Family history

Being male

Neil A. Campbell, Lawrence G. Mitchell, and Jane B. Reece, *Biology*, p. 436

# What Is a Contemporary Issue?

To review, critical thinking is a careful, thoughtful way of dealing with events, issues, problems, decisions, or situations. It requires flexibility, a clear purpose, organization, time and effort, asking questions and finding answers, research, and coming to logical conclusions. At this point, you have a good idea of what all of these characteristics mean and how they can be applied to the ordinary circumstances of everyday life. They can also be used in a broader sense as a way of dealing with and making better sense of topics of concern in the world around you, which are commonly called **contemporary issues.**

In this context, it is probably easiest to think of *contemporary* as a fancy word for "current." And an *issue* can be defined as a point, matter, or question to be disputed, decided, or debated—in other words, subject to very different and often conflicting interpretations, which we can call **opposing viewpoints.** A *contemporary issue*, then, is a current point, matter, or question that is debatable and therefore subject to opposing viewpoints.

Of course, we do not have to look very far to find a host of contemporary issues. Race relations, abortion, capital punishment, gay rights, violence in music, sexual harassment, teenage pregnancy, welfare, and gun control are obvious examples. It is precisely because they are debatable and often arouse our emotions when we read and talk about them that contemporary issues are appropriate topics for the careful, thoughtful treatment involved in critical thinking.

At the end of each chapter in this textbook, you will be asked to read about, think about, write about, and discuss some of the controversies surrounding many contemporary issues. Our approach to them will involve all of the characteristics of critical thinking that we have been discussing. In each case, you will:

1. Determine what is at issue
2. Distinguish among opposing viewpoints
3. Express a personal viewpoint

This three-step approach should enable you to understand the various viewpoints on the issues while at the same time giving you the opportunity to think carefully about your own point of view.

In many of the courses that you will be taking in your college career, you will be asked by instructors to read, write, or think about contemporary issues. For example, you may be required to read about racism for sociology, discuss the spread of AIDS in health, or write a paper on capital punishment for a criminal justice course. In addition, as an educated person, you will want to be able to speak knowledgeably with others about the major issues of the day, including the reasons behind the various points of view and your own personal viewpoints. For instance, you may find yourself in a position to discuss these matters with children and other family members or with colleagues on the job. As you can see, thinking critically about contemporary issues is useful to you not only as a college student but in the other roles that you play in life as well, both now and in the future. It is a skill that will serve you well throughout your life.

Before turning to a more detailed discussion of the three-step approach we will be using, read the following excerpt, which was taken from a typical college health textbook. Pay particular attention to the labels in the margins. Refer to this passage often as you read the explanation that follows it.

Topic (title)

# Euthanasia

1    Medical science is now capable of prolonging the functioning of bodily systems long after the systems would normally have failed. It is not unusual to see patients in institutions living as near-vegetables for months and even years. Such individuals create a definite problem for family members and physicians: Would it not be better to put these patients out of their misery?

Context definition

2    On the question of this sort of "mercy killing," or *euthanasia,* Americans are divided into three groups. One group consists of the people who insist that all possible efforts be made to prolong the life of seriously ill patients. Those who take this stance maintain that any tampering with human life is a form of playing God and that the result is either murder or, if the patient concurs, murder combined with suicide.

Central message
First viewpoint

Rationale

Context definition

3    A majority of Americans, on the other hand, admit to a belief in *indirect euthanasia,* sometimes referred to as negative euthanasia. In forms of indirect euthanasia, death is not directly caused or induced; rather, it is allowed to take place through the withdrawal of specific treatments. Such indirect euthanasia is not uncommon in medical practice, though it is rarely acknowledged by doctors for fear of legal complications. This position has considerable authoritative backing, including that of the late Pope Pius XII, who declared that no extraordinary means need be taken to prolong human life.

Second viewpoint

Rationale

4    The third—and smallest—group consists of those who believe in *direct euthanasia.* The number of people who actually practice direct euthanasia is difficult to ascertain. Some physicians admit in private to having done so—either directly, by administering a lethal drug, or indirectly, by allowing the patient, the family, or the support staff to cause the death.

Third viewpoint

5    Such life-and-death decisions are far easier to make in the classroom than in the reality of a traumatic situation with a loved one. The primary difficulty does not involve logic so much as the poignancy of the environment in which decisions are made. Decision makers, plagued by long-standing illness, weary and bleary-eyed, emotionally drained, with daily life disrupted for many weeks or months (and perhaps feeling guilty, financially pressured, and involved with unfinished business), do not easily resort to the

Rationale

usual logic. Many a theoretically strong pro-life stance melts into a belief in euthanasia as soon as one is confronted with a loved one who is screaming in agony or lying in a comatose state amid life-sustaining machinery. On the other hand, one who has firmly believed in euthanasia may balk when the patient is one's own parent or child.

*Essentials of Life and Health,* pp. 331–333

## Determining What Is at Issue

Whenever you read about a contemporary issue, you must determine first what specifically is at issue, keeping in mind that occasionally there may be more than one issue at hand. Furthermore, some issues may not be as obvious as others because they are not discussed in great detail. For example, you may be reading a magazine article that deals with the debate surrounding the possible benefits resulting from the medical use of marijuana. However, in discussing the issue, the writer may talk about the U.S. government's threat to prosecute doctors who prescribe marijuana and go on to say that if the government took that action, it could be a violation of both freedom of speech and privileged communication between doctor and patient. Consequently, you would want to address those two issues as well, even though they are not the dominant ones. As you deal with each of the passages in this chapter—and contemporary issues in general—remember to look for secondary issues.

It is also important that you be as specific as possible when identifying issues. In the example just given, for instance, identifying "marijuana" as the dominant issue would be too general. There are several issues surrounding marijuana, including legalization, mandatory prison terms for its possession, and possible benefits resulting from its medical uses. Instead, you would be correct if you focused on this last topic because that is precisely what the article discusses. As you consider each of the passages presented here, remember to be very specific when identifying issues and be on the lookout for secondary ones.

How, then, do you determine what is at issue? First, it is a good idea to identify the *topic* of the passage by answering the question "What is this about?" As you know from our discussion in Chapter 1, the topic can usually be stated in one word or a phrase, and often it is the title or part of the title. It is the subject matter of most, if not all, of the sentences in a given passage, and most of the time it is indeed the issue, but only in a very general sense. In the excerpt from the health textbook, the topic is "euthanasia" or "mercy killing." It is easy to identify because of the title and the fact that the entire passage deals with that subject. Notice how the surrounding words define the term for you. Remember from Chapter 1 that the context often provides a quick, useful way of uncovering word meanings.

After determining the topic, you should identify the *central message* of the passage by answering the question "What is the central message that the writer is communicating about the topic?" The central message, as you should remember from Chapter 1, represents the specific aspect of the topic that the writer wishes to discuss, and often it can be found in one or more sentences. If it is not explicitly stated, it can be determined by a careful reading of the sentences in the passage, many of which generally provide direct support for the central message. In the textbook passage that we are using, the central message is provided in the sentence "On the question of this sort of 'mercy killing,' or *euthanasia*, Americans are divided into three groups." Most of the rest of the sentences in the passage lend direct support to it by providing details that develop or explain it further. The central message always tips you off to the major issue discussed in the passage, and it does it in a much more specific fashion. Hence in our example, an accurate statement of the issue would read something like "Americans have three different viewpoints regarding euthanasia." In this particular passage, there are no secondary issues.

## Distinguishing Among Opposing Viewpoints

In addition to determining what is at issue in each passage, you will be asked to state the differences among the opposing viewpoints. This will involve not only identifying the viewpoints but also providing the **rationale,** or specific reasons, that support each of them. For instance, if the issue has to do with whether capital punishment deters or prevents murder, you would provide the reasons offered in support of the viewpoint that says yes and the reasons offered in support of the viewpoint that says no. However, sometimes a complete explanation for each of the opposing viewpoints is not provided. In those instances, you may have to use your knowledge or perhaps do some research to help you come up with the missing information. For example, in a class discussing whether capital punishment deters murder, one student mentioned the viewpoint that the death penalty does serve that purpose. She went on to provide one reason in support of that point of view: If a convicted murderer were put to death, indeed he would not be able to kill again. In that specific case, capital punishment would deter murder. Although the reason she gave for the viewpoint was not mentioned in the passage read by the class, she was able to offer it from her knowledge of the issue. As you deal with contemporary issues, there may be occasions when you too can provide missing reasons for a particular viewpoint.

Also remember that as a critical thinker, you should be aware of your own feelings toward the issues and the various viewpoints that you will be dealing with in the coming pages. You need to show flexibility by considering carefully *all* opposing viewpoints and the reasons behind them, no matter what your personal feelings are. With regard to the example of capital punishment, even if you are in strong support of one of the two viewpoints mentioned, you would be just as thorough and objective in presenting the viewpoint you do not support. In fact, as a result of doing so, you might change your initial point of view. As you know, that is a characteristic of the critical thinker.

How, then, do you determine the opposing viewpoints and the reasons for them? By focusing on the information that lends direct support to the central message. As you recall, the central message of the textbook passage that we are using is "On the question of this sort of 'mercy killing,' or *euthanasia*, Americans are divided into three groups." The passage then proceeds to define and explain the three viewpoints, including some of the rationale for each. Did you notice how some of the details are organized in a simple-listing-of-facts pattern of organization? Good for you!

The first viewpoint is held by individuals who oppose euthanasia. Americans who support it "insist that all possible efforts be made to prolong the life of seriously ill patients." Their rationale is "that any tampering with human life is a form of playing God and that the result is either murder or, if the patient concurs, murder combined with suicide." We can use our knowledge of this issue to add here that miracles do occur, particularly with modern medicine, and therefore patients should be given every opportunity to survive.

The second viewpoint is favored by people who believe in indirect or negative euthanasia, in which "death is not directly caused or induced; rather, it is allowed to take place through the withdrawal of specific treatments." This point of view, according to the passage, has "considerable authoritative backing, including that of the late Pope Pius XII." Apparently, this "backing" is an important reason for the Americans who favor this particular position. If we have some background knowledge of this issue, we might add here that this viewpoint has the general support of the medical community and the courts, which is not the case with regard to direct euthanasia. This in turn could explain further why some people favor indirect over direct euthanasia.

The third viewpoint is supported by people who believe in direct euthanasia, which involves a doctor's "administering a lethal drug" or "allowing the patient, the family, or the support staff to cause the death." Although the passage gives no specific rationale for those who favor direct euthanasia, it does provide some additional reasons for people who favor both kinds of euthanasia: guilt, disruption of daily life, or the emotional, physical, and financial burden that go along with prolonged illness of a loved one. Thus we could guess that a possible rationale on the part of those favoring direct euthanasia would involve a quicker end to a terrible situation.

The details that support the central message of the passage have provided us with the opposing viewpoints and at least some of the rationale for each. We also have added some possible reasons of our own. As a critical thinker, you should always be prepared to do the same thing when dealing with contemporary issues.

## Expressing a Personal Viewpoint

After determining what is at issue and distinguishing among opposing viewpoints, you can then express your personal viewpoint regarding the issue. Undoubtedly, you have your own opinions regarding many of the contemporary issues of the day, including those covered in this textbook. In fact, you will be asked to express your initial feelings toward each issue covered in this book *before* completing the three-step approach. Thus you can determine if your personal viewpoint changes after you have thoroughly considered the opposing viewpoints surrounding a given issue.

As already mentioned, it is important as a critical thinker that you be aware of your initial opinions and not permit them to interfere with a careful consideration of all viewpoints. For instance, you may have strong feelings of support or opposition regarding one or more of the viewpoints discussed in our textbook example dealing with euthanasia. That is fine, provided that you keep an open mind when distinguishing among the viewpoints, give careful thought to each of them, and at least consider the possibility that you might change your initial feelings after reading and thinking about the rationale for all points of view.

Having done that, you are in a better position to express your personal viewpoint even if it has not changed, because you have opened yourself up to other possibilities. When discussing your viewpoint, be sure to provide the reasons why you favor it over the others. For example, suppose that you support indirect euthanasia because you do not believe that extraordinary measures, such as a feeding tube or ventilator, should be taken to keep a person alive. Furthermore, in answer to those who do not favor any form of euthanasia, you believe that by using extraordinary measures, they are indeed playing God by preventing nature from taking its course. In addition, by doing so, they are perhaps prolonging a hopeless situation indefinitely, thereby placing loved ones under a tremendous physical, emotional, and financial burden. To those who support direct euthanasia, you respond that you do not favor that course of action because you believe it is playing God by deliberately bringing about certain death, to say nothing of the fact that it is both illegal and morally wrong.

Thus you have given your personal viewpoint regarding euthanasia and the reasons why you support it over the other two. Some of those reasons were mentioned in the passage you read, and others were not. It is always permissible to use your knowledge of an issue to supply additional rationale for your point of view.

Furthermore, you could have just as easily come out in favor of one of the other viewpoints or even some combination of them as long as you provide your reasons for doing so. For instance, in discussing this issue, one student supported indirect euthanasia only after three different doctors certify that the situation is hopeless; otherwise, she did not favor it at all. She wanted to be reasonably sure that there was little chance of improvement. Another student agreed with the use of a feeding tube to keep someone alive but was opposed to the attachment of a ventilator. Although he agreed with preventing a patient from starving, he did not support the use of a machine to do all of the patient's breathing. In other words, he considered only the second option to be extraordinary. Thus under one set of circumstances he was not in favor of indirect euthanasia, while under another set of circumstances he was.

Turning to the issue of capital punishment, there are people who oppose it under all circumstances no matter what the crime. On the other hand, some people support it for certain crimes, such as premeditated murder, but oppose it for others, like causing death in the course of a robbery. The possibilities for combinations of viewpoints are considerable when dealing with contemporary issues. As you focus on contemporary issues both in this textbook and in your daily life, do not stick automatically to just one point of view before considering others or some combination of them.

## ACTIVITY 16

Read the following six passages, and in your notebook answer the questions that follow them. The *comprehension questions* will ask you to state the topic and central message of each passage before proceeding to determine what is at issue, distinguish among opposing viewpoints, and express a personal viewpoint. In addition, you will be asked to compare your personal viewpoint before and after you have thoroughly considered the opposing viewpoints brought out in the passages. Finally, to show flexibility, you will write a few paragraphs *in support of the viewpoint that you do* not *favor*. Keep in mind that some of the selections may deal with more than one issue.

The *thought and discussion questions* will often place you into *hypothetical* or imaginary situations involving the issues brought out in the passages. After thinking about them, feel free to discuss the questions with your classmates and together come up with possible answers. Finally, you will be asked to contribute any questions of your own that come to mind when reading the passages. You should be prepared to discuss possible answers to both your questions and those of your classmates.

### 1

## Down with Casual Fridays!
*Can Laid-Back Clothes Set Working Women Back?*
*Don't Dress Down Until You Read This*

JOHN T. MOLLOY

1   Many working women today are happy that so many businesses have adopted dress-down days, or even casual dress all week long. But women shouldn't rejoice. The world's most clever male chauvinist could not have designed a more effective strategy to keep women out of power.

2       For more than 20 years, my company's research on wardrobe has shown that when women dress casually, their authority and competence are more likely to be challenged. In the 1970s, I found that women working in companies with strict dress codes earned almost one third more than those who had the same levels of education and experience but worked in companies where they were allowed to dress casually. I redid the survey a dozen times, most recently in 1992. The gap between

the salaries of women who dress formally and casually has narrowed—but only by 11 percent.

3     To figure out why, my firm used photographs of a man and a woman dressed professionally—the woman in a skirted suit and the man in a traditional men's suit. When we showed the pictures to businesspeople and asked which person was the vice president and which was the assistant, a slight but not overwhelming majority labeled the man the vice president. But when we showed respondents pictures of the same man and woman *without* their jackets, 80 to 90 percent of those questioned identified the man as more senior. When men dress casually, they lose some of their authority; when women do the same, they lose most of theirs.

4     The key to that authority—especially for women in male-dominated fields—is the jacket. In our latest survey, more than 90 percent of businesspeople assumed that women wearing jackets outranked those without. (Wearing a jacket especially helped young, petite women get taken seriously.)

5     So why ask women to dress for failure? The advocates of casual dress codes have wrapped their cause in virtue. A number of executives we talked to said they instituted casual days to build team spirit. True: If *everyone* wears jeans, including the company president, the change may have a positive effect on corporate culture. However, casual dress codes only break down hierarchies when they are first introduced. Within a year, most people in authority begin to dress more formally to identify their positions. If you go into these companies on a casual Friday, you can tell at a glance who is in charge.

6     A second claim in favor of dressing down is that employees have to spend less on clothing for work. This argument has a great deal of validity—for men. Take the experience of one of our clients. As far as Martha was concerned, she had to buy a second work wardrobe when her company instituted casual Fridays. Her husband and the other men at the company just started wearing their golf outfits to work, but Martha felt her weekend clothes would not do; many women's casual outfits are more revealing or sexier than men's, and Martha felt that as a manager, she had to maintain a professional image.

7     She's right. Many executives use casual days and social affairs as a way to appraise up-and-coming young people. The president of a Fortune 500 company openly admitted to me that when young employees, male and female, wore suits to work, they looked so cookie-cutter that he had a problem figuring out which of them would fit in best at corporate headquarters. He started using company outings—when employees were in more personal attire—to decide who was top-echelon material.

8     If your company institutes casual days, you can't ignore the new rules; you may look as if you're boycotting the program. But businesswomen are learning that to go to work in jeans and a T-shirt is a dangerous proposition. Many told us that when they dressed casually at work, they began to receive second-rate treatment; many started to dress as professionally as possible on casual days. They also adopted a wise strategy: keeping a jacket handy in case someone important shows up.

9     If the country's workplaces continue to go casual, jeans manufacturers will undoubtedly make money. But I doubt women will. When companies institute casual workdays, they are changing the rules of dress, but not the rules of nature. When executives tell you that you can wear anything you want to work, they are telling you

that you will not be officially censured for dressing as you wish. They are *not* telling you that you will be taken just as seriously as if you were dressed professionally.

10      It is up to women to make sure that casual days do not undermine their hard-won clout.

*Glamour,* October 1996, p. 196

## Comprehension Questions

1. What is the topic of the passage?
2. What is the central message of the passage?
3. Determine what is at issue. What is your initial personal viewpoint?
4. Distinguish among opposing viewpoints, and provide the rationale for each.
5. Think carefully about the viewpoints. Express a personal viewpoint, and give the reasons why you favor it. Does it differ from your initial personal viewpoint? Why or why not?
6. Write a few paragraphs *in support of the viewpoint that you do not favor*.

## Thought and Discussion Questions

1. Use the context to figure out what the author means when he states, "The world's most clever male chauvinist could not have designed a more effective strategy to keep women out of power."
2. As a businesswoman, how would you react if your company adopted casual dress all week long? Why? As a businessman, how would you react if your company adopted casual dress all week long? Why? If you answered these two questions differently, explain why.
3. List any questions that came to mind while you were reading this selection, and be prepared to discuss possible answers to them.

## 2

## The Question of Reproductive Rights

*Few issues have been as controversial over the past 20 years as whether women have the right to control their own reproduction, specifically, whether birth control and abortion should be available on demand. At the heart of this issue is a crucial question about individual rights: whether the mother has a right to individual self-determination or whether the rights of the unborn baby should be protected by the state. Two views follow, presenting both sides of this volatile question.*

### SELF-DETERMINATION: A BASIC RIGHT

1    In 1973 the Supreme Court, in the landmark *Roe* v. *Wade* case, declared that abortion, like birth control, is included in the fundamental right to privacy that belongs to all individuals. The Court ruled that the decision to have an abortion

during the first 3 months of pregnancy must be left to the pregnant woman and her doctor.

2    This ruling was based on the premise that our society values freedom and self-determination as a basic right. For this reason, the Court attempted to place the decision to bear a child—a decision inextricably related to the right of self-determination—beyond the reach of government. This ruling, along with earlier decisions allowing access to birth control, correctly leaves the choice to the individual most involved, the mother.

3    The mother is the person most closely concerned with the many issues concerning childbirth: Does she have the support a new mother needs? Will she be able to provide the child with a good home? How will an additional member affect the rest of her family? It is the mother who runs the emotional, social, spiritual, and physical risks of abortion or of not having the procedure.

4    Before *Roe* v. *Wade* millions of American women had dangerous and sometimes fatal illegal abortions, often driven to this extreme by poverty or fear. Since *Roe* v. *Wade* millions of women have taken advantage of their right to a safe, legal abortion. Considering the explosive growth in world population, this is a positive step contributing toward our stewardship of the planet.

5    There is no doubt that abortion is an emotionally charged and complex issue. However, the rights of the pregnant woman are paramount. She must have the right to choose and the fundamental right to control her own body and life.

## PROTECTING THE RIGHTS OF THE UNBORN IS THE STATE'S DUTY

6    Beginning in the nineteenth century and extending through much of the twentieth, most states in the United States passed laws restricting or forbidding abortion. These laws were based on two general principles: the state's duty to protect those who cannot protect their own rights and the idea that life itself is an ultimate good.

7    Although various cases preceding *Roe* v. *Wade* established the right to birth control, there is a fundamental difference between birth control and abortion. The Supreme Court itself has declared that the decision to abort a fetus is inherently different from the decision to prevent a pregnancy, because a pregnant woman "cannot be isolated in her privacy." In other words, the pregnant woman is not just an individual but the source of a potential human life whose rights are equally important. Since the fetus cannot safeguard its own rights, it is the state's duty to intervene to ensure that they are protected.

8    Those who oppose abortion believe that the unborn child has a right to its own life and that this life begins at conception. No one has the right to take the life of an unborn child. To those who argue that a woman should not have to raise a child she does not want or cannot afford, they point to the thousands of childless couples who are desperate to adopt babies. The rights of the fetus, then, are of such importance that they must take precedence over the individual rights of the mother.

Marvin R. Levy, Mark Dignan, and Janet H. Shirreffs, *Life and Health*, p. 248

## Comprehension Questions

1. What is the topic of the passage?
2. What is the central message of the passage?

3. Determine what is at issue. What is your initial personal viewpoint?

4. Distinguish among opposing viewpoints, and provide the rationale for each.

5. Think carefully about the viewpoints. Express a personal viewpoint, and give the reasons why you favor it. Does it differ from your initial personal viewpoint? Why or why not?

6. Write a few paragraphs *in support of the viewpoint that you do* not *favor.*

## Thought and Discussion Questions

1. Is there a possible third viewpoint that is a combination of the two opposing points of view presented in the passage? If so, what is it?

2. In the debate over abortion, some people oppose it in all circumstances while others oppose it except in cases of rape, incest, an abnormal fetus, or risk to the mother's health. Discuss these two viewpoints *objectively* by providing the rationale for each.

3. List any questions that came to mind while you were reading this selection, and be prepared to discuss possible answers to them.

## 3

## Are We Puppets of Society?

1  Through socialization we internalize the norms and values of society. Does this imply that we become puppets of society, individuals who basically enjoy giving up freedom and following the rules society sets down? The answer is yes and no.

2  In many respects, we do behave like society's puppets. We are glad to follow society's expectation that we be friendly to our friends and love our parents. We are happy to do many other similarly nice things every day as expected of us by society. It just happens that we enjoy doing all these things because others have made us happy by responding positively when we do them. Living in a highly individualistic society, though, we do not see ourselves as society's puppets when we act in these ways.

3  But we may also do things differently than dictated by society. We may get drunk, fool around a bit too much, protest what we perceive to be a social injustice, or do other similar things that raise others' eyebrows. By engaging in such activities, we express the unsocialized aspect of our "self," no longer behaving like puppets. Dennis Wrong (1961) has suggested that we can never be puppets all the time because it is impossible to be entirely socialized. There are at least four reasons why socialization can never turn us into total puppets:

4  First, we have certain "imperious biological drives" that always buck against society's attempt to mold us in its image.

5  Second, the socializing influences are not always consistent and harmonious with one another. Our ethnic group, social class, and professional and occupational associations may not socialize us in the same way. They may teach conflicting roles, norms, and values.

6    Third, even if society could consistently and completely socialize us, we would still violate its laws and rules. In the very process of learning to obey the rules, we may also learn how to break them without getting caught, which is a great temptation for most if not all people. Even some of the most "respectable" citizens have committed crimes.

7    Finally, if we were completely socialized, we would become extremely unhappy and probably neurotic or psychotic. This is why, as Sigmund Freud said, civilization tends to breed discontent in the individual. No normal persons want their drives for self-expression, freedom, creativity, or personal eccentricity to be totally suppressed.

Alex Thio, *Sociology: A Brief Introduction,* p. 75

## Comprehension Questions

1. What is the topic of the passage?
2. What is the central message of the passage?
3. Determine what is at issue. What is your initial personal viewpoint?
4. Distinguish among opposing viewpoints, and provide the rationale for each.
5. Think carefully about the viewpoints. Express a personal viewpoint, and give the reasons why you favor it. Does it differ from your initial personal viewpoint? Why or why not?
6. Write a few paragraphs *in support of the viewpoint that you do* not *favor.*

## Thought and Discussion Questions

1. Use the context to figure out the meaning of the word *socialization,* and explain how important it is in our society.
2. Are there any ways in which you behave like society's puppet? If your answer is yes, explain how. If your answer is no, explain why not.
3. List any questions that came to mind while you were reading this selection, and be prepared to discuss possible answers to them.

## 4

## Childless by Choice

JEANNE SAFER

1    This year, the first wave of the baby boomers turns 50. For many of the 38 million women born during the baby boom, the biological clock so many watched anxiously is winding down forever.

2    But what about the 15 percent of those women—I am one—who intentionally never produced a baby boom of our own? Because our decision not to have children violates norms of feminine conduct, we face a different psychological task from our peers who became mothers or were infertile.

3    According to my own experience and the interviews I conducted with 50 women who are also childless by choice—the majority of them baby boomers—most of us have never been happier.

4      Contrary to popular assumptions, most women I've talked to who have made conscious decisions not to reproduce for personal or professional reasons are approaching their milestone birthdays with few regrets and with a lot of relief and excitement about the future.

5      At 35, Jane, a dancer, married a man who did not want children. At 40, she went to medical school. She has now established a child psychiatry practice and repaid her loans. "I make a difference in children's lives and still go out at night," she told me.

6      "My life is really beginning at 50," said Anna, an acupuncturist, as she and her new husband prepared for an around-the-world trip.

7      Reviewing a decade as a war correspondent in the Muslim world, one woman told me: "I've had such an eventful time I wouldn't mind dying now. Would I have been able to go into Afghanistan with the rebels if I'd had a child waiting at home?"

8      Robin, a secretary living in a Long Island suburb surrounded by other people's children, says: "There's no gene for motherhood. I'm happy with my life. I feel no need to undo what I didn't do—and I will leave lots of love behind me."

9      Lauren, a housewife and community activist, believes she has given up "a kind of self-knowledge you only get from having kids," but has gained "time to reflect that most people don't have."

10     It is only now as she approaches 50 that Leslie, a gallery owner, can volunteer that she chose not to be a mother. "I felt a stigma in my earlier years," she said. "I was afraid people would judge me or feel sorry for me, because I mistrusted my decision to be different. Now I know that I made that choice out of strength."

11     Many women attributed their satisfaction specifically to their decision to remain childless, a choice they believe has offered them rare opportunities for self-expression, service and creativity. Their need to be the center of their own attention is not based on selfishness or coldness, as is often assumed, but reflects a healthy wish to focus on their own lives.

12     All of them say they feel proud that they actively grappled with their motherhood dilemma. They say they do not regret the outcome, even though many had to mourn lost possibilities and accept being permanent outsiders to a principal preoccupation of their peers. Each told me she now enjoys her unconventional life, the intimacy of her marriage, her uncommon degree of freedom and privacy.

13     Conventional wisdom, the religious right and the psychologist Erik Erikson (who wrote, "A woman who does not fulfill her innate need to fill her uterus with embryonic tissue is likely to be frustrated or neurotic") are wrong. These "barren" women feel fully womanly as they reach menopause; many see themselves as models for the next generation, demonstrating that women can finally make informed choices about reproduction, see motherhood as a vocation that may or may not suit them, and be fulfilled whichever life they chose.

*The New York Times,* January 17, 1996, p. A19

## Comprehension Questions

1. What is the topic of the passage?
2. What is the central message of the passage?
3. Determine what is at issue. What is your initial personal viewpoint?

4. Distinguish among opposing viewpoints, and provide the rationale for each.

5. Think carefully about the viewpoints. Express a personal viewpoint, and give the reasons why you favor it. Does it differ from your initial personal viewpoint? Why or why not?

6. Write a few paragraphs *in support of the viewpoint that you do* not *favor.*

## Thought and Discussion Questions

1. Is the writer of the passage being evenhanded or biased in her presentation of the material? Why?

2. Would you marry someone who did not want to have children? Why or why not? How would you handle the situation if you disagreed on that point?

3. List any questions that came to mind while you were reading this selection, and be prepared to discuss possible answers to them.

# 5

## Shot in the Arm

JOHNNY TOWNSEND

1 I cried yesterday upon leaving the doctor's office.

2 I know, it sounds melodramatic. Men in our society aren't supposed to cry. It's just that the news was so devastating.

3 My bill was $120.

4 I had received "two" injections of cortisone in my left shoulder for tendinitis. (Technically, it was one injection but included a dose of anaesthetic.) Each dose cost $6. That seemed reasonable to me.

5 But the office visit cost $45—a bit steep considering the doctor wasn't there for more than three minutes, and a minute of *that* consisted of his leaving the room to get the hypodermic and medicine. I understand there is a flat fee for office visits; shouldn't there then be a designated minimum amount of time that the doctor spends with each patient? This doctor ignored my questions, handed me the bill, and left while I was still putting on my shirt. Is it right to make me pay for his running behind schedule, when I've paid a fair fee?

6 As it was, I had waited an hour past my scheduled appointment to see him as it was. Even if I'm just a peon, my time is still worth a good $5.50 an hour. Can't I deduct that?

7 But the really painful part of the bill was the $63 for actually performing the injection, which lasted all of eight seconds. If I'm paying $63 for his skill, what was the $45 for—his ability to tell me to remove my shirt? (Don't tell me it was for his diagnosis, because he'd made that a month earlier when he gave me my first injection at a cost of $81.)

8      Basically, since the doctor was only in the room with me for two minutes, at $120 I paid him a dollar a second to see me. At those rates, maybe I should be glad he didn't stay longer.

9      My shoulder had been hurting for three months before I finally went to the doctor. I'd been hoping it would get better on its own, but when I tried to reach for something and realized I could no longer stretch my left arm as far as my right, I became frightened. I suppose this is the way most poor people let problems develop too far.

10     I have a couple of friends I take down to charity hospital every few weeks—one for arthritis and another for a shattered bone that won't heal. I took a third friend there when he got the flu. Their waits of four, five, and six hours were demeaning and dehumanizing. Usually (except for the flu), they wouldn't even get to see a doctor but only set up an appointment to see one a month or two down the line. And when they showed up for *these* appointments, they had another four- to five-hour wait. Then they were diagnosed but often had to return in another few weeks to receive any treatment, with yet another four- to five-hour wait ahead of them.

11     I grew up in a middle-class home and just couldn't bear to go through all that myself. I am spoiled. I have three college degrees in English and work professionally as a college English instructor, where I earn $6,500 a year, with no benefits. I can't afford insurance. I don't know how I even saved enough for these two office visits, but they are the last.

12     After I had paid the $120, I walked in a daze to my car. I have finally become a complete nothing, I realized. People with money are everything, and people without it are nothing. It's certainly been said before, but I finally realized what it meant.

13     I don't expect anyone to feel sorry for me. As someone who frittered away his life on something so frivolous as English, I know exactly what society thinks of me. But as someone who grew up middle class, despite my miserable income of the past several years, I still managed to see myself as part of *us,* not *them.*

14     I, too, looked down on the poor somewhat, as ignorant or lazy or whatever. Oh, it's true that because of my liberal-arts background I was very nice and sensitive to *them,* but I hung on as long as I could to being part of *us,* believing I was only an honorary *them.* I was only clinging to respectability by my fingernails, but that doctor bill ripped my fingernails right off.

15     I was raised conservative but became much more liberal as an adult. Still, I am an odd mixture and maintain some strong views on both sides. I do think that entitlement programs and welfare too often promote dependence and lack of ambition, as well as punish those who try to escape poverty.

16     But honestly, how many people are going to say, "You know, the government is paying for my health care, so I think I'll go out and get appendicitis today"? Do people really say, "I hate rich people. I want them to pay more taxes for me. I was going to let that lump in my breast just sit there, but I think I'll go get it checked just to be spiteful"? Has anyone really been heard to remark, "Since I don't have to pay for it, I think I'll go develop some intestinal polyps. A colonoscopy sounds like a lot of fun. It'll liven up my boring, lazy week"?

17     The fact is that many people will never earn more than minimum wage and will be forever stuck in jobs with no benefits. And most people, even if they do work

hard, will never be able to afford health care. If I'd had a torn rotator cuff, my doctor said it could cost a couple of thousand dollars to repair. We dregs of society may deserve to live in cruddy apartments and shop for clothes at thrift stores, but do we really deserve to wait half a year to be treated for something others are cured of in a week? Do only those who are smart enough or talented enough or lucky enough (or brutal enough or avaricious enough) to become wealthy deserve health care?

18    I've been back at school for a year now, taking my pre-med prerequisites with a grade-point average of 4.0. With or without health-care reform, I'm going to get the health care I deserve. It would be nice to think, though, that maybe the millions of other Americans without health care might get some, too. No matter where we stand as individuals on the issue of reform, it is clear that the health-care system on some substantial level needs a shot in the arm.

*The Humanist,* November 1995, p. 4

## Comprehension Questions

1. What is the topic of the passage?
2. What is the central message of the passage?
3. Determine what is at issue. What is your initial personal viewpoint?
4. Distinguish among opposing viewpoints, and provide the rationale for each.
5. Think carefully about the viewpoints. Express a personal viewpoint, and give the reasons why you favor it. Does it differ from your initial personal viewpoint? Why or why not?
6. Write a few paragraphs *in support of the viewpoint that you do* not *favor.*

## Thought and Discussion Questions

1. If you were a doctor, how would you react to a patient who could not afford to pay your fees? Why? Would you agree to provide medical care to a homeless person? Why or why not?
2. If you were a doctor, what possible rationale would you give if you were accused of charging high fees?
3. List any questions that came to mind while you were reading this selection, and be prepared to discuss possible answers to them.

## 6

## Should There Be Prayer in Our Public Schools?

LYNN MINTON, MODERATOR

*We spoke with a group of New York University students about the controversial issue of whether there should be prayer in our public schools. The students were taking part in an honors seminar on religion and the Constitution with John Sexton, dean of the NYU*

*School of Law. They were Gregory A. Belinfanti, 19, of Elmont, N.Y.; Shaheen A. Khal-fan, 20, of Searingtown, N.Y.; Victoria Kopolovich, 20, of Brooklyn, N.Y.; Molly Cowan, 20, of Fort Worth, Tex.; Brian J. Fitzpatrick, 20, of Brooklyn, N.Y.; Christopher Hughes, 20, of Secaucus, N.J.; Elie Fink, 21, of Bridgeport, Conn.; and Brooke E. Bell, 20, of San Jose, Calif.*

1   **Greg:** Yes. Throughout our history, religion and the United States are intermingled—the first people who came here came to escape religious persecution. Every session of Congress begins with a prayer; on every coin is "In God we trust"; when we say the pledge of allegiance, we say "under God." If you say, "No, you can't have prayer in the schools," you're negating the country's history.

2   **Shaheen:** I was born in Tanzania, and in Muslim countries religion is an inherent part of the school system. But I don't think that a public school education in America should have religion mixed in. You don't want to turn around one day and have the government tell you, "Now, you have to do *this* prayer." It's like you're brainwashing children. And I don't think the government should be saying, "I want you to believe in God." Or, "I want you to say this prayer before you start your school day." It may not even be your prayer. Who made up this prayer? Why should you have to say it if you don't believe in it?

3   **Greg:** At least 99% of the people, including the government, accept that there is this Being—and we'll call him God—who, as a nation, we live under. And all I'm saying is, at the beginning of the day, those of us who would like to say a nondenominational prayer should be given the opportunity. If you don't want to say the prayer, then don't say it.

4   **Victoria:** For you to say, "Well, you don't have to pray—you can leave the room" . . . well, we'll be looked upon as different. And it is our right to have an education in this country, and it is our right to stay in class. And I don't believe that there is such a thing as a general prayer that everyone could be part of.

5   **Molly:** That's the problem with school prayers—they try to combine all these religions, and so the prayer doesn't really represent any religion. A Christian prayer would say, "In Jesus' name I pray," but they're not going to say that in a public school. It's like the state is forming this pseudo-combo religion.

6   **Brian:** But even a nondenominational prayer to begin the school day is not constitutional—even a "moment of silence or voluntary prayer" is not allowed. It seems to me that in this country now there is a very strong anti-religious thread. There's this feeling that anyone who believes strongly in their religion is a fanatic, which of course isn't true. There is this feeling that if religion is allowed in schools, you're going to brainwash the children, which is ridiculous.

7   **Shaheen:** I don't mind a moment of silence, because a person can—if they want to—just sit and think about their plans for the day. But then the teacher should just announce a moment of silence. Not say, "We'll have a moment of silence or voluntary prayer." Just the fact that you're getting prayer involved with a public school education—it shouldn't be there.

8   **Molly:** Some people forget that you can pray anywhere. You don't need the school to "give" you time for prayer. You can sit in your class and pray. You can pray in the hall. Nobody's saying that they're going to hunt you down, listen to your thoughts and say, "No prayer!"

9   **Greg:** Perhaps you don't have the time. Perhaps you'd like to do it with your school-mates. But the Supreme Court said you can't have a moment of silence that is designed for meditation or voluntary prayer.

10  **Victoria:** I think it's just like, you give them a little bit, and then they'll want a lot. Then they'll start with spoken prayer. So the Supreme Court said, "No. We're stopping right here. We're drawing the line."

11  **Chris:** I'm definitely for a moment of silence. For meditation too. School is such a rat race, that's the last thing on your mind—to stop and collect your thoughts for a minute. So maybe it's like a reminder. And if you want to pray during that moment, then that's your choice.

12  **Lynn Minton: What about people who don't pray silently? Or who kneel when they pray?**

13  **Chris:** Those people can think about something else.

14  **Elie:** When you bring religion in any form into the public schools, it creates an opportunity to have the religion of the majority enforced. Children are very susceptible to peer pressure, and there's no way to regulate what goes on in every classroom.

15  **Brooke:** Once you bring religion into the schools, religious persecution will probably follow.

16  **Shaheen:** This country was founded to get away from religious persecution.

17  **Elie:** Even during a moment of silence, maybe some of the students are crossing themselves and others aren't—some kids could be ostracized.

18  **Greg:** Let's stop kickball too, because kids can be ostracized—a kid gets picked last, and he's got to stand against the fence.

19  **Brian:** We've heard religious persecution being thrown around. I don't think in this country, in this day and age. . . .

20  **Brooke:** I don't mean the Holocaust happening in P.S. 20 or whatever, but I do think it can cause tension between kids and cause insults to be thrown around.

21  **Brian:** Those insults are around anyway. Let's say there's a Sikh, and he's wearing a turban. You don't think he's already going to have comments made to him, whether or not there are prayers in school?

22  **Greg:** Persecution doesn't stem from prayer. It stems from what's already in your head.

23  **Chris:** I don't think spoken prayer should be allowed.

24  **Brian:** I do.

25  **LM: Who'd write the prayer?**

26  **Brian:** Perhaps each district school board. Preferably with input from the students' parents—all working on a very local level.

27  **LM: Would you be comfortable with their prayers?**

28  **Brian:** It depends on what prayers they write. Let's just say the word "God" is used.

29  **LM: Why is this important to you?**

30  **Brian:** I feel religion in a group setting is very important.

31  **LM: How about church?**

32  **Greg:** You can't go to church on weekdays.

33  **Elie:** I go to synagogue every day.

34  **Greg:** And my grandmother goes to church every day. But I don't think it's realistic to expect high school kids to go to church every day.

35   **Molly:** Is it the responsibility of the government to bring the church to the school every day?

36   **Greg:** All they'd be doing is saying that we acknowledge that we are a religious people and that some people enjoy prayer before they start their day, and we will set aside this moment of time, and here is a prayer. If you don't want to say the prayer, you don't have to.

37   **Brian:** The idea of the First Amendment was not to deny people the right to say prayer. It was to prevent the government from meddling in and controlling people's lives.

38   **Victoria:** And prayer is not meddling?

39   **Greg:** The government is not supposed to tell people which religions to choose or to set up a national religion. By establishing prayer in the schools, the government is not doing those things.

40   **Molly:** You're saying you'd love to see prayer in school. There *is* prayer in school. I've done it. You could ask tons of students who have prayed in school.

41   **Brian:** But it's illegal.

42   **Molly:** It's not illegal! A private prayer, in class, in the hall . . .

43   **Brian:** Why should people be afraid to freely announce their faith in God? Why should they have to go in the corner or in the hallway and secretly say it to themselves?

44   **Victoria:** They don't have to go into a corner. They don't have to pray silently—they can do what they want. But the government can't do it. The school can't do it.

45   **Greg:** It's sort of taboo to express your religious beliefs among your friends while you are at school, and I think it all stems from a misinterpretation of the First Amendment, which says "Congress shall make no law respecting an establishment of religion, or prohibiting the free exercise thereof." It does not say that the government can't say that we are *for* religion.

46   **LM: Have you ever had a coach who held a pre-game prayer meeting in school?**

47   **Chris:** Before every single game, our JV basketball coach would say, "All right, guys, hands in." And we'd say "The Lord's Prayer." And in the locker room, before every game, I would put my head down, say a prayer. A lot of kids would.

48   **Brooke:** I have a problem with the coach leading a prayer. Here the team is supposed to go out together and play, and yet right before, you divide up the group: If you want to pray, stay. If you don't . . .

49   **Chris:** You have to realize, I went to a high school where almost everybody was Catholic.

50   **LM: Is it okay where it's a public school, but everybody is the same religion?**

51   **Molly:** I don't know. I mean, if none of the students have any problem with it, then it's okay.

52   **LM: What if Elie moved into town and was on your team?**

53   **Chris:** Actually, there were one or two Jewish kids on the JV team.

54   **Brian:** If no one objected, why would there be a problem?

55   **Elie:** The government has to worry about the guy who's sticking his hand in because he doesn't want to be different—but he really doesn't want to.

56   **Chris:** The coach knew that there were two Jewish kids on the team, but it wasn't an issue. If you do object, you could take that to him and say, "Listen, it really offends me that you say 'The Lord's Prayer.'"

57  **LM: I'm thinking it takes a lot of courage to tell a coach, "I don't like the way you're doing that!"**

58  **Greg:** We keep on saying that if you allow prayer in the school, some people will feel different. Well, the fact is that if you're not a Christian in the United States, then you're different. Because the majority, we're a Christian nation. If Elie went to a public school in my district, he'd be different. Regardless of whether there's prayer in the school.

59  **Brian:** It's a Judeo-Christian nation.

60  **Shaheen:** Are we all just putting aside that this country was established for religious freedom? Are the rest of us just going to have to go away?

61  **Greg:** You have religious freedom in a country that's a Judeo-Christian nation. We're not establishing a Judeo-Christian nation, we *are* one.

62  **Brooke:** What about the minority?

63  **Brian:** So what should we say—that it's Judeo-Christian-Islamic-Hindu . . . ?

64  **Brooke:** No. You can just say it's a nation of different religions. What's wrong with that?

65  **Brian:** All you have to do is look at our motto, look at the prayer before Congress begins.

66  **Molly:** I'm uncomfortable just because I *am* part of the Christian majority. I know how I feel, but you have to consider how other people are going to feel. And there's something else: When you're in the majority and you don't take care of the minority's rights, then who is to say that, someday, somebody's not going to come along and take away *your* rights? And who will protect you?

*Parade*, November 27, 1994, pp. 4–5

## Comprehension Questions

1. What is the topic of the passage?
2. What is the central message of the passage?
3. Determine what is at issue. What is your initial personal viewpoint?
4. Distinguish among opposing viewpoints, and provide the rationale for each.
5. Think carefully about the viewpoints. Express a personal viewpoint, and give the reasons why you favor it. Does it differ from your initial personal viewpoint? Why or why not?
6. Write a few paragraphs *in support of the viewpoint that you do* not *favor.*

## Thought and Discussion Questions

1. How would you respond if your instructor asked the class to say a prayer today? Why?
2. Assume for a moment that you are a teacher who has been ordered by the school district to start each school day with a prayer. How would you react to a student who refused to do so because he does not believe in God? Why?
3. List any questions that came to mind while you were reading this selection, and be prepared to discuss possible answers to them.

## ACTIVITY 17

As a semester project, choose a contemporary issue that is of interest to you, and write an essay in which you discuss what is at issue, distinguish among the opposing viewpoints, and express a personal viewpoint. When you have completed your essay, you will be asked to make copies available for your classmates to read. After they have had an opportunity to consider what you have written, you will lead a classroom discussion of the issue during which you will present your conclusions and answer any questions that your fellow students may have.

## ACTIVITY 18

Your instructor is going to divide the class into groups, each of which will choose a contemporary issue to investigate. Each group will then be divided into two debate teams for the purpose of representing the major opposing viewpoints regarding the issue. Toward the end of the semester, the two teams will debate the issue in class, with your instructor serving as the moderator.

## LOOKING BACK

With two of your classmates, come up with a list of the most important points you learned from this chapter, and determine how they can be put to use in other classes. Be prepared to discuss both the list and the uses.

## THINK AGAIN!

Suppose that you are alone in the forest with a friend, and you are both riding horses. An argument starts over whose horse is slower. After several minutes of bickering, you make a $100 bet and decide to have a race immediately. However, the race does not work because you each make your horse go as slowly as possible on purpose so that you can win the money. Assuming that you want to settle the matter right there on the spot, can you figure out a fair way to determine whose horse is slower?

## MASTERY TEST 3

A. Fill in the blanks and answer the questions.

1. _____ thinking has no clear purpose or objective.

2. Critical thinkers are in a better position to _____ what is going on around them, avoid costly _____ , and _____ whatever they set out to do.

3. What is critical thinking?

   _____

   _____

   _____

4. Name the characteristics of critical thinking, and describe each of them in a sentence or two.

   _____

   _____

   _____

   _____

   _____

   _____

   _____

   _____

   _____

   _____

   _____

   _____

   _____

   _____

5. When using the Internet for research, the critical thinker
   a. should first make sure that a particular source is both appropriate and thorough
   b. should try to use material from *.edu*, *.gov*, and *.mil* sites because they are most likely to be reliable
   c. should look for the professional affiliation and bibliography of the author
   d. should always be aware of possible bias
   e. all of the above

6. What is a contemporary issue?

   _____

   _____

7. As a critical thinker it is important that you be aware of the _____ , or specific reasons, for a given viewpoint.

8. What is the central message of the following memo?

MEMO

TO ALL OUR VALUED CUSTOMERS
DUE TO AN OVERLOAD OF PAPERWORK ALL CREDIT REQUESTS WILL BE HANDLED BY MS. HELEN WAITE.
SO IF YOU WANT CREDIT GO TO HELEN WAITE

MEMO

Central message: _____

_____

_____

B. For each of the following passages, determine what is at issue and distinguish among the opposing viewpoints, including the rationale for each.

### 9. PRO & CON: Putting Pig Parts into Human Bodies

*Should researchers be permitted to experiment with the transplanting of pig cells or organs into humans?*

[asks] *John O'Neil*

**YES**

The possibility of infection by retroviruses is a hot topic, given Ebola and AIDS, but virologists say the risk is very small. Some people want to halt experiments—but halt them until when? It's almost impossible to identify a risk when you have no experience of something. It's true that if the benefits are not going to outweigh the risks, then any risk will be too great. But 60,000 people are waiting for organs in this country this year. About 12,000 are waiting for livers, but only 4,000 will get them. Even if everyone in the nation donated organs who could there wouldn't be enough. Where else do we have a life and death circumstance that's rationed? We can't create livers, hearts or kidneys. That's the reason to move forward, but cautiously.

Dr. Ronald Ferguson is *chairman of the surgery department at Ohio State University Medical Center.*

**NO**

I'm all for basic research in this field, but not human research. Before that, we have to consider who is going to be put at risk, and there's no argument that this risk exists. The danger, which nobody can quantify, is that a pig's infectious particle will infect a human recipient, mutate and infect the public in a way not unlike AIDS. The question then becomes an ethical one. If the general population is to be put at risk, shouldn't the population be informed about the risk and shouldn't there be a way of getting public input on whether clinical trials should go forward? We have suggested a moratorium on human trials until we find a way to involve the public. Lab experiments are fine, but don't impose risk on people to find out what the risk is.

Dr. Fritz H. Bach is an *immunobiologist and the Lewis Thomas Professor at Harvard Medical School.*

*The New York Times,* October 27, 1998

Issue: _____

_____

Opposing viewpoints and rationales: _____

_____

_____

_____

_____

_____

_____

_____

_____

_____

## 10. Do You Trust the Media?

1   These days, more and more news is *about* the news, thanks to a wave of media malfeasance that has Americans wondering whether they can trust anything they read, watch or hear. Among the biggest scandals: CNN and *Time*'s admission that their joint report about the United States' use of nerve gas in Vietnam had little basis in fact; the firing of a *Boston Globe* columnist and a *New Republic* writer for making up quotes and events; and prestigious news outlets caught spreading unfounded rumors during the early days of the Clinton-Lewinsky brouhaha.

2   These exposés arrive amid a growing credibility crisis. The percentage of Americans who think that news outlets usually get the facts straight has plummeted from 55 to 34 over the past 13 years, according to The Pew Research Center for The People & The Press.

3   Some say news quality is compromised by the intense, often minute-to-minute competition among a growing number of outlets, including cable shows, Internet sites and some dozen TV newsmagazines. As *Nightline*'s executive producer recently said, "Everybody is ratcheting up the speed and that's totally wrong. . . . You can work too fast and make mistakes."

4   Others say the battle for ratings and advertising dollars also affects the news. "We're moving from journalism as a profession toward news as marketing," says Jim Naureckas of Fairness & Accuracy In Reporting, a watchdog group. Big-business media, he argues, would rather run "sensationalist stories that can be played for tears, fears or outrage" than cover serious political and economic issues.

5   Journalists' own biases are part of the problem too, adds Deborah Lambert of Accuracy in Media, a watchdog group that monitors the media for liberal bias. To "make a splash," she charges, some reporters give vent to personal passions instead of presenting information fairly. "To these journalists, truth has become a quaint relic."

6    Yet many believe news gathering is better than ever. "We never had a 'good old days' when no one made mistakes on deadline," says Dick Schwarzlose, a professor at Northwestern University's Medill School of Journalism. Nor are competition, sensationalism or bias anything new (the term *yellow journalism* was coined in the late nineteenth century); it's just that today, reporters as well as their audience are far more aware when the media falls short. Says Schwarzlose, "The vast majority of people in the news business are doing their best to provide good information."

7    Robert Lichter, Ph.D., who heads the Center for Media and Public Affairs, questions whether bias-free news is ideal. The founding fathers' vision of a free press wasn't a few respected sources spooning out "objective" facts, he notes, but a welter of conflicting sources and viewpoints—precisely what today's consumer faces.

8    Journalism's defenders point out that most people know which sources are usually trustworthy and which play the news for thrills. The Pew survey, for example, found that 93 percent of Americans have little or no faith in the accuracy of supermarket tabloids. Meanwhile, believability of serious news outlets is becoming more of a concern—especially now that members of the media are watchdogging each other, says Bill Kovach, curator of Harvard's Nieman Foundation journalism fellowships. "When you make ratings your number-one priority and credibility number two, eventually you get slammed," he says. "I hope CNN and the others have learned that lesson by now."

9    Is the media less trustworthy than ever?

*Glamour,* October 1998, p. 240

Issue: _____

_____

Opposing viewpoints and rationales: _____

_____

_____

_____

_____

_____

_____

_____

_____

## 11.  A Small Plea to Delete a Ubiquitous Expletive
### *Can't We Get Along Without the "F" Word?*

ELIZABETH AUSTIN

1    Oh, f—.

2    The "F" word, as it's called in more polite circles (including magazines such as this one), is increasingly hard to escape. Those who rarely use it themselves nonetheless hear it frequently—on the street, on the job, at the health club, at the movies—anywhere two or three disgruntled citizens might gather. Most people have uttered the word; everyone can define it. But even those who aren't particularly shocked by it don't want to hear it all the time. The toughest of tough guys cringes inwardly when somebody says it in front of his mother. Becoming a parent induces instant hypersensitivity to the word's ubiquitous presence in movies, on cable TV, in music, and in the loose talk of childless friends.

3    In its simplest and oldest usage, the "F" word refers to copulation. This usage has a long, frequently jolly, occasionally distinguished history. Shakespeare made glancing puns about it, and Scottish poet Robert Burns included it in his racier verses. More commonly today, though, the "F" word is used to express not desire but derision, not heat but hostility. Even when used as a kind of verbal space holder, a rougher, hipper equivalent of "you know" (as in "I f——ing love that f——ing movie," or in the Army patois that has been common for decades), it carries a rude message. It is both a gauge and an engine of our ever plummeting standards of civility. Yet enough people are fed up with it that it's possible to erase the "F" word from public parlance and civil discourse.

### LAST WORD

4    A couple of generations back, calling for a public elimination of the "F" word would have been preposterous, since the word was never uttered in polite company (loosely defined as anywhere middle-class women were likely to hear it). In the late '60s, however, the loud, open use of the "F" word became a true shibboleth, dividing the student radicals from the Establishment "pigs" they delighted in tweaking. In Jerry Rubin's words, the "F" word was "the last word left in the English language. Amerika cannot destroy it because she dare not use it."

5    But America took that dare. From the early '70s on, the "F" word started turning up with increasing regularity in movies, literature, and real life, according to Jesse Sheidlower's exhaustive volume, *The F-Word*. Many linguists and social critics celebrated the "F" word's coming out as a healthy abandonment of prudishness; a few still do. But civic virtuecrats today make a stronger case that public use of the word is a prime example of the "broken window" theory of social decay. When we put private frustrations and the right to be foulmouthed ahead of public order and civility, we coarsen society and risk an avalanche of rage and violence. Despite its near universality, the "F" word remains a fighting word.

6    So let's get rid of it. Scholars of social norms say all that's necessary to remove offensive language from public speech is a critical mass of people willing to take up cudgels against it. University of Chicago law Prof. Randal Picker describes such sudden overthrows of social standards as "norms cascades." If society is ripe for change, he contends, a single, powerful catalyst can engineer

swift, widespread transformation. Picker cites Jesse Jackson, whose call for a switch from "black" to "African-American" changed the nation's nomenclature almost overnight. A more subtle but equally effective norms cascade was engineered by a handful of feminist writers in the early 1970s. Author-activist Robin Morgan remembers furiously listing words then commonly used to describe women, both in conversation and in print. "Produce and animals is what we were," she recalls. "We were 'chicks' and 'lambs' and 'birds' and 'bitches,' and there was always the infamous 'cherry."' When Morgan and other feminist leaders publicly insisted on being called women, they started a norms cascade that eventually erased not only chick and bitch but girl and lady as well.

7      The "F" word seems like a particularly ripe target for a new generation of linguistic activists from both sides of the ideological divide. Erasing the word from civil discourse is one goal that Phyllis Schlafly could share with Andrea Dworkin. Here are a few modest proposals to help make that happen:

- Police should start ticketing drivers who use the "F" word (or the correlating hand gesture), thereby boosting civility and calming road rage simultaneously. Although this could raise some First Amendment hackles, keep in mind that "fighting words" are not protected speech. One simple test of the fighting-words concept is whether a fight actually ensues. Slapping a $100 ticket on a driver whose uplifted finger sparked a collision should pass any constitutional test.

- The Motion Picture Association of America movie rating system should be overhauled to give an automatic NC-17 rating to any film that uses the "F" word even once. An NC-17 rating all but guarantees diminished viewership. Writers and directors who considered the word necessary to their artistic expression could still get their movies made; they'd just have to make the decision to trade lucrative ticket sales to teenagers for their artistic license.

- Authors who salt their books with gratuitous "F" words should get the same critical treatment as those who sprinkle their prose with casual racial epithets. Certainly, there are times when the "F" word expresses precisely what a writer means to convey. But we need literary critics who understand the distinction between necessary frankness and the adolescent desire to shock.

- Most important, we must delete the "F" word from our own lives. The most lasting shifts in social standards are those that begin at cocktail parties and around water coolers. We can wipe out the "F" word simply by refusing to use it ourselves and quietly but firmly objecting when others use it within earshot. The next time someone uses the "F" word in casual conversation, Judith Martin, better known as Miss Manners, suggests responding: "I'm not used to that sort of language." (If you can't say that line with a straight face, try: "We don't use that word anymore.")

8      Objecting to the "F" word isn't censorship. You can still use it as a punch line, if you like. You'll just risk the freezing silence and icy glares now reserved for white people who use the "N" word in public. Similarly, you're free to use it among your intimates, as a term of (in Sheidlower's words) "endearment, admiration, [or] derision." The rules of public civility have always included the naked-and-sweaty exemption. How you talk in the locker room or bedroom is up to you.

9    Ultimately, a social norm is nothing more, and nothing less, than the sum of individual decisions. In reconsidering the "F" word, you may prize your right to say it above your neighbor's right not to hear it. But personally, I'm swearing off.

(U.S. News and World Report, April 6, 1998, pp. 58–59)

Issue:  _____

_____

Opposing viewpoints and rationales:  _____

_____

_____

_____

_____

_____

_____

_____

_____

_____

## GO ELECTRONIC!

For additional readings, exercises, and Internet activities, visit our Website at:

### http://longman.awl.com/englishpages

If you need a user name and password, see your instructor.

**Take a Road Trip to** the American Southwest! Be sure to visit the Critical Thinking module in your Reading Road Trip CD-ROM for multimedia tutorials, exercises, and tests.

# Chapter Four

# BASIC PROBLEM SOLVING

## Chapter Outline

What Is a Problem?

What Is a Solution?

How Do You Solve Problems?

Problem Solving and Critical Thinking

A Basic Method for Personal Problem Solving

   *Step 1: Identifying the Problem*

   *Step 2: Gathering Information and Determining If the Problem Can Be Broken Down*

   *Step 3: Thinking About Possible Solutions and Weighing the Advantages and Disadvantages of Each*

   *Step 4: Choosing a Possible Solution*

   *Step 5: Checking Back on the Problem and the Possible Solution*

Applying the Method to a Typical Problem Situation

# THINK ABOUT IT!

What *specific* problem is being addressed on each of the signs in the photographs below? Discuss your answers with your classmates.

(1)

(2)

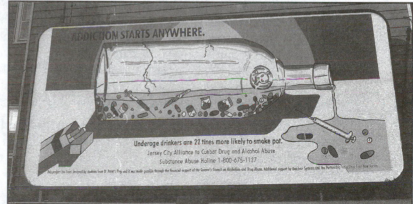

(3)

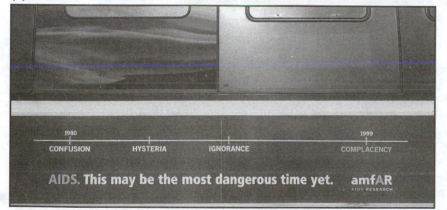

---

## Chapter Outcomes

After completing Chapter 4, you should be able to:
- Define *problem* and *solution*
- List and describe the five steps involved in the basic method for personal problem solving
- Apply the method to a typical problem situation
- Continue to find topics and central messages in passages on contemporary issues to determine what is at issue, distinguish among opposing viewpoints, and express personal viewpoints

---

## Problem-Solving Exercise

For purposes of giving you the opportunity to practice both your thinking and problem-solving skills together, an exercise like this will be presented at the beginning of all of the remaining chapters in this textbook. The exercises will deal with a variety of hypothetical situations.

### Hypothetical Situation

Suppose that you would really like to date a fellow student who is in one of your classes, but that person shows absolutely no interest in you. Every attempt that you make to start a conversation has failed. In fact, your glances and smiles are ignored with little or no eye contact in return. Nevertheless, you continue to be very attracted to your classmate and interested in starting a relationship because you think that this could be the "love of your life."

Think about this situation for a few moments, and then write a short essay in which you discuss how you would resolve it. Feel free to discuss your thoughts with your classmates.

## What Is a Problem?

"I have a problem!" "We have a problem!" "You have a problem!" "She has a problem!" "There is a problem!" How often have you heard statements like these? Probably quite often. Problems are a big part of life. As one student aptly put it, "To have problems is to be alive." In that we cannot avoid them, what exactly do we mean when we talk about problems?

The dictionary defines a **problem** as "a question, matter, situation, or person that is perplexing or difficult" or "any question or matter involving doubt, uncertainty, or difficulty." These definitions are fine, but they really do not describe what it feels like to have a problem. We all have a wide variety of problems as we go through life yet really never think about an accurate definition of what it is we are experiencing.

To put it in simple terms, there is a problem when we feel uncertain, dissatisfied, or upset with things, persons, or circumstances because they are either not doing what we think they should be doing or not going the way that we want or expected. Thus we experience such problems as an automobile that will not start, a good friend that has been ignoring us lately, a boss that does not value our work, and an inability to stop smoking even though we want to quit. We can try to ignore problems like these and hope that they disappear, but usually they will not go away by themselves. Furthermore, they remain *our* problems and do not necessarily become anyone else's. Hence we are often forced to search on our own for possible solutions.

## ACTIVITY 1

Make a confidential list of personal problems that you have experienced recently.

## What Is a Solution?

The dictionary defines a **solution** as "the act, method, or process of solving a problem" or "the act or process of explaining, settling, or disposing of a difficulty, problem, or doubt." In other words, solutions are the means by which we rid ourselves of problems. As a result, we no longer feel uncertain, dissatisfied, or upset with the things, persons, or circumstances that were either not doing what we thought they should be doing or not going the way that we wanted or expected.

The means that we choose to get us out of difficult situations will vary greatly. For instance, returning to the examples of the problems mentioned earlier:

The automobile that will not start can be fixed, junked, or traded in for another.

The good friend can be approached to talk about reasons for the change in behavior in order to come up with possible remedies, or the friendship can be ended if that is what is decided.

A discussion can be held with the boss to determine why our work is not appreciated, a higher-up can be consulted, or another job can be found.

Attempts can be made to stop smoking by wearing a nicotine patch, through the use of hypnosis, or by joining a support group.

There are always at least a few possible solutions to consider before deciding which one has the best chance of succeeding in eliminating a given problem.

## ACTIVITY 2

List the solutions that you came up with to solve the personal problems you noted in Activity 1.

## How Do You Solve Problems?

In Activities 1 and 2, you listed problems that you experienced recently and their solutions. Is there a specific approach that you follow consistently when trying to solve problems? For example, do you run down all the possible solutions before choosing one, or do you go from one solution to the next by using trial and error? What approach did your classmates and you use to resolve the hypothetical situation presented in the problem-solving exercise at the start of the chapter?

Your approach to problem solving may not be clear to you and easy to describe. In fact, it is possible that you do not turn consistently to a definite method at all. Perhaps you use past experiences to help you sort things out. Maybe there are instances in which you do nothing, hoping that problems will go away by themselves. In short, there are different ways of dealing with problems, and we all have our individual preferences. However, we do agree on one thing: We want our problems to disappear quickly.

## ACTIVITY 3

Take a few moments to think carefully about the lists of problems and solutions that you drafted for Activities 1 and 2. See if there are any similarities in how you arrived at the solutions. Did you use a specific approach, several different approaches, or no approach at all? Your instructor will ask for volunteers to discuss individual approaches to problem solving, without necessarily going into any details regarding the personal problems.

## Problem Solving and Critical Thinking

In Chapter 3, we noted that critical thinkers are careful and thoughtful in their approach to the world and that this enables them to make the most of limited time and helps them handle the complexities of life. That carefulness and thoughtfulness is particularly important when dealing with problems, because as a result of thinking critically, you place yourself in a stronger position to come up with the best solutions. In fact, all of the seven characteristics of critical thinking described in Chapter 3 are necessary ingredients for effective problem solving: flexibility, a clear purpose, organization, time and effort, asking questions and finding answers, research, and coming to logical conclusions.

## A Basic Method for Personal Problem Solving

The structured five-step approach to problem solving that follows may not eliminate all of your problems or guarantee perfect solutions, but it does provide a basic, simple, organized way of trying to deal with the things, persons, or circumstances that are disturbing you. As we proceed with the discussion, you may in fact discover that you are already using at least some of the steps as part of your approach to problems.

## Step 1: Identifying the Problem

Before attempting to solve a problem, you have to make sure that you know what the problem is. This may seem obvious, but sometimes it is difficult to uncover what exactly is bothering you. For example, you may be angry at a friend who owes you money not because of the money itself but because she has ignored your constant reminders. Thus the real problem involves the fact that she is apparently not paying attention to you or not living up to her part of the bargain. In short, you may feel that you are being treated with a lack of respect or that a trust has been broken.

When defining a problem, you must be careful to go beneath the surface, to be very specific and not confuse means (ways of accomplishing goals) with the ends (the goals themselves). In the example just mentioned, the repayment of the money by your friend could simply be a means that really does not get at the overall problem of being ignored or treated with a lack of respect.

As part of this step, it is important to realize that the problem is yours and not necessarily anyone else's. *You* are the one who is uncertain, dissatisfied, or upset, and *you* have to take action to make things better. If other persons are involved, they may be perfectly happy to keep things exactly as they are. In fact, others may not even be aware that you are feeling unhappy about something. To take our example, your friend may not realize that you are angry about the money situation, or if she is aware of it, she may be quite willing to let things continue as they are indefinitely. With regard to the situation described in the problem-solving exercise at the beginning of the chapter, the problem of the fellow student not showing any interest in you may be very clear from your vantage point, but your classmate probably sees no problem at all and thus feels no need to take any kind of action.

Even if other people are not involved in what is bothering you, you must still come to terms with the fact that the solution to the problem requires action on your part. You may seek the advice of others, but ultimately you are the one who must do something to eliminate a given problem. Problems usually do not disappear by themselves.

## Step 2: Gathering Information and Determining If the Problem Can Be Broken Down

After identifying the problem and defining it very specifically, you need to gather as much information about it as possible. Depending on the nature of the problem, this could involve doing research and include discussions with various people who are knowledgeable about it, particularly those who have actually caused the problem or perhaps been involved in it in some other way. They can be very helpful in providing clarification.

As mentioned in Chapter 3, you must take into account whether the information gathered is relevant, factual, and unbiased. This may involve determining the motivations or purposes of the sources that you are using. Once you have evaluated and given careful thought to the information that you have gathered, you are in a much better position to proceed toward a solution.

As part of this step, you should determine if the problem can be broken down into smaller problems that can be worked on one at a time. Frequently, the solving of those smaller problems can lead to the solution of the overall one. For instance, you may be dissatisfied because you have a C average in your psychology course, and you really want to get a higher grade. Perhaps this problem can be broken down by subdividing it into smaller ones that are more specific and perhaps more manageable, such as ineffective note taking, poor test taking, lack of comprehension of the textbook, or not enough time spent on preparation for the class. By subdividing your problem, you can then focus on the problem areas that need improving and come up with strategies or solutions for them, thereby, ideally, resolving the overall problem. For example, you can take a note-taking or test-taking workshop to learn new techniques, improve on your reading skills by getting tutorial help and practicing, or simply spend more hours on course preparation. Over time, any of these could lead to a better grade in the course, thereby solving the major overriding problem of an average that is below what you want.

Looking back at the problem-solving exercise at the beginning of the chapter, after doing some research and gathering information from friends or other students, perhaps you find that your classmate is ignoring you because of involvement in another relationship or simply as a result of shyness. These facts help you break the problem down so that you can then decide whether to continue your pursuit and, if that is the case, arrive at a strategy such as getting involved in the same outside activities as your classmate. That might allow you to get acquainted in a more casual, less threatening atmosphere. As a result of breaking the problem down, you are in a better position to resolve it.

### Step 3: Thinking About Possible Solutions and Weighing the Advantages and Disadvantages of Each

After you have identified the problem, defined it very specifically, gathered the facts, and determined if it can be broken down, you need to come up with a list of possible solutions. If the problem involves another person, as it often does, it is often advisable, if possible, to get that person involved at this stage even if he or she was already approached for information in Step 2. This is important for at least two reasons: First, the other party would likely supply additional information that is helpful when trying to devise a solution, and second, it is unrealistic to expect someone to cooperate with a given solution if the person had little or no part in the process through which it was decided on. In fact, as a result of not consulting with that other person, the proposed solution is likely to become no solution at all!

Obviously, to get another person involved, you have to communicate *your* specific definition of the problem—why *you* are uncertain, dissatisfied, or upset—and any of the information that you may have gathered concerning it. A *mutually* agreeable time has to be set up for that purpose. It is useless to try to discuss a problem if the other person is preoccupied with something else. In short, for this method to work, all concerned parties must be ready and willing to talk.

Whether you are working alone or with others, it is at this stage that a list of possible solutions is drawn up, indicating the advantages and disadvantages of each. It may help to write these out so that they can be properly analyzed and revised as you think them over. This is not something that can be rushed, so enough time should be set aside to review the options thoroughly. Remember, critical thinking is by definition a lengthy process, especially when trying to deal with problems.

Looking again at the problem-solving exercise at the beginning of this chapter, you might decide to take the direct approach and get your classmate involved at this stage by being totally honest about your interest in going out on a date. The big advantage of doing this is that it gets the matter out in the open and brings it to a head quickly. However, if the lack of interest has been a result of another relationship or shyness on the part of that student, then at this early stage, this possible solution could make matters even worse for you by scaring off your classmate. For that reason, it might be better in this particular situation for you to consider other possible solutions on your own.

Another possibility is to forget about the whole thing. This has the advantage of saving time and energy but the disadvantage of depriving yourself of the opportunity to date someone who is very appealing to you. Also, you may not want to accept defeat at this early stage without giving it your best shot.

One final possible solution was mentioned in Step 2, and it involves your finding out your classmate's interests so that you can participate in the same activities outside of class. The advantage of this possible solution is that you may get to know each other better, and your classmate may become friendlier after recognizing that you have similar interests. The major disadvantage involves your expenditure of much time and energy participating in activities that may not really excite you.

### Step 4: Choosing a Possible Solution

After enumerating the advantages and disadvantages of as many potential solutions as you can think of, you select the one with the greatest chance of succeeding. This is likely to be the solution with advantages that outweigh the disadvantages. If the problem involves other people, the solution must of course be arrived at after discussion with them. Everyone concerned must agree that this is the very strongest possible solution at the time, the one that has the best chance of solving the problem. Once a decision has been made—whether you make it alone or with others—it is crucial that the solution chosen be supported completely and that the reasons for its selection be kept in mind always.

Turning once again to the problem-solving exercise, at this point you would choose the possible solution that you think has the best chance of resolving the problem to your satisfaction—in other words, the one that will result in a date with your classmate. Of the three possible solutions discussed in

Step 3, the one that seems to be the strongest without having any important disadvantages involves your participation in some of the same outside activities as your classmate. As a result of this apparent interest in similar activities, the hope is that you would get to know each other, which in turn could lead ultimately to a date. The only real disadvantage is the time and energy you would use to participate in additional activities that you would not normally choose to do. Under the circumstances, that seems like a small price to pay, considering your strong desire to go out with your classmate.

### Step 5: Checking Back on the Problem and the Possible Solution

You never know for sure if the possible solution chosen is going to work until you try it. For that reason, both the problem and the proposed solution must be reconsidered after enough time has gone by to allow the latter a chance to succeed. Once again, when others are using this approach with you, it is necessary to discuss together the extent of the progress made. If the solution is not correcting the problem, either it has to be revised or another one has to be selected. This will necessitate that at least one or perhaps all of the previous steps be revisited.

Considering the problem-solving exercise one last time, if your involvement in those activities does seem to be changing your classmate's reaction to you, you will want to continue with your chosen solution, at least for a while longer. On the other hand, if there is no change after a reasonable period of time, you may want to turn to either of the remaining possible solutions that we discussed. For example, you could attempt the direct approach, thinking that at this point you have nothing to lose by being blunt, or decide instead to simply give up and go on with your life. Giving up the fight would not result in a date, but at least the problem has been eliminated to the extent that you can turn your attention perhaps in a more promising direction.

## Applying the Method to a Typical Problem Situation

Let us look at one more example of how the basic five-step problem-solving approach was used in a personal situation. Richard and Susan have been married for 30 years and have experienced all the ups and downs that go along with a marriage of that duration. In recent years, Richard has been getting up at 4 A.M. to run 5 miles for health reasons. After finishing the run and taking a shower, he would take clean clothes from the dresser drawers in the bedroom. Unfortunately, Richard got into the bad habit of leaving the drawers half-open, which was starting to upset Susan. Although she mentioned it to him on several occasions, Richard did not attach much importance to the matter and continued to leave the drawers open.

### Step 1: Identifying the Problem

Things went on like that for a while until Susan realized that this was her problem, because Richard was perfectly willing to continue what he was doing indefinitely. When she thought about it more thoroughly, it was not the half-open drawers per se that bothered her but the fact that Richard was apparently ignoring her. Furthermore, she saw no reason why she had to be the one to close them when Richard was perfectly capable of doing that for himself. After all, she was his wife, not his servant! The situation clearly required action on her part, or it would never be resolved to her satisfaction.

## Step 2: Gathering Information and Determining If the Problem Can Be Broken Down

Because of the nature of this problem, Susan did not have to do research or consult other people about it, but she thought it appropriate to ask Richard why he was leaving his dresser drawers half-open. As it turned out, it was a good thing that she bothered to ask him, because he explained that the drawers stick, and he was afraid that by forcing them closed, he would make too much noise, thereby disturbing her sleep at that early hour. By making Susan aware of his thoughtful motivations, Richard clarified the situation for her. Although she appreciated his consideration, Susan continued to feel dissatisfied about the drawers' being left open and Richard's apparent assumption that it is her responsibility to close them. At this stage, she could not think of any way to break down the problem, so Susan proceeded to the next step.

## Step 3: Thinking About Possible Solutions and Weighing the Advantages and Disadvantages of Each

Susan approached Richard on the matter, and they agreed to sit down and discuss it at length. She explained that even though she appreciated his consideration about not making too much noise in the morning, the fact that he continued to leave the dresser drawers half-open was upsetting to her. Susan was careful to emphasize that the real issues surrounding the problem involved his ignoring her constant complaints and his apparent belief that she was responsible for closing the drawers.

They agreed to consider the advantages and disadvantages of some possible solutions to the problem. One possible solution was for Richard not to run so early in the morning, but he explained that he could not fit a run in at any other time. Besides, he liked exercising at that early hour. For those two reasons, that proposed solution was unacceptable. Another possible solution was for Richard to force the drawers closed even if that made noise. Susan rejected that possibility because she was sure that it would disturb her sleep. A final possible solution involved Richard's taking out his clean clothing the night before so that he would not even have to go into the drawers in the early morning hours. Although this had the minor disadvantage of adding some clutter, it had the advantage of enabling Richard to adhere to his exercise schedule without disturbing Susan while at the same time eliminating her dissatisfaction with dresser drawers left half-open.

## Step 4: Choosing a Possible Solution

After much discussion, they agreed that the third possible solution was the most acceptable because its advantages far outweighed its disadvantages. Apparently, it would solve the problem without creating any serious new problems for either Susan or Richard. They decided to give it a try.

### Step 5: Checking Back on the Problem and the Possible Solution

Richard and Susan discussed both the problem and the agreed-on solution two weeks later after it became obvious that Richard was still leaving the drawers half-open at least some of the time. He explained that it was not intentional, but he was having a difficult time remembering to put his clothes out the night before. Because they had both thoroughly explored the other possible solutions and found them wanting, they decided to try to revise the one that they were currently using rather than going back through all the steps to find another solution. Susan certainly did not want to start nagging Richard about taking his clothes out the night before, so they came up with the idea that he would write a reminder to himself on the large message board in the kitchen until he got into the habit of gathering his clothes at night. With this slight adjustment, the problem was finally solved. Richard could run his heart out and have clean clothes while Susan slept in peace in a bedroom with closed dresser drawers.

Not all personal problems get resolved this easily, and of course there are much more serious ones that people face every day. Nevertheless, this example serves as a demonstration of how this basic method can be used to solve problems. The five-step approach is only one way of trying to deal with the complexities and difficulties of life that confront us all. When using it for the first several times, try to be very structured by following all of the steps in order. After a while, you will see that the steps can often be combined because the lines between them are not exact. In short, some flexibility is not only possible but desirable in most circumstances.

## ACTIVITY 4

With two of your classmates, decide on a hypothetical problem, and apply the basic method for personal problem solving to it. Make sure that you use all five steps to try to solve it.

## ACTIVITY 5

Using the five-step approach, try to come up with possible solutions in the following problem situations. In each case, write an essay explaining step by step how you went about arriving at the solution. As you go through the steps with Problem 1, make sure that you identify specifically what *you think* the problem is after considering the various possibilities. Because the problem is not explicitly stated in this particular situation, you will have to come to a logical conclusion about what is wrong.

## Problem 1

James is a good friend of yours, but lately he has been acting strange. His behavior is erratic, and his mood swings from silliness to depression to anger. He does not seem to care about college anymore, which has led to low grades and the strong possibility of his failing out. Furthermore, James has lost his part-time job because of continual tardiness and absenteeism. Consequently, he is often broke, yet he always seems so desperate for money. He no longer talks with you much and is hanging around with a different group of friends. You are very concerned about his well-being.

## Problem 2

In this situation, as in the first one, identify the problem by considering carefully the information presented and drawing a logical conclusion. Put yourself in Anita's place as you proceed through the five steps. After you have completed your essay, your instructor will pair you off with a classmate *of the opposite sex* so that you can exchange essays and discuss your work.

1   Andy passed Anita's locker every morning on his way to first period class. He began by just staring at her when he walked by. Then she noticed that when he passed her in the hallways or stairwells, he kept on looking.

2      At first, the 14-year-old thought Andy was flirting, but as she paid more attention to his gaze, she realized something didn't feel right. Anita felt uncomfortable with Andy's looks. It felt dirty, as if Andy had some kind of X-ray vision and was trying to see through her clothes to what was underneath.

3      One morning. Anita was standing by her locker. Suddenly, from behind she felt a guy's body pressed full front up against her. As she turned to see who it was, she felt Andy Porter's hand grabbing tightly on her behind and squeezing it. Anita spun around with anger to look Andy in the eye. He glared at her with that ugly intensity she had experienced in the past. A sly smile emerged on Andy's lips, and Anita could feel her insides buckling.

4      Thoughts of Andy and his behavior distracted Anita in school for the next two weeks. She had difficulty concentrating. She found herself drifting off in class, thinking of ways she could avoid Andy. Her Spanish teacher remarked about the decline in her class participation and the impact that would have on her "B" average. Mr. Marks, her history teacher, talked with Anita about her lateness to class and the negative consequences should she continue this behavior.

5      When Monday morning arrived, Anita once again experienced the gnawing knot of fear in her stomach as she approached the high school. Anita had shared her upset feelings with her close friends, but they just didn't understand. They thought she was lucky to have Andy Porter interested in her. He was one of the "hot" senior guys and having him "flirt" with her could only improve Anita's social status.

6      Anita could not relate to their opinion at all. She felt horrible. She lingered in the parking lot waiting for the first bell to ring. Although Anita realized she would be late again for Mr. Marks' class, she also knew that her tardiness would assure her of missing Andy in the hallway.

7      Anita finally entered the building and walked rapidly to her locker, head down, books held tightly against her chest. Suddenly overtaken by anger, she slammed her

locker closed. Anita's eyes began to well up with tears, and the knot in her stomach began throbbing.

*MJEA Review,* March 1995, pp. 28–29

## Problem 3

Last academic year, you took a science course in which a term paper was required. You spent much of the semester doing research and writing what turned out to be a 20-page paper. All of your effort and hard work paid off, because the instructor was very pleased with the result and gave you an A. During the summer, your best friend informed you that she will be taking the same course during the spring semester and expects to fulfill the term paper requirement by submitting your paper with her name on it. She believes strongly that favors like this one are what friends are for.

## Problem 4

Your mother is suffering from malignant cancer and is in pain much of the time. Day after day, she remains in a near-comatose state but occasionally does awaken for short periods. During those times, she is fairly lucid when you have conversations with her. Although her doctors refuse to predict when she will die, they do not offer much hope for her survival. Because she is having difficulty breathing and is steadily losing weight from her inability to eat, the hospital has asked for your permission to attach a ventilator and feeding tube. These measures could keep her alive indefinitely, although they probably would not improve her deteriorating condition. You have no brothers or sisters, and your father, who has Alzheimer's disease, is in a nursing home. Furthermore, your mother does not have a living will, nor has she ever made her wishes known.

## Problem 5

For the problem situation discussed in the following article, put yourself in the shoes of Anna and Camille as you go through the five steps.

## Love in the Time of AIDS

CAMILLE McCAUSLAND

1   Devin sat on her great-uncle Richard's lap, playfully poking her fingers into his face. Richard took it in good humor, gurgling happily at his niece. That is, until her tiny fingers came away from his nose covered with blood. Then he gripped her arms while nine-month-old Devin struggled to get her fingers into her mouth.

2   "Hey, I need help," Richard yelled, his voice edging toward hysteria. Ignoring the blood running from his nose, he continued holding Devin's arms. "Get me a goddamned rag," he screamed.

3   "It only took a minute," my friend Anna said, when she told me this story. "I got a rag and disinfectant and cleaned her up. Still, it's scary." And scary it is, because Richard has AIDS.

4   Anna's voice faded into the background as I thought of my four-year-old daughter, Lauren, playing with Richard. Along with her dresses, she wore scraped knees, skinned elbows, and various other scratched parts common to toddlers. And I

thought of AIDS. For a moment, I swear it was only a moment, I thought of not bringing Lauren around until Richard was gone.

5   Lauren's squeals, erupting as Richard chased her around the yard, interrupted my thoughts. I was reminded that Lauren's laugh always rings out when Richard is visiting. I remembered her tears that Richard dried when she fell off her bike. I remembered her joy when Richard hand-washed her muddied outfit so she could still wear it to school the next day. And I remembered Richard, old friend, almost family, loved one. Somehow, for that brief moment, I had forgotten Richard and what his life might be like without children in it.

6   Sanity returned as Richard came into focus: cropped hair, jeans, leather coat, T-shirt sleeves rolled just so. I thought of his annoyingly cheerful voice in the morning, his willingness to listen, and the advice bound to follow. And the laugh, never far away, making it impossible to stay mad at him for long.

7   Sanity returned, but it left behind a trace of fear so easily condemned in others.

8   I knew, standing in her yard, that Anna wouldn't be telling this story to any of her other friends. Most of Anna's friends were patiently awaiting Richard's departure to resume their visits. Just days before, I had told Anna what I thought of them. "The truth is," I had righteously claimed, "they prefer their ignorance to your company."

9   Now I am not so sure. Unlike Anna's other friends, I've known Richard for years. Diagnosed with ARC during a 1978 hepatitis B study and rediagnosed in the early '80s with HIV, Richard has lived with his disease for as long as I've known him. Years before my daughter was born, I was used to Richard's illness and had already lost other friends to AIDS. I've had plenty of time to adjust. And still I felt, that afternoon at Anna's, the fear that can erase a person simply by its presence. It was not born of ignorance.

10   The fact is that Anna's fear for her daughter was well founded. If Richard had been less careful of his disease than he was, Devin could have put blood carrying the HIV virus into her mouth. My own fear, while not as well founded, was certainly reasonable. For years I have equated that kind of fear with ignorance and bigotry. And then I felt it myself.

11   I wish I could say that my momentary lapse would not have been any longer even if I had not known Richard. But I am not so sure.

*New Age Journal,* October 1995, p. 176

## Problem 6

As you proceed through the five steps with the problem stated here, read the two articles that follow it as a way of gathering information for Step 2.

You are a single parent with a full-time job and an 8-year-old son. Thomas is a hyperactive child who is consistently disruptive in school. The teacher has called you several times about his behavior, and you have met with the principal regarding the matter. You have warned Thomas several times, but he just seems to be ignoring you. In fact, he has started to question your authority in other areas as well and constantly talks back to you. He refuses to follow your instructions, such as your request that he put his dirty clothes in the hamper. You have become angry and impatient with him, and you are starting to lose your temper. In fact, you have threatened to spank him on more than one occasion unless he changes his behavior.

# Spanking Is Becoming the New Don't

CLARE COLLINS

1   Have you ever spanked your child? Perhaps a better question is, would you admit to it?

2   "We spank as a last resort, when the children are either very rebellious or very rude," said Kellie Nienajadly, a Syracuse mother of a 2-year-old and a 3-year-old. "There's only so much reasoning you can do with children this young."

3   On the other hand, Rose Zagaja, who lives outside Hartford and has two children, ages 7 and 8, adamantly opposes spanking. "I think it's degrading and infuriating" to the child, she said.

4   Ms. Nienajadly's and Ms. Zagaja's differing views point to an emotional debate over a form of discipline that few of today's adults escaped as children. Is spanking merely a quick and decisive form of discipline, or is it to be shunned as ineffective, even cruel?

5   A recent Harris poll found that spanking is far from an uncommon parental act: 80 percent of the 1,250 adults surveyed said they had spanked their children. And 87 percent of those polled said that spanking is sometimes appropriate.

6   The telephone poll, conducted between Feb. 6 and 9, had a margin of error of plus or minus three percentage points. It did not ask respondents how frequently they spanked, nor did it define spanking.

7   The poll's findings run counter to the advice handed out by a growing number of child development experts who say spanking not only is ineffective but also breeds aggression.

8   "Spanking teaches kids that when someone is doing something you don't like and they won't stop doing it, you hit them," said Murray A. Straus, a professor of sociology at the University of New Hampshire in Durham and the author of *Beating the Devil out of Them: Corporal Punishment in American Families* (Lexington Books, 1994), which argues against spanking.

9   Dr. Straus said that studies he had conducted found that children who are frequently spanked are more likely to act aggressively toward their peers and may then go on to be aggressive teenagers and depressed, abusive adults.

10   According to Dr. Straus's definition, spanking refers to any kind of swatting or slapping "intended to cause a child physical pain but not injury, for purposes of correction or control."

11   "Spanking is very subjective," Dr. Straus said. "Some people think you have to hit hard enough to leave a mark that doesn't last very long. Others would define that as abuse." He would like to see corporal punishment outlawed in this country. Spanking is illegal in many European countries.

12   "Parents spank young children because they don't know what else to do," said Alvin Rosenfeld, a child psychiatrist in Manhattan and co-author of *The Art of the Obvious* with the late Bruno Bettelheim. "Spanking does work. It puts a stop on certain behaviors. But the question is, does it achieve what you're trying to achieve?"

13   Even the strongest of statements against physical punishment usually stop short of condemning parents who have spanked. "We're all human," said Linda S.

Budd, a St. Paul psychologist and the author of *Living with the Active Alert Child* (Parenting Press, 1993). "The fact that you lost it once and smacked your child doesn't mean you've ruined him for life. It does indicate a need to slow down and stop before you act."

14    Some experts condone spanking, usually on an extremely limited basis when the issue is safety or willful disobedience. One of the most widely quoted is James C. Dobson, the author of *The New Dare to Discipline* (Tyndale House Publishers, 1992).

15    Dr. Dobson, who writes that his theories are firmly rooted in Judeo-Christian beliefs, advocates spanking for children between the ages of 18 months and 10 years who directly challenge a parent's authority. He states in his book that spanking—which should be done in a calm, "I'm doing this for your own good" fashion— "is the shortest route to an attitude adjustment."

16    John Rosemond, a psychologist, supports spanking but suggests it be followed by consequences appropriate to the misbehavior. For instance, if a child leaves the house when told not to and is spanked, the parent should then take away television or other privileges. Mr. Rosemond says spanking can be far less detrimental than extreme verbal abuse or overly severe punishment.

17    More and more, though, spanking is emerging as the don't of the 1990's.

18    Dr. Budd said that she and most of her colleagues had given up on forms of therapy that change behaviors out of fear. She favors alternative methods of disciplining like time-outs and the taking away of privileges.

19    Although still a majority, the number of parents who spank is on the decline, said Dr. Straus, whose first study, in 1968, showed that "94 percent of the adult U.S. population believed it was sometimes necessary to give a child a spanking."

20    In a survey he conducted in 1994, Dr. Straus found that only 68 percent of the adult population—even fewer than in the Harris poll—believed in spanking. "In my line of work, that's actually an astronomical speed of social change," he said.

21    The Harris poll seems to support his contention that spanking is on the decline. It found that among the newest generation of parents—ages 18 to 24—31 percent said they had never spanked, compared with 19 percent among all parents. That trend is likely to continue, since the survey also found that most parents who were not spanked have not spanked their children.

22    Parents who do spank often feel they can't admit to it without risking harsh criticism. In a recent forum on Compuserve, the on-line service, only a handful of parents who responded to a query about spanking would speak for attribution. "It used to be parents who *didn't* spank were the ones who wouldn't be quoted," Dr. Straus said. "They were seen as the crackpots."

23    Spanking, Dr. Rosenfeld said, does nothing to further the long-term goal of successful parenting: raising happy, well-socialized adults. "Spanking deprives you of an opportunity to show your child that you have superior reasoning skills," he added.

24    "I came to the realization that spanking isn't all that effective," said Jebbie Crowe of Mystic, Conn., who is the mother of six children ages 14 to 28. She spanked her oldest children but changed her theory with her youngest. "My kids actually preferred it to other punishments because it was over quickly," she said. "It was an easy way out for both of us."

25      Dr. Budd says she believes that many parents spank because they have unrealistic expectations. "Often, parents just don't understand child development," she said. "They spank a child for being developmentally appropriate."

26      Dr. Budd said she had seen parents slap a toddler's hand because she kept pushing her plate off the highchair tray. "It would be better to just take the plate away," she said.

27      But what about matters of safety? "If a child is running in the street, it would be better to make her go inside for a while every time she does that, until she understands the limit," Dr. Budd said.

28      And rather than spanking a child who is rude or otherwise out of control, Dr. Rosenfeld recommended saying: "You must go to your room. I'm so disappointed in the way you're behaving. You are a good boy, a smart boy, but you are annoying me."

29      "In the long run," he added, "removing your approval works much better than spanking."

30      What if despite your best intentions, you do lose it? "Apologize," Dr. Budd said. "Own up to your mistake. That's parenting at its best."

*New York Times*, May 11, 1995

## Are You a Wimpy Parent?

DEBBIE KENT

1      "Time to put the toys away," my friend Julie called to her eight-year-old shortly after my family and I arrived at her house for dinner. Her son, Michael, had spread his Lego blocks all over the dining room table and was now off in another room playing video games. "C'mon, honey," she said. "Put your toys away so we can have dinner." Michael was in no rush to comply with his mother's request. "*You* put them away," he yelled back. "It was your idea to get out that stuff in the first place."

2      Julie was undaunted. "Michael, if you don't get up here this minute and clear these blocks off the table I'm going to put them away in my closet and you won't be able to play with them for a week!" Michael never did put his toys away. His mother did. And after dinner when he asked to play with them again, she let him. So much for consequences. "It's easier this way," Julie confessed. "Now he'll keep himself busy and we can talk without interruptions." Though I was grateful for the chance to have a quiet conversation with my friend, one word immediately came to mind: *Wimp*.

3      It takes one to know one, of course. I can't begin to count the times my husband and I have caved in on all kinds of issues. When my fourth-grader phones from school because he forgot, yet again, to take his homework, I drive it there myself despite our rule that taking homework to school is his responsibility, not mine. When my daughter faces a five-minute time-out in the dining room, she knows that with enough hysterical screaming I'll let her off after only a minute.

4      "Parents today find it hard to set boundaries for their children and even harder to apply consequences when those boundaries are violated," says Raymond Guarendi, PhD, a clinical psychologist in Canton, Ohio, and the author of *You're a Better Parent than You Think*. (Fireside/Simon & Schuster). "As a result," he says,

# Are You Tough Enough?

Do your kids know who's in charge or do they wheedle and whine their way out of just about anything? To test your wimpitude, give yourself a point for each statement that applies to you. Next add up your points and see how you score below.

1. I try to reason with my children when I give out consequences, but they use that as an opportunity for endless arguing—and they often win.
2. My children cannot readily answer this question: "What are the rules in this house about clothes left on the floor?"
3. I often feel powerless with my kids.
4. I have trouble seeing my child unhappy because he's been deprived of something. After all, that's why I earn money.
5. I just can't follow through with a consequence if it makes my child cry.
6. Sometimes I blow up after a problem has gone on too long and give out a punishment that's too harsh. Then I let my children off the restriction before the time is up.
7. My child has such a temper that many times I'll let things slide rather than risk her getting angry at me.
8. My children don't have to do a lot of chores. I believe childhood should be fun and carefree.
9. I try to gratify my child's every need. I don't want her to grow up thinking I don't love her.
10. I want to be my child's best friend, not act like some kind of boss.

## SCORING

**0–1 point:** Your kids know who's in charge—nearly all the time.

**2–4 points:** You're a relatively firm parent but you may want to work at being in control more consistently.

**5–7 points:** Your wimp factor is dangerously high. Sure, the kids will balk at first if you strengthen your resolve. But rest assured they will come around.

**8–10 points:** Your kids are running the show. Maybe it's time to demonstrate who's boss. They'll thank you for it—later.

Adapted from *Raising a Responsible Child: How Parents Can Avoid Overindulgent Behavior and Nurture Healthy Children* by Elizabeth Ellis, PhD (Birch Lane Press).

---

"many parents don't enjoy their kids as much as they could, thanks to constant discipline and authority problems."

5    How do you know if you're a wimpy parent? If your child regularly gets you to change your mind when you know you shouldn't, you fit the bill. (To test yourself, see "Are You Tough Enough?") When confronted by a crying, nagging, pouting, demanding or persistent youngster, pushover parents tend to buckle under in defeat and frustration. Those who manage to establish a few rules are often convinced to waive them. In a nutshell, wimpy parents just can't say no.

6    But if wimps are at one end of the spectrum, authoritarian parents are at the other. They tend to be rigid and have endless rules. They believe that children, like well-trained puppies, should obey on first command or be punished. Kids raised by authoritarian parents, research shows, often wind up unhappy, withdrawn and mistrustful of others.

7    What we ought to aim for, say the experts, is a middle ground—neither wimpy nor rigid but *authoritative*. Such parents are fair but firm, according to Elizabeth Ellis, PhD, a psychologist in private practice in Atlanta and the author of *Raising a Responsible Child: How Parents Can Avoid Overindulgent Behavior and Nurture Healthy Children* (Birch Lane Press). They determine the core rules central to the family's values and make sure their kids know these rules by heart. They set reasonable limits and consistently dole out fair consequences when those limits are violated.

8    Unlike parents who constantly stretch like Silly Putty to accommodate their children, authoritative parents are flexible only when they need to be. They choose

their battles wisely and know when to let things slide—a skill that seems to elude wimpy parents, who can never figure out when to yield and when to hold the line. "Authoritative parents are calm, self-assured and always in control without being controlling," says Ellis. "Even if it's easier to acquiesce and avoid conflicts, an authoritative parent knows that giving in when she shouldn't only makes for more problems in the long run."

### THE ROOTS OF WIMPINESS

9    Given the behavioral difficulties wimpiness can create, why do so many parents surrender their authority to their children? Here are the major factors:

### Convenience

10    When my friend allowed her son to play with his Lego toys despite an earlier threat to take them away, she bought herself an hour of relaxed conversation. In my case, driving my son's homework to school was easier than arguing with him on the phone about why I wouldn't do it.

### Fatigue

11    "When you've been working all day and you're tired, of course it's easier to let things go," says James Windell, a psychotherapist who works with children and adolescents in Bloomfield Hills, Michigan, and is the author of *8 Weeks to a Well-Behaved Child* (Macmillan). He's right. When I'm exhausted I'm much more likely to ignore transgressions such as a sneaked pudding snack right before dinner or an extra round of Wolfenstein when it's homework time.

### Guilt

12    It's hard to stick to your guns when you feel guilty about being preoccupied with work or spending too much time away from home. "Working brings women an enhanced sense of freedom and control over their lives, but for some women these gains have been purchased at a high price—guilt," says Ellis. "And guilt is one of the most common causes of overindulgence."

13    That's certainly the case for Jane Pierce, a travel industry sales manager in Memphis who takes eight to 10 business trips a year. "If I've been out of town, once I get home I'll wimp out in situations where I'd normally be firm," says Pierce, explaining that she'll let her three-year-old sleep in her bed or eat messy food on the couch, two no-nos in the Pierce household. "When I travel I feel so bad for being away that it makes me more vulnerable as a parent."

### Fear of Meltdown

14    Some parents wimp out because they simply can't bear to see their children express intense negative emotions. Whether it's because it tugs at the heartstrings, grates on the nerves or is frightening, the prospect of a whining, bawling or stomping child is enough to make some parents cave in. "Wimpy parents want harmony," says Ellis, "and they'll avoid direct confrontation in their effort to achieve it."

### Reaction to One's Upbringing

15 Perhaps the most compelling reason parents interviewed for this article gave for routinely acquiescing is rooted in childhood. Pushover parents frequently admit they've made a conscious effort to be different from their own parents who were, in effect, models of what *not* to be. "You see this reaction in people raised by rigid or abusive parents, or parents who were cold, critical, uninvolved," says Windell. "They'll say 'When I have kids, I won't have all those rules. I won't be so strict.' Or 'My kids will never doubt that I love them. I'll always treat them with respect.'"

16 But because these parents felt so oppressed and victimized as children, they tend to go overboard in making their youngsters feel like equals. They want to be a friend, not the adult in charge. They want to reason with their kids instead of laying out clear-cut rules. Above all, they want their children to *like* them.

17 Filled with only the best intentions, many of these parents tragically end up in parent/child relationships as troubled as the ones they grew up in.

18 "I never wanted to be the kind of mother I had, someone who never listened to anything I said, who never wanted to hear my side of the story," says Elaine Chaiken, a fund-raiser in New York City and mother of 12-year-old Michael. "I decided that I would be a different kind of mother. I wanted to hear my son's every thought. His feelings and opinions mattered as much as mine did."

19 But her method didn't work; her son only became spoiled and disobedient. From skipping homework to shirking chores, he usually got his way, while Chaiken felt manipulated and resentful. Even though she had set out to be the perfect parent, using her own mother as the antimodel, Chaiken wound up in an equally stressful relationship with her child.

20 Today Chaiken is working hard to turn the tide. With the help of a parent support group, she is learning how to be firm and is earning her son's respect in the process. She also realizes now that she did her son no favors by indulging him: He's struggling in school, thanks to so many missed homework assignments.

### HOW KIDS ARE HURT BY WIMPINESS

21 The effects of wimpy child-rearing go far beyond kids getting away with not picking up toys or gaining an extra hour of television-viewing. Youngsters who are raised without limits firmly in place often feel insecure and confused; it's hard for them to make sense of the world when they don't know what the boundaries are. Not only that, but it can be downright scary for a child to think he may be running the show; children feel safe and secure knowing their parents are in charge. Little wonder, then, that the kids of wimpy parents are often disruptive, unhappy and low in self-esteem. "The most miserable children I've seen," says clinical psychologist Guarendi, "are the ones whose parents don't set limits—or who don't stick to the ones they've set."

22 Children are hurt by wimpy parents in another way. Though many pushover parents like to think of themselves as warm and loving, ironically they are often the screamers, the naggers, the ones who find themselves blurting out things they quickly wish they hadn't said. "I think of myself as a loving parent, but sometimes I get really nasty," admits one Southwestern mother. "My son just keeps pushing until I lose it and say things like 'What have I done to deserve a kid like you?' or 'You

selfish brat!' Even as I'm saying those words I can't believe they're coming out of my mouth because I'm such a softy."

23    "When you can't control your child because you're trying to be sweet and gentle all the time, you're going to wind up screaming and threatening," notes Guarendi. "Your kids push you to that point. Authoritative parents, on the other hand, don't spend a lot of time yelling. They don't have to because their kids know *beyond a shadow of a doubt* that if they don't behave, consequences will be meted out firmly and calmly."

### FROM WIMP TO WINNER

24    As Chaiken has discovered, it is never too late to take your rightful place as head of the household. Consider these insights from the experts:

### Determine Your Family's Bottom-Line Rules

25    It's hard to hold the line when you don't know exactly where it is. The first step, then, is for you and your spouse to decide what's really important and come up with some rules based on those beliefs. For example, you might have rules about bedtime and the morning routine, completing homework and doing chores. Once you've determined these limits, communicate them clearly to your children to avoid "that's not what you said" conflicts. Some families find it helpful to write down their basic rules and post them on the refrigerator.

### Stand Firm

26    Before giving in, ask yourself: Am I letting my child do or have something I know she shouldn't? Am I compromising my values or violating an important guideline? If the answer is yes—even if you're tired or it seems more convenient or assuages your guilt to acquiesce—that's the time to draw on your reserves and stick to your guns. Remind yourself of the consequences of caving in: a less secure, more disobedient child. Remember that children raised with firm limits are more apt to become self-reliant, self-disciplined adults.

### Don't Fear Your Child's Intense Emotions

27    If you find yourself wimping out because you can't bear to see your child cry, scream or yell, tell yourself it's OK for kids to feel negative emotions. "It helps to remember that a child's anger and unhappiness will pass in a few minutes, but in that time they will have learned an important lesson about limits," says psychologist Ellis. "Children need to experience boundaries. The world is full of them and they might as well learn that early on."

### Expect Kids to Resist

28    "How can an eight-year-old understand your reasons for disciplining him?" asks Guarendi. "Some experts will tell you that if you're really psychologically savvy your child will say 'Thank you, Mother. These are tools that will help me in my socialization.' Nonsense. The only thing your child needs from you is loving rules, not lengthy explanations. It doesn't matter what he thinks of you when he's eight. What matters is what he thinks of you when he's 25. Children *will* understand some day. But not now."

### Avoid Compensating for Your Parents' Mistakes

29    "You need to separate lousy child-rearing from healthy limit-setting," says James Windell. "Rejecting limits because your parents were rigid, authoritarian or abusive is like throwing the baby out with the bathwater." Guarendi puts it this way: "If you want to compensate for your parents' harsh discipline, do it by offering loving discipline. When you put a child in her room, do it firmly; don't yell and scream as your parents might have done. Discipline is action, not words."

30    Inspired by the experts I interviewed for this article, I was eager to stake my claim as head of our household. My opportunity came last night, after my daughter had scattered her Polly Pocket dolls around the floor of the family room. I was bending to pick them up when I realized that was *her* job, not mine. "Lisi," I called out, "come pick up your dolls." She flashed one of her megawatt smiles and said in her sweetest voice, "Can you do it, Mama, please? I'm tired."

31    I knew if I persisted I'd be in for a battle, and I didn't have the energy for a fight. But tonight, I decided, would be different. "No, Lisi. You pick them up, and then we can have fun reading a bedtime story."

32    "But Mommmmmm," she whined.

33    "No arguments. Just pick them up now," I responded, surprising myself with a commanding tone that felt alien, yet oddly satisfying. Even more surprising was my daughter's reaction. She seemed almost happy to comply.

34    I could get used to this.

*Working Mother*, February 1996, pp. 28–33

## ACTIVITY 6

During the course of the semester, try to solve two of your personal problems by using the five-step approach. Toward the end of the semester, your instructor will ask each student to discuss how well the approach worked. *You will not be asked to reveal the details of your personal problems.*

## ACTIVITY 7

For the following passages on contemporary issues, use the same procedure as in Chapter 3. First, answer the comprehension questions, which ask you to state the topic and central message of each passage before proceeding to determine what is at issue, distinguish among opposing viewpoints, and express a personal viewpoint. In addition, you will be asked to compare your personal viewpoint before and after you have thoroughly considered the opposing viewpoints brought out in the passages. Finally, to show flexibility, you will write a few paragraphs *in support of the viewpoint that you do* not *favor.* Once again, keep in mind that some of the selections may deal with more than one issue.

You will then proceed to answer the thought and discussion questions before contributing any questions of your own that may come to mind while reading the passages. Feel free to discuss all of the questions with your classmates and together come up with possible answers.

# 1

## Why the Poor Become Poorer

1   In recent years the poor have gotten *poorer,* particularly in big cities. Again, there are two contrasting explanations. One is sociological, attributing the increase in poverty to forces beyond the control of the individual. Over the last 30 years the middle class has largely left the cities for the suburbs, taking much of the tax base with them. Many well-paying, low-skilled jobs in manufacturing industries have also left the cities. As a result, the poor who are left behind jobless have become poorer.

2   According to another explanation, a new version of the old "blame the victim" theory, poor people have gotten poorer because they do not want to work. There are still many jobs that match their skills, such as working in sweatshops, in fast-food restaurants, and as maids or servants. But poor people today consider these jobs demeaning and prefer to be on welfare instead, not seeing the first jobs as stepping-stones from which to advance. Such an attitude is said to scorn the traditional view that almost any honest job, however unpleasant, confers independence and therefore dignity, and is better than taking something for nothing (Mead, 1992).

Alex Thio, *Sociology,* p. 154

### Comprehension Questions

1. What is the topic of the passage?
2. What is the central message of the passage?
3. Determine what is at issue. What is your initial personal viewpoint?
4. Distinguish among opposing viewpoints, and provide the rationale for each.
5. Think carefully about the viewpoints. Express a personal viewpoint, and give the reasons why you favor it. Does it differ from your initial personal viewpoint? Why or why not?
6. Write a few paragraphs *in support of the viewpoint that you do* not *favor.*

### Thought and Discussion Questions

1. If you were the president of the United States, what policies would you recommend to help the poor? Why?
2. Can you think of any other instances in which the "blame the victim" theory has been used as an explanation?
3. List any questions that came to mind while you were reading this selection, and be prepared to discuss possible answers to them.

## 2

## The Future of the Family

1    The death of the family has been predicted for decades. In 1949 Carle Zimmerman concluded from his study on the family that "We must look upon the present confusion of family values as the beginning of violent breaking up of a system." By the "confusion of family values," Zimmerman (1949) referred to the threat that individualism presented to the tradition of paternalistic authority and filial duty. He assumed that individualism would eventually do the family in. Today, many continue to predict the demise of the family, pointing out as evidence the increases in divorce, out-of-wedlock births, cohabitation, and singlehood. But the family is alive and well. The flaw in the gloomy forecast is that it confuses change with breakdown.

2    Many of the traditional families—with husbands as breadwinners and wives as homemakers—have merely changed into two-career families, which still hang together as nuclear families rather than disintegrate.

3    Despite the increased number of people staying single, an overwhelming majority of those who now live alone will eventually marry. Although divorce rates have doubled over the last two decades, three out of four divorced people remarry, most doing so within three years of their marital breakup. Most of the young adults who live together before marriage will also marry eventually. It is true that single-parent families, especially those resulting from out-of-wedlock births, do pose problems for many mothers and their children. But the problems stem more from economic deprivation than from single parenthood as a new form of family.

4    Evidence from public opinion polls also points to the basic health of the U.S. family. Asked to describe their marriages in a recent national survey, 60 percent of married individuals said "very happy," 36 percent said "pretty happy," and only 3 percent said "not too happy" (NORC, 1994).

5    What will the U.S. family be like in the next 20 years? Most likely it will be much the same as it is today: manifesting *diversity* without destroying the basic family values. The continuing acceptance of these values comes through clearly in two studies. One shows that, compared with Europeans, people in the United States are more likely to tie the knot, to marry at an earlier age, and to have slightly larger families, despite their higher incidence of divorce and single-parent families (Sorrentino, 1990). Another study is longitudinal, having tracked changes in U.S. family attitudes and values from the 1960s to the 1980s. It shows that the vast majority of young people in the United States still value marriage, parenthood, and family life, and plan to marry, have children, and be successful in marriage (Thornton, 1989).

Alex Thio, *Sociology*, p. 357

## Comprehension Questions

1.  What is the topic of the passage?
2.  What is the central message of the passage?
3.  Determine what is at issue. What is your initial personal viewpoint?
4.  Distinguish among opposing viewpoints, and provide the rationale for each.

5. Think carefully about the viewpoints. Express a personal viewpoint, and give the reasons why you favor it. Does it differ from your initial personal viewpoint? Why or why not?

6. Write a few paragraphs *in support of the viewpoint that you do* not *favor.*

## Thought and Discussion Questions

1. In paragraph 3, the author writes: "It is true that single-parent families, especially those resulting from out-of-wedlock births, do pose problems for many mothers and their children. But the problems stem more from economic deprivation than from single parenthood as a new form of family." Do you agree? Why or why not? Do you see any additional problems other than economic deprivation?

2. In your view, what will the family be like in the future?

3. List any questions that came to mind while you were reading this selection, and be prepared to discuss possible answers to them.

## 3

## A True Crime Story
### *A Tragic Moment in New Mexico: Reflections on a Nation Gripped by Violence*

KEN ENGLADE AND TONY HILLERMAN

1   Five Points, in a seedy South Valley section of Albuquerque, New Mexico, is a convergence of five streets, littered parking lots, and shopping centers half boarded up. A still, deserted place at 5:40 A.M. on a dark, 20-degree Sunday morning, January 9, 1994.

2   A man in his 60s enters one of the lots on his morning exercise walk, heading south. A Buick Riviera recently stolen by its two teen occupants cruises slowly along Five Points Road, also heading south. The car circles the lone figure.

3   On its fourth drive-by one of the youths jumps from the car, holding a police baton, demands money and clubs the man several times. The flat crack of a pistol shot pierces the air and Eddie Torres, 16, falls back and runs to the car, which screeches away. Dean Kern, 63, blood running down his cheek, gun in hand, staggers off looking for assistance.

4   Kern is hailed as a hero. Torres—after he has been arrested in the hospital and later sent to prison for aggravated battery—is dubbed a thug. But the phenomenon—civilians arming themselves and teens doing hard time—appears less a solution than a desperate, even dangerous, stopgap.

5   That a 63-year-old would resort to such drastic action is supported by a recent *USA Today*/CNN/Gallup poll: Americans have finally had it with youthful offenders. Sixty percent of respondents said a teen convicted of murder should get the death penalty, and more than 20 states (among them New Mexico) have or are planning tough new juvenile laws.

6   Meanwhile, because of crime's prevalence many older people are avoiding activities they felt safe taking part in a few years ago. That may be why those 65 and

over are, according to 1992 Bureau of Justice statistics, the least likely victims of violent crimes or theft. But at what cost to their quality of life?

7    To many, like Dean Kern, locking themselves indoors is not an option, yet continuing their activities as before is risky at best. . . . Some believe their only recourse is to arm themselves when going out. Is this, truly, the final and only option?

8    Today Kern is cautious and fearful—he wouldn't allow his face to be photographed. Torres is bitter and vengeful—and could be released from prison as early as next year. Exactly what did happen between the two of them may unfortunately raise more questions than it can answer.

9    What *is* clear is that we generally perceive crime from one point of view, and from that perspective solutions may appear straightforward, even simple.

10    But if we examine this crime from all vantage points—and face its tempestuous issues of violence, an armed populace, and justice itself—it becomes evident that finding a viable solution is as complex as the moment of crime itself.

11    For 17 years Dean Kern has risen habitually at 4:30 and begun his day with a rigid physical regimen. In 1976 he suffered a severe heart attack. As part of his recovery program he took up jogging five miles a day around the perimeter of Kirtland Air Force Base where he used to work as manager of the telephone exchange.

12    After he retired in 1986, his knees could no longer take the hard pounding so he gave up jogging for swimming and walking. Three days a week he swam laps at a neighborhood pool; the other four days he walked a five-mile circle around his home, a tiny but comfortable bungalow he built in 1955 with a GI loan.

13    Shortly after 5:00 A.M. on Sunday, January 9, the tall, slim, sandy-haired man whose sartorial preferences run to jeans and Western-style snapfront shirts zipped up his padded down jacket, put on his hand-knit wool stocking cap (a gift from a neighbor grateful for a favor), and grabbed his .25 caliber Colt automatic from the top shelf of the hall closet.

14    Years earlier Kern had developed the habit of carrying the fist-sized pistol he originally bought for his wife but later appropriated for his own use because it was small and light—just the right size to fit in his jogging-suit pocket. He took it then to protect himself in case he encountered any of the stray or wild dogs that inhabited the desert around the Air Force base.

15    He continued to pack the weapon after he retired because part of the South Valley neighborhood where he walked in the mornings had become a campsite for the homeless, some of whom Kern feared might be strung out on drugs one day and come looking for a handy source of revenue.

16    About ten minutes into his route he came upon Five Points. "I was just walking, thinking, lining out my day." As he turned south on Sunset Road and was cutting through one of the parking lots, he suddenly became aware of a car.

17    "It came to the traffic signal but didn't want to wait for the light, so it cut across the lot I was in. Passed right in front of me, maybe 20 feet away." The windows were tinted and rolled up, but a street light showed two heads silhouetted in the front seat. The car exited the lot onto Sunset a block away. Then hesitated. Then turned around.

18    "When I saw it do that, I picked up my pace and crossed Sunset to get to the other side. It passed by again on the street."

19      The car backed up, turned around, and went by him a third time. "I knew then I was in big trouble." Kern was in front of a furniture store. Parked nearby was a truck with a FOR SALE sign on it. "They made a U-turn and came back toward me again. I walked behind the truck to keep it between me and them."

20      When he came around the truck, a figure had already jumped out of the car and was slapping a sidehandled police baton in his hand.

21      Kern took off running. But workmen had been repaving the parking lot and planting trees there, and sand and gravel covered the pavement. Kern slipped and almost tumbled to the ground. Before he could regain his balance the attacker was all over him.

22      He felt one sharp blow bounce off his skull, two thud against his arm. He tried to outrun his assailant but couldn't. The baton cracked him two more times on the head. Despite Kern's thick cap and heavy jacket, the blows "took the hide off my arm and broke the skin on my head. I told myself, 'If I go down, I'm in bad shape.'"

23      Not able to get away, still being pummeled and honestly fearing for his life, Kern finally yanked the pistol from his pocket. "I put it against him and pulled the trigger."

24      The effect was instantaneous. The attacker cried out and threw up his arms, staggered backward, then ran back to the car. Tires screaming, the car spun around and sped away.

25      Kern stood there, dazed, and said a silent prayer. If it hadn't been for the wool cap's cushioning effect, he probably would have been knocked unconscious or his brains might have been leaking onto the sidewalk. Staggering to a pay phone, he dialed 911.

26  A lot of people think ironing is women's work, but it always gave Eddie Torres considerable pleasure. While his friends may have laughed if they had seen him hunched over the ironing board on the night of January 8 in the small trailer he shared with his mother, Torres wasn't worried about his macho image. Holding up his party shirt to inspect, he smiled in self-congratulation. A *cholo* (street-wise young Latino male) had to be respected. Looking sharp definitely earned him respect.

27      Torres was really pumped up for the party he was going to that night. Throwing it was an "older" woman (she was 25, he 16) he had met shortly after arriving in New Mexico two months before.

28      The party was everything he'd hoped for—good music, good booze, good dope. Then something happened that would change Eddie Torres's already grim life for the worse. "I was talking with the girl when somebody told me to chill out with her and swung me around," he said. Torres was more surprised than hurt. That would've never happened in the Los Angeles suburb where he'd grown up. Known by his fellow cholos there as "Crook," he had a reputation as someone to be reckoned with. His gang, East Side Paramount, was one of the largest and most violent in all of Los Angeles County, and its name was tattooed across the back of his neck and shoulders in inch-tall letters.

29      "I hit him, and they took him to the bathroom. A few minutes later the girl told me to leave." Drunk and upset, he stormed outside with two homeboys: one called "Gino," and Kevin Baca, 17, whom he'd met a month before.

30  Torres wandered into a nearby parking lot—and his eyes locked onto a solitary Buick Riviera. Quicker than most people can adjust the rear-view mirror, Torres broke in, hot-wired it, and had the Riviera quietly rolling down the street.

31  Baca dropped Gino off at his home and Torres followed Baca's car to Baca's house. Then Baca jumped behind the wheel of the Buick and the pair went looking for some action, which meant a fight. "I was still hyper about what happened at the party. Then I see this *vato* (guy)."

32  There, in the middle of Five Points, a lone figure was crossing the parking lot. "The guy was acting crazy. He had his hand in his jacket like he had a gun, like he was tough or somethin'. I said, 'Go back towards him, I'll show him who's tough.'"

33  They drove back and passed real close, and the stranger stared at Torres. *"Me vió."* ("He looked at me.") Torres thought the man had challenged, or "mad-dogged," him. "I wanted to beat him up," Torres said.

34  They circled the man twice more ("I was scoping it out for cops") before Torres felt safe. Spotting a police baton under the seat of the Riviera, he grabbed it and lunged out of the Buick. "I don't know why I didn't just let him go," he said. "But I was drunk, I just wanted to get him." Blocking the man's path and smacking the polished wooden club, Torres barked, "Give me your money!"

35  "He tried to run away," Torres recalled later, "but I hit him [with the nightstick] on the head and shoulder."

36  All of a sudden the man straightened up and swung toward *him*. "I heard something real loud," Torres said. "There wasn't much pain, but I got dizzy. I felt something inside me."

37  He lurched back to the car and screamed at Baca to take him home. "I couldn't breathe. I said to myself, 'I'm going to die.'"

38  They picked up his mother at home and minutes later found a pay phone. As Torres waited, bleeding and shivering, his mother dialed 911.

39  The youngest of four gang-member brothers, Torres's indoctrination into their world started early on. He had his first serious brush with authorities—for breaking into a car—at eight. He went on to pile up arrests for burglary, auto theft, narcotics violations, and assault and battery ("I used to look for innocent-looking kids coming out of school and just beat 'em up. I knew it wasn't right, but it was what I liked to do").

40  There was a time, Torres says, when things might have turned out differently. For a while his father, Eddie Sr., a butcher, was able to keep his brothers clean and straight. "He was real strict, man, the way he grew my brothers up. He kept them in the right direction. Couldn't cuss, couldn't go out, nothin'."

41  And then, as in so many families, the arguments between their parents began, escalated, then eventually forced their mother, Dorie, to leave and take the boys. "After that, Mom would say the same things to us, but we wouldn't listen. That's when I started kicking back with my brothers and homeboys. I saw the things they were doing and thought it was all right."

42  Hoping to get her youngest son away from his brothers' and gang's influence and into a more stable environment, Dorie took Eddie Jr. to Albuquerque, where her sister lived.

43   Nine days after the shooting, while Torres was recuperating in the hospital, police arrested him on charges of aggravated battery with a deadly weapon, armed robbery, and conspiracy to commit armed robbery. Nancy Neary, the assistant district attorney, saw Torres as a classic sociopath. "Empathy is not a concept this kid has within himself," she said. "He was totally without remorse. He would kill Mr. Kern or anyone else the same way I'd swat a fly."

44      Feeling the county judges were lenient with juveniles and would never give him the maximum on all three counts, Neary made the boy an offer: Plead guilty to aggravated battery and she'd drop the other charges. Torres agreed. In New Mexico, victims have the right to be heard. So Kern drafted a letter that read, in part: "I feel I need to take this opportunity . . . to plead with you to keep this man away from us for as long as the law permits. . . . There is no way [law-enforcement officials] can prevent these types of crimes or protect us from these kinds of preditors [*sic*]. Only you can do that, Judge. Please put this young man away for as long as you can. Please keep him off us."

45      The Children's Court Judge Tommy E. Jewell has a reputation as a "liberal" jurist, always willing to give an offender a break if he believes the person can be rehabilitated. When Torres's case showed up on his calendar, however, the youth's record painted a grim picture. Jewell later stated that Torres was "a threat to society" and he was "pessimistic" that the young man would be changed by the experience.

46      The judge sentenced Torres to three years in prison. In a very few specified cases, courts can also add time to a sentence when there are "aggravating circumstances" for such things as the age of the victim. Because Kern was 63, Jewell tacked an extra year on to Torres's sentence. It was remarkably stiff considering the judge's reputation. When asked if such incarceration may only teach Torres to be a better criminal, Jewell replied, "A new and improved Eddie Torres in the crime-producing world is really a frightening thought." (As for Kevin Baca, he pleaded guilty to conspiracy to commit armed robbery and was eventually sentenced to two years' probation.)

47      According to Janet Velazquez, Torres's attorney, incarceration may actually be the young man's best—and last—chance to turn his life around. She noted that Torres tended to do well in structured environments, such as juvenile camps, where he got A's and B's. To date he's finished 10th grade, an anomaly in the gang world. "In school he's bright," she said. "But take him out of that structure . . ."

48   The Southern New Mexico Correctional Facility is a medium-security prison built to house 480 men (and holding 570 at the time of this interview). It is surrounded not by walls but by two tall chain-link fences, one topped, the other covered, with razor wire. It sits low and half-hidden amid the pale desert scrub just off Interstate 10, a few miles west of Las Cruces.

49      On the day of his interview for this article, Eddie Torres strolls into the visitor's room in a lazy, liquid cholo gait. His eyes, sparkling in the bright overhead lights, reflect a detached, but shrewd, awareness. At 5-foot-8 and 140 pounds, he isn't physically threatening, but he certainly looks bigger and older than the average 16-year-old. He speaks quietly, with control—uncommonly mature for a youth his

age—as he recalls the incident that had brought him there. "I was drunk," he says. "I knew I shouldn't have gone out there. I didn't want to rob him."

50    *Did you know at the time you were beating a 63-year-old?*

51    "I saw him, but I didn't know he was an older man. I regretted that *big time* afterwards. I knew how I'd feel if it had been my uncle or somebody."

52    *Are you bitter about being sent to prison?*

53    Torres slowly pulls his shirttail out and lifts it, exposing a long, ugly scar running from his navel to his sternum. "That *vato* didn't have to shoot me. He could've just pointed the gun at me or fired it in the air—I would've run away. I only wanted to beat him up. I wasn't trying to kill him."

54    *Do you understand why he felt he had to shoot you?*

55    "He wasn't wrong to shoot me, but he didn't have to tell the police. I wouldn't have said nothing. I told 'em it was a drive-by."

56    *Mr. Kern has become a local hero for how he defended himself. Do you think he's a hero?*

57    "F—no, he's no hero! Shooting someone doesn't make anyone a hero. A lot of old people think if they go out and [shoot criminals], they're protecting society. *That pissed me off.* My brothers got real mad after they heard about that; they wanted to come out here and get the old guy."

58    *If you stay out of trouble when you get out, what do you want to do with the rest of your life?*

59    "Get a good job, a house, a lady and kids. Maybe my own business. Construction business. I'd like to build houses.

60    "But I'll probably be back [in prison] for something else."

61    *What would you do if you ran into Mr. Kern again?*

62    [*Softly*] "I'll probably kill him if I ever see him again."

63    Today, nearly a year after the crime, Dean Kern still worries about Torres's street philosophy of revenge, called *venganza* in the barrios. But what disturbs him more is the specter of the next "Torres" lurking in the early morning mist where he walks. "Suppose it happens again?" he asks. "Are people going to say, 'Ol' Dean must be out there trolling for these guys'?"

64    Kern poses the question but never answers it. Although carrying a concealed weapon in Albuquerque can be punishable by 90 days in jail and a fine, little was said about it during the proceedings. Defense attorney Velazquez, although asserting that carrying a concealed weapon "is a crime in my book," opted not to pursue the issue. "That was up to the prosecutor and D.A. By ignoring it, though, [they put] a stamp of approval on vigilante behavior. My concern is that *that* will be the message."

65    Prosecutor Neary shrugs off the violation. "Although Mr. Kern technically did something illegal, as far as I'm concerned he did nothing wrong. He didn't shoot immediately—he fired only after he'd been hit several times and couldn't get away. If it had been my mother-in-law, those blows would have destroyed her."

66    For his part, Kern admits he has changed his pre-dawn route—"I don't walk where cars go anymore"—but not his means of self-protection: He still carries his pistol.

67   To some experts and sociologists, youths like Eddie Torres seem destined to follow the criminal path on which—to whatever extent—family, culture or society has pushed them. They seem to have refused, or been unable, to resist their fate.

68      The fate of victims like Dean Kern, however, seems changed forever. After the incident he received more than 50 telephone calls and numerous letters applauding his action. "I didn't get one negative comment," he says.

69      One woman wrote saying that he was her hero. "But," he adds with a chuckle, "she also offered some advice: 'Practice, man, practice!'"

70      It's easy to be so sure, so brazen, from a comfortable distance. But ask Kern today how he feels about his entrance into the world of *venganza:* "I have no remorse; I was defending myself. But I'm worried about his friends. He knows what I look like—and that's enough."

*Modern Maturity,* January-February 1995, pp. 22–31

## Comprehension Questions

1. What is the topic of the passage?
2. What is the central message of the passage?
3. Determine what is at issue. What is your initial personal viewpoint?
4. Distinguish among opposing viewpoints, and provide the rationale for each.
5. Think carefully about the viewpoints. Express a personal viewpoint, and give the reasons why you favor it. Does it differ from your initial personal viewpoint? Why or why not?
6. Write a few paragraphs *in support of the viewpoint that you do* not *favor.*

## Vocabulary Question

Use the context to define the following words: *cholo, vato, me vió,* mad-dogged, *venganza.*

## Thought and Discussion Questions

1. If you were Eddie Torres, what would you have done in a similar situation? (Keep in mind his background and what happened at the party.) Why?
2. If you were Dean Kern, what would you have done in a similar situation? Why?
3. Is there any hope now for Eddie Torres? Why or why not?
4. What can we do as a society to prevent conflicts like the one in this article from occurring?
5. List any questions that came to mind while you were reading this selection, and be prepared to discuss possible answers to them.

## 4

## The Politics of Paternity Leave
*Why Government Isn't Always the Problem*

TOM MCMAKIN

1    Valerie's asleep now, having snacked most of the morning, fussed and finally closed the brightest blue eyes I've ever seen. Quiet moments like these are rare when you are taking care of a 4-month-old. When she sleeps, it's time for me to mix more formula, wipe the counter, call about life insurance and then, if time allows, break open the laptop and sit down to write for a few minutes. Welcome to paternity leave, a spicy stew of belches and smiles, DPT shots, heavy warm diapers and the odd moment of reflection.

2    The idea that fathers should take time off from work to be with their newborn children is a relatively new one, but it's an idea that is long overdue. Two years ago, time at home with Valerie would not have been possible. But thanks to the Family and Medical Leave Act of 1993, here I am changing my daughter's diapers and enjoying her first gurgles and giggles. Who would have thought it? A bunch of faraway lawmakers passed legislation, and it profoundly affected my life. Their law, PL103-3, requires that companies with more than 25 employees allow them to take up to 12 weeks of uncompensated time off to care for their children. Because of this legislation my life is richer.

3    Much richer. This bundle of sweet smells I call my daughter has given me the gift of new sight. A trip to the supermarket used to be a dreaded errand; now it is the highlight of my week. Valerie has taught me to look beyond our store's confusion of brands and hype and focus on the colors, shapes and happy chatter that make each visit a carnival of sight and sound. We squeal at the celery, spit heartily at the dairy rack and shrink in terror at the sight of the frozen turkeys. The moving counter by the cash register is a revelation.

4    A walk downtown has been similarly transformed. Everyone loves a baby. And we love them back for it. People I've never spoken with, but have passed on the street many times before, smile and ask how old she is. To be a baby, I've learned, is to live in a friendly, welcoming world. But it's not just her world; it's mine too. Because of my time home with Valerie, I'm also much more understanding of children and parents. I rush to help a mom with a stubborn car door or a dad whose youngest is on the verge of straying. I smile at mischievous kids, happy to see them speeding off in this direction or that, ruining their parents' best-laid plans.

5    I have paternity leave to thank for teaching me these and other lessons (never dump formula in cold water—it doesn't mix). I am grateful to my wife and to my employer for encouraging me in my decision to stay home and am grateful to a government that made taking this time possible.

6    Sadly, when Valerie and I walk downtown and stop at the local coffee shop, we hear people talking about government in two ways, neither of them very good. They say that government is either ineffective or misguided, with most agreeing that it is

both. It is not hard to understand why the ranchers and business people clustered around the small Formica tables think this way. In our state of Montana, the public owns 39 percent of all land. That means there are legions of federal, state and local managers running around doing surveys, convening task forces, forming policy and interpreting regulations. With so much at stake and with so many bureaucrats in action, it is inevitable that these well-intentioned civil servants make mistakes. When they do, the mistakes are widely discussed and greatly criticized.

7    That's a shame. Somewhere in the rush to criticize, we have failed to see the forest for the trees. While Bozo the Clown may run a public agency or two, I cannot escape the fact that my sitting here today trading coos with my daughter is a salute to the possibility inherent in public action. On Feb. 5, 1993, our representatives in Washington decided it was important that families be allowed to spend time together when they most needed it and, more important, that wage earners should not lose their jobs while caring for a dying mother or recuperating from a serious operation or spending time with a newborn. In my book, that bad boy of American culture, Congress, did something right when it passed this law.

8    The citizenry of this country has expanding and contracting tastes in what it wants its government to do, not unlike the members of the credit union to which I belong. One year we may ask the credit union's management to make sweeping changes, add more services and expand the types of loans it is willing to make. And then that energy runs its course and the membership elects a new board or hires a new manager to trim costs and services. When we ask the credit union to add services, we are not suggesting that credit unions ought to take over the world. By the same token, when we ask it to cut services, we are not saying credit unions are worthless. It's more like riding a horse up a hill: you might go to the left for a while and then to the right, but, even with the zigs and zags, you are still headed in one direction—toward the top.

9    In this current season of scaling back government—both Republicans and Democrats seem to agree that this is a good thing these days—my hope is we remember that government is capable of doing things and doing them well. I work 40 hours a week because my great-grandfather voted for a reform Congress at the end of the last century. My savings at the credit union are insured because my grandmother voted for FDR. My dad put Eisenhower and a forward-looking Congress in place in the late '50s. As a result, it takes me one hour to travel to Butte and not two, on an interstate-highway system. Government isn't bad in and of itself. It isn't some malevolent Beltway-girdled ogre perched on the banks of the Potomac. It is, rather, an expression of our collective will.

10    But wait. Valerie is stirring. Little wet slimy hands await. I need to warm a bottle, find a fresh diaper, pad upstairs and quietly make sure she is serious about ending this nap, and finally peek over the side of the crib and drink in that bright, beautiful smile that never fails to remind me why I so like being a dad at home.

*Newsweek,* September 25, 1995, p. 26

## Comprehension Questions

1. What is the topic of the passage?
2. What is the central message of the passage?

3. Determine what is at issue. What is your initial personal viewpoint?

4. Distinguish among opposing viewpoints, and provide the rationale for each.

5. Think carefully about the viewpoints. Express a personal viewpoint, and give the reasons why you favor it. Does it differ from your initial personal viewpoint? Why or why not?

6. Write a few paragraphs *in support of the viewpoint that you do* not *favor.*

## Thought and Discussion Questions

1. Should fathers take time off from work to be with their newborn children? Why or why not?

2. Do you agree with the statement "To be a baby . . . is to live in a friendly, welcoming world"? Why or why not?

3. In your view, is the author expressing happiness, sadness, or both? Why?

4. List any questions that came to mind while you were reading this selection, and be prepared to discuss possible answers to them.

## 5

## Why Women Make Better Cops

Tessa De Carlo

1   It's Friday night in Madison, Wisconsin, and officers from the police department's Blue Blanket team—a special drug, gang and gun squad—are cruising past an East Side low-income neighborhood, a site they've often had occasion to visit. Tonight the mood in the neighborhood, whose residents are mostly African American, is tense; a rumored party hasn't materialized and about 50 young people are now hanging around waiting for something to happen.

2       Just then an emergency call comes in, reporting that a young man has beaten up his girlfriend. As the officers, led by Sergeant Tony Peterson and Detective Marion Morgan, approach the crowd to see if they can find him, several kids cry out, "Marion! Marion!" She is the only black officer in the group, and the young people's voices are somewhere between affectionate and mocking.

3       The police approach a teenager who partly fits the reported batterer's description: young, black male; tall; denim jacket. But the man, who's apparently been drinking, isn't in any mood to cooperate. "I want to talk to my lawyer," he yells. "You're just doing this because I'm black!"

4       "We can do this the easy way, but now we're going to have to do it this way," says Peterson, as he and another officer deftly snap the man into handcuffs and lead him over to a police car to pat him down, check for outstanding warrants and ask a few questions. It turns out he isn't the man they're looking for, and after a few minutes he's released.

5       But in the meantime, one of his friends, another teenager in a black-and-red University of Wisconsin team jacket, has begun complaining loudly about the police,

and a group of younger kids gathers around. Morgan puts her hand on the arm of the older boy, who towers over her. She's arrested him before on various charges, none of them very serious.

6    "You know we're here so everyone can live peacefully and safely," she tells him in a firm but not angry voice. "If *you* called in a complaint, you'd want us to come and deal with it. It doesn't help when someone like you, with standing in the neighborhood, cops an attitude and gets all these shorties going"—she nods toward the kids standing around. "I'm just telling you how it felt to me, and it felt like you were disrespecting me."

7    "I wouldn't disrespect you, you know that," the young man says, abashed.

8    She pats him on the arm, and he shrugs, looking a little embarrassed.

9    "We're not the enemy," she says.

10    "I know that," he answers.

## A BETTER KIND OF COP?

11    According to many law enforcement officials, stories like this one show why women in police work aren't just as good as men—they're sometimes better.

12    "There's such an obvious need for more women in this business," says Nick Pastore, chief of police in New Haven, Connecticut. In his view, when it comes to the skills that really count, "women are much more effective."

13    America celebrates strong-arm police officers in movies and TV shows, but in real life, too much macho causes more problems than it solves. When police departments are permeated by "good old boy" attitudes and filled with what Pastore calls "young, male, suburban adventure-seekers eager to bash heads," they tend to confuse the war on crime with a war on minorities, women, gays and the rest of the community they're supposed to be serving.

14    Until two decades ago, a woman's only entrée into the hypermasculine world of policing was to become a clerk, or a "policewoman" restricted to working with juveniles. The passage of the Equal Employment Opportunity Act of 1972 prompted a flood of discrimination lawsuits and court orders that forced the stationhouse doors open—but not very far. Women still make up less than ten percent of the nation's police officers and about three percent of police supervisors.

15    That's a loss not only for women who want to be police officers but for everyone who wants safer communities and better policing. Because women—precisely because they don't conform to the locker-room mores of traditional law enforcement—often make better cops.

16    "Women officers are less authoritarian and use force less often than their male counterparts. They're better at defusing potentially violent confrontations, possess better communication skills and respond more effectively to incidents of violence against women," said Katherine Spillar, national coordinator for the Feminist Majority Foundation, in testimony before a commission investigating police brutality in Los Angeles.

17    Many police veterans agree. "Women officers are no less tough or strong or capable of dealing with the world of the streets," says Hubert Williams, president of the Police Foundation and former chief of police in Newark, New Jersey. "But on the whole they're better listeners, with a special knowledge of families and children,

able to engage effectively and develop working relationships. That's why they're so valuable to law enforcement."

## WOMEN FIGHTING CRIMES AGAINST WOMEN

18   The woman had called police in the Louisiana town several times before. Her marriage had fallen apart but her husband refused to leave. He hit her and threatened her and sabotaged her car so that she needed him to drive her to and from her job.

19   "This man beats me up, and the officers won't do anything," the woman sobbed when the police arrived yet again.

20   But this time the two officers who answered the call were women. "We told him, 'Look, whatever it was you did to her car, you get out there now and undo it,'" one of the officers recalls. "He was angry. If we'd been men, he would have fought. But I told him, 'I'm just a little-bitty person, so if you come at me, I'm not going to fight—I'll just shoot.'' The man decided to cooperate.

21   The officers wouldn't leave until he replaced the distributor cap on his wife's car. "Then we told him that if she ever called us again, we'd come back and kick his butt," the officer says.

22   The woman didn't call again, but a few months later one of the women officers ran into her on the street. Her husband had agreed to a divorce and moved out of state.

23   Why hadn't any of the other police who'd visited this woman helped her out? "This is an old-fashioned, good-old-boy place," says the Louisiana cop, who doesn't want her name used. "When the male officers go on a domestic, I hear them saying things like, 'The bitch don't keep the house clean—you *ought* to be whuppin' her ass.'"

24   Domestic violence is one of the most pressing issues in police work. A 1993 federal inquiry estimated that more than 21,000 domestic assaults, rapes and murders are reported to police each week. By some estimates, "family disturbances" account for more calls received by police each year than any other kind of crime.

25   But traditional male-dominated police departments take these calls less seriously than robberies and other crimes involving strangers. A study conducted by the Police Foundation cited police failure to make arrests in family violence cases as one of the most serious aspects of the nation's domestic violence problem.

26   One reason for poor police performance in this area may be that male officers are particularly prone to domestic violence themselves, and therefore resist treating it as a serious crime. "There's a lot of domestic violence being committed by officers," says a female cop from a large Southeastern city. "It's that macho image, saying, 'I'm the authority and I'm above the law.'"

27   Research bears her out. One 1991 study found that while violence—ranging from slapping to punching to stabbing—is an element in 16 percent of U.S. marriages, the rate among a sample of 425 police officers, 90 percent of them male, was as high as 41 percent.

28   A third study—concerning 72 male officers in the Midwest—bolstered a suspicion long held by observers of law enforcement: that the more violent an officer is at home, the more prejudiced he is against victims of domestic violence and the less likely he is to make arrests in such cases.

29      Arrest rates are influenced by many factors, including local laws and whether prosecutors are willing to bring cases to trial. But officers' attitudes do play a role. "Studies in the past 20 years show that women officers take domestic violence calls more seriously and treat it more seriously as a crime," says Katherine Spillar, who's now on the advisory board of the National Center for Women and Policing.

30      New Haven's Pastore noticed a difference in this area after he fast-tracked eight women into detective positions in his department. "These women have really concentrated on abuse against women and sexual assault," he says—crimes Pastore believes were given less focus when the system was all male. "Twice in the past year the same thing has happened: Friends of the accused have come to me and said, 'Since when do you have women doing these cases? They're so tenacious. . . . Chief, can you take some heat off?' Their performance in this area alone is worth the presence of women on the force."

## ARE WOMEN COPS TOUGH ENOUGH?

31      The belief that women are less violent—and therefore less able to stand up to force or dish it out when necessary—used to be a prime argument for a male-only police force. But once affirmative action opened policing to women, extensive research confirmed that although women are, in general, smaller and less powerful than men, especially in terms of upper-body strength, they are just as capable of policing as men.

32      For example, a 1987 study of 3,701 violent conflicts between police and citizens in New York City, including both assaults and gunplay, confirmed that female cops were just as brave as males. "Female officers, whether with a partner or alone, are more than willing to get involved in violent confrontations apparently without any fear of injury or death," the study concluded.

33      Take the case of San Francisco inspector Holly Pera, who before joining the force was a member of the San Francisco Ballet and then a teacher. A specialist in cases involving children, Pera teamed up with Inspector Kelly Carroll, a six-foot-one-inch male, to arrest a recently released ex-con who had reportedly robbed and sodomized several boys. High on crack cocaine, the man resisted arrest, attacking both officers. During the struggle, the suspect managed to get hold of Carroll's gun and was about to shoot him from a few feet away when Pera stepped between them. She and the ex-con both fired: His shots missed and hers hit him in the chest. He died of his wounds at the hospital. "I have never witnessed a single more courageous act," says Carroll. "There's no doubt she saved my life."

34      But the same research that showed women cops are as tough as their male colleagues discovered something equally important: Women officers *misuse* violence far less. In another study of New York City cops, for example, this one in 1989, researchers found that although female officers were involved in just as many violent confrontations as male officers, they received fewer civilian complaints, were involved in fewer shootings and used deadly force less often.

35      Women officers are frequently more effective in volatile situations because they focus on cooling everyone down, rather than asserting their own authority.

36      "I'm not going to get fired up because they call me a whore or a dyke," says a female trooper from Connecticut. "I just say, 'Forgive me, I have to be here. Now

give me your side of the story.' Whereas a lot of male officers are going to say, 'What did you call me?' and—whoomp!—you've got another fight going."

37    "We tell officers that when you lose your temper, *you* are in danger," says Sheriff Jackie Barrett of Fulton County, Georgia. Staying cool and sidestepping unnecessary physical confrontations, she says, are "a function of maturity and of strength—*inner* strength."

38    Often courage can mean *not* using force and still getting results. In the Midwest two officers, a woman and a man, were called to a bar late at night by two frightened female bartenders. A nearby club had just let out, and although it was closing time at the bar, too, suddenly the bartenders were faced with a crowd of more than 200 people. With most of them drunk and refusing to leave, the scene was turning ugly.

39    The woman officer went into the bar and didn't notice until too late that the male officer had stayed outside. But there was no turning back. Using what she calls her mom voice ("You may not even like your mom, but you obey her"), she told the barful of rowdies, "It's time for you to go home now." Anyone who didn't leave would immediately be arrested, she told the crowd. "There are five police cars outside"—as far as she knew, there were only two, including hers—"and the doors will be locked and you'll all be processed right here."

40    "I got some lip," she recalls, "but everybody left. There were no fights and I didn't have to arrest a single person."

41    When she went outside she found four male officers standing around in the street. "They were waiting to see if I could handle the call," she says. "I'm considered not aggressive enough because I don't rush in and arrest the first person I see. But I don't get into fights, either, and I don't need 15 other officers for backup."

## LOS ANGELES: BOYS IN BLUE

42    Of course the absence of a Y chromosome doesn't automatically make someone a good cop, any more than it makes her a good mother or a bad driver. Some female officers are hot tempered and high-handed, and plenty of male cops are caring, compassionate people with excellent interpersonal skills.

43    However, traditional policing still tends to devalue those skills—in men as well as women—in favor of bullyboy aggressiveness and an "us against them" attitude toward not only crooks but the public at large. The result can be that police become part of the crime problem themselves.

44    This has been vividly demonstrated in Los Angeles, where cops were notorious for manhandling citizens long before the videotaped beating of Rodney King by four police officers in 1991. The gigantic cost of community ill will toward the L.A. Police Department was clear during the riots a year later, when police couldn't even enter riot-torn areas and citizens trying to defend their lives and property had to fend for themselves.

45    The independent commission formed to investigate the LAPD in the wake of the beating condemned the department's authoritarian, often confrontational policing style and found a direct connection between its proclivity for violence and its attitude toward women.

46    "Traditional views concerning the nature of police work in general—that is, that police work is a male-oriented profession with a major emphasis on physical

strength—foster a climate in which female officers are discouraged," said the commission's final report. "A corollary of that culture is an emphasis on use of force to control a situation and a disdain for a more patient, less aggressive approach."

47      Transcripts of computerized transmissions between police cars show just how brutal the LAPD's internal culture had become. "I hope there is enough units to set up a powwow around the suspect so he can get a good spanking and nobody c it . . ." was one typical computer transmission. Said another, "U wont believe this . . . that female call again said susp returned . . . I'll check it out then I'm going to stick my baton in her."

48      But one group of cops in L.A. did not succumb to run-amok machismo. The independent commission reported that female LAPD officers were much less likely to resort to use of excessive force. In 1991 women made up about 13 percent of the LAPD, but the commission found that of the 808 officers involved in frequent use of force, women accounted for only 30, or 3.7 percent. Among the 120 officers with the most use-of-force reports, not a single one was a woman.

49      As Katherine Spillar notes, one officer tried to stop the beating of Rodney King, "but the men told her to stay out of it."

50      The commission's findings aren't unique to Los Angeles. "In every department there's a small number of cops who get a huge number of civilian complaints," says Samuel Walker, a criminologist at the University of Nebraska at Omaha. "In all the cases where we've gotten information on who the bad boys are, female officers never show up on the list."

51      The Los Angeles City Council, which is currently paying out $28 million a year to settle civilian complaints against police, got the message. In 1992 it called on the LAPD to bring its percentage of female officers up to 43 percent—the percentage of women in the city's overall workforce, and far higher than that of any police department in the nation. Last year the council took the additional step, making 43 percent the LAPD's annual hiring goal.

## MADISON: HUMAN BEINGS, NOT ROBOCOPS

52  Right now, the city with one of the highest percentages of women cops is Madison, Wisconsin. Twenty-seven percent of its force is female; in addition, a third of its detectives and 25 percent of all those ranked above officer status are women.

53      Chief Richard Williams says women officers are essential to the department's community-oriented style of policing. "We want to reflect the community, and 50 percent of the people out there are women," he explains. "We want people to see us as human beings, rather than Robocops with dark glasses and no feelings." Williams says his department is doing that, not just by adding women to police ranks but by redefining what a police officer is.

54      Instead of recruiting eager young warriors with high-school educations and a couple of years in the military, Madison is voting for maturity and independent thinking by favoring candidates ages 25 to 29 with college degrees and well-developed communication skills.

55      Although women officers in Madison say the department isn't free of sexism, they describe many of the male officers as what Officer Carren Corcoran calls '90s

guys: "They have good relationships with their wives, good communication with citizens, they don't try to take over our calls and they talk to suspects instead of just
smashing the guy against the car."

56      The respect Madison officers feel for each other is paralleled by the force's relations with the community. In Los Angeles, officers often demand that suspects lie
prone on the pavement. In Madison, officers address everyone as Sir or Ma'am and
ask politely for identification and permission to pat a suspect down. Most of the
time permission is given, and what is elsewhere a ritual of dominance and submis-
sion becomes a surprisingly good-natured interaction.

57      Madison officers say being respectful of citizens makes their job easier. "If you
rip someone's self-respect and self-esteem away from them, that doesn't get you
anywhere," says Sergeant Patricia Rickman.

58      Officers from Milwaukee and Chicago, whose departments are run on more traditional lines, "think we're all pansies here because we talk too much," she adds,
laughing. "That's fine—we talk and we don't get hurt."

59      In other cities, social worker is the worst thing you can call a cop, but officers
in the Madison Police Department see much of what they do in exactly those terms.
Officer Sue Armagost has a master's degree in social work and worked with battered
women for three years before becoming a cop. She says, "This is social work with a
gun and a little more authority and a whole lot more job security."

60      Forget the gunfights and car chases in the movies and cop shows. Here are the
crime-fighting highlights of one three-day weekend in Madison last fall:

- A six-year-old boy is accused of stealing a $1.99 toy gun from a supermarket.
- A man has beaten up his girlfriend. He leaves the house when she calls the
  police and has to be pursued for several blocks before he is arrested. The officers explain to the girlfriend her legal options for seeking protection from
  him in the future.
- A worried mother files a missing-person report on her pregnant 15-year-old,
  who has disappeared with a boyfriend. (She turns up six hours later.)
- A 17-year-old boy from a nearby farm town is hanging around a neighborhood at one o'clock in the morning with two small children in the back of
  his truck. He says they are from a nearby homeless shelter and that he gave
  their father a lift here, supposedly so he could cash a money order. The officers convince the boy to hand the children over to them and go home. They
  also call his parents.
- The children's parents are found a half hour later. The father has crack cocaine hidden in his mouth and is arrested. The mother and children are
  given some phone numbers for social services and taken back to the homeless shelter.
- A man reports he's been robbed, then admits he made up the story because
  he has spent his mother's bus money on drugs. He threatens suicide and
  must be taken to a crisis center.
- A confused 65-year-old woman turns up on a residential street several miles
  from where she lives. The officer finds her caregiver and returns the woman
  to her home.

61      This scenario is not unique to Madison. Even in the nation's largest, toughest cities, an officer on patrol spends 80 to 95 percent of work time answering service calls, talking to citizens and writing reports. Cops who don't like "social work" aren't well-suited to their jobs.

## TOUGHING IT OUT

62   Despite their advantages, women police officers are still relatively rare. Although a 1990 Police Foundation survey of about 200 large municipal departments found that some 20 percent of police-academy applicants and graduates are now women, most major police department's female ranks remain stuck around the ten to 12 percent mark. *The Police Chief* magazine reports that women still make up only 8.6 percent of new hires nationally.

63      The biggest reason is that hostility to women officers is still rampant. A survey of 280 male officers in Washington, Oregon, Idaho and Montana, published in *The Police Chief* last year, found that 68 percent object to the idea of having a woman partner.

64      Often hostility takes the form of harassment. The LAPD is currently the target of a class-action lawsuit charging deliberate and systemic discrimination against women and minorities, ranging from rudeness and name-calling to sexual assault. Male resistance can sometimes take even harsher forms. In a story published last year about alleged harassment within the Maryland State Police, *The Baltimore Sun* reported one female trooper's charges about what happened when she refused a superior officer's requests for a date: He sent her into a riot situation with no backup. Baltimore attorney Kathleen Cahill, who is representing two female officers in sexual harassment suits against the agency, says one of her clients has received death threats that appear to have come from fellow officers. "If a woman speaks out in an office setting and her superiors retaliate, that's very serious," she says. "But women who blow the whistle on law enforcement are afraid they're going to die. When the police threaten your life, who do you call for help?"

65      Yet police departments are changing, whether the old guard likes it or not. And those changes will almost certainly mean an ever bigger role for women.

66      First, rising educational standards for police officers mean departments must recruit from the widest possible pool. "Agencies in major cities reject, on average, more than 90 percent of candidates," says the Police Foundation's Williams. "We would not be able to keep the police cars rolling without women."

67      Second, the future of policing is brain power, not muscle, which helps level the playing field for women. "In the future the really good cops are going to be preventing crime and disorder by understanding those things in an analytic way," predicts Karin Schmerler, a former researcher with the Police Executive Research Forum, a nonprofit law enforcement think tank. "Policing is becoming proactive rather than reactive, and therefore more of a thinking, creative kind of job."

68      One example of that is offered by Austin, Texas, chief of police Elizabeth Watson, one of only two women chiefs in major American cities. Old-style, control-oriented policing, she points out, has failed to stop drug dealing in residential neighborhoods. Unless police devote long hours to surveillance (unlikely in this budget-slashing era), they can't make arrests that hold up in court because they

can't catch dealers in the act. As a result, says Watson, more and more police departments are helping local residents to organize and take action, for example, by slapping nuisance suits on crack-house landlords, agitating for better street lighting and creating citizen surveillance teams that can provide police with photos of drug deals, license-plate numbers and other evidence.

69     "We need to work in partnership with communities and other agencies, using problem-solving, communication and other interpersonal skills," says Watson. "Those are characteristics that were not considered as critical for officers in the past but that women are generally very good at."

70     Finally, women cops love their work with a fervor that can't help but attract more women to the ranks. Interviews with more than 30 women officers from around the country yielded many stories of harassment and discrimination, of on-the-job injuries and brushes with death. But not one of these women wishes she were doing anything else.

71     One lieutenant, the only woman supervisor in her Midwestern agency, has suffered intense harassment, including being stalked by a former fellow officer, but has never considered changing careers. "When you're on patrol you have a lot of autonomy; you're pretty much your own boss," she says. "You're taking care of people, helping them when they're hurt, protecting them. It's different each day. It's the best job in the world."

72     As a girl, Marianne Scholer noticed that women in TV crime shows were always the victims. "I didn't want to have to be helped—I wanted to do the helping," she says. "I knew that being feminine didn't have to mean being helpless." A lieutenant in the Orange County, Florida, sheriff's office, she recently won a medal of valor for rescuing three people, including a child, from a burning building. "This is what I want to do," she says. "Every day, every hour brings an opportunity for you to be there for somebody."

*Glamour,* September 1995, pp. 260–273

## Comprehension Questions

1. What is the topic of the passage?
2. What is the central message of the passage?
3. Determine what is at issue. What is your initial personal viewpoint?
4. Distinguish among opposing viewpoints, and provide the rationale for each.
5. Think carefully about the viewpoints. Express a personal viewpoint, and give the reasons why you favor it. Does it differ from your initial personal viewpoint? Why or why not?
6. Write a few paragraphs *in support of the viewpoint that you do not favor.*

## Thought and Discussion Questions

1. Should the police have put handcuffs on the teenager who partly fit the reported batterer's description? Why or why not? What would you have done if you had been one of the police officers present? Why?

2. In your view, are women cops tough enough? Why or why not?

3. Would you rather have a male or a female cop patrolling your neighborhood? Why?

4. In your view, does the author deal with the subject matter of the article in an unbiased way? Why or why not?

5. List any questions that came to mind while you were reading this selection, and be prepared to discuss possible answers to them.

## LOOKING BACK

With two of your classmates, come up with a list of the most important points you learned from this chapter, and determine how they can be put to use in other classes. Be prepared to discuss both the list and the uses.

## THINK AGAIN!

The following problem was given to me by one of my critical-thinking students:

Suppose you bought a house with two floors, plus a basement and an attic. There are three separate lights in the attic that are controlled by three separate switches in the basement.

One night you are all alone and decide to match *each* of the three switches in the basement with the specific light in the attic that it controls. Assume that you want to accomplish this task immediately and that you can only make one trip to the basement and one trip to the attic. Can you figure out how you would go about doing it?

## MASTERY TEST 4

A. Answer the questions and fill in the blanks.

1. What is a problem?

   _____

   _____

   _____

2. What is a solution?

   _____

   _____

   _____

3. Name and describe briefly the steps involved in the basic method for personal problem solving.

   _____

   _____

   _____

   _____

   _____

   _____

   _____

   _____

   _____

4. When identifying a problem, it is important not to confuse _____ (ways of accomplishing goals) with the _____ (goals themselves).

5. If your problem concerns another person, is it necessary to get that person involved in all steps? Explain your answer.

6. What is the specific problem discussed in the following story?

## Whose Job Is It?

This is a story about four people named Everybody, Somebody, Anybody, and Nobody. There was an important job to be done, and Everybody was asked to do it. Everybody was sure Somebody would do it. Anybody could have done it, but Nobody did it. Somebody got angry about that, because it was Everybody's job. Everybody thought Anybody could do it, but Nobody realized that Everybody wouldn't do it. It ended up that Everybody blamed Somebody when Nobody did what Anybody could have done.

Problem: _____

_____

_____

_____

B. Using the five-step approach, try to come up with possible solutions in the following problem situations.

7. You have been dating the "love of your life" for the past year, and the two of you have decided to get married. One evening, while talking over wedding plans, you express your overwhelming desire to have children. During the course of the conversation, you are shocked to find out that your prospective spouse does not want kids. Even though the subject has never been discussed before, you always assumed that there would be no disagreement. You are madly in love but at a loss as to what to do because having children has been a lifelong dream.

_____

_____

_____

_____

_____

_____

_____

_____

_____

_____

_____

_____

_____

_____

_____

## 8. The Eggs, Embryos and I

*After Years of Infertility, IVF and Now Three Children, I'm Struggling with a Difficult Choice*

Melissa Moore Bodin

1   I have six potential children on ice in a hospital in southern California, and I don't know what to do with them. For seven years my husband and I suffered with the '90s affliction—infertility. Our problem started in 1986 when we threw out the diaphragm; the next month I was pregnant. Unfortunately, the embryo didn't make the whole journey. It started to develop in one of my tubes, and emergency surgery was necessary to remove it. "Don't worry, this happens, try again," the experts told us.

2   Eight months later, pregnant—again in the fallopian tube. More surgery. After an evaluation, we were told that my tubes weren't clear (what a surprise) but that an operation could help. By now I knew I was never wearing a bikini again, so what's another scar? After the procedure, we kept on trying, with no results. Then it was time for a little chemical help. I tried Clomid, a drug that increases the production of eggs from the normal one per month to four or more. The rationale is that the more eggs out there, the better the odds of hitting the jackpot. Finally, after a year and a half of monthly ovaries the size of softballs, another tubal pregnancy that needed surgery. You hit yourself in the head with a phone book enough times and something tells you to stop.

3   The last stop on the Infertility Highway is in vitro fertilization. IVF is expensive and not covered by insurance, but we scraped together every penny and went for it. To begin, I had to shut down my regular reproductive hormones by giving myself a shot in the thigh every morning for 10 days. It wasn't too bad, since I used a tiny diabetic needle. Then I moved on to the big guns, Metrodin and Pergonal, to chemically regulate my cycle. These drugs are suspended in sesame oil, so they have to be injected into the big gluteus muscles with a *large*

needle. Now the husband comes into play, reluctantly. Although it was my body on the receiving end of the needle, David had a very hard time making the plunge. We had to do these injections twice a day for 10 days. One side effect: a lot of bruising and a huge lump at the site of each injection. Not a pretty picture, but since actual sex was not part of the process, looks weren't that important.

4    The big day came, and the infertility clinic harvested 15 eggs, an operation more unpleasant than it sounds. The eggs were then  mixed with my husband's sperm in a petri dish. For 36 hours we waited to hear that we'd made 11 embryos. The doctor decided that six was the magic number for us and froze the other five. The only really happy part of the whole ordeal was that before the six embryos were placed in my womb, my husband was allowed to look through a microscope and see the tiny cells waiting to go home. Afterward I had to lie in an uncomfortable position: on my stomach, feet much higher than my head, for four hours in a dark room by myself. The nurse said to think positive thoughts—all I could think about was the enormous dent the end of the gurney was putting in the top of my head. The trip home was a sight to behold; suffice it to say I kept my feet higher than my head in the car, too. I stayed in bed for a week and watched afternoon talk shows about multiple births. Another week went by before the blood test.

5    Ever heard that you can't be "a little bit pregnant"? Wrong. The pregnancy test was positive, but the "numbers" weren't high enough. The test measures the level of a hormone in the mother's blood, and the doctors want to see a number around 100. Mine was 54. We spent a horrible week before the next blood test, half pregnant. In the end, the one tenacious embryo out of six slipped away. We had our frozen embryos left over, but only three survived the thaw, and that attempt was unsuccessful.

6    It took two years to recover from the failure, but after promising my husband that it would be the last attempt, we tried IVF again. The day of the pregnancy test I felt premenstrual and crampy, certain I wasn't pregnant. I made my husband call for results. "Does positive mean positive?" he said into the phone. Nine months later Jesse was born. When Jesse had his first birthday, I began thinking about the 18 frozen embryos left over from this IVF cycle. I never thought I had a shot of succeeding (my odds were about 11 percent), but we went ahead and had six of the thawed embryos "put back." (Six others did not survive.) Two weeks later, when I had the pregnancy test, I'd already grown out of my bra, so I knew something was up. Not only was I pregnant, but the hormone level was 412. Our twins, Paul and Samuel, were born nine months later.

7    I am 42 and my husband is 50. We have three children in diapers—exactly three more than we ever thought we'd have. In Jesse's preschool class we're always 15 to 20 years older than the other parents. My silver-haired husband shows his buddies baby pictures and their response is "Are these your grandkids?" Parents in the play group are worried about buying their first house; I'm worried about menopause. Most parents are concerned about saving for college; we're concerned about being able to feed ourselves when the kids are college age. We've already spent their college money to get them. Our bank account is

empty, and we're both going to have to work full time until we're in our 90s. Of course, we have three of the most wonderful, intelligent, beautiful children on earth, so none of this really matters.

8    But we still have six frozen embryos. We have only two choices—donate or destroy. As painful as the infertility was, we never considered adoption an alternative. Giving our embryos to another infertile couple would be like giving our children up for adoption. We know this is a very selfish attitude and have struggled mightily with the issue. After all we've gone through, the concept of destroying the embryos is hard to imagine.

9    So we pay our $50 a month storage fee, raise our boys and wonder what we are going to do.

*Newsweek,* July 28, 1997, pp. 14–15

_____

_____

_____

_____

_____

_____

_____

_____

_____

_____

_____

_____

_____

_____

Along with your partner, read the second part of "The Adventure of the Three Students," and then answer the questions that follow it.

---

# The Return of Sherlock Holmes
## *The Adventure of the Three Students: Part Two*

A. CONAN DOYLE

Holmes shook his head impatiently.

"Let us be practical," said he. "I understand you to say that there are three students who use this stair and are in the habit of passing your door?"

"Yes, there are."

"And they are all in for this examination?"

"Yes."

"Have you any reason to suspect any one of them more than the others?"

Soames hesitated.

"It is a very delicate question," said he. "One hardly likes to throw suspicion where there are no proofs."

"Let us hear the suspicions. I will look after the proofs."

"I will tell you, then, in a few words the character of the three men who inhabit these rooms. The lower of the three is Gilchrist, a fine scholar and athlete; plays in the Rugby team and the cricket team for the college, and got his Blue for the hurdles and the long jump. He is a fine, manly fellow. His father was the notorious Sir Jabez Gilchrist, who ruined himself on the turf. My scholar has been left very poor, but he is hard-working and industrious. He will do well.

"The second floor is inhabited by Daulat Ras, the Indian. He is a quiet, inscrutable fellow, as most of those Indians are. He is well up in his work, though his Greek is his weak subject. He is steady and methodical.

"The top floor belongs to Miles McLaren. He is a brilliant fellow when he chooses to work—one of the brightest intellects of the University, but he is wayward, dissipated, and unprincipled. He was nearly expelled over a card scandal in his first year. He has been idling all this term, and he must look forward with dread to the examination."

"Then it is he whom you suspect?"

"I dare not go so far as that. But of the three he is perhaps the least unlikely."

"Exactly. Now, Mr. Soames, let us have a look at your servant, Bannister."

He was a little, white-faced, clean-shaven, grizzly-haired fellow of fifty. He was still suffering from this sudden disturbance of the quiet routine of his life. His plump face was twitching with his nervousness, and his fingers could not keep still.

"We are investigating this unhappy business, Bannister," said his master.

"Yes, sir."

"I understand," said Holmes, "that you left your key in the door?"

"Yes, sir."

"Was it not very extraordinary that you should do this on the very day when there were these papers inside?"

"It was most unfortunate, sir. But I have occasionally done the same thing at other times."

"When did you enter the room?"

"It was about half-past four. That is Mr. Soames's tea time."

"How long did you stay?"

"When I saw that he was absent I withdrew at once."

"Did you look at these papers on the table?"

"No, sir; certainly not."

"How came you to leave the key in the door?"

"I had the tea-tray in my hand. I thought I would come back for the key. Then I forgot."

"Has the outer door a spring lock?"

"No, sir."

"Then it was open all the time?"

"Yes, sir."

"Anyone in the room could get out?"

"Yes, sir."

"When Mr. Soames returned and called for you, you were very much disturbed?"

"Yes, sir. Such a thing has never happened during the many years that I have been here. I nearly fainted, sir."

"So I understand. Where were you when you began to feel bad?"

"Where was I, sir? Why, here, near the door."

"That is singular, because you sat down in that chair over yonder near the corner. Why did you pass these other chairs?"

"I don't know, sir. It didn't matter to me where I sat."

"I really don't think he knew much about it, Mr. Holmes. He was looking very bad—quite ghastly."

"You stayed here when your master left?"

"Only for a minute or so. Then I locked the door and went to my room."

"Whom do you suspect?"

"Oh, I would not venture to say, sir. I don't believe there is any gentleman in this University who is capable of profiting by such an action. No, sir, I'll not believe it."

"Thank you; that will do," said Holmes. "Oh, one more word. You have not mentioned to any of the three gentlemen whom you attend that anything is amiss?"

"No, sir; not a word."

"You haven't seen any of them?"

"No, sir."

"Very good. Now, Mr. Soames, we will take a walk in the quadrangle, if you please."

Three yellow squares of light shone above us in the gathering gloom.

"Your three birds are all in their nests," said Holmes, looking up. "Halloa! What's that? One of them seems restless enough."

It was the Indian, whose dark silhouette appeared suddenly upon his blind. He was pacing swiftly up and down his room.

"I should like to have a peep at each of them," said Holmes. "Is it possible?"

"No difficulty in the world," Soames answered. "This set of rooms is quite the oldest in the college, and it is not unusual for visitors to go over them. Come along, and I will personally conduct you."

"No names, please!" said Holmes, as we knocked at Gilchrist's door. A tall, flaxen-haired, slim young fellow opened it, and made us welcome when he understood our errand. There were some really curious pieces of mediæval domestic architecture within. Holmes was so charmed with one of them that he insisted on drawing it on his note book, broke his pencil, had to borrow one from our host, and finally borrowed a knife to sharpen his own. The same curious accident happened to him in the rooms of the Indian—a silent, little, hook-nosed fellow, who eyed us askance and was obviously glad when Holmes's architectural studies had come to an end. I could not see that in either case Holmes had come upon the clue for which he was searching. Only at the third did our visit prove abortive. The outer door would not open to our knock, and nothing more substantial than a torrent of bad language came from behind it. "I don't care who you are. You can go to blazes!" roared the angry voice. "To-morrow's the exam., and I won't be drawn by anyone."

"A rude fellow," said our guide, flushing with anger as we withdrew down the stair. "Of course, he did not realize that it was I who was knocking, but none the less his conduct was very uncourteous, and, indeed, under the circumstances rather suspicious."

Holmes's response was a curious one.

"Can you tell me his exact height?" he asked.

"Really, Mr. Holmes, I cannot undertake to say. He is taller than the Indian, not so tall as Gilchrist. I suppose five foot six would be about it."

"That is very important," said Holmes. "And now, Mr. Soames, I wish you good-night."

Our guide cried aloud in his astonishment and dismay. "Good gracious, Mr. Holmes, you are surely not going to leave me in this abrupt fashion! You don't seem to realize the position. To-morrow is the examination. I must take some definite action to night. I cannot allow the examination to be held if one of the papers has been tampered with. The situation must be faced."

"You must leave it as it is. I shall drop round early to-morrow morning and chat the matter over. It is possible that I may be in a position then to indicate some course of action. Meanwhile you change nothing—nothing at all."

"Very good, Mr. Holmes."

"You can be perfectly easy in your mind. We shall certainly find some way out of your difficulties. I will take the black clay with me, also the pencil cuttings. Good-bye."

When we were out in the darkness of the quadrangle we again looked up at the windows. The Indian still paced his room. The others were invisible.

"Well, Watson, what do you think of it?" Holmes asked, as we came out into the main street. "Quite a little parlour game—sort of three-card trick, is it not? There are your three men. It must be one of them. You take your choice. Which is yours?"

"The foul-mouthed fellow at the top. He is the one with the worst record. And yet that Indian was a sly fellow also. Why should he be pacing his room all the time?"

"There is nothing in that. Many men do it when they are trying to learn anything by heart."

"He looked at us in a queer way."

"So would you if a flock of strangers came in on you when you were preparing for an examination next day, and every moment was of value. No, I see nothing in that. Pencils, too, and knives—all was satisfactory. But that fellow *does* puzzle me."

"Who?"

"Why, Bannister, the servant. What's his game in the matter?"

"He impressed me as being a perfectly honest man."

"So he did me. That's the puzzling part. Why should a perfectly honest man—well, well, here's a large stationer's. We shall begin our researches here."

There were only four stationers of any consequence in the town, and at each Holmes produced his pencil chips and bid high for a duplicate. All were agreed that one could be ordered, but that it was not a usual size of pencil and that it was seldom kept in stock. My friend did not appear to be depressed by his failure, but shrugged his shoulders in half-humorous resignation.

"No good, my dear Watson. This, the best and only final clue, has run to nothing. But, indeed, I have little doubt that we can build up a sufficient case without it. By Jove! my dear fellow, it is nearly nine, and the landlady babbled of green peas at seven-thirty. What with your eternal tobacco, Watson, and your irregularity at meals, I expect that you will get notice to quit and that I shall share your downfall—not, however, before we have solved the problem of the nervous tutor, the careless servant, and the three enterprising students."

Holmes made no further allusion to the matter that day, though he sat lost in thought for a long time after our belated dinner. At eight in the morning he came into my room just as I finished my toilet.

"Well, Watson," said he, "it is time we went down to St. Luke's. Can you do without breakfast?"

"Certainly."

"Soames will be in a dreadful fidget until we are able to tell him something positive."

"Have you anything positive to tell him?"

"I think so."

"You have formed a conclusion?"

"Yes, my dear Watson; I have solved the mystery."

"But what fresh evidence could you have got?"

"Aha! It is not for nothing that I have turned myself out of bed at the untimely hour of six. I have put in two hours' hard work and covered at least five miles, with something to show for it. Look at that!"

He held out his hand. On the palm were three little pyramids of black, doughy clay.

"Why, Holmes, you had only two yesterday!"

"And one more this morning. It is a fair argument that wherever No. 3 came from is also the source of Nos. 1 and 2. Eh, Watson? Well, come along and put friend Soames out of his pain."

The unfortunate tutor was certainly in a state of pitiable agitation when we found him in his chambers. In a few hours the examinations would commence, and he was still in the dilemma between making the facts public and allowing the culprit to compete for the valuable scholarship. He could hardly stand still, so great was his mental agitation, and he ran towards Holmes with two eager hands outstretched.

"Thank Heaven that you have come! I feared that you had given it up in despair. What am I to do? Shall the examination proceed?"

"Yes; let it proceed by all means."

"But this rascal ____ ?"

9 "He shall not compete."

"You know him?"

"I think so. If this matter is not to become public we must give ourselves certain powers, and resolve ourselves into a small private court-martial. You there, if you please, Soames! Watson, you here! I'll take the arm chair in the middle. I think that we are now sufficiently imposing to strike terror into a guilty breast. Kindly ring the bell!"

*The Complete Original Illustrated Sherlock Holmes,* pp. 570–574

## Questions

1. Who are the suspects? Name and describe each of them.

2. At this point, do you suspect any one of them more than the others? Why or why not?

## GO ELECTRONIC!

For additional readings, exercises, and Internet activities, visit our Website at:

### http://longman.awl.com/englishpages

If you need a user name and password, see your instructor.

**Take a Road Trip to** the American Southwest! Be sure to visit the Critical Thinking module in your Reading Road Trip CD-ROM for multimedia tutorials, exercises, and tests.

# Critical Reading: Evaluating What You Read

# Chapter Five

# USING INFERENCE

**Chapter Outline**

What Is Critical Reading?

Drawing Inferences
*Using Knowledge to Infer*
*Using Experience to Infer*
*Using Clues to Infer*

Looking at the World with a Questioning Mind

Using Inferences with Contemporary Issues and Problem Solving

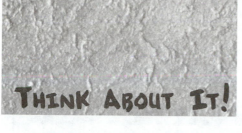

# THINK ABOUT IT!

Look at the message on the sign in the photograph below. Use your knowledge, experience, and the clues to make an "educated guess" regarding what the advertisement is really urging husbands to do. Discuss it with your classmates.

(1)

Assuming that you do not speak Spanish, make an "educated guess" regarding what the message on the sign in the photograph below is urging you to do. Discuss it with your classmates.

Make an "educated guess" why the author decided not to purchase a wall-to-wall carpet from the store in the photograph below. Discuss your guess with your classmates.

(2)

(3)

(4)

Make an "educated guess" why someone might be offended by the restaurant sign in the photograph to the right. Discuss your guess with your classmates.

(5)

Make an "educated guess" why the cars in the photograph to the right were parked on the lawn in front of a high school. Discuss your guess with your classmates.

---

## Chapter Outcomes

After completing Chapter 5, you should be able to:

- Continue to apply the basic method for personal problem solving

- Define critical reading

- Define inference

- Use knowledge, experience, and clues to draw inferences in problem situations and when reading passages concerning contemporary issues

- Continue to find topics and central messages in passages on contemporary issues to determine what is at issue, distinguish among opposing viewpoints, and express personal viewpoints

## Problem-Solving Exercise

Using your notebook, apply the basic method for personal problem solving to the following hypothetical situation. Make sure to label each step clearly as you discuss what you would do.

### Hypothetical Situation

You are very close friends with a married couple whom you have known for many years. While driving through town, you spot one of them entering a restaurant with a person of the opposite sex. The following afternoon, you see them once again going into the same restaurant together. They seem to be very comfortable with each other and in a rather jovial mood.

# What Is Critical Reading?

As a college student, you are expected to derive meaning from whatever information you encounter in textbooks and other sources. In Chapters 1 and 2, we reviewed a number of reading skills:

➤ Using context to determine word meanings
➤ Distinguishing main ideas, major details, and minor details
➤ Recognizing patterns of organization
➤ Uncovering the central message of a selection
➤ Overviewing a textbook
➤ Previewing a textbook chapter
➤ Developing questions from chapter headings and answering them
➤ Underlining or highlighting

All of these skills help you comprehend reading material better, particularly material found in textbooks.

**Critical reading** can be defined as very high-level comprehension of written material requiring interpretation and evaluation skills that enable the reader to separate important from unimportant information, distinguish between facts and opinions, and determine a writer's purpose and tone. It also entails using inference to go beyond what is stated explicitly, filling in informational gaps, and coming to logical conclusions. All of this permits a very high level of comprehension of written material. These various skills require much thought, and that is why critical reading is dependent on critical thinking. Indeed, all of the characteristics of critical thinking discussed in Chapter 3 can be applied to critical reading.

You have already had some practice in separating important from unimportant information, particularly when answering questions developed from textbook chapter headings and when dealing with contemporary issues. In the remaining chapters, you will continue to practice that skill. The other critical reading skills—using inference, distinguishing between facts and opinions, and uncovering purpose and determining tone—are covered here in Part III. Let's begin with a discussion of inference.

## Drawing Inferences

Pretend that you have had Professor Arlene Brown as a mathematics instructor for the past two semesters. She is a friendly person who always greets her classes in a warm manner. This past Tuesday, Professor Brown gave a rather difficult midterm examination in your algebra course. It covered rather complex material, and many of your classmates were concerned about their grades.

When the class met again on Thursday morning, Professor Brown arrived late, and when she came through the door she was not smiling at all. In fact, she walked briskly to the front of the room, slammed her briefcase on the desk, gruffly told the students to take out their notebooks, and began to cover new material immediately. Consequently, most of your classmates concluded that Professor Brown was upset about something.

They based that conclusion on three factors: first, their *knowledge* of the way people in general behave when they are upset; second, the *experience* they have had with Professor Brown in previous sessions; third, their using her behavior or actions as *clues*. That she was upset was a reasonable conclusion because it rested solidly on their knowledge and experience and flowed logically from the clues or facts at hand.

Some students went one step further by concluding that Professor Brown was upset because the class had done poorly on the midterm exam. Therefore, they became even more concerned about their test scores. However, you were skeptical and reluctant to go along with that line of reasoning. Although your classmates based their conclusion on knowledge and experience, you felt that it was not as solid as the previous one because there was a lack of specific clues pointing in that direction. They may ultimately end up being correct, but without additional information, their hunch was by no means certain. So it was probably wise for you to be cautious.

Now let's add some information to the story. Suppose Professor Brown, after slamming her briefcase on the desk, blurted out, "Men!" Could you then conclude reasonably that she had had an argument with her husband? Maybe, but you certainly might end up being wrong, because once again there are not enough clues. She could just as easily have had an argument that morning with some other male, such as a driver who cut her off on the way to school, her automobile mechanic, the dean, or another faculty member.

What if, instead, she had shouted, "Men, they are impossible to live with!" Would you then feel safe concluding that she had had an argument with her husband? Although that conclusion would be more likely in that it does rest on an additional clue, it might also turn out to be incorrect because she could be living with a boyfriend, son, brother, father, or roommate. It would become a much stronger conclusion if she had exclaimed, "Men, they are impossible to live with! Don't ever get married!" There would finally be enough clues to support the original conclusion that she had had a disagreement with her husband.

What we have been discussing here are **inferences,** which are "educated guesses" by which we go beyond what is explicit in order to fill in informational gaps, come to logical conclusions, and make sense of the world around us. They are "educated" because they are not wild guesses but are instead based on knowledge, experience, and the clues or facts of the situation. In short, the more knowledge, experience, and clues we have, the better our chances of coming up with sound inferences and hence logical and reasonable conclusions.

## Using Knowledge to Infer

Knowledge of different subjects or topics varies from person to person: It comes down to what we have learned and experienced through the years. In that sense, knowledge really cannot be separated from experience because the latter adds to our knowledge base. On the other hand, our knowledge helps shape the way we interpret our experiences.

It follows, then, that the more we know and the more we have experienced, the easier it will be to draw inferences, depending of course on the circumstances. There will be occasions when we are in a much better position to make educated guesses and other occasions when we will not be able to do so with any degree of confidence. For example, look at the following photograph:

Certainly, most of us have enough knowledge to realize that this is a picture of a bus that is used for sightseeing purposes. However, what if I asked you to infer where the photograph was taken? There is one clue, and that is the name "Beantown." If you know the name of the city that is called "Beantown,"

you would feel very secure answering that the photograph was probably taken in the city of Boston. Thus your knowledge helped you use the clue to answer the question. People without that knowledge would be forced either to do some research or to take a wild guess. If they took a wild guess, the chances are fairly high that they would be wrong.

This is just one example of how knowledge can play a significant part when it comes to drawing inferences. We all need to accept the fact that we do not know everything, and no two people will possess the same degree of knowledge on every matter. In other words, we should not be embarrassed if we do not have enough knowledge in certain situations to draw inferences, and in those instances, it is probably better not to because there is a greater chance of being wrong. Keep in mind that there will be other situations in which we will find ourselves in a better position to come to logical conclusions. Furthermore, knowledge is not a constant but increases as we go through life.

### Using Experience to Infer

We have already discussed the relationship between knowledge and experience. Our experiences add to our knowledge base and place us in a better position to come to logical conclusions about our surroundings. Once again, our experiences vary from person to person and therefore with regard to how much they help us draw inferences in different situations. For instance, look at the photograph below, and see if you can determine where it was taken.

If you have had the experience of visiting New York City around Christmastime, you probably came to the conclusion that the photograph is of the Christmas tree in Rockefeller Center. The Santa Claus, angels, size of the tree, and general layout of the buildings serve as clues. But if you have never had the experience of visiting Rockefeller Center in person at Christmastime, seen pictures of it in newspapers or magazines, or been introduced to it on television, it was much more difficult for you to make an accurate educated guess. Thus experiences—or lack of them—have an important effect on our ability to draw inferences.

## Using Clues to Infer

As you have seen, in addition to knowledge and experience, we all depend on clues to help us draw inferences. The clues or facts present in a given situation interact with our knowledge and experiences, thus enabling us to make sense of our surroundings. For example, look at the following photograph, and list in your notebook at least three possible characteristics of the person who uses the study in the picture. When you are done, proceed to the explanation.

Although you do not know for sure, you can conclude reasonably that the person is a hockey fan because of the puck on the desk and the picture on the wall. In fact, judging by the uniform in the photograph, it would appear that the person is a New York Rangers fan. Furthermore, the other pictures on the wall suggest that he or she is a parent or that children are in some way an important part of his or her life. Also, the person obviously makes use of a portable computer, which is clearly visible on the desk. Finally, the can on the desk seems to indicate that the person drinks ale at least some of the time, and the golf clubs next to the desk would lead logically to the conclusion that he or she plays golf.

As you can see, by using the clues in the photograph in combination with your knowledge and experiences, you were able to infer some things about the person who uses the study. Much like a detective, you pieced together some important information that gave meaning to what you were observing. We all do this kind of exercise very often without even realizing it, and much of the time, our inferences are correct. Obviously, the more clues available in a given situation, the better the chances of our inferences' being accurate.

## ACTIVITY 1

For this activity, your instructor will divide the class into three groups. Each group will read only one of the three paragraphs that follow and use knowledge, experience, and clues to try to infer what person is being described. The paragraphs vary in terms of the clues that they provide, so be careful not to jump to a hasty conclusion unless your group is reasonably sure of that conclusion.

## One Solitary Life

1   He was born in an obscure village, the child of a peasant woman. He grew up in another obscure village, where He worked in a carpenter shop until He was thirty. Then for three years He was an itinerant preacher. He never had a family or owned a home. He never set foot inside a big city. He never traveled two hundred miles from the place He was born. He never wrote a book, or held an office. He did none of the things that usually accompany greatness.

2   While He was still a young man, the tide of popular opinion turned against Him. His friends deserted Him. He was turned over to His enemies, and went through the mockery of a trial. He was nailed to a cross between two thieves. While He was dying, His executioners gambled for the only piece of property He had—His coat. When He was dead, He was taken down and laid in a borrowed grave.

3   Nineteen centuries have come and gone, and today He is the central figure for much of the human race. All the armies that ever marched and all the navies that ever sailed and all the parliaments that ever sat and all the kings that ever reigned, put together, have not affected the life of man upon this earth as powerfully as this "One Solitary Life."

## Looking at the World with a Questioning Mind

In Chapter 3, we noted that critical thinking involves asking questions, persistence in trying to find answers, and coming to logical conclusions that are based on sound reasoning and the information or evidence that has been gathered. In other words, to be a critical thinker, you must always be inquisitive about what is going on around you and constantly seeking answers. This in turn sometimes involves filling in the gaps by using your knowledge, experience, and the clues that are present to come to logical conclusions.

Now you see the connection between inferences and critical thinking, because in most instances in order to infer you must first question and then think carefully about what you see, hear, or read. Most of the time, no one is going to supply you with questions, so it is up to you to look at the world with a questioning mind. Then you must evaluate the information gathered to determine if you can answer your questions. It is at this point that you decide whether it is necessary to use inferences to help you.

## Using Inferences with Contemporary Issues and Problem Solving

When we read critically, it is often necessary to "read between the lines" by using inferences to fill in the gaps. We have already reviewed the importance of understanding a writer's stated and unstated messages in Chapter 1 when we talked about main ideas and central messages. As already mentioned, you will be introduced to facts/opinions, purpose and tone later on in this textbook.

In Chapter 3, when dealing with contemporary issues, you used inferences at times to help uncover unstated secondary issues, opposing viewpoints, and the rationale for those viewpoints. For example, for Selection 5, "Shot in the Arm," you not only had to infer the secondary issue involving how patients are treated by doctors but also had to supply reasons for one of the opposing viewpoints regarding why doctors often charge high fees.

Inferences can also be useful in basic problem solving. For instance, in Problem 1 in Activity 5 in Chapter 4, you were advised that because the problem was not stated explicitly, you would have to draw a logical conclusion about what was wrong. In other words, you were asked to use your knowledge, experience, and the facts that were given to infer what was bothering James. After thinking about the situation and discussing it in class, it was decided that one of the most likely possibilities was that James had some kind of substance abuse problem. Problem 2 in the same activity also required that you come to a logical conclusion by inferring from the information given that sexual harassment was the problem that Anita was experiencing.

Finally, in the hypothetical situation for the problem-solving exercise at the beginning of this chapter, you had to be very careful to gather additional information as part of Step 2, *before* trying to infer the nature of your friend's relationship. You could not possibly address the situation with any degree of certainty until completing that important step. Thus you saw the importance of questioning what you observe and the necessity for caution when using inferences.

As you make your way through college, remember to read and think with a questioning mind. This is a very important part of being both a critical reader and a critical thinker! Go beneath the surface, and do not accept information at face value. Use your knowledge, experience, and the clues available to help you draw inferences so that you can fill in some of the gaps and come to logical conclusions. However, remember not to go too far beyond the information presented, because your conclusions may not have a solid foundation, and therefore they could be wrong.

## ACTIVITY 2

Your instructor is going to divide the class into small groups in order to apply the basic method for personal problem solving to the following situation. This was a real-life problem I encountered that required the use of inference skills in order to come to a logical conclusion regarding the doctor's motivations. When discussing the situation in your group, try to figure out what logical conclusion the author came to and what solution he decided on. Because this problem actually occurred, your instructor will let you know what I found in Step 5 when I "checked back on the problem and the possible solution." In other words, your instructor will tell you how the entire episode turned out.

You are in the surgeon's office with your daughter three weeks after he operated successfully on her for a thyroid tumor, and you ask him to recommend an internist because you have a lump on the side of your neck. Dr. Rosin informs you that the neck area is one of his specialties and starts immediately to examine you. After about two minutes, he advises you that one of your salivary glands is swollen. He proceeds to prescribe two antibiotics, schedules an X-ray for you at the hospital to determine if there is a stone in the gland, and sets up another appointment with him in three weeks.

On your return visit, you tell Dr. Rosin that you think the lump changes in size and is smaller at least some of the time. After reexamining you for about three minutes, he declares that the X-ray showed no evidence of a stone, the antibiotics have been ineffectual, and in his opinion the lump has gotten bigger. You ask him if the X-ray showed anything else, and he advises you that he was only testing for a stone. Furthermore, Dr. Rosin warns that either the gland is inflamed or it has a tumor that has a 50-50 chance of being malignant. Even if it is just inflamed, he continues, you will probably wake up one morning in excruciating pain with the lump three times bigger. He adds that he would not wish that kind of pain on his worst enemy.

Dr. Rosin explains further that he could do a needle biopsy in his office to determine if the lump is malignant, but he does not advise doing that because in his opinion those kinds of biopsies usually do not give accurate readings. He urges you to have surgery and explains how the operation will be performed, adding cautiously that he will not know for three days after surgery whether or not the lump is malignant. Finally, Dr. Rosin explains that the chances are high that during surgery, a nerve in your neck will get severed, affecting your lower lip when you smile. However, he assures you that the functioning of your mouth will not be affected. After listening, you tell him that you will have to think about what to do, and he agrees with that course of action. As you are leaving, he concludes by saying that if you decide on the operation, you should schedule it through his office. Otherwise, he would like to see you in about a month.

## ACTIVITY 3

Read the following passages, and answer the questions that follow. Continue to use inferences, when needed, to draw logical conclusions.

### 1

## Killing Animals
### *Raising of Fenced-In Quarry for "Hunters" Spawns a Debate*

Alfred Lubrano

1   Beer was waiting. Now was the killing time.

2   "I wanna peg one of these babies and get to my Silver Bullet," Rex Perysian shouted, fitting an arrow into his crossbow.

3   The beefy redhead and his four buddies arranged themselves in a semicircle around an animal feeder in a clearing at the Renegade Ranch Hunting Preserve.

4   In the frigid nowhere of northern Michigan, the 300-acre ranch is a fenced patch of snow and jack pines stocked with buffalo, exotic deer and other trophy animals that can be killed for a price. Today, the men—dressed in camouflage and sporting walkie-talkies—were shooting for Russian boars, normally $450 per head, marked down to $350.

5   To help the hunt, the ranch owner's son chased a snorting black line of boars along an animal trail toward the boars' breakfast bin, and the poised arrows.

6   Hiding behind a tree, Perysian fired first, hitting the first boar in line in its hindquarters. The 250-pound animal writhed and squealed as the whizzing arrow pierced skin and muscle with a muffled whack. The boar hobbled up a ridge toward an 8-foot fence, staining the snow with its blood.

7   Unable to escape, the animal cried, startling three rams out of a stand of trees. Perysian delivered a second arrow, then a third, both from closer than 10 feet. The boar shuddered and twitched, then lay still, four minutes after the first arrow hit.

8   "I was pumpin', man," Perysian, 31, a commercial-sign installer from Michigan, said into the camcorder his buddy pointed at him. "The first arrow was high. The second hit liver. The third took lung. I like it."

9   Perysian stood astride the boar and, after cleaning blood off its nose, lifted its head by the ears for the camera. "I'll grab it like I grab my women," he told his pals.

10  Then Perysian dropped the animal's head and bellowed into the woods, boasting that the kill had sexually aroused him. His voice echoed in the woods and frightened the rams, who ran off. In the next 30 minutes, three more boars would go down at Renegade

11      They're known pejoratively as "canned hunts," a different kind of killing experience.

12      People without the time, ability or inclination to spend days in the woods tracking trophy-quality animals visit fenced-in places like Renegade to bag their prey.

13      "It's like taking a gun to the zoo," said Michael Carlton, a former hunting writer who visited the fenced-in Stony Fork Hunts in Wellsboro, Pa., 25 years ago, then vowed never to hunt again.

14      The hunts are fomenting national debate. Animal-rights activists are appalled. Members of pro-hunting groups that advocate "ethical," non-fenced hunting label the hunts "despicable." Meanwhile, breeders of animals used in the hunts defend their $100 million-a-year industry, saying it's their right to raise animals for whatever purposes they desire. Similarly, canned-hunt owners say no one can tell them what to do on their property. Even Congress has weighed in, with a proposed bill that would criminalize the use of animals for such hunts.

15      What riles most opponents of canned hunts is how the deck seems stacked against the animals. Many such hunts guarantee a kill. Customers rarely need hunting licenses and may hunt any time of the year.

16      As at Renegade, many ranch owners set up hunting blinds where shooters can sit and await their prizes near the troughs where the animals eat. It's so easy to kill an animal that a few places, like the J.W. Hunting Preserve in Henryetta, Okla., specialize in wheelchair hunts. At Hunters Quest Game Ranch in southern Michigan, a disabled hunter who can't use his arms fires his rifle by pulling with his teeth on a leather strap attached to the trigger.

17      At canned hunts, many animals are accustomed to seeing and being fed by people daily, which means they may not flee hunters as truly wild animals would. If they do run, they can't get far: The ranches are surrounded by high fencing.

18      Sometimes, Pennsylvania Game Commission officials report, ranch owners drug animals to make them easier to handle. "At one hunt, they stood up a drugged sheep like a silhouette, and guys shot arrows at it and it didn't even flinch," said Jim Beard, assistant director of the commission's Bureau of Law Enforcement.

19      Some animals aren't given the chance to wander preserves—they are shot by hunters in—or just outside—their cages, Beard and others said.

20      Most of the animals in the camps are known as exotics—species of deer and antelope, sheep, goat, boars, gazelles, yaks and other creatures not native to the United States.

21      Many are grown on ranches and sold to hunting camps by people like Bill Dyroff, an Austin, Pa., math teacher who found that raising fallow deer for hunts is more profitable than raising cattle. "Only people who don't put pork chops on their plates can criticize," he asserted.

22      Other animals are believed to come from circuses and—less frequently—from zoos.

23      Canned hunts are legal in 39 states, including Pennsylvania, which is believed by the Humane Society to be among four states that have the most hunting preserves. The Humane Society estimates that Texas has more than half of the nation's 1,000 hunting preserves, although no one knows the exact number. The hunts are outlawed in 11 states, including New Jersey.

24    Lately, there's been movement to make the hunting of captive exotics illegal everywhere. Two bills being considered by the U.S. House of Representatives and the Senate would prohibit the transport and possession of exotics held in captivity on a ranch with fewer than 1,000 acres for "purposes of allowing the killing . . . of that animal for entertainment or the collection of a trophy."

25    The House version—co-signed by Pennsylvania Democrats Robert Borski and Thomas Foglietta, and Republican Curt Weldon—has been getting some bipartisan support. Hearings in the House Judiciary Committee's subcommittee on crime are scheduled to begin in the spring.

26    Canned hunts are so controversial, many "legitimate" hunters rail against them.

27    "It's cheating," said Lark Ritchie, a Cree Indian who guides hunts in northern Ontario. "The men involved do it to show off [their manhood], for status. There's a lot of 'hunters' I call killers."

28    Some believe canned hunts violate the widely held hunting ethic of "fair chase," which demands that a hunter pursue and take wild game in a manner that doesn't afford him improper or unfair advantage.

29    The Boone and Crockett Club, a hunting and conservation organization founded by Teddy Roosevelt that keeps track of wild-game hunting records (biggest antlers, widest head) won't allow the entry of any animal taken in a hunting preserve into its books. Fences, club members say, render the chase unfair.

30    The National Rifle Association's federal lobbyist, Heather Wingate, said, "We are not in favor of canned hunts." Still, the NRA is opposing the proposed captive-exotics legislation, for fear it could lead to restrictions on all forms of hunting.

31    While Perysian went after the first boar at Renegade, 25-year-old Eric Heiss aimed for the second.

32    "I never shot an animal before," said Heiss, who works for a Michigan chemical company. His eyes were wide, he spoke rapidly. "But I shot an artery with the first arrow. You can see the blood. The second shot slashed heart and lung. I was more scared than anything. But it was a rush."

33    Beaming for the camcorder, Heiss said to his buddies: "I used to raise hogs for the state fair. I once won a blue ribbon." He paused, allowing the irony to float away. "Oh, well. How's my hair?"

34    A ranch hand came by to gut the animal, pulling its internal organs into a pile. The hunters told Heiss to sit astride his boar and lift up its head for the camera, as Perysian had.

35    "Poor thing, abusing it like this," Heiss suddenly said.

36    Jim Kurdziel, the videographer, was puzzled by the remark: "You shoot him, then you feel bad?"

37    As the men spoke, vapor from the boar's newly hollowed body cavity wafted into the freezing air, like the smoke from a barbecue.

38    Some hunters feel that hunting on game ranches is a perversion of a noble American sport.

39    "I feel most alive when I'm hunting," said the Rev. Theodore Vitali, chairman of the philosophy department at St. Louis University, an avid hunter, and a member of the Boone and Crockett Club. But Father Vitali finds "canned hunts despicable."

40     "I'm celebrating life. There is no life without death. When I kill an animal, my immediate response is gratitude to the animal and nature . . . for giving me his life. It's the dialectic of life and death. There's no other game in town."

41     Asked whether killing animals is at odds with being a priest, Vitali, who mounts the heads of the animals he's killed on his walls to "honor them," said: "It's not against Christianity to kill, unless we take illicit pleasure in it."

42     His friend Dan Pletscher, a biologist at the University of Montana, said hunting was natural for a predator like man. Still, he added, "Predation is hard to understand because it is not pretty. But if you eat meat, you're part of the food chain. I always feel better because when I hunt, I know where it comes from."

*Newark (N.J.) Star-Ledger,* February 11, 1996, pp. 39–40

## Comprehension Questions

1. What is the topic of the passage?
2. What is the central message of the passage?
3. Determine what is at issue. What is your initial personal viewpoint?
4. Distinguish among opposing viewpoints, and provide the rationale for each.
5. Think carefully about the viewpoints. Express a personal viewpoint, and give the reasons why you favor it. Does it differ from your initial personal viewpoint? Why or why not?
6. Write a few paragraphs *in support of the viewpoint that you do* not *favor.*

## Thought and Discussion Questions

1. Would you ever participate in a "canned hunt"? Why or why not?
2. What can you infer from the article regarding Rex Perysian's view of women? Why?
3. How do you interpret the statement "Only people who don't put pork chops on their plates can criticize" (paragraph 21)?
4. List any questions that came to mind while you were reading this selection, and be prepared to discuss possible answers to them.

## 2

## An "Amos 'n' Andy" Christmas

HENRY LOUIS GATES JR.

1     The Christmas season—that perilous time between Thanksgiving indigestion and midnight Mass on Christmas Eve—is an emotional gauntlet for me. It's a month of almost irresistible appeal for "essential" items that I can't afford and could easily have done without—followed by the sticker shock of credit card statements after New Year's. Besides, I find relentless holiday cheer inexpressibly depressing.

2    It wasn't always so.

3    Last year, determined to recapture the warm glow of childhood memories, I decided to spend Christmas back home in Piedmont, the West Virginia village in the Allegheny Mountains where I spent my first 18 Christmases.

4    It was a hard sell with my two daughters, who are 12 and 14 years old. No manual for parenting ever prepares you for the battle of wills when you try to persuade adolescents to spend a vacation away from their friends. Reason soon fails, leaving only the recourse of the desperate: "Because I say so, that's why." (One of the cruelest features of parenthood is the gradual discovery that your children have lives—their own lives.) "Going back to Piedmont is like traveling in a time machine," Liza, the younger child, remarked tartly. "A time machine to nowhere." The cruelty of youth!

5    Walking with my wife, Sharon Adams, and daughters down the main drag, Ashfield Street, which resembles those frontier sets you see in bad Westerns, I sorted through my abundant reserves of nostalgia to find my happiest Christmas memory.

6    As we passed what used to be the five-and-ten-cent store—it's now a warehouse—I remembered Christmas 1956, when I was 6 years old. That year, my father invited me to "ring the bell" for the Salvation Army sidewalk appeal, installed between the two double doors of the five-and-dime. Although it meant standing in the snow, half-frozen, I enjoyed myself—more because my father kept me supplied with hot cocoa than because shoppers were tossing money into the red kettle.

7    I was gulping my umpteenth cup of cocoa when an old black man walked by. His name was Mr. Smoke Clagett. "Evenin', Mr. Smoke," my father said. "How's it going today?"

8    "White man still in the lead," Mr. Smoke mumbled as he tossed a quarter into the kettle, then shuffled off through the snow.

9    "What's that mean, Daddy?" I blurted. My father laughed.

10    "He always says that," he replied. "I'll explain later." I don't know that he ever did; he must have realized I was bound to figure it out on my own one day. We had other things on our mind just then.

11    Back home, while I was still shivering and about drowned in all that hot chocolate, my parents consoled me by letting me and my older brother open one present early. We picked a big box, ripped open the wrapping paper to find a record player and a package of 45's that came with it. While my brother sang "The Great Pretender" along with the Platters, his arms spread wide and his eyes closed, I tried to puzzle out what kind of thrill Fats Domino had found up on Blueberry Hill.

12    But the big event of Christmas Eve was always the "Amos 'n' Andy" Christmas television episode, "Andy Plays Santa Claus." We watched it on a 12-inch set, which seemed mammoth in those days.

13    The episode opens with the miserly Kingfish visiting his friends' homes, pulling out a Christmas card, reading it out loud, then leaving. "I just bought one," he explains, proud of his thrift, "and I goin' around readin' it."

14    But what really captivated me was that in the all-black world of Amos 'n' Andy's Harlem, there was an all-black department store, owned and operated by black attendants for a black clientele, whose children could sit on the lap of a black Santa Claus—even if that Santa was a red-robed and white-bearded Andy (that's Andrew H. Brown to you). Andy had taken the job late on Christmas Eve just so he could buy

a present for Amos's daughter, Arbadella: an expensive talking doll, which Amos "just couldn't afford this year."

15 And then I saw it. As the camera panned across an easel and paint set (marked $5.95) and a $14.95 perambulator set, there in the heart of Santa Claus Land, perched high on the display shelf, was Arbadella's talking doll. She was wearing a starched, white fluffy dress, made all the brighter by contrast with the doll baby's gleaming black skin. A black doll! The first I'd ever seen.

16 How fortunate those people in Harlem are, I thought. Not only do they have their own department stores; those department stores sell black dolls! My cousins had about a zillion dolls, but none of them black, brown or even yellow. You could bet your bottom dollar that Piedmont's five-and-ten would stock no such item. That Arbadella was one lucky little girl. And Andy Brown was not as dumb as he looked.

17 Last Christmas, in Piedmont, I found myself struggling against the gravitational force of family and time, feeling drawn into the same old family roles, helplessly watching the re-emergence of "little Skippy" Gates as we assembled for dinner with so many aunts, uncles and cousins that our children needed a scorecard to tell the players.

18 Somehow childhood anxieties were easier to tap than childhood merriment. "Have you washed your hands?" Uncle Harry asked me as we sat down, as if I were still 6. I realized that to him I would always be stuck in a time zone of ancient Christmases. Then I remembered our collection of "Amos 'n' Andy" videotapes and decided to show it to the girls.

19 While the dishes drip-dried in the kitchen, I set up the VCR and told Liza and Maggie to take off their CD headphones and discover that marvelous world of warmth and solidarity that makes the "Amos 'n' Andy" Christmas show such a rare and poignant memory. I found myself laughing so hard at Kingfish's malapropisms and Andy's gullibility that it took me a while to realize that I was laughing alone.

20 They'll get it—eventually—I thought. Just wait until they see Arbadella's doll and the scene when Amos tucks his daughter in bed and teaches her the Lord's Prayer while the kindhearted Andy sneaks the doll under the Christmas tree.

21 So how did these two post-modernists, reared on "A Very Brady Christmas," Kwanzaa festivals, multicultural Barbies and a basement full of black dolls with names like Kenya and Kianja, respond to my desperate effort to drag them down my memory lane?

22 "It was garbage," Liza pronounced, to my disbelief. Maggie volunteered, "Fake, pathetic and stupid." Liza added: "No 8-year-old's gonna lay there while their father recites them the Lord's Prayer. Yeah, Amos, cut the prayer stuff."

23 Then Maggie demanded, "Why can't we watch *Ernest Saves Christmas*?"—a 1988 movie for children about a goofy white Florida cabdriver who helps to find Santa's successor.

24 My father, who had entered the room near the end of the program, listened quietly to this aftermath. "Looks like the white man's still in the lead," he said.

*The New York Times*, December 23, 1994

## Comprehension Questions

1. What is the topic of the passage?
2. What is the central message of the passage?

3. Determine what is at issue. What is your initial personal viewpoint?

4. Distinguish among opposing viewpoints, and provide the rationale for each.

5. Think carefully about the viewpoints. Express a personal viewpoint, and give the reasons why you favor it. Does it differ from your initial personal viewpoint? Why or why not?

6. Write a few paragraphs *in support of the viewpoint that you do* not *favor.*

## Thought and Discussion Questions

1. How do you interpret the statement "White man still in the lead" (paragraphs 8 and 24)?

2. Why did the author believe that Piedmont's five-and-ten would not stock black dolls?

3. Relate the following statement to the article: "The more things change, the more they stay the same." What things changed? What things stayed the same?

4. Was the author wrong to make his children go back with him to Piedmont for Christmas? Why or why not?

5. List any questions that came to mind while you were reading this selection, and be prepared to discuss possible answers to them.

# 3

# In Autumn We All Get Older Again

GARRISON KEILLOR

1  It is cold in the Midwest, winter is coming, and despite our best efforts, we are still getting older. The fabulous anti-aging vitamin *cathline-b,* discovered in burdock and the fiddlehead fern, was discovered too late for us; bales of burdock wouldn't make us a minute younger. In the pasture, where our burdock grows, Holsteins recline, chewing their cud. Cud is food previously eaten, then regurgitated into the mouth for further chewing. This is how a cow's digestive system works, how we get milk. A Holstein lies in the pasture, eating vomit, thinking about her career.

2  Holsteins are hardworking Danish cows who make it possible for well-disciplined families to earn a living from ground not good enough to grow corn or soybeans. Dairying is not a sentimental line of work, however, and a cow's productivity chart hangs by the stall where she can see it: she knows that when her output declines she's dead meat; retraining will not be an option. Dogs and cats, when hunting became too hard, retrained as house pets, but a large hoofy animal that chews its own vomit will never be welcome in the American home.

3  So Holsteins are trapped in their profession, which is declining anyway, and someday a brilliant geneticist will engineer an enzyme that can be thrown into a tank of silage to produce a nonfat miracle milk that makes people younger, and the Holstein breed will face a bleak future, perhaps as a game animal for the slower

hunter. A sad fate for a virtuous creature who lets down her milk twice a day and never is a problem to anybody.

4      Time catches up suddenly to us all. One day you're young and brilliant and sullen to your elders, and the next you're getting junk mail from the American Association of Retired Persons and people your very own age are talking about pension plans and the prostate. Last week, on the southwest windowsill of my studio, I found a note written in tiny strokes in the dust, with two exhausted houseflies lying beside it:

5      *go ahead and kill us god what are you waiting for you bashed our friends so whats two more you dont care youre a lousy god anyway you put us here in this beautiful world and just when life starts to get good you kill us so go do it just dont expect us to admire you for it*

6      I got a rolled-up newspaper and killed them both. In the time it would have taken to explain things, they would have died anyway.

7      Fall is gone; winter comes soon, and a freezing rain. And as your wife fixes a casserole of Spam and pineapples and hashbrowns, you go out to put salt on your sidewalk and slip, your arms waving like windmills, and something in your lower back twists loose, and you never attend the opera again. You spend the rest of your life in search of pain relief and wind up in India, penniless, lying on a mat at the Rama Lama Back Clinic, as the Master's disciple places the sacred banana on your back—ice can do this to a person, make you much older very suddenly.

8      I'll never forget what George Gershwin told me about aging. He was 37 at the time. I met him because I had gone to New York City to be honored for my heroism in riding my bike across a frozen lake to rescue a lost child, and my bicycle, the Schwinn, had been invented, of course, by Gershwin's father. Gershwin was pacing the floor of his apartment on Riverside Drive, trying to write "Love Walked In" when I came through the door, except he was calling it "Truth Walked In." He said, "Listen to this, kid," and sang it. I said, "Mr. Gershwin, I'm only 14, but I know that truth doesn't walk right in and drive the shadows away, and it doesn't bring your sunniest day either. I wonder if you don't mean love."

9      After he corrected the song, he and I walked out onto the roof. The lights of Manhattan twinkled beneath us. His hair was slicked back, just like in the pictures, and he was holding a Manhattan and a cigarette. He said, "When I was your age I owned the moon and the stars, I could do anything, and now I'm lonely as a hoot owl and my mouth tastes of cold ashes. Thirty-seven is depressing, kid. My life is half over. What am I supposed to do now?"

10     A kid can't answer that question, but I can now.

11     A sense of mortality should make us smarter. Life is short, so you do your work. You spend more time attending to music and art and literature, less time arguing polities. You plant trees. You cook spaghetti sauce. You talk to children. You don't let your life be eaten by salesmen and evangelists and the circuses of the media. The Trial of the Century was a pure waste of time. It was a tar pit, and nobody who went into it came out smarter or kinder or happier or more enlightened. It had no redeeming aspects; it taught nothing. Midwestern farm boys can get 18 years in prison for raising marijuana; rich people can walk away from murder: everyone knew that. Time to get back to work.

## Comprehension Questions

1. What is the topic of the passage?
2. What is the central message of the passage?
3. Determine what is at issue. What is your initial personal viewpoint?
4. Distinguish among opposing viewpoints, and provide the rationale for each.
5. Think carefully about the viewpoints. Express a personal viewpoint, and give the reasons why you favor it. Does it differ from your initial personal viewpoint? Why or why not?
6. Write a few paragraphs *in support of the viewpoint that you do* not *favor*.

## Thought and Discussion Questions

1. How did the manufacturer come up with the name "Schwinn" for its bicycle?
2. What was the "trial of the century," and what can you infer about the author's opinion regarding the verdict? Why?
3. Who supposedly wrote the note that the author found on the windowsill in his studio? How do you interpret it?
4. List any questions that came to mind while you were reading this selection, and be prepared to discuss possible answers to them.

# 4

## Animals, Vegetables and Minerals
### *I Love Animals and Can Still Work with Them in a Research Laboratory*

JESSICA SZYMCZYK

1   I've been a vegetarian (an ovo-lacto vegetarian, to be exact) since I was 13 years old. I don't wear cosmetics. I won't buy or wear fur. I refuse to wear or use leather if at all possible. And I absolutely love animals. I live with fish, a mouse, a pony, a horse and cats, and I'm looking for the perfect dog to complement my other companion animals. Oh, yes. I also love rats. I've had rats for pets. The last was a big black-and-white-hooded rat. I even nursed an abandoned baby mouse, whose eyes had not yet opened, until she reached adulthood.

2       So why am I working in a biomedical research lab that uses animals in its experiments? No, I am not an infiltrator from the so-called "animal rights" movement. I love what I do, and I get angry when I hear the terrible things animal-rights groups like People for the Ethical Treatment of Animals say about me and my colleagues and how we supposedly treat laboratory animals.

3       If you buy into the stories of some animal-rightists, I am the last person you would expect to find working at an animal research lab. Well, not only are these groups wrong about me and my profession; they are also grossly mistaken about my colleagues, our work and the conditions under which we keep our animals.

4        The work we do with animals is crucial. It's important to me as a woman, as a human and as an animal lover. Although most of my work as a veterinary technician involves rodents, two new studies I find pretty exciting involve dogs. In one, my dogs undergo a minor surgical procedure and take one pill a day of a promising drug that may regenerate bone in victims of osteoarthritis, a condition that cripples many elderly folks. In the second, we're investigating a drug that stimulates T-cell and white-blood-cell production, something of vital importance to AIDS patients.

5        Both would likely be condemned by the rightists as cruel and unnecessary. Let me tell you the extent of the "cruelty" my dogs undergo. In the first study, they play with a lab technician for an hour every day. The other experiment requires that they drink a tiny amount of an extremely diluted drug, about a fifth of a teaspoonful, every day for eight days, and have some blood drawn. When I draw blood, the dogs are happy to see me and they romp about like bouncy pups. Contrary to popular belief, all animals are not euthanized at the end of a study. Those that are receive the same treatment from a veterinarian that your pet would in a veterinary hospital.

6        How do I justify my profession in view of my beliefs? I want to dispel any idea that I do what I do for the money. I've wanted to work with animals—horses, actually—since I was old enough to think such thoughts. My first job out of high school was working for a wonderful and compassionate veterinarian for $4 an hour. Until then I had always imagined myself working on a farm where I could train and ride horses.

7        I guess you could say my desire to work with animals caused me to go back to school, where I earned a degree in equine veterinary science with a minor in animal science. I spent a few years as a vet tech in private practice taking care of sick animals, assisting with surgery and dealing with the pet owners. From that experience I can honestly say at least 25 percent of pet owners should never be allowed near any animals. The stories I could tell about pet mistreatment are not fit for any ears.

8        I'd never considered working in a biomedical lab until a friend invited me to apply where he worked. I did not know what to expect. TV images of dark, dirty, water-dripping dungeons floated in and out of my imagination. I didn't really want to go, but I knew he was a good person and wouldn't be associated with a bad place, so I applied. The moment I stepped into the lab was an eye-opener. I was impressed with how clean, well lit and modern the facilities are. It's more like a human hospital. The monitoring equipment, the sterile technique used in the surgery area, the anesthetics and painkillers for postoperative recovery are identical to what you would find in most hospitals for humans.

9        The animals themselves are frisky, playful and happy to see the animal techs, who play with them whenever they have a free moment. All the dogs have play toys. Do you know of any other hospital where the patient is held in a nurse's arms until he or she awakes and is steady enough to walk alone? That is part of what I do for every animal undergoing anesthesia, whether it's a rat, mouse, cat or a dog.

10       What impressed me then, and still does now that I am a part of the team, is the absolute honor, respect and devotion all of us have for the animals. Love for the animals is the rule, not the exception. The protective clothing worn by visitors to the lab is to protect the animals.

11       I take my profession very seriously. And I get angry when I hear people who don't know what they are talking about rant and rave about "torture" and duplica-

tion of tests. The research we do is essential to humans and animals. Test duplications are sometimes needed to show that the results of the first study aren't a fluke. Less than 5 percent of our studies require any pain relief at all. A full 95 percent are less painful than a visit to the doctor for you or me.

12    I've thought about the difference between animal welfare and animal rights. The whole issue of moral and ethical treatment of animals has been one that has shaped how I live my life. But there are some animal-rightists whose definitions and priorities are so extreme that they just don't apply. PETA, I've read, envisions a future where I would not be allowed to keep my pets. And it considers a rat, a mammal, the equal of a child, so deciding to save one or the other would be a flip of a coin. I cannot accept this. My love for animals matches anyone's, but there's no question in my mind as to who would come first.

13    Biomedical research has become my life. I know how researchers treat lab animals, including mice and rats. I see how the work we are doing truly benefits everyone, including animals. Today, dogs and cats can enjoy a three-to-five-year increase in their life expectancies thanks to research and the vaccines and medicines we've developed. I'm glad to be working with animals and other animal lovers to find ways to make life better for both.

*Newsweek,* August 14, 1995, p. 10

## Comprehension Questions

1. What is the topic of the passage?
2. What is the central message of the passage?
3. Determine what is at issue. What is your initial personal viewpoint?
4. Distinguish among opposing viewpoints, and provide the rationale for each.
5. Think carefully about the viewpoints. Express a personal viewpoint, and give the reasons why you favor it. Does it differ from your initial personal viewpoint? Why or why not?
6. Write a few paragraphs *in support of the viewpoint that you do* not *favor.*

## Thought and Discussion Questions

1. In your view, what is the difference, if any, between animal welfare and animal rights? Does your view differ from that of the author? Why or why not?
2. Would you work in a biomedical research laboratory? Why or why not?
3. Is it safe to conclude that the author believes that animals and humans are of equal value? Why or why not?
4. Based on your reading of the selection, can you infer that biomedical research laboratories are clean and humane? Why or why not?
5. List any questions that came to mind while you were reading this selection, and be prepared to discuss possible answers to them.

## LOOKING BACK

With two of your classmates, come up with a list of the most important points you learned from this chapter, and determine how they can be put to use in other classes. Be prepared to discuss both the list and the uses.

## THINK AGAIN!

The following passage came from a psychology textbook. After reading it carefully, use your inference skills to figure out what suggestion the colleague made to remedy the backward curtain problem without having to replace the motor.

## The Case of the Backward Curtain

A colleague of mine was in the hospital suffering from a bad back. He was confined to his bed and was dependent upon others to do many things for him. One of the few tasks he could do for himself was to open and close the curtains in his room by pressing buttons on a console beside his bed. But when he pressed the button labeled "Open," the curtains closed; pressing "Close" opened the curtains. A hospital maintenance man was called to fix the mechanism. He defined the problem as a defective motor that controlled the curtain and began to disconnect the motor when my colleague suggested, "Couldn't we look at this problem differently?"

Anthony F. Grasha, *Practical Applications of Psychology,* p. 93

## MASTERY TEST 5

A.  Answer the question and fill in the blanks.

1. A very high level comprehension of written material requiring interpretation and evaluation skills is called
   a. critical thinking
   b. inference
   c. literal comprehension
   d. critical reading
   e. none of the above

2. Inferences are _____ guesses by which we go beyond what is
   _____ in order to fill in informational _____ , come to
   _____ conclusions, and make sense of the _____ around us.

3. Inferences should be based on _____ , _____ , and _____ .

B.  Use your inference skills to answer the following questions.

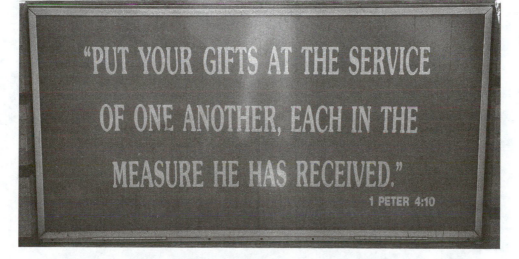

"PUT YOUR GIFTS AT THE SERVICE OF ONE ANOTHER, EACH IN THE MEASURE HE HAS RECEIVED."
1 PETER 4:10

4. What gifts are being referred to on the sign in the photograph above?
   How do you interpret the rest of the message?

   _____

   _____

   _____

   _____

   _____

5. What war is being discussed in the following passage?

1   The war affected black Americans in many ways. Several factors operated to improve their lot. One was their own growing tendency to demand fair treatment. Another was the reaction of Americans to Hitler's barbaric treatment of millions of Jews, which compelled millions of white citizens to reexamine their views about race. If the nation expected blacks to risk their lives for the common good, how could it continue to treat them as second-class citizens? Black leaders pointed out the inconsistency between fighting for democracy abroad and ignoring it at home. "We want democracy in Alabama," the NAACP announced, and this argument too had some effect on white thinking.

2       Blacks in the armed forces were treated more fairly than they had been in World War I. They were enlisted for the first time in the air force and the marines, and they were given more responsible positions in the army and navy. The army commissioned its first black general. Some 600 black pilots won their wings. Altogether about a million served, about half of them overseas.

John A. Garraty, A Short History of the American Nation,  p. 473

6. Read the passage; then answer the questions following it.

As a group, they are a very special breed apart from the rest of us. They have one goal on their minds from the moment they wake up in the morning until the moment they go to sleep at night. Although promises make up a big part of their speeches, those promises are seldom kept. Their remarks are often couched in glowing terms that are difficult to understand but always focused on the things they think we want to hear. We can't trust them! It has been that way for centuries, and it is not going to change any time soon.

a. What group is the writer discussing?
b. What goal is the writer referring to?
c. Is the writer optimistic or pessimistic about the future?
d. Is the passage mostly fact or mostly opinion?

7. Read the passage; then answer the questions following it.

I have been here for so many years that I can barely remember what it is like on the outside. The fight has been long and hard, but it all comes to an end at midnight. Although there is one last chance, that chance now seems slim at best. How I wish I could turn back the clock to that warm day in July when everything went up in smoke. If only I had ignored what he did, it might have turned out differently. Will God forgive me?

a. What is going to happen to the person in the passage?
b. What is her "one last chance"?
c. How did she get into this situation?
d. To whom is she speaking?

8. What is the central message of *all* the people quoted here?

_____

_____

_____

_____

1   **Diane:** I had a sinus infection, so I called one of the doctors on my HMO's list. When I checked in with the receptionist, she couldn't find my name on the computer, and she told me I'd have to pay. Since I had run out of the house with only $20 in my pocket, I argued with her a little. She summoned the doctor in charge of the entire clinic, the doctor I was supposed to see. He proceeded to tell me, in front of everyone, how he hated managed care and how my HMO owed him hundreds of thousands of dollars. Meanwhile I'm standing there with my head pounding, my sinuses clogged. I wanted to walk out and say, "Screw you and your clinic," but I knew I needed antibiotics. It made me feel so small and powerless.

2   **Cathleen:** I was pregnant and I started spotting, something that hadn't happened in my first pregnancy. It made me nervous, so I called my doctor's office, even though it wasn't during office hours. When she called me back she was clearly irritated that I had bothered her. She said. "Oh well, a lot of people miscarry at this stage, you had to have known that." She was very matter-of-fact. When I asked her what I could do, she told me if the bleeding got really heavy to call back and we could confirm the miscarriage with a sonogram. She was exasperated with my emotions.

3   **Cynthia:** I was going through infertility treatment. I didn't like the doctor very much, but he was highly recommended and there are continuous hormonal cycles involved, so it's hard to break away. One day he was inseminating me with my husband's sperm, and he said, "Now that's what I call a quickie." It was so disdainful I never went back. I gave up trying to have a baby for a year. It was just so offensive.

4   **Jerry:** My father was dying, supposedly of complications from diabetes, and I moved home to take care of him. I learned how to change IV's, I was dealing with a lot of body fluids. It was only later that I found out he had AIDS. His doctors knew he hadn't told me, knew I was doing all this stuff, but they never warned me about the risk of infection. I think under the circumstances that they should have told me *something*.

5   **Rebecca:** My mother had been pushing me to get a nose job. I didn't really think I needed one, but I went for the consultation anyway. She sent me to a family friend, a plastic surgeon. When I walked into his office, the first thing he said was, "What took you so long?" I felt that he disapproved of my imperfection, that any imperfection was an offense to his eye. He had a little God complex going. I blame myself because I didn't have the courage or self-esteem to

say, "I'm out of here." I felt I was at his mercy. He knew how to prey on everything I was worried about with regard to my appearance.

6    **Joanne:** I was at the gynecologist's for the first time, being fitted for a diaphragm. I was uncomfortable, and I must have squirmed. The doctor was irritated. He said, "Would you sit still so I can examine you?" Then he told me I'd better go on the Pill because if I couldn't sit still for an exam, I'd never be able to use a diaphragm. I was humiliated. He made me feel like a baby.

Elizabeth De Vita, "The Decline of the Doctor-Patient Relationship," *American Health*, June 1995, pp. 63–67, 105

## GO ELECTRONIC!

For additional readings, exercises, and Internet activities, visit our Website at:

**http://longman.awl.com/englishpages**

If you need a user name and password, see your instructor.

**Take a Road Trip to** the Great Lakes! Be sure to visit the Inference module in your Reading Road Trip CD-ROM for multimedia tutorials, exercises, and tests.

## Chapter Six

# Distinguishing Between Facts and Opinions

**Chapter Outline**

Why Distinguish Between Facts and Opinions?

What Is a Fact?

What Is an Opinion?

Facts and Opinions in Combination

Relating Facts and Opinions to Problem Solving and Contemporary Issues

# THINK ABOUT IT!

Look carefully at photographs 1, 2, and 3 below. Then for each, write a paragraph in your notebook in which you describe what you see in detail. What caption or title would you give each of the photographs?

After you have written your paragraphs and captions, read them carefully, and try to distinguish between the facts and your opinions. Discuss your conclusions with your classmates.

(1)

(2)

(3)

Is the central message of the sign in photograph 4 below a fact or an opinion? Discuss your answer with your classmates.

(4)

---

### Chapter Outcomes

After completing Chapter 6, you should be able to:
- Continue to apply the basic method for personal problem solving
- Define *fact* and *opinion*
- Define *unbiased*
- Distinguish between facts and opinions and understand why it is important to do so, particularly when dealing with problems and contemporary issues
- Continue to find topics and central messages in passages on contemporary issue to determine what is at issue, distinguish among opposing viewpoints, and express personal viewpoints

---

## Problem-Solving Exercise

Using your notebook, apply the basic method for personal problem-solving to the following hypothetical situation. Make sure to label clearly each step as you discuss what you would do.

### Hypothetical Situation

You are a single parent living alone with a 2-year-old child. This past September, you enrolled as a full-time college student with the hope of pursuing a career in social work so that you can make a better life for you and your son. So far, college has been a challenging but rewarding experience.

Because you have no immediate family living in this part of the country, you have to bring your son to a day-care center while you attend classes. Although financial aid covers your books and tuition, you are forced to work at home as a typist for an agency to support the two of you. However, there never seems to be enough money to make ends meet.

Furthermore, it is very difficult to get either typing or schoolwork done with your son running around the apartment. Thus you are living under a great deal of stress, which is affecting your performance at school and your relationship with your child. You lose your temper often and yell at him constantly. Things have to change quickly.

## Why Distinguish Between Facts and Opinions?

Read the list of ten statements below, and place an *O* next to the ones that you think are opinions, an *F* next to those that you think are facts, and an *O* and an *F* next to the items that are both opinions and facts.

1. Washington, D.C., which is the capital of the United States, is a beautiful city.
2. World War II was the last major war to be fought in the twentieth century.

3. The winters in Canada are really horrible because they are usually very cold.

4. Ronald Reagan, who was the fortieth president of the United States, was a wonderful leader.

5. The Berlin Wall, which separated East from West Berlin, has been taken down.

6. There are 50 states in the United States, and it is a widely accepted fact that Puerto Rico will become the fifty-first.

7. Experts tell us that the Mercedes-Benz is the best automobile on the market today.

8. Carbon monoxide is a poisonous gas that can be extremely deadly.

9. The United States is the most powerful country in the world.

10. Heart disease, which strikes people of all ages, can be caused by high blood pressure, smoking, and lack of exercise.

Now let's examine the responses.

Statement 1 combines both *fact* and *opinion* because Washington *is* the capital of the United States, but whether or not it is a beautiful city is a matter of opinion. Certainly, some people would agree that it is beautiful while others may not. It could depend on both the definition of the word *beautiful* and the other cities to which Washington is being compared.

Statement 2 is an *opinion* because it could be argued convincingly that there have been other major wars fought since World War II, including the one in Vietnam, which caused the loss of many American and Vietnamese lives. Furthermore, it really depends on one's definition of the word *major*. For example, does it mean many casualties, number of countries involved, or something else?

Statement 3 is a combination of *fact* and *opinion* because although it is true that the winters in Canada are usually very cold, some people would argue that cold does not necessarily make them horrible. For instance, many Canadians like cold weather because it enables them to earn a living or do things that they enjoy doing, such as skiing, skating, and playing hockey.

It is a fact that Ronald Reagan was the fortieth President of the United States, but not everyone is of the opinion that he was a wonderful leader. Thus statement 4 is also a combination of *fact* and *opinion*.

Statements 5, 8, and 10 are all *facts* that can be supported by checking various sources. They can be proved and are generally accepted by everyone.

Statement 6 is a combination of *fact* and *opinion*. Whereas the first part of the statement is obviously a fact, the second part is an opinion because it is a prediction and a matter of conjecture that Puerto Rico will become the fifty-first state. Also, the use of the word *fact* in the sentence does not necessarily prove that the information is indeed factual.

Statement 7 is an *opinion* for two reasons: First, the "experts" are not identified, so we do not know if they are reliable, and second, no data are presented that would indicate how the word *best* is being used in the sentence.

© 2000 Addison-Wesley Educational Publishers, Inc.

For example, does it refer to economical gas mileage, reliability, extensive safety equipment, exceptional good looks, or all of those pluses taken together?

Finally, statement 9 is also an *opinion* because the meaning of the word *powerful* as used in the sentence is not clear. If it refers to military power, a strong case can be made for the accuracy of the statement, although some people would argue that as long as other countries possess nuclear weapons, no single country, including the United States, is all-powerful. By contrast, if it refers to economic power, more people might argue that the United States is indeed *not* the most powerful country in the world.

As you can see, it is sometimes not simple to distinguish between opinions and facts, yet if you expect to think and read critically, you must be able to separate fact from opinion as part of evaluating what you see, hear, and read. In other words, you should not automatically accept information without first considering its accuracy, its source, and the motivations of whoever is presenting it. Otherwise, you are in danger of accepting opinions as facts, and that could have a negative effect on the decisions you make in life. For example, you could end up taking the wrong course, choosing the wrong solution to a problem, accepting the wrong version of a story, buying the wrong product, dating the wrong person, or voting for the wrong candidate. Thus the cost of confusing facts and opinions can be quite substantial. Let's take a closer look at how to distinguish between them.

## What Is a Fact?

A **fact** is something that can be or has been proved, verified, or confirmed in an unbiased manner. As you know, *unbiased* means "evenhanded," "objective," "impartial," or "without prejudice." You can prove, verify, or confirm a fact by personal observation, by using the observations of others, or by checking with reliable sources, such as studies that have been conducted, reputable books that have been written, or noted experts in a given field.

Personal observation simply involves checking something for ourselves, such as going to a person's home to verify that the person lives there. However, for practical reasons, we sometimes have to rely on the observations of others who serve as witnesses when we are unable to be present ourselves. For information about an event that occurred in the past or one that is happening in a far-off place that we cannot get to—such as the taking down of the Berlin Wall in Germany—we must rely on the eyewitness accounts of others. Finally, sometimes we must rely on written materials or other people who have more expertise than we do in a particular subject to determine if something is indeed factual. For instance, most people would rely on what they have read in the medical literature, including the results of studies conducted by prominent physicians, to conclude that statement 10, dealing with heart disease, is factually accurate.

One of the keys to uncovering facts, then, is our determination that they have been or can be proved in an unbiased way. In other words, we have to be reasonably certain that the observations, experts, and any additional sources that we use or that are presented to us by others are as evenhanded as possible and not clouded by personal opinion.

Also, keep in mind that facts can change over time as conditions change, resulting in the elimination of some facts and the addition of others. For example, it was once a fact that there were 48 states in the United States, but that was no longer a fact after the addition of the states of Alaska and Hawaii in 1959, thereby bringing the total to 50. Thus one fact was replaced by another. In short, determining whether or not something is a fact is an ongoing process that involves careful evaluation and continuous reevaluation, both of which are important characteristics of critical thinking.

## ACTIVITY 1

In your notebook, list ten facts, and be prepared to discuss them in class.

## What Is an Opinion?

An **opinion** is someone's personal judgment about something that has not been proved, verified, or confirmed in an unbiased manner. In the more obvious cases, words like *good*, *bad*, *right*, or *wrong* are often used with opinions. However, sometimes people are more subtle when offering their opinions, which makes them more difficult to recognize. For example, the statements "George Bush was a bad president" and "George Bush, as president, left something to be desired" both express negative opinions, but the first is stronger and more obvious than the second.

Also, be on the lookout for opinions that are couched in factual terms, such as "The fact of the matter is that abortion is wrong!" Just because the word *fact* is used does not make the statement a fact. You saw another example of an opinion couched in factual terms in statement 6, which asserted that "it is a widely accepted fact that Puerto Rico will become the fifty-first [state]."

Finally, opinions can sometimes turn into facts after they have been proved, verified, or confirmed in an unbiased manner. For instance, a week before your birthday, you can claim that it is going to rain on that day, which is your opinion. However, if it does rain on that day, your original claim has become a fact, which can now be proved. Thus opinions, like facts, can change over time and should therefore be reevaluated.

When dealing with opinions in general, you should not automatically disregard them. First of all, you need to take into consideration who is offering a given opinion. An expert or some other person who has extensive education, training, or experience in a given area is in a strong position to offer an opinion in that area. That kind of opinion, sometimes called an **informed opinion,** should be taken seriously. For example, the foreign policy views of the chair of the U.S. Senate Foreign Relations Committee are worth careful consideration, as are those of a cancer researcher if the subject involves the causes of that disease. Opinions in general are also worth looking at because they can give you new ideas and viewpoints that you may not have thought about before. In short, always make it a practice to evaluate the opinions you encounter and give special consideration to their sources.

## ACTIVITY 2

In your notebook, list ten opinions, and be prepared to discuss them in class.

## Facts and Opinions in Combination

As you saw at the beginning of this chapter, often facts and opinions are used in combination, which makes it more difficult to distinguish between them. Sometimes this is done inadvertently when we are trying to express ourselves orally or in writing, but it can also be an intentional device to influence or persuade others. Commercials that influence our decisions as to what to purchase or whom to vote for and propaganda that attempts to persuade people to think in a certain way or support a certain course of action come to mind immediately as examples of how this technique can be used effectively.

For instance, a political commercial that states "Inflation is rising dramatically. But don't worry—our candidate has the answer! Remember that when you vote next Tuesday!" is probably a combination of fact and opinion. A rising inflation rate can be proved by published statistics, but whether or not the candidate has the answer to the problem is not so simple to prove, at least not at this time. Of course, the whole purpose of the commercial is to get you to vote for that candidate. If indeed the official does eventually solve the inflation problem after the election, the latter part of the original commercial has become a fact. Once again, you must carefully evaluate and continuously reevaluate what you see, hear, and read.

## ACTIVITY 3

In your notebook, list ten statements that combine facts and opinions, and be prepared to discuss them in class.

## Relating Facts and Opinions to Problem Solving and Contemporary Issues

When engaged in problem solving, you are already aware of the importance of gathering information as part of Step 2 of the approach that we have been using. No matter where the information comes from, it is crucial that it be as factual as possible. Otherwise, you could base your possible solutions on opinions or biased information, in which case they may not turn out to be solutions at all.

For example, if you are trying to solve the problem of a car engine that is smoking and you accept the opinion of a person who knows little about car engines, you are likely to waste your time, effort, and money. But if you consult a reliable car repair manual or take the advice of a reputable mechanic, you will probably end up with a solution to the problem. In short, the more you base possible solutions on facts, the better your chances of resolving problems.

As you already know, the ability to distinguish between facts and opinions is an important part of critical reading in general, no matter what kind of material you have in front of you. When you read, you should know whether or not you are dealing with information that is reliable and factual. Textbook material, for the most part, fits into that category due to its educational focus and because it is usually reviewed and approved by publishers and scholars prior to publication. When doing other kinds of reading, you need to be more vigilant, because facts and opinions are often interspersed.

That is certainly the case with contemporary issues, which tend to arouse emotions and bring out an array of opinions and opposing viewpoints. Furthermore, the ratio of facts to opinions will vary widely from passage to passage. Some will consist mostly of facts, some will consist mostly of opinions, and some will fall somewhere in between.

In addition, writers will not always make their purpose, tone or mood, obvious or mention the sources from which they have gotten their information. In those instances, you will either have to do research yourself or make a decision on the spot regarding the credentials of the writer and the reliability of the publication in which the information appeared. As you know, you can spend a great deal of time doing research, and sometimes that will be necessary if your purpose, for example, is to write a term paper for one of your courses. However, on other occasions, when you may be reading for pleasure, you can use your inference skills to come to a logical conclusion as to the writer's purpose and the reliability of the publication so that you can ultimately determine if the information is unbiased.

We will deal more thoroughly with purpose and tone in Chapter 7, but keep in mind at this point that recognizing purpose is an important part of determining what proportion of the material before you is factual and how much is opinion. As you can see, uncovering bias is not an exact science. It does require time and effort on your part, but that is what critical reading and critical thinking are all about.

## ACTIVITY 4

Refer to the information you gathered for Step 2 in the problem-solving exercise at the beginning of this chapter. Was it mostly fact, mostly opinion, or a combination of both? Why?

## ACTIVITY 5

Write a three-paragraph essay on a contemporary issue of your choice. Make the first paragraph mostly fact, the second paragraph mostly opinion, and the third paragraph a combination of both. Be prepared to read your essay aloud in class.

## ACTIVITY 6

The following problem was taken from a psychology textbook. After reading and thinking about it carefully, get together with one of your classmates to discuss how to gather facts to solve it.

> Suppose that you live in a town that has one famous company, Boopsie's Biscuits and Buns. Everyone in the town is grateful for the 3B company and goes to work there with high hopes. Soon, however, an odd thing starts happening to many employees. They complain of fatigue and irritability. They are taking lots of sick leave. Productivity declines. What's going on at Boopsie's? Is everybody suffering from sheer laziness?

> Carol Tavris and Carole Wade, *Psychology in Perspective*, p. 437

## ACTIVITY 7

Read the following passages and answer the questions that follow. When reading each passage, try to make a determination as to what is fact and what is opinion. As part of that process, it will be helpful for you to take note of the writer's credentials if they are included, any sources mentioned, and the publication from which the passage was taken. Also, remember to use inference skills when appropriate.

### 1

## It's More Influential Than TV Advertising. So Why Do They Call It "Junk Mail"?

1   Any advertising medium that can influence consumers better than television deserves more respect.

2       And, in fact, most people like direct mail advertising. More than half the population read it promptly and completely, and say they find it useful. Some even say they'd like more. Over half the people in America order goods and services through catalogs or other advertising that comes by mail.

3       All of which is probably why direct mail is the U.S. Postal Service's fastest-growing business. Marketers large and small like it because it's inexpensive, goes

straight to specific customers, invites response and gets results. And direct mail pays for itself, which is reassuring to customers who think first-class postage rates subsidize third-class mail.

4      Direct mail is an essential component of the American retail economy. It benefits marketers and consumers alike. In 1995, it generated almost $385 billion in sales revenues for marketers. And it brought happiness to a lot of people who like browsing through catalogs, discovering unique products, or finding out about neighborhood bargains without leaving the comforts of home.

5      And now direct mail is going international. In 1995, the U.S. Postal Service sent to Japan the one millionth package for a major catalog retailer who is building a customer base there. And that helps the balance of payments.

6      So, call it Direct Marketing, call it Ad Mail—but please, don't call it junk mail.

*United States Postal Service. We Deliver For You.*

## Comprehension Questions

1. What is the topic of the passage?
2. What is the central message of the passage?
3. Determine what is at issue. What is your initial personal viewpoint?
4. Distinguish among opposing viewpoints, and provide the rationale for each.
5. Think carefully about the viewpoints. Express a personal viewpoint, and give the reasons why you favor it. Does it differ from your initial personal viewpoint? Why or why not?
6. Write a few paragraphs *in support of the viewpoint that you do* not *favor.*

## Thought and Discussion Questions

1. Would you prefer to call this mail "junk mail," "direct marketing," or "ad mail"? Why?
2. If you had the option of never receiving this kind of mail again, would you take that option? Why or why not?
3. Do you think the information presented is mostly fact, mostly opinion, or a combination of both? Why? Provide specific examples.
4. Do you think the article is unbiased? Why or why not?
5. List any questions that came to mind while you were reading this selection, and be prepared to discuss possible answers to them.

## 2

# A Simple Act

1      When our family—my wife Maggie, our 4-year-old Eleanor, and I—drove through Messina, Sicily, to our hotel in the early hours of the morning one day last September, I felt I had never been in a bleaker place. We didn't know a soul, the streets

were deserted, and we were leaving at the hospital our 7-year-old son in a deep and dreadful coma.

2    We wanted only to go home, to take Nicholas with us, however badly injured, to help nurse him through whatever he faced, to hold his hand again, to put our arms around him.

3    It had been the worst night of our lives.

4    The next morning we took a bus back to the hospital. There had been no deterioration but no improvement either. "You know, there are miracles," said the man who had been appointed to act as our interpreter, but the doctors looked grave. In lives that only a few hours before had been full of warmth and laughter, there was now a gnawing emptiness.

5    Within days our intensely personal experience erupted into a worldwide story. Newspapers and television told of the shooting attack by car bandits, Nicholas' death, and our decision to donate his organs. Since then streets, schools, scholarships, and hospitals all over Italy have been named for him. We have received honors previously reserved largely for kings and presidents, prizes that go mainly to Nobelists and awards usually given to spiritual leaders of the stature of Mother Teresa. Maria Shriver, who all her life has been told by people where they were when President Kennedy was shot, told us where she was when she heard about Nicholas. Strangers come up to us on the street still, tears in their eyes.

6    We have received letters from about a thousand people around the world, written with a simple eloquence possible only when it comes straight from the heart. A 40-year-old American, who recently became blind, said our story had given him the strength to resist despair. One man who was close to death now has a new lung because someone was moved by what happened to Nicholas. A woman who lost her 4-year-old daughter imagines the two children playing happily together in a place where there is no violence.

7    All this for a decision that seemed so obvious we've forgotten which of us suggested it.

8    I remember the hushed room and the physicians standing in a small group, hesitant to ask crass questions about organ donation. As it happens, we were able to relieve them of the thankless task. We looked at each other. "Now that he's gone, shouldn't we give the organs?" one of us asked. "Yes," the other replied. And that was all there was to it.

9    Our decision was not clouded by any doubts about the medical staff. We were convinced they had done everything in their power to save Nicholas. To be sure, we asked how they knew his brain was truly dead, and they described their high-tech methods in clear, simple language. It helped. But more than that, it was the bond of trust that had been established from the beginning that left no doubt they would not have given up until all hope was gone.

10    Yet we've been asked a hundred times: How could you have done it? And a hundred times we've searched for words to convey the sense of how clear and how right the choice seemed. Nicholas was dead. He no longer looked like a sleeping child. By giving his organs we weren't hurting him but we were helping others.

11    For us, Nicholas will always live, in our hearts and our memories. But he wasn't in that body anymore.

12    His toys are still here, including the flag on his log fort, which I put at half-staff when we returned home and which has stayed that way ever since. We have assembled all his photographs, starting with the blur I snapped a few moments after he was born. Nicholas now lies in a peaceful country churchyard in California, dressed for eternity in the kind of blue blazer and neat slacks he liked and a tie with Goofy on it.

13    Donating his organs, then, wasn't a particularly magnanimous act. But not to have given them would have seemed to us such an act of miserliness that we don't believe we could have thought about it later without shame. The future of a radiant little creature had been taken away. It was important to us that someone else should have that future.

14    It turned out to be seven people's future, most of them young, most very sick. One 19-year-old within 48 hours of death ("We'd given up on her," her physician told me later) is now a vivacious beauty who turns heads as she walks down the street. The 60-pound 15-year-old who got Nicholas' heart had spent half his life in hospitals; now he's a relentless bundle of energy. One of the recipients, when told by his doctors to think of something nice as he was taken to the operating theater, said, "I am thinking of something nice. I'm thinking of Nicholas." I recently visited him at school; he's a wonderful little fellow any father would be proud of and, I admit, I did feel pride. The man who received one of Nicholas' corneas told us that at one time he was unable to see his children. Now, after two operations, he happily watches his daughter fencing and his son play rugby.

15    We are pleased the publicity this incident has caused should have led to such a dramatic arousal of interest in organ donation. It seems unfair, however, to the thousands of parents and children who, in lonely hospital waiting rooms around the world, have made exactly the same decision. Their loss is indistinguishable from ours, but their willingness to share rather than to hoard life has remained largely unrecognized.

16    I imagine that for them, like us, the emptiness is always close by. I don't believe Maggie and I will ever be really happy again; even our best moments are tinged with sadness. But our joy in seeing so much eager life that would otherwise have been lost, and the relief on the families' faces, is so uplifting that it has given us some recompense for what otherwise would have been just a sordid act of violence.

Reg Green
Bodega Bay, Calif.

JAMA, Vol. 273, No. 22 (June 14, 1995), p. 1732

## Comprehension Questions

1. What is the topic of the passage?
2. What is the central message of the passage?
3. Determine what is at issue. What is your initial personal viewpoint?
4. Distinguish among opposing viewpoints, and provide the rationale for each.
5. Think carefully about the viewpoints. Express a personal viewpoint, and give the reasons why you favor it. Does it differ from your initial personal viewpoint? Why or why not?
6. Write a few paragraphs *in support of the viewpoint that you do* not *favor.*

**Thought and Discussion Questions**

1. If you had been Nicholas's parent, what decision would you have made? Why?

2. What decision have you made regarding the use of your organs after you die? Why?

3. If a member of your family needed one of your kidneys right now to survive, what would you do? Why?

4. Do you think the information presented is mostly fact, mostly opinion, or a combination of both? Why? Provide specific examples.

5. Do you think the article is unbiased? Why or why not?

6. List any questions that came to mind while you were reading this selection, and be prepared to discuss possible answers to them.

# 3

## Making the Grade
### *Many Students Wheedle for a Degree as If It Were a Freebie T-Shirt*

KURT WIESENFELD

1    It was a rookie error. After 10 years I should have known better, but I went to my office the day after final grades were posted. There was a tentative knock on the door. "Professor Wiesenfeld? I took your Physics 2121 class? I flunked it? I wonder if there's anything I can do to improve my grade?" I thought: "Why are you asking me? Isn't it too late to worry about it? Do you dislike making declarative statements?"

2    After the student gave his tale of woe and left, the phone rang. "I got a D in your class. Is there any way you can change it to 'Incomplete'?" Then the e-mail assault began: "I'm shy about coming in to talk to you, but I'm not shy about asking for a better grade. Anyway, it's worth a try." The next day I had three phone messages from students asking *me* to call *them*. I didn't.

3    Time was, when you received a grade, that was it. You might groan and moan, but you accepted it as the outcome of your efforts or lack thereof (and, yes, sometimes a tough grader). In the last few years, however, some students have developed a disgruntled-consumer approach. If they don't like their grade, they go to the "return" counter to trade it in for something better.

4    What alarms me is their indifference toward grades as an indication of personal effort and performance. Many, when pressed about why they think they deserve a better grade, admit they don't deserve one but would like one anyway. Having been raised on gold stars for effort and smiley faces for self-esteem, they've learned that they can get by without hard work and real talent if they can talk the professor into giving them a break. This attitude is beyond cynicism. There's a weird innocence to the assumption that one expects (even deserves) a better grade simply by begging for it. With that outlook, I guess I shouldn't be as flabbergasted as I was that 12 students asked me to change their grades *after* final grades were posted.

5     That's 10 percent of my class who let three months of midterms, quizzes and lab reports slide until long past remedy. My graduate student calls it hyperrational thinking: if effort and intelligence don't matter, why should deadlines? What matters is getting a better grade through an unearned bonus, the academic equivalent of a freebie T shirt or toaster giveaway. Rewards are disconnected from the quality of one's work. An act and its consequences are unrelated, random events.

6     Their arguments for wheedling better grades often ignore academic performance. Perhaps they feel it's not relevant. "If my grade isn't raised to a D I'll lose my scholarship." "If you don't give me a C, I'll flunk out." One sincerely overwrought student pleaded, "If I don't pass, my life is over." This is tough stuff to deal with. Apparently, I'm responsible for someone's losing a scholarship, flunking out or deciding whether life has meaning. Perhaps these students see me as a commodities broker with something they want—a grade. Though intrinsically worthless, grades, if properly manipulated, can be traded for what has value: a degree, which means a job, which means money. The one thing college actually offers—a chance to learn—is considered irrelevant, even less than worthless, because of the long hours and hard work required.

7     In a society saturated with surface values, love of knowledge for its own sake does sound eccentric. The benefits of fame and wealth are more obvious. So is it right to blame students for reflecting the superficial values saturating our society?

8     Yes, of course it's right. These guys had better take themselves seriously now, because our country will be forced to take them seriously later, when the stakes are much higher. They must recognize that their attitude is not only self-destructive, but socially destructive. The erosion of quality control—giving appropriate grades for actual accomplishments—is a major concern in my department. One colleague noted that a physics major could obtain a degree without ever answering a written exam question completely. How? By pulling in enough partial credit and extra credit. And by getting breaks on grades.

9     But what happens once she or he graduates and gets a job? That's when the misfortunes of eroding academic standards multiply. We lament that schoolchildren get "kicked upstairs" until they graduate from high school despite being illiterate and mathematically inept, but we seem unconcerned with college graduates whose less blatant deficiencies are far more harmful if their accreditation exceeds their qualifications.

10    Most of my students are science and engineering majors. If they're good at getting partial credit but not at getting the answer right, then the new bridge breaks or the new drug doesn't work. One finds examples here in Atlanta. Last year a light tower in the Olympic Stadium collapsed, killing a worker. It collapsed because an engineer miscalculated how much weight it could hold. A new 12-story dormitory could develop dangerous cracks due to a foundation that's uneven by more than six inches. The error resulted from incorrect data being fed into a computer. I drive past that dorm daily on my way to work, wondering if a foundation crushed under kilotons of weight is repairable or if this structure will have to be demolished. Two 10,000-pound steel beams at the new natatorium collapsed in March, crashing into the student athletic complex. (Should we give partial credit since no one was hurt?) Those are real-world consequences of errors and lack of expertise.

11    But the lesson is lost on the grade-grousing 10 percent. Say that you won't (not can't, but won't) change the grade they deserve to what they want, and they're fre-

quently bewildered or angry. They don't think it's fair that they're judged according to their performance, not their desires or "potential." They don't think it's fair that they should jeopardize their scholarships or be in danger of flunking out simply because they could not or did not do their work. But it's more than fair; it's necessary to help preserve a minimum standard of quality that our society needs to maintain safety and integrity. I don't know if the 13th-hour students will learn that lesson, but I've learned mine. From now on, after final grades are posted, I'll lie low until the next quarter starts.

*Newsweek,* June 17, 1996, p. 16

## Comprehension Questions

1. What is the topic of the passage?
2. What is the central message of the passage?
3. Determine what is at issue. What is your initial personal viewpoint?
4. Distinguish among opposing viewpoints, and provide the rationale for each.
5. Think carefully about the viewpoints. Express a personal viewpoint, and give the reasons why you favor it. Does it differ from your initial personal viewpoint? Why or why not?
6. Write a few paragraphs *in support of the viewpoint that you do* not *favor.*

## Thought and Discussion Questions

1. In your opinion, is "hyperrational thinking" ever acceptable? Why or why not? Have you ever engaged in it? When and why?
2. Do you agree with the author that the erosion of quality control with regard to academic standards can be socially destructive? Why or why not?
3. If you were a college instructor, would you permit students to raise their grades by doing extra credit work? Why or why not?
4. Do you think the information presented is mostly fact, mostly opinion, or a combination of both? Why? Provide specific examples.
5. Do you think the article is unbiased? Why or why not?
6. List any questions that came to mind while you were reading this selection, and be prepared to discuss possible answers to them.

## 4

## Fertility for Sale

1   *As reproductive technology has advanced, the law of supply and demand has inevitably clicked in. Some clinics have had trouble finding women to donate their eggs for implantation in infertile women. That has led to a medical and ethical debate over*

*whether donors should charge for their eggs and, if so, how much. The St. Barnabas Medical Center in Livingston, N.J., recently accelerated that debate by offering $5,000 for donors, double the rate of many clinics. A variety of experts were asked whether women should be permitted to sell their eggs on the open market:*

**Robert Wright** *is* the author of The Moral Animal: Evolutionary Psychology and Everyday Life.

2    Is a woman who gets several thousand dollars for a few eggs being exploited? The claim is not on its face ridiculous; a donor undergoes an unpleasant and risky procedure that is invasive both physically and in a less tangible sense. What *is* ridiculous is the idea that the woman is more exploited if she gets $5,000 than if she gets $2,000. Yet that is the implicit logic of some who argue for limiting fees lest we degrade women by turning their eggs into commodities.

3    Critics of high fees say it's all right to compensate donors, just not to entice them. But that distinction faded years ago, when infertile women began paying more than a few hundred dollars for eggs. They found that if they didn't pay real money, they'd get no eggs. This is the market at work: a willing buyer, a willing seller. Is there any reason to get between them?

4    Sometimes society plausibly says yes, as with drug sales and prostitution. Personally, I don't see a comparably strong argument in this case. If there is one, maybe we should take eggs off the market. But what's the point of pretending they aren't already there?

**Cynthia Gorney** is the author of Articles of Faith: A Frontline History of the Abortion Wars.

5    A precedent for limiting compensation for egg donation was set 15 years ago, when the most heated argument in infertility circles was about surrogate mothers—women who volunteered to undergo artificial insemination and carry a baby to term for infertile couples. The ethical consensus then was that if a woman offers to lend out her own reproductive system because she wants to help someone else, we suppose we can't stop her, but she shouldn't be tempted to do it because she wants or needs money: a surrogate should be paid for medical expenses and lost time at work, and perhaps offered some modest extra cash to offset the physical discomfort of pregnancy. But the money should not be generous enough to make surrogacy an attractive line of work.

6    And as a rule, surrogate mothers still don't collect much money, nor should they. To be sure, this is partly because they deliver up fully developed human beings, which by law and venerable tradition may not be bought and sold. But it is also because surrogate mothers deliver up their own bodily organs—their eggs and the use of their wombs—and we have equally venerable tradition forbidding people to sell their body parts for profit.

7    Galloping technology and the escalating hopes of infertile couples are working together to push us much too far, too fast. There has got to be a point at which society declares to the infertile couple: We are sorry for your situation, but you cannot buy everything you want. We will not let you offer that young woman $10,000 for some of her eggs, just as we will not let you offer her brother $10,000 for one of his kidneys. The potential cost to both of them—and to all the rest of us—is too high.

**Lee M. Silver,** a biology professor at Princeton, is the author of Remaking Eden: Cloning and Beyond in a Brave New World.

8    Why are physicians and bioethicists—who are mostly male—trying to limit monetary compensation to women who donate their eggs? In no other part of the economy do we limit the amount of money that can be paid to people who participate in risky or demeaning activities. Indeed, college students have long been enticed by high fees into participating in risky medical experiments.

9    But society expects women to be altruistic, not venal. And it insists that women be protected from themselves, on the assumption that they are unable to make rational decisions about their own bodies. And perhaps men feel threatened by the idea that women now also have a way to spread their seed upon the earth.

**Robert Coles,** a physician, is a professor of social ethics at Harvard and the author, most recently, of The Youngest Parents: Teen-Age Pregnancy as It Shapes Lives.

10    We really don't know the long-term medical consequences for women who donate their eggs. There have been a few reports of serious side effects, like renal failure. But have researchers studied carefully enough what exposure to these fertility drugs does to women? If poor women become repeat donors because the process keeps getting more lucrative, will they increase their risk down the line for ovarian cancer? These are unanswered questions.

11    Most important, the widening divide between the rich and the poor poses an ethical dilemma: can we condone the "harvesting" of eggs from poor women, who may be putting their health at risk, for the benefit of the affluent?

**Elizabeth Bartholet,** *a professor at* Harvard Law School, is the author of Family Bonds: Adoption and the Politics of Parenting.

12    The selling of human eggs puts at risk the donors' health and sacrifices their human dignity. It also encourages women to bear children who are not genetically related to them, so that their mates can have genetic offspring. This practice produces children who have lost one genetic parent—in a world that already has an abundance of orphans who need homes.

13    We need to call a halt to further commercialization of reproduction to give policy makers a chance to consider the ethical issues involved in reproductive technology like egg selling, cloning and sex selection. We should follow the lead of other countries and establish a national commission to resolve these issues rather than leave them to the market.

**Lori Arnold** is a doctor at the Fertility and I.V.F. Center of Miami.

14    Most women who donate their eggs at our clinic do so because they want to help provide the gift of life. Many have children of their own; they want to help others experience the joys of motherhood.

15    The motive is altruistic, but that should not blind anyone to the practical difficulties. Donors are required to undergo treatment with fertility drugs, counseling, screening, ultrasound monitoring, blood work and numerous office visits. It takes weeks. And retrieving the eggs from their ovaries is a surgical procedure.

16    Also worth factoring in is that the donors are giving a couple the chance to have a family, with a child who has the father's genetic makeup. The donor also

gives the recipient a chance to experience pregnancy, delivery and breast-feeding, thereby facilitating mother-baby bonding.

17    Thus compensation given to an egg donor is well deserved. Of course, there comes a point when a fee becomes self-defeating, since the cost is paid by the recipient—few couples can afford to pay an unlimited amount. But donors deserve something more than a token. Ours receive $1,500 to $2,000; no one should begrudge them that.

*The New York Times,* March 4, 1998

## Comprehension Questions

1. What is the topic of the passage?
2. What is the central message of the passage?
3. Determine what is at issue. What is your initial personal viewpoint?
4. Distinguish among opposing viewpoints, and provide the rationale for each.
5. Think carefully about the viewpoints. Express a personal viewpoint, and give the reasons why you favor it. Does it differ from your initial personal viewpoint? Why or why not?
6. Write a few paragraphs *in support of the viewpoint that you do* not *favor.*

## Thought and Discussion Questions

1. If your spouse and you were infertile, would you agree to having a surrogate mother carry a baby to term for you? Why or why not?
2. If your spouse and you were infertile, would you agree to having donor eggs implanted? Why or why not?
3. If you are a woman, would you agree to be a surrogate mother or an egg donor if the price were right? Why or why not? If you are a man, would you support your wife's decision to be a surrogate mother or an egg donor if the price were right? Why or why not?
4. Do you think the information presented is mostly fact, mostly opinion, or a combination of both? Why? Provide specific examples.
5. Do you think the article is unbiased? Why or why not?
6. List any questions that came to mind while you were reading this selection, and be prepared to discuss possible answers to them.

## LOOKING BACK

With two of your classmates, come up with a list of the most important points you learned from this chapter, and determine how they can be put to use in other classes. Be prepared to discuss both the list and the uses.

## THINK AGAIN!

Assume that *you* are the person making the statement "Brothers and sisters, I have none. But that man's father is my father's son." What is the relationship of *that man* to you? Get together with a classmate, and discuss the possibilities.

## MASTERY TEST 6

A. Answer the questions and fill in the blanks.

1. What is a fact?

_____

_____

2. What is an opinion?

_____

_____

3. A statement is *unbiased* when it is
   a. evenhanded
   b. objective
   c. impartial
   d. without prejudice
   e. all of the above

4. You can prove or verify a fact by personal _____ , by using the observations of _____ , or by checking with reliable _____.

5. "As a critical thinker, you must disregard all opinions." Is this statement true or false?

6. An _____ opinion is one given by a person with extensive education, training, or experience in the particular area being discussed.

B. After each statement, indicate whether it is a fact, an opinion, or a combination of both.

7. It is a fact that capital punishment serves as a deterrent to murder. _____

8. Although the Supreme Court has made a landmark decision regarding abortion, the issue is far from settled. _____

9. The Clinton-Lewinsky matter was given extensive coverage by the media. _____

10. The Soviet Union no longer exists, but there still is much instability in Europe. _____

11. Women's rights have improved greatly because of the feminist movement. _____

C. Place an *O* next to the paragraph that consists of opinion and an *F* next to the paragraph that consists of fact.

12. When Nixon became president in 1969, the major economic problem facing him was inflation. It was caused primarily by the heavy military expenditures and "easy money" policies of the Johnson administration. Nixon cut federal spending and balanced the 1969 budget, while the Federal Reserve Board forced up interest rates in order to slow the expansion of the money supply. When prices continued to rise, there was mounting uneasiness. Labor unions demanded large wage increases. In 1970 Congress passed a law giving the president power to regulate prices and wages.

John A. Garraty, *A Short History of the American Nation,* p. 52

13. Surely there is no more cherished, yet humbling, idea than the conviction that parents hold in their hands the power to shape their child's tomorrows. And the evidence for it is as impossible to ignore as the toddler throwing a tantrum in the grocery store when Daddy refuses to buy him M&Ms: setting reasonable, but firm, limits teaches children self-control and good behavior, but being either too permissive or too dictatorial breeds little brats. Giving your little girl a big hug when she skins her knee makes her feel loved and secure, which enables her to form trusting relationships when she blooms into a young woman. Reading and talking to children fosters a love of reading; divorce puts them at risk of depression and academic failure. Physical abuse makes them aggressive, but patience and kindness, as shown by the parents who soothe their child's frustration at not being able to play a favorite piano piece rather than belittling him, leaves a child better able to handle distress both in youth and in adulthood. Right?

Sharon Begley, "The Parent Traps," *Newsweek,* September 7, 1998, p. 53

D. The two passages that follow deal with the same issue. What is that issue? Alongside each passage, indicate whether it consists of mostly fact, mostly opinion, or a combination of both.

14. Perhaps the most unfortunate victims of drug prohibition laws have been the residents of America's ghettos. These laws have proved largely futile in deterring ghetto-dwellers from becoming drug abusers, but they do account for much of what ghetto residents identify as the drug problem. Aggressive, gun-toting drug dealers often upset law-abiding residents far more than do addicts nodding out in doorways. Meanwhile other residents perceive the drug dealers as heroes and successful role models. They're symbols of success to children who see no other options. At the same time the increasingly harsh criminal penalties imposed on adult drug dealers have led drug traffickers to recruit juveniles. Where once children started dealing drugs only after they had been using them for a few years, today the sequence is often reversed. Many children start using drugs only after working for older drug dealers for a while. . . . Legalization of drugs, like legalization of alcohol in the early 1930s, would drive the drug-dealing business off the streets and out of apartment buildings and into government-regulated, tax-paying stores. It also would force many of the gun-toting dealers out of the business and convert others into legitimate businessmen.

Ethan A. Nadelmann, "Shooting Up," *The New Republic,* June 1988

15. All studies show that those most likely to try drugs, get hooked, and die—as opposed to those who suffer from cirrhosis and lung cancer—are young people, who are susceptible to the lure of quick thrills and are terribly adaptable to messages provided by adult society. Under pressure of the current prohibition, the number of kids who use illegal drugs at least once a month has fallen from 39 percent in the late 1970s to 25 percent in 1987, according to the annual survey of high school seniors conducted by the University of Michigan. The same survey shows that attitudes toward drug use have turned sharply negative. But use of legal drugs is still strong. Thirty-eight percent of high school seniors reported getting drunk within the past two weeks, and 27 percent said they smoke cigarettes every day. Drug prohibition is working with kids; legalization would do them harm.

Morton M. Kondracke, "Don't Legalize Drugs," *The New Republic,* June 27, 1988

E. For each of the longer selections that follow, indicate whether the information presented is mostly fact, mostly opinion, or a combination of both.

16. ## America's Favorite Food: The Hamburger

1   It's not only the President who enjoys a good hamburger.

2      Americans consume some 38 billion hamburgers a year. And, according to a fast food expert, they account for nearly 60 percent of all sandwiches sold over the counter, replacing the hot dog as the nation's most popular food item.

3      "Hamburgers are popular because they are great tasting and basic, yet can be adapted to suit various tastes," suggested Linda Vaughan, vice president of new products for Jack in the Box restaurants, which sold 200 million hamburgers last year.

4      Americans consume about 25 percent of their meals away from home, and about half of that in fast food restaurants, she said. So it's no wonder that nearly five billion hamburgers and cheeseburgers were served in commercial restaurants in 1993, according to the National Restaurant Association.

5      No one can claim the exact date the first hamburger was made, but America's favorite sandwich got its name in the 18th century from German immigrants from the city of Hamburg who brought their popular broiled chopped steak to the United States. The rest is hamburger history.

6      What makes today's hamburger perfect is a matter of debate, but no matter. Variety in hamburgers has become the norm, Vaughan said. Though some restaurants specialize in basic burgers, others pride themselves on making every condiment count.

7      But whether it's a secret sauce or bacon and onion rings that draws people to hamburgers, Americans have many ways of creating a sandwich unique to them. "They can be made to suit individual tastes from the basic to the exotic," said Vaughan.

8      "In our research, we discovered many people literally crave the taste of a hamburger, some claiming that they can eat a good burger every day of the week." In fact, she said, Jack in the Box, a fast food chain targeted primarily to

more adult tastes, is refocusing its efforts on the hamburger in its many varieties as a business strategy. "It's a taste people don't get tired of, even as food trends come and go."

*Smart Publications,* September 16, 1995, p. 13

## 17. Wasn't the Congo Green?

SUNNY PLUTZER

1   A long time ago, my grandmother would sigh and say, "What was, isn't." I, being young, wanted to tell her, "It's all about progress, Grandma. Onward, upward, forward." But it wasn't prudent in those days to contradict your grandmother.

2   Then, faster than the speed of light it seemed, I became a grandmother myself. The French are wrong when they say, "The more things change, the more they stay the same." *Au contraire.* I say the more things change, the more they change. What was, isn't. My grandmother was a sage.

3   Consider the map. Early in my academic life, a map of the world hung rolled up above the blackboard and beneath the penmanship strip at the front of my classroom. It was frayed along the edges, cracked and wrinkled from countless pull-downs, but except for minor adjustments after the Great War, it was for us a constant. The U.S.S.R. was the huge pink section, the Belgian Congo was green, and the British Empire was blue and, well, everywhere. Israel, Bangladesh, and Zimbabwe weren't around yet. I refer only to change here, not to the better or worse of things. There was comfort in knowing where you were.

4   There were no malls in those days. That needs no further comment—but I have one anyway: Do you ever yearn for quiet stores, salespeople older than your children? While being addressed as "Ma'am" took some getting used to, it isn't nearly as jarring as "Can I help you guys?"

5   I admit that calculators and market scanners are fabulous, but they lack character. When our grocery man took the pencil stub from behind his ear and scribbled your items' prices on your large brown bag, you marveled at his speed and accuracy—and the philosophy he always dispensed. You won't get that from a computerized cash register today.

6   The advent of the clothes dryer probably falls somewhere between dinosaurs and the Stone Age. My children wouldn't be able to identify a wooden clothespin. But for me, the time spent folding sun-kissed laundry, when the house was still and everyone was asleep, was my downtime. Time to think, dream, plan, and re-sort my thoughts. A half hour to be me. Somehow, the walk to the trashcan with a rolled-up disposable diaper is easier, but too short.

7   Don't get me wrong; I'm not for rolling back time. Scientific advances are truly miraculous, and life is longer and better—mostly. But don't you sometimes long for the nights when you truly saw a face on the moon and your mobile phone consisted of two milk cartons and a string? When you addressed your parents' friends as Mr. and Mrs. and drugs were only what you bought to cure an ailment? Before fat grams and lowfat yogurt? When the private lives of public servants and celebrities were indeed private, and nobody had dreamed of the *National Enquirer?*

8       Back then, Claudette Colbert's ankle could stop a truck, and there was no doubt in anyone's mind what Rhett Butler was carrying Scarlett O'Hara up that magnificent stairway *for*. Today, Howard Stern's private parts wouldn't slow traffic. And frankly, my dears, I don't give a damn.

*Modern Maturity*, November-December 1998, p. 92

## GO ELECTRONIC!

For additional readings, exercises, and Internet activities, visit our Web site at:

### http://longman.awl.com/englishpages

If you need a user name and password, see your instructor.

**Take a Road Trip to** the American Southwest! Be sure to visit the Critical Thinking module in your Reading Road Trip CD-ROM for multimedia tutorials, exercises, and tests.

# Chapter Seven

# RECOGNIZING PURPOSE AND TONE

## Chapter Outline

The Importance of Recognizing Purpose

*To Inform*

*To Persuade*

*To Entertain*

*Combination of Purposes*

The Importance of Recognizing Tone

*Matter-of-Fact Tone*

*Humorous Tone*

*Angry Tone*

*Sad Tone*

*Ironic Tone*

# THINK ABOUT IT!

What is the purpose of the message on each of the signs in the following photographs? Discuss the purposes with your classmates.

(1)

(2)

(3)

---

### Chapter Outcomes

After completing Chapter 7, you should be able to:
- Continue to apply the basic method for personal problem solving
- Define *purpose* and *tone*
- Recognize the various kinds of purpose
- Recognize the various kinds of tone
- Continue to find topics and central messages in passages on contemporary issues to determine what is at issue, distinguish among opposing viewpoints, and express personal viewpoints

---

## Problem-Solving Exercise

Using your notebook, apply the basic method for personal problem solving to the following hypothetical situation. Be sure to label each step clearly as you discuss what you would do.

### Hypothetical Situation

For several weeks, you have been enrolled in an introductory business course that is required in your program of study. From the beginning of the semester, you have not been comfortable with the instructor. His lectures are difficult to follow, and he is gruff and impatient when you ask questions, both in and out of class. Furthermore, you feel that he grades your test papers unfairly by taking off too many points for answers that are basically correct. In short, you get the impression that he simply does not like you.

Although you have a C– average, you need a much higher grade in your major courses in order to continue your education and eventually secure a better job. In fact, you have not received a grade lower than B in all the other courses that you have taken to this point. You fear that this predicament is not going to get any better, and you are at a loss as to what to do about it.

## The Importance of Recognizing Purpose

Throughout this textbook, we have emphasized the importance of evaluating what you see, hear, and read as a necessary part of critical thinking. You have been cautioned not to rush to judgment by accepting everything at face value but instead to take the time to consider what you have before you, regardless of your personal viewpoint. When reading, part of the evaluation process involves recognizing the writer's **purpose**, or reasons for writing. That, in turn, can help you distinguish between facts and opinions, uncover bias, and assess the overall reliability of information.

Although writers always have a purpose for writing, they usually do not come right out and say what it is. Consequently, it is up to the reader to make an inference or an educated guess regarding their motivations, based on:

➤ Author's background or affiliation
➤ Publication in which the writing appears
➤ The information itself
➤ How the information is presented

For example, a physician who is a member of the American Medical Association may write a piece in a popular magazine dealing with the high cost of malpractice insurance in order to persuade readers to be sympathetic to rising medical fees. In doing so, she may not state that purpose explicitly but instead present convincing information that supports that point of view without providing any contradictory information. Thus the reader could infer her purpose by taking into consideration the fact that she is a physician who is affiliated with the major medical association representing doctors, by keeping in mind that the article appears in a magazine that is read widely by the general public, and by recognizing that the information provided appears to be one-sided.

Generally speaking, a writer's purpose for writing is usually to *inform*, to *persuade*, to *entertain*, or some combination of the three. The ease with which you will be able to recognize these purposes will often depend on how obvious a particular writer chooses to be in the presentation of the material. As noted, it will sometimes be necessary for you to use your inference skills. Let us look more closely at each of the three purposes.

### To Inform

When the purpose is to inform, a writer simply provides facts, data, or information about a given subject so that you can learn more about it. Textbook writers generally have this as their overall purpose. For example, read the following passage from a biology textbook:

## Biology Is Connected to Our Lives in Many Ways

1   Global warming, air and water pollution, endangered species, genetic engineering, test-tube babies, nutrition, aerobic exercise and weight control, medical advances, AIDS and the immune system—is there ever a day that we don't see several of these issues featured in the news? These topics and many more have biological underpinnings. Biology, the science of life, has an enormous impact on our everyday life, and it is impossible to take an informed stand on many important issues without a basic understanding of life science.

2      Much of biology's impact on modern society stems from its contributions to technology and medicine. Technology is the *application* of scientific knowledge. Many discoveries in biology have practical applications. The technology of modern birth control, for instance, grew out of an understanding of the structure and function of the human reproductive system.

3      One of the newest applications of biology is the development of techniques for artificially transferring genes (DNA) from one organism to another. Popularly called genetic engineering, this technology is being used today for producing certain

medicinal drugs. It also has potential use in curing certain human diseases and in increasing crop productivity.

4     Perhaps the most important application of biology to our lives today is in helping us understand and respond to the environmental problems we currently face. One of our biggest environmental challenges is the possibility of global changes in weather and climate. Rain forests, which we have featured in this chapter, have a major effect on climate. In this capacity, tropical rain forests are vital to life as far away as Siberia and Antarctica. . . . Every year, vast areas of tropical rain forest are destroyed for agriculture or mining, as human demands for farmland and mineral resources increase. And at least 85% of North America's rain forests have been heavily logged. Destroying rain forests kills off untold numbers of species. It also produces large amounts of carbon dioxide ($CO_2$) gas. The $CO_2$ traps heat from sunlight and can warm the atmosphere. Many scientists contend that the destruction of rain forests at the current rate, coupled with $CO_2$ increases from other sources (such as industrial pollution), is raising global temperatures. Higher temperatures might melt glacial and polar ice, cause worldwide flooding, and alter the world's climates even more drastically.

5     Evaluating news reports on problems of this magnitude requires critical thinking and familiarity with many aspects of biology. For instance, in considering the possible effects of rain forest destruction, it is useful to know something about whole plants, cells, and molecules, as these subjects relate to photosynthesis and other kinds of energy transformation. It is also useful to know about carbon and water cycling in ecosystems, the growth patterns of the human population, and the effect of climate and soil conditions on the distribution of life on Earth.

6     Biology—from the molecular level to the ecosystem level—is directly connected to our everyday lives. It may also help us find solutions to the many environmental problems that confront us. Biology offers us a deeper understanding of ourselves and our planet, and a chance to more fully appreciate life in all its diversity.

Neil A. Campbell, Lawrence G. Mitchell, and Jane B. Reece, *Biology*, p. 12

The writer's purpose here is to inform the reader about the many important connections that the subject of biology has to our everyday lives, including its contributions to technology and medicine and its help in finding solutions to environmental problems. Several examples are provided for support and clarification.

Keep in mind that sometimes a writer wants to inform us in order to suggest, in a subtle way, that we do something. For instance, as you read the following passage, think about its purpose.

## Getting Help When Anger Turns Inward

THOMAS H. MATTHEWS

1   When Jerome W. was 13 years old, he tried to kill himself. He thought that pressures in his life had grown so large that ending his life was the only solution.

2     He had thought for weeks about how he would do it. Then one day, with family gathered around him, he simply walked to the window of his fifth-floor apartment in Brooklyn and began to crawl to the ledge. As he poised for the jump, his mother realized what Jerome was doing and pulled him back into the house.

3    "I was very serious," Jerome said. "I wanted to die. I began to ask myself, 'Why am I here?'"

4    Jerome said his problems stemmed from his relationship with his mother. After he was 9, there was no father in his house, so he was responsible for his brother and sister. He helped care for them, making their breakfast every day and taking them to and from school. He felt a great deal of pressure trying to go to school himself and care for his siblings.

5    He also began to feel that his mother was turning against him.

6    "There was a fight every day," he said. "I couldn't figure out why she was doing this to me."

7    After the suicide attempt, his mother chided him, saying that if he tried it again, she would let him. And that response, coupled with the ongoing arguments, he said, caused Jerome to shut down and say, "No more."

8    "I couldn't believe she said those things to me," he recalled. "From that day on, I blocked my mother out. I no longer showed any emotion. I didn't expect it to go as far as it did."

9    It went on for more than 10 years.

10    A psychotherapist for Jerome was recommended by the UJA-Federation of New York, one of seven agencies supported by The New York Times Neediest Cases Fund, now in its 84th year. The Times pays the fund's administrative costs, so donations go directly to the charities.

11    The therapist, Kiki Vouyiouklis, quickly realized that Jerome had successfully isolated himself from the world. "He had lost touch with everyone," she said.

12    While seeing Ms. Vouyiouklis over a 10-month period, Jerome was able to let out what he had held back for years. "I was forced to hate, but I was able to release all of that," he said. "It was a big-time relief."

13    "I've come such a long way," said Jerome, 25, who now works as a freelance production assistant in the television and movie industry. "I'm proud of what I have been able to do. I feel like a whole person now."

*The New York Times*, February 16, 1996, p. B2

This passage is intended for the most part to inform the reader about how Jerome W. overcame much adversity and developed into a successful person. However, the reader is also told that he was able to accomplish this through the help of one of seven agencies supported by The New York Times Neediest Cases Fund, which depends in part on donations. Hence, in a subtle way, the writer is suggesting that others like Jerome could be helped similarly if readers of the passage would donate money. It is not unusual for writers to present facts with the intention of encouraging us to do something.

## ACTIVITY 1

Write a short informational essay in your notebook dealing with a contemporary issue in which you present only facts. Then, using the same essay, add some material that encourages the reader to do something.

## ACTIVITY 2

Bring to class an example of a passage that was written to inform readers.

### To Persuade

When a writer's purpose is to persuade, the writer is trying to get the reader to think in a certain way or take a particular action. Although some facts may be presented, the writer's real intention is to get others to agree with the opinion being expressed or to engage in some activity in support of that point of view. For instance, as you read the following passage, think about the author's purpose.

## The Littlest Killers
### Lord of the Flies, *Chicago Style*

BRENT STAPLES

1   Imagine the terror of a 5-year-old child, dangling 14 stories above the pavement, as his brother tries fruitlessly to save him from two other boys, ages 10 and 11, who are determined to see him drop.

2   The image of Eric Morse, hurled to his death in Chicago in 1994, has been a recurrent one in both local and national politics. Newt Gingrich cited it in speeches. Henry Cisneros, the Secretary of Housing and Urban Development, called it a clinching fact in the Government's decision to take over the Chicago Housing Authority, deemed by Federal authorities the most dangerous and ill managed in the country. The Illinois Legislature easily passed a bill permitting 10-year-old children to be charged with murder and—as "super predators"—sent to maximum-security jails. The rush to jail young children is catching on elsewhere as well. Nationwide last year, 700 pieces of legislation were introduced aimed at prosecuting minors as adults.

3   The judge who last week sent Eric Morse's killers to jails for juveniles came near to rending her robes as she described Eric's plunge and asked how the boys who caused his death had become so indifferent to human life. No one who has spent time in, or even near, Chicago public housing projects should need to ask such a question. Eric's fall—and the world he lived in—bears a disturbing resemblance to *Lord of the Flies*, William Golding's novel about a band of British schoolboys marooned on a jungle island. Without adults to keep them in check, the boys turn to blood lust and murder. A boy who tries to reason gets his skull split open when he is thrown from a cliff.

4   Eric was killed for refusing to steal candy for his tormentors. The public housing complex where he died qualifies as an "island" in Golding's sense—an island of poverty and pathology, cut off from the city proper. Of the 15 poorest census tracts in America, 11 are Chicago public housing communities. The city designed and treated them as pariah states, even while they were bright, shining steppingstones for the black middle class. Public housing was far too densely built, walled off with freeways and railroad lines used as ghetto walls. As the poverty deepened, there was simply no way to dilute it.

5    Chicago's Ida B. Wells housing development has few adult men. The women are disproportionately teenagers. At the time of Eric's death, a third of the complex's 2,800 apartments were abandoned, used primarily by drug dealers who hawked heroin from the windows. In a survey at a nearby high school, half the students said they had been shot at; 45 percent said they had seen someone killed. The boys who dropped Eric from the window did not originate the act. The gangs, which both boys knew well, occasionally used such punishment on members who tried to quit. Bear in mind that this environment is sustained with Federal dollars.

6    The conduct of the two young killers was all the more understandable given that they have I.Q.'s of 60 and 76, with perhaps less emotional maturity than 5-year-old Eric. The judge in the case has ordered psychiatric treatment and follow-up care. But in light of what experts describe as Illinois's poor record with treatment—and its high failure rate with juveniles—the prospects for treatment seem poor. In Massachusetts or Missouri, the two would have been sent to facilities with fewer than two dozen beds and extensive psychiatric help. In Illinois, the boys could go to lockdowns with hundreds of others—many of them gangsters who will re-create the projects behind bars.

7    Few things are more horrifying than the murder of a child. But in view of the antecedents, Eric Morse's death was almost a naturally occurring event. The projects have become factories for crime and killers, with homicide taking younger and younger victims each year. The judge who sentenced Eric's killers called it "essential to find out how these two young boys turned out to be killers, to have no respect for human life and no empathy for their victim." We know quite well what made them killers. What we need is the political will to do something about it.

*The New York Times*, February 6, 1996, p. A22

The passage does present facts regarding the murder of Eric Morse by two other boys and the very poor conditions in the Chicago public housing projects that have led to crimes like that. However, the writer concludes by stating: "We know quite well what made them killers. What we need is the political will to do something about it" (paragraph 7). We can infer from those statements that the writer is urging readers to support measures that will help correct the conditions in the housing projects or politicians who favor such measures. In short, he is trying to get us to agree with his point of view regarding the causes of crimes like the murder of Eric Morse and asking us to take action to eliminate them.

## ACTIVITY 3

Write a short essay in your notebook dealing with a contemporary issue in which you try to persuade the reader to think in a certain way or take a particular action.

## ACTIVITY 4

Bring to class an example of a passage that was written to persuade readers.

### To Entertain

A writer whose purpose is to entertain must try to bring enjoyment to readers by treating a topic in a light, cheerful, funny, or laughable manner. For example, as you read the passage that follows, think about its purpose.

## The Look-Alike Years

CALVIN TRILLIN

1    A neighbor of mine named David Rothenberg, who has managed to reach the age of 62, informed me with some pride recently that he is now eligible for the senior-citizen discount at many movie theaters.

2    "How do they know you're 62?" I asked him. Could it be, I was wondering, that the accumulation of regulations in this country has reached the point at which citizens are regularly carded at both ends?

3    "Most ticket sellers are about 18," he said. "To them, we all look alike."

4    A lot of people are unenthusiastic about becoming eligible for the slim privileges that go with age. A 50-year-old man who receives an invitation to join an organization that offers vitamin discounts for the mature may resent it as a harbinger of that dreaded day when he takes his wife's hand during an evening stroll through the park and overhears some college kid on a nearby bench saying, "Isn't that cute!"

5    David, on the other hand, seemed to consider his movie discount what people in Washington would call an entitlement, richly deserved and untouchable. He spoke of it with such youthful enthusiasm that I found myself wondering, just for a moment, whether there was any possibility at all that someone could hold off the ravages of age by repeated viewings of Hollywood movies at half price.

6    There is some evidence against David's notion that in the eyes of younger people everyone born before the Inchon landing melds together into a single blob of undifferentiated old coot. There is, for instance, my favorite theory about why Ronald Reagan, the most successful oldie-but-goodie candidate in recent times, did so poorly in the Iowa caucuses in 1980, compared with 1976—a theory quickly forgotten after he reclaimed his microphone and his future in New Hampshire.

7    According to the theory, the Iowa voters of 1976, catching the campaign on TV screens that had more snow than the back 40, assumed that Reagan still looked like the Gipper. Four years later they had cable.

8    "Do you really get the geezer discount without question every time?" I asked David.

9    A few days earlier, he said, he'd requested a senior-citizen ticket from a ticket seller who was "a woman of some years." There are a few of them left. They now have legal recourse if management tries to ease them out, as Forbes discovered when he fired his secretary for unauthorized aging.

10    "Do you have any identification?" the ticket seller asked. Was she going to card him?

11    "Madam, you flatter me," David said in reply.

12    She smiled and waved him in.

13    It occurred to me that one of the resources available to people of some years is a certain polished charm.

*Time,* February 19, 1996, p. 22

The passage deals with reaching the age when one is eligible for senior-citizen discounts, particularly those offered by movie theaters. For the most part, the writer presents the material in a humorous manner designed to bring enjoyment to the reader. Phrases like "single blob of undifferentiated old coot" (paragraph 6) and "geezer discount" (paragraph 8) are two of the most obvious examples. They are funny and meant to entertain by making us laugh.

## ACTIVITY 5

Write a short essay in your notebook dealing with a contemporary issue that has entertainment as its purpose.

## ACTIVITY 6

Bring to class an example of a passage that was written to entertain readers.

### Combination of Purposes

Sometimes a writer has more than one purpose, as illustrated in the passage dealing with Eric Morse. As you recall, the writer provided factual information but also tried to persuade readers to accept his viewpoint and take action. This is not at all unusual, especially when you are reading material that deals with controversial contemporary topics.

When there is a combination of purposes, try to uncover and concentrate on the writer's *overall* or *main purpose* by focusing on the most important messages and the information that lends direct support to them. Remember that recognizing the purpose (or purposes) helps you evaluate the reliability and objectivity of reading material. This is very important when dealing with issues that involve conflicting, debatable, and sometimes emotional viewpoints.

## ACTIVITY 7

Write a short essay in your notebook dealing with a contemporary issue that demonstrates a combination of purposes.

## ACTIVITY 8

Bring to class an example of a passage that has a combination of purposes.

## ACTIVITY 9

Read the following passages and answer the questions. When reading each passage, keep in mind the writer's background or affiliation, the publication in which the writing appears, and how the most important information is presented, all of which should help you recognize the writer's purpose. Remember to use inference skills when appropriate.

## 1

### A New Sales Incentive

ISADORE BARMASH

1    A creative brainstorm recently came to me during a period of personal discomfort. Waiting endlessly for my wife to finish her shopping in a cavernous department store, it occurred to me that the patient men and women who accompany their spouses when they shop are really the forgotten consumers of today. The partners who give moral support to shoppers, cheerfully hold bags, stare into space, concentrate on where they parked and keep their eyes on the time so that dinner doesn't slip by unnoticed, desperately need some support of their own. America's 1 million-plus stores—which constitute the nation's biggest industry—are just over their exhausting, frustrating, agonizing Christmas season. Now they are balefully looking ahead to the new year, hoping that it may bring an improvement. Anything positive they do will surely help to stem the downsizings, closings and mergers that have dogged American retailing in the last few years. Any new wrinkle that retailers can offer to create more good will and turn a discomfited grouser into a gratified shopper's companion makes good sense.

2    Let's examine why, in addition to business reasons, it's important morally and socially to please those who accompany their partners when they buy that merchandise. We are forbearing. We provide moral support just in case our companion wants some advice (even if it is usually ignored). We are security symbols when the two of us go into the parking lot. If need be, we stand as a credit confirmation. If the salesclerk has some doubts, they vanish as she or he sees us standing stolidly beside the shopper. And we are a sort of sober authority figure, flashing indignant, even threatening expressions to a clerk giving our companion a hard time. We're a great backup.

3    So what should the merchants do for us? They should provide some physical comforts. Some chairs or benches, preferably inside the store and preferably in the most popular departments, would be useful, so that our backs and feet do not protest so badly that our patience just oozes away, leading to a potential argument with our spouses when they come up for air. It wouldn't take much room, but it would be so

welcomed. The bigger the stores, the more flexibility they offer for such amenities. Actually, one reason that they range to as much as two or three football fields is that it allows them the capability of easily moving things around, like a giant stage. Aisles, nooks and crannies, corners, and dead ends flourish in the big stores.

4    Going a bit further, it would be very pleasant to find a large store setting aside a small area as a lounge for men (and women) as in airports. A TV, the latest newspapers, perhaps some magazines could be placed there, along with a few upholstered chairs and perhaps a couple of vending machines. One per floor—OK, one per store—would be appreciated. Is it really too much to ask? I'm not asking for a Dow-Jones stock ticker or a Bloomberg news wire. But if the store wants to provide them, who would say no?

5    As a couple, my wife and I have traveled a bit and seen chairs and benches made available to shoppers at the Mitsukoshi stores in the Ginza in Tokyo and at Stockmann's, the big department store in Helsinki. If they can do it, why can't we?

6    To be fair, when my wife and I were recently in a Macy's, I began wandering around while waiting and experienced a pleasant shock. The store actually has two upholstered chairs and two wooden chairs on the main selling floor. Sitting there were four men with soulful looks as if savoring a celestial pleasure. Would that one would have given a seat to a well-dressed soul nearby whom I observed leaning up against a post, his face pressed against it as if in terminal despair. Anecdote's moral: great, but give us more chairs!

7    Not so long ago, in another department store, I was waiting as usual when a woman wandered by. She glanced at me and announced, "I've lost my husband." I answered, innocuously enough, "And I am waiting for my wife." But she didn't hear me because she was wandering around, shouting, "Maurice, Maurice!" What an argument they are going to have when they finally meet, I thought.

8    Why is it, I wondered, that the sexes have such a hard time with each other in the nation's stores? Women buy about three times as much merchandise as men, but it is not a problem of socio-demographics. What it is, I concluded, is just a matter of (1) comfort and (2) communications. Marital relations would certainly blossom if the man were happily ensconced in a leisure area while his wife shopped. At least she would know where he was.

9    But better yet, what the retailers might well consider are walkie-talkies so that shopping companions can keep in touch with each other. It's manageable—show credit cards, get a pair of walkie-talkies, return them when leaving. Ridiculous? Maybe, but think how many arguments it would avoid. After all, when you have these multi-football-field-size sites, communications are vital, aren't they?

10    Stores lately seem to love initials in their display signs. In the women's department, they have LIZ, DKNY and I.N.C., and others in the men's wear department. So how about SCSC, for Shoppers' Companion Support Center? It may not directly beef up a store's business, but can it hurt? What it will do is improve good will, something that retailers pay a lot for when they swallow up one another, as they have been doing a lot lately. Yet it is something that can't be truly measured in dollars but in the intangibles that really count. What is certain is that it would relieve those tired, aimless souls who just wait around but would like nothing better than to fade into the woodwork.

11     And consider how it would motivate shoppers knowing their companions were relaxing in comfort, not brooding or nursing anger. They might even buy more.

*Newsweek,* January 29, 1996, p. 12

## Comprehension Questions

1. What is the topic of the passage?
2. What is the central message of the passage?
3. Determine what is at issue. What is your initial personal viewpoint?
4. Distinguish among opposing viewpoints, and provide the rationale for each.
5. Think carefully about the viewpoints. Express a personal viewpoint, and give the reasons why you favor it. Does it differ from your initial personal viewpoint? Why or why not?
6. Write a few paragraphs *in support of the viewpoint that you do* not *favor.*

## Thought and Discussion Questions

1. In your view, do men and women shop differently? Why or why not?
2. In your view, is this article sexist? Why or why not?
3. What is the author's *overall* or *main purpose*? Give specific reasons for your answer.
4. List any questions that came to mind while you were reading this selection, and be prepared to discuss possible answers to them.

# 2

## Why Americans Hate the Media

JAMES FALLOWS

1  *Why has the media establishment become so unpopular? Perhaps the public has good reason to think that the media's self-aggrandizement gets in the way of solving the country's real problems.*

2  In the late 1980s public-television stations aired a talking-heads series called *Ethics in America.* For each show more than a dozen prominent citizens sat around a horseshoe-shaped table and tried to answer troubling ethical questions posed by a moderator. The series might have seemed a good bet to be paralyzingly dull, but at least one show was riveting in its drama and tension.

3     The episode was taped in the fall of 1987. Its title was "Under Orders, Under Fire," and most of the panelists were former soldiers talking about the ethical dilemmas of their work. The moderator was Charles Ogletree, a professor at Harvard Law School, who moved from panelist to panelist asking increasingly difficult questions in the law school's famous Socratic style.

4    During the first half of the show Ogletree made the soldiers squirm about ethical tangles on the battlefield. The man getting the roughest treatment was Frederick Downs, a writer who as a young Army lieutenant in Vietnam had lost his left arm in a mine explosion.

5    Ogletree asked Downs to imagine that he was a young lieutenant again. He and his platoon were in the nation of "South Kosan," advising South Kosanese troops in their struggle against invaders from "North Kosan." (This scenario was apparently a hybrid of the U.S. roles in the Korean and Vietnam wars.) A North Kosanese unit had captured several of Downs's men alive—but Downs had also captured several of the North Kosanese. Downs did not know where his men were being held, but he thought his prisoners did.

6    And so Ogletree put the question: How far would Downs go to make a prisoner talk? Would he order him tortured? Would he torture the prisoner himself? Downs himself speculated on what he would do if he had a big knife in his hand. Would he start cutting the prisoner? When would he make himself stop, if the prisoner just wouldn't talk?

7    Downs did not shrink from the questions or the implications of his answers. He wouldn't enjoy doing it, he told Ogletree. He would have to live with the consequences for the rest of his life. But yes, he would torture the captive. He would use the knife. Implicit in his answers was the idea that he would do the cutting himself and would listen to the captive scream. He would do whatever was necessary to try to save his own men. While explaining his decisions Downs sometimes gestured with his left hand for emphasis. The hand was a metal hook.

8    Ogletree worked his way through the other military officials, asking all how they reacted to Frederick Downs's choice. William Westmoreland, who had commanded the whole U.S. force in Vietnam when Downs was serving there, deplored Downs's decision. After all, he said, even war has its rules. An Army chaplain wrestled with how he would react if a soldier in a morally troubling position similar to Downs's came to him privately and confessed what he had done. A Marine Corps officer juggled a related question: What would he do if he came across an American soldier who was about to torture or execute a bound and unarmed prisoner, who might be a civilian?

9    The soldiers disagreed among themselves. Yet in describing their decisions they used phrases like "I hope I would have the courage to . . ." and "In order to live with myself later I would . . ." The whole exercise may have been set up as a rhetorical game, but Ogletree's questions clearly tapped into discussions the soldiers had already had about the consequences of choices they made.

10    Then Ogletree turned to the two most famous members of the evening's panel, better known even than Westmoreland. These were two star TV journalists: Peter Jennings, of *World News Tonight* and ABC, and Mike Wallace, of *60 Minutes* and CBS.

11    Ogletree brought them into the same hypothetical war. He asked Jennings to imagine that he worked for a network that had been in contact with the enemy North Kosanese government. After much pleading Jennings and his news crew got permission from the North Kosanese to enter their country and film behind the lines. Would Jennings be willing to go? Of course, he replied. Any reporter would—and in real wars reporters from his network often had.

12    But while Jennings and his crew were traveling with a North Kosanese unit, to visit the site of an alleged atrocity by U.S. and South Kosanese troops, they unexpectedly crossed the trail of a small group of American and South Kosanese soldiers. With Jennings in their midst the Northern soldiers set up an ambush that would let them gun down the Americans and Southerners.

13    What would Jennings do? Would he tell his cameramen to "Roll tape!" as the North Kosanese opened fire? What would go through his mind as he watched the North Kosanese prepare to fire?

14    Jennings sat silent for about fifteen seconds. "Well, I guess I wouldn't," he finally said. "I am going to tell you now what I am feeling, rather than the hypothesis I drew for myself. If I were with a North Kosanese unit that came upon Americans, I think that I personally would do what I could to warn the Americans."

15    Even if it meant losing the story? Ogletree asked.

16    Even though it would almost certainly mean losing my life, Jennings replied. "But I do not think that I could bring myself to participate in that act. That's purely personal, and other reporters might have a different reaction."

17    Ogletree turned for reaction to Mike Wallace, who immediately replied. "I think some other reporters *would* have a different reaction," he said, obviously referring to himself. "They would regard it simply as another story they were there to cover." A moment later Wallace said, "I am astonished, really." He turned toward Jennings and began to lecture him: "You're a *reporter*. Granted you're an American" (at least for purposes of the fictional example; Jennings has actually retained Canadian citizenship). "I'm a little bit at a loss to understand why, because you're an American, you would not have covered that story."

18    Ogletree pushed Wallace. Didn't Jennings have some higher duty to do something other than just roll film as soldiers from his own country were being shot?

19    "No," Wallace said flatly and immediately. "You don't have a higher duty. No. No. You're a reporter!"

20    Jennings backtracked fast. Wallace was right, he said: "I chickened out." Jennings said that he had "played the hypothetical very hard." He had lost sight of his journalistic duty to remain detached.

21    As Jennings said he agreed with Wallace, several soldiers in the room seemed to regard the two of them with horror. Retired Air Force General Brent Scowcroft, who would soon become George Bush's National Security Advisor, said it was simply wrong to stand and watch as your side was slaughtered. "What's it *worth?*" he asked Wallace bitterly. "It's worth thirty seconds on the evening news, as opposed to saving a platoon."

22    After a brief discussion between Wallace and Scowcroft, Ogletree reminded Wallace of Scowcroft's basic question. What was it worth for the reporter to stand by, looking? Shouldn't the reporter have said *something*?

23    Wallace gave a disarming grin, shrugged his shoulders, and said, "I don't know." He later mentioned extreme circumstances in which he thought journalists should intervene. But at that moment he seemed to be mugging to the crowd with a "Don't ask me!" expression, and in fact he drew a big laugh—the first such moment in the discussion. Jennings, however, was all business, and was still concerned about the first answer he had given.

24    "I wish I had made another decision," Jennings said, as if asking permission to live the past five minutes over again. "I would like to have made his decision"—that is, Wallace's decision to keep on filming.

25    A few minutes later Ogletree turned to George M. Connell, a Marine colonel in full uniform. Jaw muscles flexing in anger, with stress on each word, Connell said, "I feel utter contempt."

26    Two days after this hypothetical episode, Connell said, Jennings or Wallace might be back with the American forces—and could be wounded by stray fire, as combat journalists often had been before. When that happens, he said, they are "just journalists." Yet they would expect American soldiers to run out under enemy fire and drag them back, rather than leaving them to bleed to death on the battlefield.

27    "I'll do it!" Connell said. "And that is what makes me so contemptuous of them. Marines will die going to get . . . a couple of journalists." The last words dripped disgust.

28    Not even Ogletree knew what to say. There was dead silence for several seconds. Then a square-jawed man with neat gray hair and aviator glasses spoke up. It was Newt Gingrich, looking a generation younger and trimmer than he would when he became speaker of the House, in 1995. One thing was clear from this exercise, Gingrich said. "The military has done a vastly better job of systematically thinking through the ethics of behavior in a violent environment than the journalists have."

29    That was about the mildest way to put it. Although Wallace and Jennings conceded that the criticism was fair—if journalists considered themselves "detached," they could not logically expect American soldiers to rescue them—nevertheless their reactions spoke volumes about the values of their craft. Jennings was made to feel embarrassed about his natural, decent human impulse. Wallace seemed unembarrassed about feeling no connection to the soldiers in his country's army or considering their deaths before his eyes "simply a story." In other important occupations people sometimes face the need to do the horrible. Frederick Downs, after all, was willing to torture a man and hear him scream. But Downs had thought through all the consequences and alternatives, and he knew he would live with the horror for the rest of his days. When Mike Wallace said he would do something horrible, he barely bothered to give a rationale. He did not try to explain the reasons a reporter might feel obliged to remain silent as the attack began—for instance, that in combat reporters must be beyond country, or that they have a duty to bear impartial witness to deaths on either side, or that Jennings had implicitly made a promise not to betray the North Kosanese when he agreed to accompany them. The soldiers might or might not have found such arguments convincing; Wallace didn't even make them.

*Atlantic Monthly*, February 1996, pp. 45–47

## Comprehension Questions

1. What is the topic of the passage?
2. What is the central message of the passage?
3. Determine what is at issue. What is your initial personal viewpoint?

4. Distinguish among opposing viewpoints, and provide the rationale for each.

5. Think carefully about the viewpoints. Express a personal viewpoint, and give the reasons why you favor it. Does it differ from your initial personal viewpoint? Why or why not?

6. Write a few paragraphs *in support of the viewpoint that you do not favor.*

## Thought and Discussion Questions

1. What would you have decided to do if you were in Frederick Downs's position? Why?

2. What would you have decided to do if you were in Peter Jennings's position? Why?

3. Do you agree with Newt Gingrich's statement: "The military has done a vastly better job of systematically thinking through the ethics of behavior in a violent environment than the journalists have" (paragraph 28)? Why or why not?

4. Has the media in this country gone too far "to get a story"? Why or why not?

5. What is the author's *overall* or *main purpose*? Give specific reasons for your answer.

6. List any questions that came to mind while you were reading this selection, and be prepared to discuss possible answers to them.

# 3

## Thinking About Racism and Our Children

RICHARD PIROZZI

1 Two African American women—a mother and her daughter—are shopping for clothing at a major department store. As they browse through the aisles trying to decide what to buy, they are followed and watched closely by the salespeople. Meanwhile, there are two Caucasian girls one aisle over who are going unnoticed as they put various articles of clothing into a shopping bag without paying for them. The mother and her daughter purchase some items and proceed to leave the store. As they reach the door, they are joined by the two white girls, who quickly go through the exit at the same time. When the alarm goes off, the salespeople rush to the door and ask the mother and daughter to return to the counter in order to check the contents of their bags. In the meantime, the two girls walk toward their car, having stolen hundreds of dollars' worth of merchandise.

2 A young professional African American man waits for a cab in the middle of New York City at midnight. As he waves, several taxis pass right by him, the drivers fearful of picking him up at that hour and possibly having to drive through an unsafe part of town. On the other hand, they do not hesitate to stop for white passengers

just a few blocks away. Growing increasingly impatient after standing in the same spot for half an hour, the man decides to use public transportation.

3    Two black college students are driving back to school along an interstate highway in the middle of the afternoon. They and the drivers of three other automobiles are traveling about five miles over the speed limit. A state trooper pulls the college students over for speeding and proceeds to question them suspiciously about drugs, while the other drivers continue down the highway on their merry way. The trooper and the drivers of the three other cars happen to be white.

4    Do these three stories sound familiar to you? If you are black, your answer is probably yes. If you are white, chances are your answer is no. Yet situations like these confront black people every day, and they cut at the very soul of the country. The result is outrage and resentment on the part of African Americans toward the white establishment, while most Caucasians display an unbelievable inability to recognize the problem, no less try to correct it.

5    This was brought home clearly by the reaction to the verdict in the O. J. Simpson trial. While many whites had a look of anger or disbelief on their faces because they felt that a guilty man had been set free, most blacks responded with spontaneous joy and much satisfaction. For many of them it was not even a question of guilt or innocence but rather a case where, at last, one of their own had won out against a tainted criminal justice system that has consistently proven itself to be prejudiced and unfair. To understand their reaction one does not have to look any further than the Rodney King episode where the four white cops who beat him on camera were exonerated by a jury devoid of any black people. Although that is one of the most blatant and well-publicized cases, it does epitomize what happens all too frequently. Consequently, for many African Americans it was a refreshing change of pace to see Simpson walk. On the other hand, the white people who thought that he was guilty felt the bitterness, frustration and disillusionment that blacks have had to deal with for a very long time. It is doubtful, however, that whites were able to make that connection and appreciate what African Americans have been coping with through the years.

6    There are those who will argue that much progress has been made in race relations in this century. Certainly, from a legislative point of view, there are laws now on the books that provide protection for minorities by eliminating the more blatant forms of racism, and they have helped to bring about at least some behavioral change over the last forty or so years. I can never forget the experience I had in the early 1950s as a six-year-old, when my mother sat me down at a table in a small restaurant located in Paterson, New Jersey. She had some more shopping to do so she asked the owner if he would keep an eye on me for fifteen minutes. While my mother was gone, a very dignified older black woman sat down across from me at my table. The owner, in an abrupt manner, immediately asked her to sit someplace else. The look of hurt on her face will stay with me forever. Then there were all those experiences in the mid-1960s when I was attending a small Southern junior college where local black people were treated by some of the students as if they were something other than human.

7    Perhaps these instances of outright racist behavior no longer occur as frequently, but how much have attitudes really changed? It seems that the most obvious examples of racism—the Rodney King episode notwithstanding—have for the most part disappeared, only to be replaced by a more subtle strain. In this day and

age, I am always amazed at the frequent use of racial epithets and stereotyping by professional and nonprofessional white people. And it certainly does not help matters when black people use those same epithets and stereotypes to refer to themselves and each other. Blacks are also guilty of stereotyping whites and perceiving them as all the same. In fact, years of mistreatment and degradation have led to such suspicion that on many of our college campuses African Americans generally prefer to stick together rather than mix with white students.

8     Can it be that deep down inside, we are all racists? What hope then is there for racial harmony in this country? There are some things that need to be done quickly. First of all, a real effort has to be made by both races to reach out, communicate and empathize with each other. Whites have to come to appreciate what has been the black experience for most of the history of this nation, and they must speak out strongly against all forms of racism whether blatant or subtle. On the other hand, blacks should never forget their history as victims of discrimination, but they must also attempt to rise above it and not assume that all whites are cut from the same mold. African Americans should also take great pride in their accomplishments against what must have seemed like insurmountable odds to their forefathers. They must keep in mind that change is often gradual and sometimes very painful for all those involved, and for that reason, animosity is frequently its by-product.

9     Most important, parents of both races must teach their children that racist behavior of any kind is totally unacceptable. Kids should know about the history of race relations in this country and be advised of the role they can play—now and as adults—to make the situation more harmonious. At the very least, this should include a familiarity with the diverse groups that make up American society. In short, parents need to go out of their way to introduce their children at an early age to people of different races so that they are better equipped to interact with them today and in the future. Progress cannot be made unless we start to really get to know each other. In the end, improvement in race relations does not rest exclusively with our generation but will depend ultimately on generations still to come.

*The Humanist*, July–August 1996, pp. 40–41

## Comprehension Questions

1. What is the topic of the passage?
2. What is the central message of the passage?
3. Determine what is at issue. What is your initial personal viewpoint?
4. Distinguish among opposing viewpoints, and provide the rationale for each.
5. Think carefully about the viewpoints. Express a personal viewpoint, and give the reasons why you favor it. Does it differ from your initial personal viewpoint? Why or why not?
6. Write a few paragraphs *in support of the viewpoint that you do* not *favor.*

## Thought and Discussion Questions

1. Do you agree with the author that racism today is more subtle than in the past? Why or why not?

2. In your view, what will race relations be like in the United States 50 years from now? Why?

3. Do you think the information presented is mostly fact, mostly opinion, or a combination of both? Why? Cite specific examples.

4. What is the author's *overall* or *main purpose*? Give specific reasons for your answer.

5. List any questions that came to mind while you were reading this selection, and be prepared to discuss possible answers to them.

# The Importance of Recognizing Tone

A writer's **tone** or **mood** is a reflection of the writer's attitude or feelings toward a given topic or issue. It is expressed by the words and phrases used in the information presented. As with purpose, it is important for you to recognize the tone, because it helps you determine a writer's motivations or reasons for writing, which can in turn make it easier to recognize bias and distinguish between facts and opinions. Furthermore, it is part of the whole evaluation process that you should use when considering not only what you read but also what you see and hear.

Thus tone is an important consideration when you deal with contemporary issues and also when you gather information from people and written sources for problem-solving purposes. When interacting face to face, a person's *tone of voice* and *body language* will sometimes reveal the person's feelings on a given matter, so you may find yourself in a better position to assess the quality of the information the person is giving you. This, in turn, may help you solve a problem more efficiently. The same benefit applies when dealing with written sources for problem solving, when you want to weigh their objectivity.

As with purpose, writers don't always come right out and say what they are feeling about a particular topic or issue. In those instances, it becomes necessary to "read between the lines" and use inference skills to help determine tone. Thus the words and phrases a writer uses will serve as the clues to the writer's attitude. As you will recall, it is often necessary to use those same clues to infer a writer's purpose when it is not explicit. In fact, tone and purpose are related, and therefore each can be used sometimes to help figure out the other. For example, if a writer's tone is humorous, it would probably indicate that the writer's purpose is to entertain and vice versa. On the other hand, if the tone is matter-of-fact, the purpose is likely to be informational.

When trying to recognize the tone, there are several possibilities to be considered. This is certainly the case when dealing with contemporary issues, where writers sometimes have more than one purpose. In addition, they may also express more than one attitude toward the subject matter. On those occasions, follow the same procedure that you used when dealing with a combination of purposes: Concentrate on the most important messages and the information that lends direct support to them. This should help you uncover the *overall tone.*

We will focus on five common tones or moods that are often expressed by writers: matter-of-fact, humorous, angry, sad, and ironic. Each one represents an overall feeling or attitude by a given writer toward a particular subject. Let us look at each of these.

### Matter-of-Fact Tone

When adopting a matter-of-fact tone, which is common in textbooks, the writer sticks to the facts and presents them in a straightforward, unemotional manner. In other words, there is a concerted attempt to be evenhanded and objective. The purpose is informational. For example, read this paragraph:

> Although progress has been made with regard to women's rights in the United States, it appears that there is room for improvement. There are still jobs not open to them, and they are sometimes paid less than men occupying the same or similar positions. Furthermore, some women have been the victims of out-and-out sexual harassment on the job. In short, it will take a while longer before we can safely say that there is equality between the sexes.

The paragraph expresses little emotion as the author attempts to present the information in a straightforward and unbiased way. For the most part, the words used are not extreme or slanted.

## ACTIVITY 10

In your notebook, write a paragraph with a matter-of-fact tone on any topic that interests you.

## ACTIVITY 11

Bring to class an example of a passage with a matter-of-fact tone.

### Humorous Tone

A humorous tone is one in which a writer presents information in a light-hearted manner designed to entertain or make the reader laugh. For instance, read the following paragraph, which deals with the same subject matter as the previous one:

> If you believe that there has been much progress with regard to women's rights in the United States, you probably also believe in the Tooth Fairy. Wake up and smell the aftershave lotion! Women are still excluded from some jobs as if they were suffering from some weird

contagious disease. And just compare their pay scales to those of men in certain positions—you could die laughing. Not to mention that some males turn into cavemen when they are around women on the job. Equality between the sexes? Give me a break!

Although the paragraph makes basically the same points as the previous matter-of-fact one, it does so in a much more lighthearted way. The use of expressions like "Tooth Fairy," "weird contagious disease," "you could die laughing," "turn into cavemen" and the various exclamations are an attempt to be funny and make the reader laugh.

## ACTIVITY 12

In your notebook, write a paragraph with a humorous tone on the same topic that you used for Activity 10.

## ACTIVITY 13

Bring to class an example of a passage with a humorous tone.

### Angry Tone

An angry tone lets you know that the writer is annoyed, irritated, or bothered in some way about the subject matter being presented. For example, read the following paragraph, which deals with the same topic as the previous ones:

I am sick and tired of hearing how much "progress" has been made with regard to women's rights in the United States. Women are prevented from filling some jobs and are paid ridiculously low wages in certain positions, compared to men. Furthermore, some men behave obnoxiously when they are around women on the job. It is absurd to say that we have achieved equality between the sexes.

Although the paragraph is similar to the other two in terms of the points being made, it presents them in a much more emotional manner. The use of the expressions "sick and tired," "ridiculously low," "behave obnoxiously," and "absurd" clearly express the writer's anger.

## ACTIVITY 14

In your notebook, write a paragraph with an angry tone on the same topic that you have been using.

Bring to class an example of a passage with an angry tone.

## Sad Tone

A sad tone presents information in a gloomy, melancholy, or sorrowful way. For instance, read the following paragraph on the same topic:

> Although some slight progress has been made with regard to women's rights in the United States, there is, regrettably, ample room for improvement. It is discouraging to realize that some jobs are still not open to women and that women are too often paid less than men occupying the same or similar positions. Furthermore, some women are still the unfortunate victims of sexual harassment on the job. In short, equality between the sexes at this point remains far beyond our grasp. What a sad state of affairs!

Once again, the points that are made in the paragraph are similar to those found in the others, but this time they are presented in a downcast manner. The use of "regrettably," "discouraging," "unfortunate," and "sad state of affairs" and the generally negative approach to the material indicate that the writer is pessimistic about the situation.

In your notebook, write a paragraph with a sad tone on the same topic that you have been using.

Bring to class an example of a passage with a sad tone.

## Ironic Tone

The dictionary defines **irony** as "a method of humorous or sarcastic expression in which the intended meaning of the words used is the direct opposite of their usual sense" or "a combination of circumstances or a result that is the opposite of what might be expected or considered appropriate." Thus an ironic message conveys its meaning by using words to mean the opposite of what they usually mean, and an ironic event is an occurrence that is the opposite or reverse of what is normally expected. We might describe a bad day in a sarcastic manner by saying "What a wonderful day I've had!" or we might observe the irony in the fact that the first ship specifically designed to be unsinkable, the *Titanic*, sank on its very first voyage. A writer generally uses irony to present messages in a catchy, unusual way so that readers will take notice and remember them. For instance, read the following paragraph, which deals once again with women's rights:

> Now that women are in business suits, why don't we just assume that no further progress needs to be made with regard to women's rights in the United States? We can simply ignore the fact that some jobs are still not open to them and that they are sometimes paid less than men occupying the same or similar positions. It really doesn't even matter that some women are still being subjected to sexual harassment on the job. Let's just proclaim equality between the sexes a *fait accompli* and get the whole issue behind us.

Notice how the writer takes what is essentially the same information but this time uses expressions that mean the *opposite* of the points he really wants to convey. By using this somewhat unusual technique, he hopes that the reader will be jolted into taking note of and remembering the *intended* messages.

Let us look at another example of irony, an occurrence that is the opposite of what is normally expected:

1   Earnest, lean Regilio Tuur, looking like a strip of copper wire with muscles, was no-nonsense as he shadowboxed outside the bloodstained ring at Gleason's Gym near the Brooklyn waterfront. But he permitted himself an ironic laugh when his workout was over and he talked about how his craft had changed.

2   He remembers when his big concern was how to keep from being cut badly. These days, he worries more when an opponent starts gushing blood. You never know anymore, said this young man, who is the World Boxing Organization's junior lightweight champion. Who can say where the other fellow has been?

3   "I've fought four times in the last year and had four H.I.V. tests, and my manager made sure that my opponents were tested, too," said Mr. Tuur, a Suriname-born Dutchman now living on Long Island. "This is a blood sport. You can't be careful enough. People talk about testing and the right to privacy, but that's a crock. We're talking about lives here. Going into the ring with some who's tested positive, that's an act of suicide, isn't it?"

Clyde Haberman, "H.I.V. Testing for Boxers: Is Rule Fair? Is Anything?" *The New York Times*, February 16, 1996, p. 132

Here the irony involves how one circumstance has changed completely in the sport of boxing. In the past, the boxer discussed in the passage was concerned about sustaining a bad cut, whereas today, with the AIDS problem, he is more worried about an opponent's getting cut. Thus what is happening is the opposite of what normally has been expected. Notice that the writer explicitly lets the reader know that there is irony in this situation by calling the boxer's laugh "ironic."

## ACTIVITY 18

In your notebook, write two paragraphs in an ironic tone on any topics that are of interest to you. In one of them, convey a message by using words to mean the opposite of what they usually mean, and in the other, discuss an occurrence that is the opposite or reverse of what is normally expected. Use the two examples in the text to guide you, and feel free to discuss your paragraphs with your classmates.

## ACTIVITY 19

Bring to class an example of a passage with an ironic tone.

## ACTIVITY 20

Read the following passages and answer the questions. When reading each passage, concentrate on the most important messages and the information that lends direct support to them to help you uncover the overall tone. Remember to use inference skills when appropriate.

# 1

## Double Exploitation

BOB HERBERT

1   With the show's rat-a-tat theme music blaring in the background, the television announcer, already planning future shows, says to the national viewing audience: "Is your teen daughter *obsessed* with sex? If so, call us at 800-93-SALLY and tell us about her."

2      For those who find enjoyment, excitement and lots of laughs in the sexual exploitation of children, I offer you the Sally Jessy Raphael experience. I had the misfortune to see last Monday's show, which was titled "My Teen Can't Go Without Sex." It was like spending an hour in an unclean bathroom.

3      The show opened with several comments like the following:

4      "Sally, my little girl is only 12 years old, but she's already had sex with 25 guys!"

5      Loud prurient cheers erupted from the studio audience and the music intensified as Ms. Raphael kicked off a show that was unrelentingly vile and degrading, and brutally abusive to its young guests. The girls (no boys) were encouraged, cajoled and all but coerced into revealing excruciating details of their promiscuity. They were then roundly denounced, cursed, reviled, laughed at and otherwise humiliated by the rowdy audience. They were even chastised by Ms. Raphael, an empty-headed and maddeningly self-righteous host.

6    A 15-year-old, who was booed because she had slept with 17 guys, wept and blurted out that she had been sexually abused by her mother's boyfriend.

7    "How far did he get?" Ms. Raphael asked. "Tell us, *Steffi*. How far?"

8    However far the abuser got, it was no reason—as far as the host was concerned—to give the girl a break. Ms. Raphael told her, "If you take all the women in the world who have been abused, they don't go and do what you've been doing."

9    Microphones were handed to members of the audience who wanted to denounce the girls. "You make me sick!" a woman shrieked at the 15-year-old. She told the girl that if she ever got pregnant, the child (apparently predestined to be female) would be a "slut" just like her mother. "There's going to be one slut in the other one," the woman said.

10    That was one of the milder comments. You got the impression that if rocks had been distributed to the nitwits in the audience, they would have eagerly thrown them at the wretched offenders.

11    That was the tenor of the entire show. The star was the 12-year-old, which was not surprising. She was the youngest and the whole point of the program was to titillate the audience by eroticizing children. The girls were heavily made up and repeated references were made to their relationships with older men, their reluctance to use condoms, and so on. It was a form of ritualized, legalized child abuse.

12    The host and the audience, equally reprehensible, attempted to immunize themselves and safeguard their enjoyment by portraying the children as demons and seductresses, rather than as the victims of the men and boys who preyed upon them, the parents who were unwilling or unable to protect them, and a society capable of viewing programs like Ms. Raphael's as entertainment, rather than as a menace.

13    A 12-year-old who has slept with dozens of boys needs professional counseling in a safe and compassionate environment, not the hoots ahd derisive shouts of a mob masquerading as an audience. If Ms. Raphael had even the slightest sensitivity to the needs of a child who had been sexually molested, she could never think that outing that child on national television was a good idea.

14    The children on Ms. Raphael's show last Monday were betrayed. By definition, they were excessively needy. That is the case with all sexually exploited children. But instead of getting help from a powerful authority figure like the host of a nationally syndicated television show, these children were brutally victimized again.

15    The abuse was not limited to the young. The mother of the 12-year-old seemed to be mentally impaired, perhaps retarded. When she made a tearful comment that was uttered with difficulty and was grammatically incorrect, the audience and Ms. Raphael broke into uncontrollable laughter. The daughter, distressed, looked on helplessly.

16    What fun. Maybe they can do an entire show on mental illness. It ought to be at least as entertaining as child sex abuse.

*The New York Times*, February 26, 1996, p. A13

## Comprehension Questions

1. What is the topic of the passage?

2. What is the central message of the passage?

3. Determine what is at issue. What is your initial personal viewpoint?

4. Distinguish among opposing viewpoints, and provide the rationale for each.

5. Think carefully about the viewpoints. Express a personal viewpoint, and give the reasons why you favor it. Does it differ from your initial personal viewpoint? Why or why not?

6. Write a few paragraphs *in support of the viewpoint that you do* not *favor.*

## Thought and Discussion Questions

1. Should shows like the one mentioned in the passage be permitted on the air? Why or why not?

2. Do you think the information presented is mostly fact, mostly opinion, or a combination of both? Why? Cite specific examples.

3. Which one of the five tones discussed is expressed by the writer when he states: "What fun. Maybe they can do an entire show on mental illness. It ought to be at least as entertaining as child sex abuse" (paragraph 16)? Give reasons for your answer.

4. What is the *overall tone* of the passage? Give specific reasons for your answer.

5. List any questions that came to mind while you were reading this selection, and be prepared to discuss possible answers to them.

## 2

## You're in My Spot

SHARON WHITE TAYLOR

1   While my husband, Cliff, and I were sitting in our car outside a restaurant recently, a man pulled into a space clearly reserved for the handicapped. When he bounded out of his car and sprinted into the restaurant, all my senses stood at attention.

2   Since becoming disabled by a stroke three years ago, I've waged a campaign against the able-bodied who are too lazy to walk extra steps. In this case, the man had a choice of nearby parking spots, but he opted for the reserved space in front of the door.

3   This wasn't the first time I have challenged a parking cheat. Often, from my car, I've spotted a nonqualified person parked illegally and have called out: "Excuse me, you are parked in a handicapped zone." I have clumped after people with my walker and chased them down with my wheelchair to point out the errors of their ways.

4   While family members agree with my reasons for pursuing my mission, they worry about my methods. One winter's day my sister, Nancy, questioned my sanity when I forced her to push my wheelchair through an icy parking lot to confront a woman without a limp (or a parking sticker) walking away from a handicapped space. Later, Nancy was glad she had given me the chance to challenge the offender. The

woman confessed: "I should know better. I'm a nurse." She moved her car. Not long ago, when I reminded another woman that she was parked in a handicapped zone, she retorted in a huff, "I know all about you people. I work in a convalescent home."

5    Most people don't apologize. Many are rude. Some offer nonsensical excuses. I confronted one man as he briskly headed into a grocery store. "My mother is handicapped," he snapped.

6    Before I joined the ranks of the disabled, I often eyed those coveted spots on rainy days or when I stopped for milk or bread after a long work day. I passed them by. After suffering a broken leg some years ago, I understood their importance. In my state permits are not issued for temporary handicaps. When my husband pulled into a typical narrow parking space, he had great difficulty trying to maneuver the wheelchair out of the car without hitting a neighboring vehicle. Pushing a wheelchair in the snow and rain or across a rutted parking lot can be hazardous.

7    The switch from temporary to permanent disability hasn't been easy. Following a brief bout with depression, I decided to accept what can't be changed. I have even learned to appreciate the perks. It is comforting to find a spot close to the store while other shoppers trek through snow or heat.

8    My adult children joke about taking me and my parking permit to concerts so they can have privileged parking. Of course, they quip, you have to wait in the car.

9    All kidding aside, others envy my parking status. One blistering hot summer day, a woman saw me getting out of my car at a crowded mall. She was obviously wilted after walking the length of the large lot. "You are so lucky," she said. "I'll trade places with you." I smiled. "Gladly," I answered. "I would love to walk."

10   Though I rarely feel sorry for myself these days, it would be nice to leave my house without wondering if my destination has stairs I can't negotiate or whether privileged parking will be available. In many places there are only one or two designated spots and they may be occupied. There have been times when being unable to find a space has meant we've had to forgo plans to attend an event. The frustration of finding the marked places filled by nondisabled drivers has spurred me to continue my battle against abusers.

11   Until recently, if I found a car illegally parked with no driver in sight, I would leave a hastily scribbled note on the windshield. Now I am armed with professionally printed, bright orange notices given to me by another family waging the same war. In large black letters the placards read: "This is not a ticket but a reminder. You are parked in a space that is reserved for the handicapped. These facilities are provided for individuals whose physical disabilities make their use a necessity."

12   Having left more than 50 handwritten notes and about a dozen printed notices, I was curious about their effect on the offenders. The very-abled man who had parked illegally in front of the restaurant would be a perfect gauge to test whether the placards made a difference.

13   I suggested to Cliff that we eat our sandwiches in the car and wait to see how the transgressor reacted. Cliff agreed, but he made me promise not to confront the man directly. Cliff is always conscious of my safety and blanches when I face off with scofflaws.

14      I'm sure he won't forget the day I spotted a burly oaf pulling a huge truck with monster tires into a reserved spot. Cliff refused to take my wheelchair out of the car and the guy was too far away to hear me shouting. I think of him as the big one that got away. I wasn't about to let that happen again.

15      So we munched our sandwiches, sipped coffee and discussed what the latest offender's reaction might be. Even though I'm an optimist, I didn't expect him to flagellate himself and cry *mea culpa*. Perhaps he would look sheepish and glance around to see if anyone had noticed the big orange flier under his windshield wiper. Maybe in the future he would be more considerate. My husband is a pessimist. His prediction proved more accurate.

16      After about 20 minutes, the man returned to his car. He saw the notice, pulled it off the windshield and quickly read it. Looking as if he had smelled something vile, he threw it down next to a trash container, spat on the ground and drove away.

17      We had our answer. People who illegally park in spaces for the handicapped also litter and spit.

18      Oh, dear, am I being politically incorrect? Have I stereotyped people who usurp handicapped parking? If you feel maligned, defend your position. Point out that you may selfishly inconvenience the disabled, but you never litter or spit in public.

*Newsweek,* February 19, 1996, p. 20

## Comprehension Questions

1. What is the topic of the passage?
2. What is the central message of the passage?
3. Determine what is at issue. What is your initial personal viewpoint?
4. Distinguish among opposing viewpoints, and provide the rationale for each.
5. Think carefully about the viewpoints. Express a personal viewpoint, and give the reasons why you favor it. Does it differ from your initial personal viewpoint? Why or why not?
6. Write a few paragraphs *in support of the viewpoint that you do* not *favor.*

## Thought and Discussion Questions

1. In your view, are handicapped parking spaces justified? Why or why not?
2. Are there any circumstances under which you would park in a handicapped parking space? Why or why not?
3. Is the writer on solid ground when she infers that "people who illegally park in spaces for the handicapped also litter and spit" (paragraph 17)? Why or why not?
4. What is the *overall tone* of the passage? Give specific reasons for your answer.

5. List any questions that came to mind while you were reading this selection, and be prepared to discuss possible answers to them.

## 3

## The F-Word . . . or, Isn't a Mink Bred to Be a Coat?

EVELYN RENOLD

1    Not long ago, my eightysomething aunt asked me if I wanted her luxurious mink
coat. She planned on leaving it to me in her will, she said, but why didn't I just take
it now? I remember feeling a rush of excitement, immediately followed by an
avalanche of anxiety: Given the fervor of the animal-rights movement, would I ever
have the courage to wear it? And how did I really feel about carving up little creatures to make a fashion statement?

2    It's not as if I'd spent my whole life lusting after fur. I grew up in Southern California, and though I can recall a few L.A. country-club types preening in their mink
stoles, fur was pretty exotic out there. Even after migrating east, I never seriously
considered such an extravagance. Fur coats, I remember thinking, were the province
of older women with more lavish lifestyles than mine.

3    Still, like every warm-blooded American girl, I fantasized. Suppose I were to acquire a posher lifestyle. What kind of fur would I choose? And how would it look on
me as I swept into charity balls and Monday nights at the opera? (Unspoken answers: *fox* and *very good indeed*.) Now and again, I would furtively try on a fur coat
belonging to a friend, if only to keep this harmless little fantasy alive.

4    Then one day, the fantasy stopped being harmless. Almost overnight, fur coats
went the way of red meat and unprotected sex—bygone relics of a more licentious,
less politically correct era. I'd missed my chance, and I felt a little cheated. If I
wanted to be considered a caring, compassionate person, fur was definitely out—
though I have to confess that its appeal was somewhat enhanced for me by its
newly forbidden status.

5    Not that I'm indifferent to furry creatures. Having cohabited with cats, I get
more than a little squeamish when I read about scientific experiments conducted on
living felines. (Yes, animal research is necessary; I just wish they'd draft rats rather
than kittens.) And I was outraged by last year's news story about the Colombian drug
dealers who smuggled cocaine into this country in a sheepdog's belly. So I understand the argument—at least I think I do—that even though minks are less charismatic than canines and cats, we ought to care about them too. Nonetheless, I've always been suspicious of people who worry more about animals than humans (the
English are notorious for this). "Get a life—a human life," I feel like telling them.

6    Pets, of course, are garnering some very good press these days, as psychologists
recognize the support and companionship they provide their human masters. But the
truth is, animals—even our favorite domesticated ones—are still animals, and they
have their limitations. You can't take them dancing or to the movies. And while many

are sympathetic listeners, they're totally useless when it comes to offering advice. More damning yet, not a single one has run for public office or contributed to the cultural life of the country (unless you count Mickey Mouse, Kermit the Frog, or the Lion King). Animals are different, and it's foolish to pretend otherwise.

7   Which doesn't mean we should kill them heedlessly, or inflict needless pain on them. But I do find myself increasingly concerned about our priorities. Recently, a British magazine declared animal rights to be the number one "hip" cause on the planet. And a reporter for an American magazine, interviewing some female members of PETA (People for the Ethical Treatment of Animals), suggested that in another era, these smart, committed young women would have been marching for civil rights or the Equal Rights Amendment—causes that, I don't think it's denigrating animals to say, seem infinitely more important.

8   Maybe we're looking to help our four-footed friends because we feel so hopeless about our two-footed ones. After all, spray-painting women in fur (a favorite PETA tactic) is a whole lot easier—and clearly more fun—than trying to figure out how to end racial strife, cure AIDS, or fix welfare. What's more, it seems to be effective. The number of mink farms in this country has declined precipitously in recent years, and fur sales are nowhere near what they were a decade ago (though they've improved some in the last couple of years). Celebrities are increasingly wary of lending themselves to the Blackglama What Becomes a Legend Most? advertising campaign. And many fashion designers have bailed out of the fur trade, partly because a large number of their steady customers now find fur offensive—and partly because of pressure from PETA.

9   What happens, exactly, to those minks (or foxes or chinchillas) on their way from the wild to the showroom that has the people at PETA so exercised? PETA claims that trappers kill most of the fur-bearing creatures that end up as coats, employing sadistic means to subdue their prey. Fur spokespeople, however, counter that the animals used for fashion come from farms that follow strict humane standards, further arguing that if the animals were mistreated, they wouldn't produce good pelts.

10   It's hard to know whom to believe. But given PETA's eccentric views, I'm not sure I would pick them. Not only do they want us to forswear fur; these fashion fundamentalists insist we lay down all clothing made of leather, suede, shearling, down, wool, and silk. Today your fur coat, tomorrow your cashmere sweater. They also want us to dispense with all food that comes from animals—including milk and eggs. Finally, and most alarming, the group opposes all forms of medical research that involve animal experimentation—even for AIDS and cancer.

11   Still, PETA has managed to make the antifur movement as trendy as push-up bras—trendier, really. Everyone has seen those bare-bottomed supermodels in the PETA ads posing under the slogan *I'd rather go naked than wear fur*. (Tell *that* to the Eskimos: I can see them now in their synthetic furs, polyester pants, and plastic shoes.) It's as though you have to be old, fat, and morally depraved to challenge the antifur dogma.

12   In truth, we live in a man-eat-chicken world—the point being that there's a food chain and we're at the top. That's nature. Speaking of which: Consider for a moment what happens to those furry creatures that are not pressed into service as

high-fashion coats. It's a mistake to believe they live out their days sipping piña co-ladas at some animal version of Club Med. Many are killed, brutally and unapologet-ically, by predators in their own habitat, while others die of equally grisly so-called natural causes.

13      And yet the antifur folks are hard to dismiss. Sometimes they get to me—like when they argue that years from now we'll have come to realize mistreating animals was no different from mistreating any other defenseless, disenfranchised minority group. As for my aunt's mink, it's still hanging in her closet. Wistfully, I think of it from time to time. And I can only make a guess as to why I haven't claimed it: cau-tion perhaps, cowardice no doubt, and maybe a tiny twinge of conscience.

*Cosmopolitan,* February 1996, p. 30

## Comprehension Questions

1. What is the topic of the passage?
2. What is the central message of the passage?
3. Determine what is at issue. What is your initial personal viewpoint?
4. Distinguish among opposing viewpoints, and provide the rationale for each.
5. Think carefully about the viewpoints. Express a personal viewpoint, and give the reasons why you favor it. Does it differ from your initial personal viewpoint? Why or why not?
6. Write a few paragraphs *in support of the viewpoint that you do* not *favor.*

## Thought and Discussion Questions

1. In your view, are civil rights or the Equal Rights Amendment more im-portant causes than animal rights? Why or why not?
2. If you are a female, would you wear a fur coat? Why or why not? If you are a male, would you buy a fur coat for your wife, if she really wanted one? Why or why not?
3. What can you infer regarding whether or not the writer will ever wear her aunt's mink coat? Why or why not?
4. What is the *overall tone* of the passage? Give specific reasons for your answer.
5. List any questions that came to mind while you were reading this se-lection, and be prepared to discuss possible answers to them.

## LOOKING BACK

With two of your classmates, come up with a list of the most important points you learned from this chapter, and determine how they can be put to use in other classes. Be prepared to discuss both the list and the uses.

**THINK AGAIN!**

The following message, along with a picture of the local museum of art, appeared on the side of a bus in Atlanta, Georgia:

**The real barrier between people and great art is not money.**
**It is parking!**

What is the purpose of the message? What is its tone?

## MASTERY TEST 7

A. Answer the questions.

1. What is a writer's purpose?

   _____

2. What is a writer's tone?

   _____

3. When a writer simply provides facts, data, or information about a subject so that we can learn more about it, the purpose is
   a. to persuade
   b. to inform
   c. to entertain
   d. all of the above
   e. none of the above

4. When a writer is trying to get us to think in a certain way or take a particular action, the purpose is
   a. to inform
   b. to entertain
   c. to persuade
   d. all of the above
   e. none of the above

5. When a writer is trying to amuse or bring enjoyment to us, the purpose is
   a. to entertain
   b. to persuade
   c. to inform
   d. all of the above
   e. none of the above

6. It is important for the critical reader to recognize a writer's purpose and tone to
   a. distinguish between facts and opinions
   b. uncover bias
   c. assess the overall reliability of information
   d. all of the above
   e. none of the above

7. When a writer sticks to the facts and presents them in a straightforward, unemotional manner, the tone is
   a. matter-of-fact
   b. humorous
   c. angry
   d. sad
   e. ironic

8. When a writer is mad, annoyed, irritated, or bothered by the subject matter presented, the tone is:
   a. sad
   b. angry
   c. humorous
   d. matter-of-fact
   e. ironic

9. When a writer presents information in a lighthearted, funny manner, the tone is
   a. ironic
   b. matter-of-fact
   c. humorous
   d. angry
   e. sad

10. When a writer presents information in a gloomy, melancholy, or sorrowful way, the tone is
    a. angry
    b. ironic
    c. sad
    d. matter-of-fact
    e. humorous

11. When a writer uses words to mean the opposite of what those words usually mean, the tone is
    a. ironic
    b. angry
    c. sad
    d. matter-of-fact
    e. humorous

B. Determine the purpose and tone for each of the passages.

12. **Happy National Apathy Day**

WILL DURST

1   Don't vote. You don't have to. No one's going to make you. This isn't the Soviet Union in the 50's. You won't be forced from your bed and dragged to the polls against your will. Relax. None of your friends are voting. And things are pretty good the way they are, right? If it ain't broke, don't fix it. What do you care if some barren deserted beach does or doesn't get blanketed by a thick film of 30-weight because of offshore drilling? Find another beach. What's the big deal?

2        Don't vote; you know you don't want to. Parking is a pain, the print is so tiny, and it's always on a Tuesday—what's that all about, anyway? Besides, haven't the pollsters already told us who's going to win? Why beat your head against a wall? It's a done deal. Out of your hands. Don't even need to wash them. It'd be totally different if it actually mattered. But it's not as it we have any real choice. If voting were effective they would have made it illegal by now.

3   Don't vote. Everyone knows the big corporations have the politicians so deep in their pockets they've got to brush the lint out of their hair before photo ops. It's common knowledge. Conventional wisdom. You'll only end up encouraging them.

4   You must have better things to do. Jog on over to the library before it gets closed down and read up on other people who never voted. Or you could work on that extra room for Grandma when Medicare fails and she has to move in. Or take a farewell trip on your local mass transit and wave bye-bye to the neighborhood rec center. That would be fun.

5   Besides, what difference does it make? One lousy little vote. A spit in the ocean. Don't worry. Be happy. Stay home. This is still a free country, last time I looked. Who cares? Not you.

*The New York Times,* November 2, 1998, p. A27

Purpose: _____

Tone: _____

---

13  **My Father's Keeper**

RICHARD PIROZZI

1   We buried my mother on my twenty-fourth wedding anniversary, after her short battle with pancreatic cancer. She succumbed to the disease a few days after surgery in the early morning hours during her stay at a hospital in southern New Jersey. Although I was prepared as much as one possibly can be for the departure of a mother, I cannot make the same claim regarding the care of my 85-year-old father. That very year he had survived open-heart surgery only to lose his wife of over 50 years. His feelings for her are best expressed by the words he uttered tearfully the day she died: "I have lost everything."

2   In fact, my mother was the centerpiece of the entire family. At a very early age, I discovered that, if you wanted to get anything done in our house, you simply had to know just one word: *Jo.* That was what everyone called my mother instead of Josephine, which was her formal name. She did everything for my father—from serving as his personal secretary to satisfying his every need. It became so extreme that, as he watched television, he would occasionally use a bell to beckon her when he needed something, which was often. I grew up wondering if my mother was a wife or a slave left over from pre–Civil War days. Not only would she be an impossible act to follow, no one even wanted to try.

3   There was little time for me to grieve her loss because we were all too busy trying, unsuccessfully, to ease my father's pain. My brother, who is my only sibling, lives with his family in Georgia, so it became painfully obvious almost immediately who would be given the responsibility of looking after my father. It was both a necessary and logical arrangement because at the time he was still living in southern New Jersey, while my home was an hour away in the northern part of the state.

4    Caring for my father for the next three years would be an experience that had moments of hilarity, moments of frustration, and moments of great sadness. Most of the lighter times were a result of his pursuit of romance, which came as a complete shock to the rest of the family. It seems he came to the conclusion that he was irresistible to women of all ages. This phase really began right after he moved to my neighborhood in order to be closer to me. I enrolled him in the senior citizens day-care center, where he met a woman whom *he* thought was to be his next true love. It did not make a bit of difference to him that she was 40 years old and already had a boyfriend. Much to everyone's chagrin, he tried unsuccessfully to talk her out of the relationship by extolling his own unlimited virtures. It was not a coincidence that she happened to be a nurse who could provide him with the necessary medical services. His affection for her explains, in no small part, why he would often claim not to be feeling well while at the center, so that he could be sent to the nurse's office. Believe me, I received telephone calls about it.

5    Next on his list was a 24-year-old whom he politely told one day that her impending marriage would be over in a year because her prospective husband was not in the same league as he. (She took a chance and went through with the wedding anyway.) Virtually all of the housekeepers I hired to clean his apartment were, according to my father, desperately trying to corral him. He called them all "bimbos" and pretended to express no real interest, although he did enjoy their supposed attention. I guess he did not want to mix business with pleasure. Then he went through a series of waitresses, ranging in age from 16 to 30, before finally settling for a 70-year-old woman whom he had met at the senior citizen residence where he lived for a few months. In fact, we went on a double date with them—the highlight of which was his attempt to kiss her goodbye. The problem was that she did not realize what he was attempting to do!

6    As startling as these escapades were, at least they involved real people. There was the time my father, in trying to find a bathroom in a restaurant, began to have a conversation with his reflection in a full-length mirror. Because of very poor eyesight, he mistook his reflection for a lovely woman (which must explain why he had the most radiant smile on his face). I waited a moment to help him, not out of indifference or cruelty but because I had not seen him so happy in years. Love does that to people.

7    There were, of course, the bad times as well that go along with aging and the loss of a lifelong partner. The obvious emptiness that he experienced at major family events, the endless appointments with doctors, the various tests that needed to be taken, and the general deterioration of my father's body and mind made his final years anything but "golden." On top of all this, I came to the sad realization that, when you are old and failing, no one seems to want to be with you anymore. I will never forget how one of my father's business associates turned around and walked in the other direction when he saw him coming; how members of his family disappeared, forgetting all the things that he had done for them through the years; and how even his sons sometimes thought of our own needs over his. There was the time, for example, when he showed up at my house on New Year's Eve with his blanket because he did not want to sleep at

the senior citizen residence. I had plans, so I angrily talked him into going back there to be with the other residents. Later, I found out that he had had an argument with the head nun earlier in the day. I can never forgive myself for not letting him sleep over that night. Unfortunately, there would be no chance to redeem myself, for it would be my father's last New Year's Eve.

8    My father was not happy at the residence because he did not like the head nun. In fact, he called her Sister Baccala to her face. (For those who do not know, *baccala* is the Italian word for dried cod fish, which has the most abominable smell.) But my father's dislike for her did not extend to the other nuns who worked there, to one of whom he proposed marriage. Apparently, he thought it was time to liberalize the rules of the Catholic church.

9    The end came almost three years to the day after my mother's death. Those intervening years saw a rapid decline in energy and spirit. A benign brain tumor called a meningioma took from May to September to kill my father. By that time, he was emaciated from weight loss: a mere shadow of the man I had affectionately called Charlie. But even in the final days, he managed to humor us twice more by coming out of a near-comatose state to yell, "Get rid of her!" when he heard me mention one of the housekeeper's names, and by defiantly holding his mouth tightly closed so the nurse could not suction it out. He could still make us laugh even when he wasn't trying to be facetious.

10    Those years as my father's keeper were difficult ones which have had a lasting effect on me. Although several people were very helpful, I was primarily responsible for his well-being, serving as his part-time moving agent, financial adviser and manager, nurse, transportation planner, chauffeur, and a host of other roles. Because of his feeble condition, I was forced to do things for him that I never dreamed I would have to do, including helping him to dress and cleaning him up after the inevitable accidents in the bathroom.

11    The obvious role reversal bothered me a great deal then, and it still does now whenever I think about it. My patience was tried to the limit, and my emotions were on a nonstop roller-coaster. There were times when I was angry, times when I was depressed, and many times when I felt guilty for not doing more. And yet, through it all, there were still humorous moments that will stay in my memory forever. In the end, perhaps they should serve as my father's legacy.

*The Humanist,* March–April 1996, pp. 47–48

Purpose: _____

Tone: _____

---

## 14.  I Was a Teen Mom

KIMBERLY EVANOVICH

1    Not long ago I was having lunch with the CEO of a software company that was considering me as a consultant for a lucrative overseas project. All had gone well, and we were waiting for the check when a very young, very pregnant woman passed by pushing a stroller and checking a bus schedule.

2      My companion snorted with disgust. "That makes me sick," he said, shaking his head. "You'd think she would stop creating new mouths for the government to feed."

3      Like most of my business associates, this man was not aware that I, at age 28, even *had* children—let alone kids old enough to be in the fourth and fifth grades. He saw my suit and my Gold Card and assumed I shared his view that teen mothers deserve no compassion. Nothing could be further from the truth.

4      When I accidentally became pregnant at 17, I was terrified. I cried when I got my first positive pregnancy test and promptly got three more. My friends encouraged me to have an abortion, but as logical as their arguments seemed (I barely knew the baby's father; I had my future to think about), I just couldn't do it. Yet the shock of becoming a parent was paralyzing. I remember looking in the mirror after my daughter was born, trying to connect my face to my new identity. Another human being was going to see me and think, "mother," but all I could think was that I wanted my *own* mother.

5      Although I was married to my daughter's father for a while—and had another child with him—I found myself completely on my own before my twentieth birthday, with no earning power and two babies in diapers. My parents were unable to offer me support, but I decided not to go on welfare; I just didn't think of that option at first, and by the time I did, I had found other ways to squeak by, working two jobs while I earned my college degree.

6      Over the years I came to accept, and love, my life as a parent. What I couldn't accept was the way I was treated.

7      While it is not unusual for two toddlers to break into noisy tears upon being denied an ice cream, when it happened with *my* children, strangers made snide comments—as if someone who couldn't control her own fertility certainly couldn't control a child. Once, an older woman who had stopped to admire my daughter's huge blue eyes—and who then noticed my young face and pregnant figure—remarked, "You poor thing. I bet you wish you were more careful with birth control." Another woman, with pro-life stickers on her van, muttered "welfare mother" after I parked my dilapidated car next to hers. What was she saying—Keep your baby alive, but keep it away from me?

8      Professionally, I soon realized that as long as I was just an ambitious student, employers were friendly and doors opened. But once I let on that I was also a mother of two, smiles faded. Some people said, "I don't understand . . . *you* have kids?" They were genuinely confused. Once they understood, I was often ushered out. They had no image of the life I was trying to live, and the stereotype they usually came up with was that of the irresponsible tramp.

9      Even pediatricians often acted as if I were to blame for my children's infrequent illnesses. Once, my four-year-old daughter woke screaming in pain and I rushed her to the emergency room. When it turned out to be a bladder infection, the doctor wanted to know if "a lot of men" used my toilet.

10     Indignant, I responded that the only males who used my toilet were my fiancé (an engineering graduate student who is now my husband) and my three-year-old son.

11     "Well then," he continued, "Is this 'boyfriend' of yours a *clean* person?"

12    His attitude was not unusual. In fact, if anyone made me doubt my future, it was the people employed to *help* young mothers and their children.

13    When my son was diagnosed with diabetes, a California children's services worker insisted that I would need her group's help in paying his medical bills for the rest of my life. When I protested that no, I had nearly finished college and had bright prospects, she laughed. "Do you realize," she said, "that only high-paying executive positions offer the medical coverage you will need? I think we can safely say that your chances of providing for your son on your own are extremely slim."

14    Two weeks before graduation, I was hired by a Big Six accounting firm. My insurance, I learned, was of the high-paying executive sort, and it was with great pleasure that I called the children's services worker to let her know that I would not, after all, be needing her for the rest of my life.

15    I now own my own marketing consulting company and am blissfully remarried; my children are happy and healthy. My daughter claims that nothing is better than having a mom who's young because you "like the same CDs and can share earrings."

16    As I near 30, remarks about teen moms simply annoy me; when I was 18, they stung. The difference between success and failure was, for me, the belief that I *could* make it—yet I often got the message that the game was already over. Why struggle to win when the world is convinced you have lost?

17    Many people think that to offer kind words to young mothers is to endorse their deviant behavior. I know otherwise. Treating teen moms as worthwhile and responsible can only help them live up to the challenge of their lives.

*Glamour,* April 1996, p. 156

Purpose: _____

Tone: _____

15. **The Irradiation Debate**
*The Food Industry Looks at a Controversial Process*

IRENA CHALMERS

1    Few words convey the emotional punch that the term *food irradiation* delivers. To be in favor of it is to announce oneself out of tune with a rousing chorus of politically correct boos and hisses. Nevertheless, it is worth taking a minute to think about the benefits of food irradiation before reflexively jerking our knees. "Whatever your politics," says Mike Wright, chairman, president, and CEO of Supervalu, Inc., a large food distribution and retail company, "it is undeniable that foodborne illness is a very serious health problem and that irradiation can become at least a part of the solution."

2    Irradiation is an important weapon against the approximately 6.5 million cases of foodborne illnesses and 9,000 related deaths that the U.S. Food and Drug Administration estimates occur in the United States each year. Food irra-

diation could go a long way toward destroying the deadly *E. coli* as well as campylobacter (the primary cause of food poisoning) and salmonella.

3    This is what happens during the irradiation process: Food is put into an enclosed chamber and exposed to an ionizing source of gamma rays, usually cobalt or cesium, which pass through the food and kill growing cells, like insects or bacteria. Irradiated food never comes in contact with radioactive material, and the gamma rays, x-rays, or electrons can't make the food radioactive.

4    Food irradiation is endorsed by the American Medical Association and the American Dietetic Association, a 70,000-member group that is the nation's largest organization of nutrition and food professionals. It has also been approved by the U.S. Department of Agriculture, the FDA, the Council for Agricultural Science and Technology, the United Nations Food and Agriculture Organization, the Institute of Food Technologists, and the *Harvard Health Letter*. The technology is highly regulated, reliable, and cost-effective. It only adds a couple of cents per pound to the overall cost of the food. So what's the problem? Fear.

5    Despite the endorsements of experts in the field, the general public remains skeptical or downright hostile to the concept of food irradiation. The general public was also, at an earlier time, downright hostile to milk pasteurization, microwaves, and fluoridation.

6    In the end, consumers will be the driving force behind industry decisions concerning irradiation. But as more and more consumers become educated on the subject, the needs of the marketplace will no doubt converge with the desires of the people to the benefit of all.

*Modern Maturity,* November-December 1998, p. 75

## Food Fight

"Food irradiation is a false solution to a serious problem," says Ronnie Cummins, director of the Pure Food Campaign. According to Cummins, irradiation not only creates dangerous chemical byproducts and destroys nutrients, it raises the specter of increased public exposure to radiation through the creation of hundreds of new irradiation facilities. "There were numerous instances," he says, "where feeding animals irradiated food produced things like heart problems, cancer, reproductive damage, and chromosome abnormalities."

According to Cummins, some if not all these effects were due to radiolytic byproducts, chemicals like benzene and formaldehyde that appear in irradiated foods. The USDA and others, however, say that the levels are insignificant.

But even if many scientists claim that the process is safe, is it really the right way to go? Not according to organizations like the Center for Science in the Public Interest, Food and Water, Inc., and the Pure Food Campaign. "Wouldn't it be better," says Cummins, "to deliver the freshest food possible?" Advocates, however, say that is exactly what is being done. They say adding irradiation would not replace safe food handling but would help achieve the highest level of hygienic quality.

*Rick Boling*

Purpose: _____

Tone:_____

C.  Read the following short story, and discuss its ironies.

16. **The Story of an Hour**

KATE CHOPIN

1   Knowing that Mrs. Mallard was afflicted with a heart trouble, great care was taken to break to her as gently as possible the news of her husband's death.

2   It was her sister Josephine who told her, in broken sentences, veiled hints that revealed in half concealing. Her husband's friend Richards was there, too, near her. It was he who had been in the newspaper office when intelligence of the railroad disaster was received, with Brently Mallard's name leading the list of "killed." He had only taken the time to assure himself of its truth by a second telegram, and had hastened to forestall any less careful, less tender friend in bearing the sad message.

3   She did not hear the story as many women have heard the same, with a paralyzed inability to accept its significance. She wept at once with sudden, wild abandonment, in her sister's arms. When the storm of grief had spent itself she went away to her room alone. She would have no one follow her.

4   There stood, facing the open window, a comfortable, roomy armchair. Into this she sank, pressed down by a physical exhaustion that haunted her body and seemed to reach into her soul.

5   She could see in the open square before her house the tops of trees that were all aquiver with the new spring life. The delicious breath of rain was in the air. In the street below a peddler was crying his wares. The notes of a distant song which some one was singing reached her faintly, and countless sparrows were twittering in the eaves.

6   There were patches of blue sky showing here and there through the clouds that had met and piled one above the other in the west facing her window.

7   She sat with her head thrown back upon the cushion of the chair quite motionless, except when a sob came up into her throat and shook her, as a child who has cried itself to sleep continues to sob in its dreams.

8   She was young, with a fair, calm face, whose lines bespoke repression and even a certain strength. But now there was a dull stare in her eyes, whose gaze was fixed away off yonder on one of those patches of blue sky. It was not a glance of reflection, but rather indicated a suspension of intelligent thought.

9   There was something coming to her and she was waiting for it, fearfully. What was it? She did not know; it was too subtle and elusive to name. But she felt it creeping out of the sky, reaching toward her through the sounds, the scents, the color that filled the air.

10  Now her bosom rose and fell tumultuously. She was beginning to recognize this thing that was approaching to possess her, and she was striving to beat it back with her will—as powerless as her two white slender hands would have been.

11  When she abandoned herself a little whispered word escaped her slightly parted lips. She said it over and over under her breath: "Free, free, free!" The vacant stare and the look of terror that had followed it went from her eyes.

They stayed keen and bright. Her pulses beat fast, and the coursing blood warmed and relaxed every inch of her body.

12   She did not stop to ask if it were not a monstrous joy that held her. A clear and exalted perception enabled her to dismiss the suggestion as trivial.

13   She knew that she would weep again when she saw the kind, tender hands folded in death; the face that had never looked save with love upon her, fixed and gray and dead. But she saw beyond that bitter moment a long procession of years to come that would belong to her absolutely. And she opened and spread her arms out to them in welcome.

14   There would be no one to live for her during those coming years; she would live for herself. There would be no powerful will bending her in the blind persistence with which men and women believe they have a right to impose a private will upon a fellow creature. A kind intention or a cruel intention made the act seem no less a crime as she looked upon it in that brief moment of illumination.

15   And yet she had loved him—sometimes. Often she had not. What did it matter! What could love, the unsolved mystery, count for in face of this possession of self-assertion which she suddenly recognized as the strongest impulse of her being.

16   "Free! Body and soul free!" she kept whispering.

17   Josephine was kneeling before the closed door with her lips to the keyhole, imploring for admission. "Louise, open the door! I beg; open the door—you will make yourself ill. What are you doing, Louise? For heaven's sake open the door."

18   "Go away. I am not making myself ill." No; she was drinking in the very elixir of life through that open window.

19   Her fancy was running riot along those days ahead of her. Spring days, and summer days, and all sorts of days that would be her own. She breathed a quick prayer that life might be long. It was only yesterday she had thought with a shudder that life might be long.

20   She arose at length and opened the door to her sister's importunities. There was a feverish triumph in her eyes, and she carried herself unwittingly like a goddess of Victory. She clasped her sister's waist and together they descended the stairs. Richards stood waiting for them at the bottom.

21   Some one was opening the front door with a latchkey. It was Brently Mallard who entered, a little travel-stained, composedly carrying his grip-sack and umbrella. He had been far from the scene of accident, and did not even know there had been one. He stood amazed at Josephine's piercing cry; at Richards' quick motion to screen him from the view of his wife.

22   But Richards was too late.

23   When the doctors came they said she had died of heart disease—of joy that kills.

*Literature for Composition*, 4th ed., Sylvan Barnet et al., Eds., pp. 12–13

Ironies: _____

_____

_____

_____

_____

_____

_____

_____

_____

_____

_____

_____

_____

## GO ELECTRONIC!

For additional readings, exercises, and Internet activities, visit our Web site at:

### http://longman.awl.com/englishpages

If you need a user name and password, see your instructor.

**Take a Road Trip to** the Getty Museum! Be sure to visit the Purpose and Tone module in your Reading Road Trip CD-ROM for multimedia tutorials, exercises, and tests.

## Chapter Eight

# Looking at Advertisements with a Critical Eye

**Chapter Outline**

Advertisements and Critical Thinking

Evaluating an Advertisement

*How Does It Try to Catch the Interest of Readers?*

*To Whom Is It Designed to Appeal?*

*What Is It Trying to Persuade Readers to Buy, Do, or Think?*

*What Benefit to Readers Is It Stressing?*

*How Convincing Is It?*

What are the following advertisements trying to get readers to do? What is the tone of each? Discuss your answers with your classmates.

(1)

No Ifs, Ands, Or Butts
Spa Lady
Fairfield 882-8211    W. Paterson 890-0777
Lyndhurst 201-935-2555

(2)

## SMELLY, LETHARGIC, INCOHERENT.

## IT'S HARD TO DETECT INHALANT ABUSE IN THE AVERAGE TEENAGER.

Is it just a phase your child is going through? Or is his life in danger?

The threat comes from inhalants, which are ordinary household products that kids sniff to get high.

Half of all 14-15 year olds have been offered inhalants and almost one in five 8th graders has tried them.

Few realize that just one sniff can cause death, or that chronic users can suffer severe and permanent brain damage.

The tell-tale signs of inhalant use include slurred speech, glassy eyes and the smell of chemicals on clothes.

Sniffers may also suffer nose bleeds, sores or rashes around the nose and mouth, or a sudden loss of appetite.

Warn your kids before it's too late, because we don't recommend the other means of detection. It's called an autopsy.

To learn more about inhalants, what they are and where in your home they can be found, we urge you to call 1 (800) 729-6686.

**PARTNERSHIP FOR A DRUG-FREE AMERICA®**

(3)

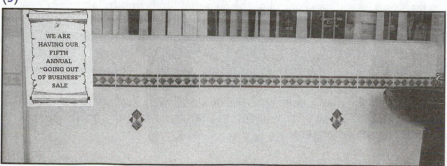

WE ARE HAVING OUR FIFTH ANNUAL "GOING OUT OF BUSINESS" SALE

## Chapter Outcomes

After completing Chapter 8, you should be able to:
- Continue to apply the basic method for personal problem solving
- Evaluate an advertisement by determining how it tries to catch the interest of readers; to whom it is designed to appeal; what it is trying to persuade readers to buy, do, or think; the benefit to readers that it is stressing; and how convincing it is
- Continue to find topics and central messages in contemporary issue passages to determine what is at issue, distinguish among opposing viewpoints, and express personal viewpoints

## Problem-Solving Exercise

Apply the basic method for personal problem solving to the following hypothetical situation. Your instructor will divide the class into four groups for purposes of dealing with the problem from the different perspectives of José, Maria, Carlotta, and Pedro. In other words, Group 1 will tackle the problem from José's point of view, Group 2 from Maria's point of view, Group 3 from Carlotta's point of view, and Group 4 from Pedro's point of view. After all four groups have completed their work, a person from each one will speak on behalf of the other members as the entire class attempts to come up with a possible solution acceptable to all groups.

### Hypothetical Situation

José and Maria have been married for many years and had three children two years apart. Their oldest son is now residing in another state, while their 23-year-old daughter, Carlotta, and their 21-year-old son, Pedro, still live at home.

Pedro, as the youngest child, has been somewhat spoiled through the years to the extent that his siblings feel a certain amount of resentment toward him. To them, Pedro has always seemed to demand and receive more attention, time, and money.

In recent years, the situation has gotten very tense at home, particularly between José and Pedro. It seems that they clash about everything and are constantly shouting at each other, which is causing much stress for the entire family. José, who gets very angry, feels that Pedro is selfish and much too demanding. As head of the family, he has decided to draw the line. Otherwise, he fears that he will lose control of the household to Pedro. In fact, on several occasions, they have almost come to blows.

Maria believes that her husband is being much too firm with Pedro, and she really does not like the way José talks to him. She has told José many times that he is using insulting, degrading language in his arguments with their son. Pedro also gets very mad at his father and always tends to go to his mother as an ally who is more receptive to his wishes. José interprets her actions as a lack of support for him, and as a result, he is losing his self-respect and has become very resentful.

Consequently, José and Maria have had some very heated arguments, which have affected the stability of their marriage. Carlotta, feeling the tension, has withdrawn from the situation and tends to stay in her room much of the time. She has become totally disgusted with the entire household!

## Advertisements and Critical Thinking

Pretend that you are a skier and read the following advertisement in the newspaper:

**Every item in every Princeton Ski Shop has been reduced to the lowest price ever. Guaranteed.**

Would you rush right out to the nearest Princeton Ski Shop and buy everything in sight? One hopes not! At the very least, you would first want to know if the advertisement is referring to the lowest prices ever at the Princeton Ski Shop or at all stores that sell those items. Furthermore, you would wonder how Princeton Ski Shop can prove to customers that the prices are indeed the lowest ever or, for that matter, how *you* would be able to find out that information for yourself. Finally, you would be interested in what the guarantee involves. For example, if you could prove to Princeton that it once sold a particular item at a cheaper price than it is now or that you can find it for less at a competing ski shop, what is the store prepared to do under the terms of its guarantee?

As a critical thinker and reader, you are very aware of the importance of evaluating what you see, hear, and read so that you are in a better position to make the best possible decisions. This is particularly important when dealing with advertisements, which are designed specifically to influence your thinking, which of course in turn has an effect on your purchasing, political, and philosophical decisions. In fact, in today's world, you are overwhelmed with advertisements which attempt to persuade you to *buy* something, *do* something, or *think* something. You are urged to buy certain products, including foods, drinks, automobiles and clothing; to take advantage of particular services, such as tax return preparation, cleaning, or pest control; to attend social affairs, workshops, or classes; to vote or not to vote for certain candidates or political issues; and to support or oppose particular viewpoints regarding such issues as abortion, health care, and school prayer. There is no end to the stream of claims and counterclaims, all designed to sell you something.

If you do not pick and choose among the products, services, and ideas pushed by advertisers, you could soon go broke, become confused about who and what to vote for, or perhaps not even know what to think. You can avoid those unattractive possibilities by taking the time to think critically about advertisements so that you can evaluate them *before* acting. In short, critical thinking can help you sift through all the information thrown your way. How, then, should you think critically about advertisements? By answering a series of questions designed to uncover their purposes and strategies.

## Evaluating an Advertisement

One way to evaluate an advertisement is to ask and answer the following questions:

➤ How does it try to catch the interest of readers?

➤ To whom is it designed to appeal?

➤ What is it trying to persuade readers to buy, do, or think?

➤ What benefit to readers is it stressing?

➤ How convincing is it?

As you know, looking at the world with a questioning mind to find answers to questions like these is an important aspect of critical thinking. This certainly applies when dealing with advertisements, which are often very clever in their attempts to sway our minds.

Although we will be concerned only with advertisements in print, the same questions are relevant to all forms of advertising. They should enable you to evaluate advertising claims more effectively so that you can make informed decisions regarding what to buy, what to do, and what to think. Let's look at each of the questions in turn.

### How Does It Try to Catch the Interest of Readers?

One of the keys to successful advertising is to catch the interest of readers. In your busy life, there is little time to read every page in front of you, so you have to be very selective. Being aware of this, advertisers go to great lengths to arouse your curiosity in what they have to say. You should know when advertisers are trying to catch your interest so that you keep in mind that they are attempting to influence you. Look at the strange advertisement on the next page.

As you can see, it is printed in reverse. Do you know what it says? That's right! The message states: "It's not the lighting. Next time Noxzema." It has been placed across from mirrors in women's restrooms so that it can be read easily by women when they look in the mirror. The point of the advertisement is that if women are not happy with the way their faces look, they should be using Noxzema. Because it is unusual, women will probably take the time to read the ad and consider its message.

### To Whom Is It Designed to Appeal?

Advertisers always have an intended audience targeted for their messages—men, women, or children of specific ages, from various ethnic groups, and with certain interests. It is important that you know to whom an advertisement is designed to appeal so that you can decide whether or not you should spend your time giving serious consideration to what it has to say. Because of its placement,

for example, the Noxzema ad was obviously meant to appeal to women. Look at the advertisement on page 324 and determine its intended audience.

If you answered that the ad is designed to appeal to students, you are correct. More specifically, it is intended for high school students who want to attend college and college students who are interested in going to graduate school. Notice how it catches their attention with the large print, which on the surface makes a connection between great test scores and looking better.

## What Is It Trying to Persuade Readers to Buy, Do, or Think?

Obviously, the whole point of a given advertisement is to get you to purchase a product, take a certain action, or think a certain way. In the examples so far,

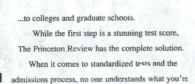

# Great test scores make you look better

...to colleges and graduate schools.

While the first step is a stunning test score, The Princeton Review has the complete solution.

When it comes to standardized tests and the admissions process, no one understands what you're going through better than we do. Our focused, personalized approach is famous for giving students an exceptional edge and top-rate scores. To find out about our intensive courses call us today at (800) 2-REVIEW or browse us at www.review.com.

Or look for our award-winning books and software at a store near you.

We'll give you a strategy make-over and enhance your chances.

GET AN EDGE.

*The Princeton Review is not affiliated with Princeton University or ETS.*

THE
PRINCETON
REVIEW

COURSES • BOOKS • SOFTWARE • SAT • ACT • GMAT • GRE • LSAT • MCAT • USMLE • MBE • CAREER

the advertisers were trying to get readers to buy Noxzema and take the Princeton Review course. It is important that you recognize the point of an advertisement so that you can determine if it has relevance to your life and is therefore worthy of your time. Read the next advertisement on page 325 to determine what it is trying to persuade readers to buy, do, or think.

The ad, which attempts to catch the interest of readers through pictures of poison ivy and marijuana leaves, is appealing to parents to talk to their

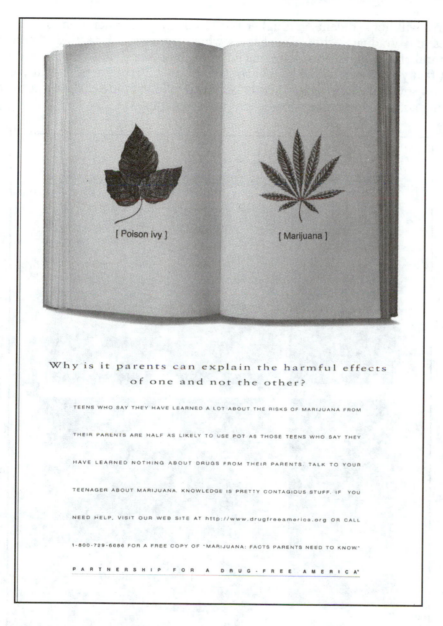

[ Poison ivy ]                    [ Marijuana ]

Why is it parents can explain the harmful effects
of one and not the other?

TEENS WHO SAY THEY HAVE LEARNED A LOT ABOUT THE RISKS OF MARIJUANA FROM

THEIR PARENTS ARE HALF AS LIKELY TO USE POT AS THOSE TEENS WHO SAY THEY

HAVE LEARNED NOTHING ABOUT DRUGS FROM THEIR PARENTS. TALK TO YOUR

TEENAGER ABOUT MARIJUANA. KNOWLEDGE IS PRETTY CONTAGIOUS STUFF. IF YOU

NEED HELP, VISIT OUR WEB SITE AT http://www.drugfreeamerica.org OR CALL

1-800-729-6686 FOR A FREE COPY OF "MARIJUANA: FACTS PARENTS NEED TO KNOW."

PARTNERSHIP FOR A DRUG-FREE AMERICA®

teenagers about the harmful effects of marijuana. Thus the target group—
parents of teenagers—are being urged to do something.

## What Benefit to Readers Is It Stressing?

An effective advertisement is very specific about the benefit to readers as a result
of their buying, doing, or thinking whatever is being urged by the ad: Applying
Noxzema will improve women's faces or looks; taking the Princeton Review

course will help students get higher test scores to gain easier admission to colleges and graduate schools; teenagers whose parents talk to them about the harmful effects of marijuana are much less likely to use it. It is extremely important that you recognize the benefit stressed by an advertisement so that you can make a sound decision as to whether or not to follow its advice. Look at the following ad, and determine what benefit it is stressing:

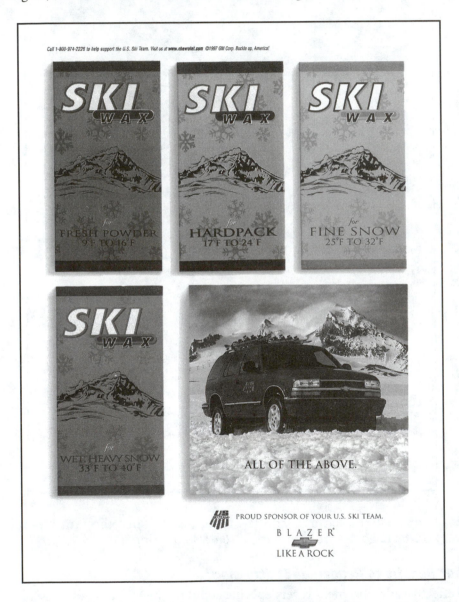

As you can see, the advertisement catches the interest of readers by pretending to be an ad for ski wax when in fact it is really making an appeal to drivers to buy a Blazer truck because it will go through all kinds of snow conditions.

## How Convincing Is It?

From your perspective as a critical thinker, the most important consideration concerning the evaluation of a given advertisement involves how convincing it is in terms of the benefit stressed. In short, your decision as to whether or not to buy, do, or think what an ad is suggesting is based almost solely on the degree to which you become convinced that the benefit to you is both relevant and valid.

The examples that we have been using do not do a very good job in that respect:

In the Noxzema ad, women are not told specifically how its use will improve their faces or looks.

Students are not informed how their enrollment in the Princeton Review course is going to result in higher test scores, nor are they given any statistics regarding success rates of other students who have completed the course.

Parents are given one statistic in the ad dealing with the harmful effects of marijuana that supports the claim that teens who have been warned by parents are half as likely to use pot as those who have learned nothing about drugs from their parents. However, they are never told how that statistic was arrived at or where it comes from. Nevertheless, at least there is an offer of additional free information from Partnership for a Drug-Free America, which *seems* like a reputable organization that favors what *apparently* is a very good cause. Hence readers have the option of investigating the matter further.

Finally, the advertisement for the Blazer gives drivers no indication how that vehicle will enable them to go through all kinds of snow conditions.

Let's take a look at the advertisement on page 328 to determine how convincing it is. This advertisement, which was posted on a college classroom door, is designed to appeal to students who are suffering from "math anxiety," and it tries to catch their interest through the use of large boldface lettering and a somewhat humorous cartoon figure. In addition, it does deal with a topic that is of obvious concern to many students. As you can see, the ad is trying to persuade readers to attend a math anxiety workshop, but it only *implies* that attendance will help students with the problem. Furthermore, there is absolutely no indication of exactly how this workshop is going to assist students who suffer from math anxiety. For instance, are certain techniques or specific methods that will help going to be suggested, or is the workshop simply a review session dealing with mathematical principles? Although some students may attend anyway because this is a rather common problem, the advertisement really does not do a very effective job of convincing readers of the benefit resulting from their attendance.

In the end, if an advertisement does not convince you of the benefit of buying, doing, or thinking what it is urging, you have no good reason to follow its advice. If you did, you might end up making a decision that you will re-

# MATH ANXIETY WORKSHOP!!!
## TUESDAY, APRIL 21ST
## 2:00 PM IN ROOM H107

# DOES MATH MAKE YOU SHAKE???

### DO YOU FREEZE DURING MATH TESTS?

### DO YOU FORGET ANSWERS TO QUESTIONS YOU KNOW?

### DOES YOUR SLEEP OR APPETITE SUFFER BEFORE A TEST?

# COME TO A MATH ANXIETY WORKSHOP:

# TUESDAY, APRIL 21ST AT 2:00 PM
# ROOM H107

gret, such as buying the wrong (for you) product or service, voting for the wrong candidate, accepting the wrong idea, or supporting the wrong viewpoint. Thus you must remember always to evaluate the advertisements you come in contact with by answering the five questions that we have been using. The time spent should make you a more informed, careful consumer who thinks before acting.

## ACTIVITY 1

Complete the following exercise, which appeared in a psychology textbook.

**What's Wrong Here?**

All of the statements below were taken from claims and assertions found in the popular media. Indicate in the space provided why you should be suspicious.

➤ "No other smoking-cessation program works better than Quitters Anonymous."

➤ "Ache-Be-Gone contains twice as much pain relief medication as its competitors, and that's why it's the most effective product on the market today."

➤ Portions of an article in the newspaper read, "*The Last Body Count* was a very successful feature film and later video store release. Unfortunately, it was ranked last in its time slot when shown on network television. A news magazine show and three situation comedies competing with it were ranked higher in the ratings. Viewers are obviously losing their taste for violence on television."

➤ "According to industry records, last year, Trans-Caribbean Airlines had the best 'on-time' record of any other airline in the industry. Fly with us, and be sure of getting to your destination on time today!"

➤ "Students who use a word processor get higher grades."

➤ "This SAT refresher course is guaranteed to raise your combined SAT scores an average of 100 points higher than your PSAT or last SAT scores."

Anthony F. Grasha, *Practical Applications of Psychology*, p. 78

For this activity, your instructor will divide the class into groups of three. Evaluate each of the following advertisements within your group by asking and answering the five questions we have been using. Be prepared to discuss your answers with the rest of the class.

(1)

When you go away, the burglars will stay.

FBI statistics show that over 26% of home burglaries occur between Memorial Day and Labor Day.*

For just $159, SND Security Systems provides the peace of mind you deserve, 24 hours a day, 365 days a year.

**Call SND today;** *THIS DEAL IS A STEAL.*

**SND Summer Sale!**

Now Only **$159**

**SND Security** SYSTEMS

*1993 FBI Uniform Crime Report

(2)

**This needs no headline. It just needs you.**

Millions of pounds of garbage are deposited in the world's waterways and on our shorelines every year. It's harming our wildlife. It's harming our planet. It's harming us.

A few hours of your time can help clean it up.

Once again, the Center for Marine Conservation will host the planet's largest volunteer cleanup effort on behalf of the marine environment. Please join us. Call 800-CMC-BEACH for local time and place. *And for your help, we'll gladly give you a Brita® Water Filtration Pitcher.*

International Coastal Cleanup Day - September 19, 1998.     CENTER FOR **MARINE** CONSERVATION     **BRITA®** WATER FILTRATION SYSTEMS

(3)

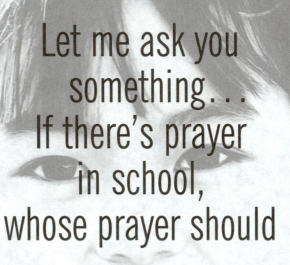

Let me ask you something...
If there's prayer
in school,
whose prayer should

it be?

Official prayer sessions in public school seem
like a good idea to many Americans,
provided they get to choose the prayer.
But in such a diverse society, how can one prayer
satisfy every religious belief?
How would you feel if your child were required to
say a Catholic prayer in school every day?
Or a Baptist prayer or Muslim prayer?
What about a Jewish prayer or a Buddhist prayer?
There are over 1,500 religious denominations
in America. How many of us would want our
children to recite someone else's prayer?
Maybe prayer is just too personal to let
the government or any one particular religious
group decide what prayers our children should
be saying in school.
Think about it.

Ira Glasser
Executive Director of the American Civil Liberties Union
125 Broad Street
New York, New York 10004
www.aclu.org

(4)

# TV is Good.

For years the pundits, moralists and self-righteous, self-appointed preservers of our culture have told us that television is bad. They've stood high on their soapbox and looked condescendingly on our innocuous pleasure. They've sought to wean us from our harmless habit by derisively referring to television as the Boob Tube or the Idiot Box.

Well, television is not the evil destroyer of all that is right in this world. In fact, and we say this with all the disdain we can muster for the elitists who purport otherwise – TV is good.

TV binds us together. It makes us laugh. Makes us cry. Why, in the span of ten years, TV brought us the downfall of an American president, one giant step for mankind and the introduction of Farrah Fawcett as one of "Charlie's Angels." Can any other medium match TV for its immediacy, its impact, its capacity to entertain? Who among us hasn't spent an entire weekend on the couch, bathed in the cool glow of a Sony Trinitron°, only to return to work recuperated and completely refreshed? And who would dispute that the greatest advancement in aviation over the last ten years was the decision to air sitcoms during the in-flight service?

Why then should we cower behind our remote controls? Let us rejoice in our fully adjustable, leather-upholstered recliners. Let us celebrate our cerebral-free non-activity. Let us climb the highest figurative mountaintop and proclaim, with all the vigor and shrillness that made Roseanne a household name, that TV is good.

(5)

# How far has Congress drifted from the rest of America?

**What Americans want... and what Congress does:**

✓ More than 70% of Americans favor more public funding for family planning...
*Congress won't adequately fund it.*

✓ Two out of three Americans support confidential teen access to family planning...
*Congress tries to block it.*

✓ 75% of Americans favor requiring health plans to cover contraceptive methods...
*Congress doesn't act.*

✓ 82% of Americans want sex education in schools...
*Congress spends millions of tax dollars on one-sided programs that teach only abstinence.*

✓ Two out of three Americans believe abortion should remain accessible to women...
*Congress tries to block access to abortion.*

Congress has drifted away from the rest of us when it comes to family planning, responsible sex education, and a woman's right to choose abortion.

The vast majority of Americans believe that decisions about these personal, private matters should be left up to individuals, their families, and their doctors.

But apparently Congress listens only to an isolated few who want to impose their choices on everyone else.

Planned Parenthood is working to put America's values into action. Our *Responsible Choices* Action Agenda advocates new state and federal policies that prevent unintended pregnancy, improve reproductive health care, ensure access to abortion, and protect our ability to make our *own* choices.

We give you the chance to make your voice heard. And show our legislators the way back home.

*"We must translate the American social consensus on family planning and reproductive health into a political consensus — and give all Americans access to the information and services they need to make responsible choices."*

—GLORIA FELDT, President
Planned Parenthood
Federation of America

Ⓟ **Planned Parenthood**
*Responsible Choices*

# Join us.

To find out how to support our *Responsible Choices* Action Agenda, contact Planned Parenthood Federation of America at 810 Seventh Ave., New York, NY 10019 • 212-261-4302 • www.plannedparenthood.org

(6)

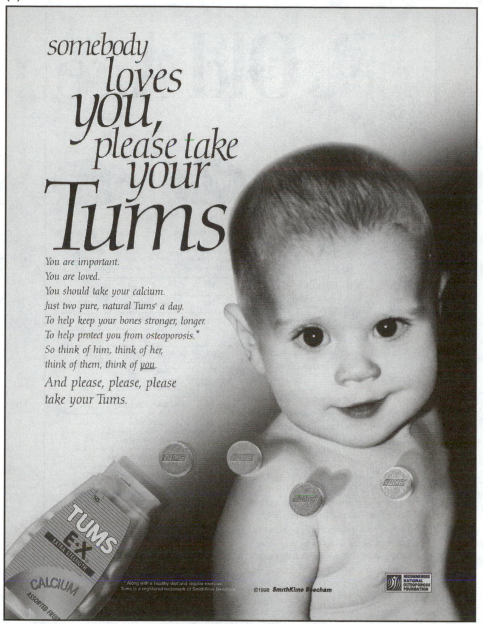

somebody
loves
you,
please take
your
Tums

You are important.
You are loved.
You should take your calcium.
Just two pure, natural Tums® a day.
To help keep your bones stronger, longer.
To help protect you from osteoporosis.*
So think of him, think of her,
think of them, think of _you_.

And please, please, please
take your Tums.

* Along with a healthy diet and regular exercise.
Tums is a registered trademark of SmithKline Beecham.

©1998 **SmithKline Beecham**

RECOMMENDED
NATIONAL
OSTEOPOROSIS
FOUNDATION

TUMS
E·X
EXTRA STRENGTH

CALCIUM

ASSORTED FRUIT

(7)

# Old Age

|  | PERCEPTIONS | REALITIES |
|---|---|---|
| Percent of Americans **18-34** who expect these things to happen when they get old. | | Percent of Americans **65 and Over** who have experienced these things. |
| 77 | More Travel | 46 |
| 76 | More Hobbies | 56 |
| 69 | Less Active | 41 |
| 64 | New Skills | 28 |
| 62 | More Respect | 53 |
| 58 | Less Stress | 50 |
| 48 | Serious Illness | 25 |
| 46 | Get Social Security | 90 |
| 47 | Can't Drive | 15 |
| 44 | Get Medicare | 80 |
| 43 | Fewer Responsibilities | 50 |
| 41 | Trouble Walking | 30 |
| 38 | Lose Bladder Control | 14 |
| 32 | Less Sex Life | 37 |
| 29 | Become Senile | 2 |
| 29 | Dependent on Kids | 5 |
| 26 | Be Lonely | 24 |
| 13 | Be Poor | 18 |

There are surprises ahead for today's young people. Old age is different than what they anticipate. This is one finding of a nationwide survey we conducted to help frame a national discussion about the future of Social Security in an aging society.

Our premise: the more we all understand about how we and our fellow citizens view old age, the easier it will be to figure out what role Social Security should play in it.

If you'd like more information, give us a call at (888) 735-ADSS (2377) or visit us on the Web at www.americansdiscuss.org. *Americans Discuss Social Security* is a non-partisan initiative to help secure the future of Social Security by publishing information, hosting discussions and helping to deliver Americans' views to America's policy makers.

SOCIAL SECURITY
Americans Discuss Social Security

A PROJECT FUNDED BY THE PEW CHARITABLE TRUSTS

2001 Pennsylvania Avenue, Suite 825
Washington, DC 20006

(8)

# Will Big Tobacco Ever Tell the Truth?

**They said smoking doesn't cause cancer, that nicotine isn't addictive, and that they don't target kids.**

**And now they say tobacco legislation won't work.**

The tobacco industry has lied for more than 40 years. Now they're pushing the idea that a comprehensive tobacco policy is a big government solution that won't help kids.

That's another lie, and the American people know it.

A new poll* shows that more than 80 percent of the public believe Congress should pass a national tobacco control policy to reduce tobacco use among kids. In fact, a large majority says the tobacco industry's opposition makes them favor legislation even more.

**It's time for Congress to pass a tough, effective tobacco bill.  No weak imitations. Don't protect Big Tobacco.**

American Cancer Society • Allergy and Asthma Network-Mothers of Asthmatics, Inc.• American Academy of Pediatrics • American Association for Respiratory Care • American Association of Physicians of Indian Origin • American College of Cardiology • American College of Physicians • American College of Preventive Medicine • American Heart Association • American Psychological Association • American School Health Association • American Society of Internal Medicine • Association of American Medical Colleges • Association of Schools of Public Health • Children's Defense Fund • Community Anti-Drug Coalitions of America • Federation of Behavioral, Psychological and Cognitive Sciences • The General Board of Church and Society of The United Methodist Church • The HMO Group • Interreligious Coalition on Smoking or Health • Latino Council on Alcohol & Tobacco • National Association of County and City Health Officials • National Association of Local Boards of Health • National Association of Pediatric Nurse Associates and Practitioners • National Hispanic Medical Association • National Mental Health Association • Oncology Nursing Society • Partnership for Prevention • Society for Research on Nicotine and Tobacco • Society of Behavioral Medicine • Summit Health Coalition

## Tobacco vs. Kids. Where America draws the line.

To learn more, call 202-296-5469 or visit our web site at www.tobaccofreekids.org.
The National Center for Tobacco-Free Kids, 1707 L Street NW, Suite 800, Washington, DC 20036

* Market Facts' TeleNation survey of 1,000 adults, April 13-15, 1998.                © 1998 National Center for Tobacco-Free Kids

(9)

(10)

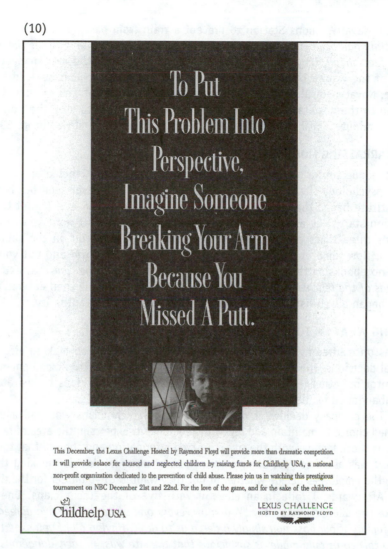

To Put
This Problem Into
Perspective,
Imagine Someone
Breaking Your Arm
Because You
Missed A Putt.

This December, the Lexus Challenge Hosted by Raymond Floyd will provide more than dramatic competition.
It will provide solace for abused and neglected children by raising funds for Childhelp USA, a national
non-profit organization dedicated to the prevention of child abuse. Please join us in watching this prestigious
tournament on NBC December 21st and 22nd. For the love of the game, and for the sake of the children.

Childhelp USA                                    LEXUS CHALLENGE
                                                 HOSTED BY RAYMOND FLOYD

## ACTIVITY 3

Read the following passages, and answer the questions. Remember to use inference skills when appropriate.

## 1

## Obedience to Authority

### HARMFUL CONSEQUENCES

1   In September of 1987, a protest against the shipment of military equipment to Nicaragua occurred outside of the Naval Weapons Station in Concord, California. Three of the protestors stretched their bodies across the railroad tracks leading out

of the Naval Weapons Station to prevent a train from passing. *The civilian crew of the train had been given orders not to stop. In spite of being able to see the protestors 600 feet ahead, they never even slowed the train.* Two of the men managed to get out of the way; a third was not fast enough and had two legs severed below the knee. Naval medical corpsmen at the scene refused to treat him or allow him to be taken to the hospital in their ambulance. Onlookers tried to stop the flow of blood for 45 minutes until a private ambulance arrived (Kelman and Hamilton, 1989).

### EMBARRASSING MOMENTS

2   A colleague sent a graduate student to be the "substitute teacher" in an introductory psychology class. The undergraduate students had never seen her before. The substitute began the class by saying, "I'm in charge today, and I want to get this session started by asking each of you to stand. Fine, now I want you to clap your hands three times and pat the person standing next to you on the shoulder five times. Now jump up and down for ten seconds. OK, sit down and put your pencils and notebooks on the floor." *Each of the 240 students in the class followed the commands of the teacher without questioning them.* My colleague then entered the room and began a well-listened-to presentation on obedience to authority.

### DOING WHAT I'M TOLD VERSUS WHAT'S RIGHT FOR ME

3   I was once hired by a company to be part of a workshop on making effective personal decisions. The company maintained and repaired electronic equipment used to monitor radiation levels in nuclear facilities. Some technicians balked at entering an abandoned facility, fearing that it was dangerous to do so.

4   The company decided it only wanted to use technicians who had made an informed choice to maintain and repair the equipment. Experts in the area of radiation as well as those familiar with the site presented information and showed that the site was safe. I was asked to provide some principles of personal decision making that would help the employees decide whether or not they wanted to volunteer for the work.

5   Afterwards, I rode in an elevator with five of the technicians. One of them broke the silence by saying, *"You know, every one of us would have agreed to enter the facility if our boss had simply ordered us to do it. Having all of you experts brought in to talk to us only made us suspicious that the site was, in fact, dangerous."*

Anthony F. Grasha, *Practical Applications of Psychology*, p. 357

## Comprehension Questions

1. What is the topic of the passage?
2. What is the central message of the passage?
3. Determine what is at issue. What is your initial personal viewpoint?
4. Distinguish among opposing viewpoints, and provide the rationale for each.
5. Think carefully about the viewpoints. Express a personal viewpoint, and give the reasons why you favor it. Does it differ from your initial personal viewpoint? Why or why not?
6. Write a few paragraphs *in support of the viewpoint that you do* not *favor.*

## Thought and Discussion Questions

1. What would you have done if you had been a member of the civilian crew of the train? Why? What would you have done if you had been one of the undergraduate students? Why?

2. Do you agree with what the naval medical corpsmen did? Why or why not?

3. Under the circumstances, would you have felt confident that the nuclear site was safe? Why or why not?

4. Is there any connection between "obedience to authority" and advertising? Why or why not?

5. List any questions that came to mind while you were reading this selection, and be prepared to discuss possible answers to them.

## 2

# A Nation of Hookers

JESSE BIER

1   Prostitution is the selling of one's person for money. I think we can all agree on that; it seems a safe enough definition. Matters turn inconvenient only when we start considering that a person can offer himself or herself as an entire self or personality for sale. The prostitution of the whole person is, after all, a far more thorough spectacle of corruption than the merely sexual. As a matter of fact, the literal streetwalker often tries to disengage himself or herself from the sex act itself in order to salvage vestiges of self-respect.

2   I emphasize these comparisons and call attention to the pertinent metaphor going the rounds in the world of advertising and entertainment, especially television. Celebrities who resist the sale of themselves for commercials are called "virgins."

3   All kinds of celebrities and people are included. I am not talking only of entertainers—although many come to mind who recruit spouse and children as well in a comprehensive family abasement for any and all products. Athletes qualify just as well, and astronauts and—well, anybody. However, it is not absolutely essential that we focus on public personalities. One of our superlatively American democratic perversions is that *anyone* can qualify as a moral prostitute, even or especially "ordinary" people—or actors posing as such—in their testimony about a dish detergent or a car or an antacid tablet. Average men confess and advertise love for their wives and sweethearts under the influence of a gerontological patent medicine; normal but aging executives press ancient "formula" into their hair in order to stay young-looking, quite literally prostituting at least part of their body for business and social purposes. And so on.

4   Still, the spectacle of celebrities in brazen cynical self-devaluation has had a certain undeniable force over the years. A lovable comedian, trading on warmth, kept saying, "Believe me . . ." about anything from coffee crystals to sweepstake lotteries. And a certain famous and rotund actor and former movie director with a

deep compelling voice solemnly linked Beethoven and California wine. One of my all-time favorites, however, comes from the world of sports. A fresh-faced champion skier changed her last name, in an ad featuring her, to "Chapstick," obliging the company by wiping herself out utterly—not quite on the ski slopes, only in life.

5    As to our general population itself, "Miss America" winners are programmed to laugh or cry at exact moments, especially at victory—a necessary forfeiture of the emotional self for the spectacle. And game-show contestants must pass virtual rehearsals demonstrating their capacity to emote in wide-mouthed commodity joy. And there are programs like "The Newlywed Game," where our scrubbed young brides and grooms recall—or should we say, expose—private and often intimate moments for public exhibition, for a price or a prize.

6    Let's not forget a species of child prostitution, to round things out. Separately, countless children advertise breakfast cereals, toys, puppy food, and the like. Or they are all put together, as by a prominent entertainer who used to mimic kids around the block but has graduated to the simpler and easier use of them in cute dessert ads. My favorite combinative ad, however, features a one-time kid now grown up to a kind of professional celebrityhood himself, as the look-alike son of one of America's most beloved twentieth-century comedians; in an endearing flashback, he recalls his father's supposed advice about natural foods—and then advertises the whole-grain cereal himself. It is brilliant reversalism: grown kids trading on their deceased parents, neatly closing the familial circle by the selling of private and precious affections.

7    There are other subtle variations of the nostalgia effect. An aging movie actor, who long ago made his name as a Frank Capra–styled honest American character, has touted the tires of the one company accused of criminal negligence in steel radials. And another all-American movie actor, dressed in his Naval Reserve uniform, has advertised for a commercial "Veterans Insurance Company," in a soft-spoken sincere exploitation of his own patriotism. As we veer toward politics, let's not overlook the former mayors, former governors, former House Speakers, and even former presidents who have sold their authority in one commercial forum or another.

8    Nothing is sacred—least of all religion. There is a whole network dedicated to smiling, glamorized personalities in slick witness to the Lord. Sooner or later I expect the ultimate ad, which will begin with a medium shot of Jesus on the crucifix. Suddenly he awakens, tears himself off the cross, and descends to us. In closeup, he plucks out a nail and says, "Only at --'s can you find old-fashioned, truly tempered precision nails. Buy some—today!"

9    Few will even object. Because by that time we shall have become so used to the vulgar sale of self, so ready to barter our most precious values, models, and icons, that any prostitution will seem only natural—the logical end of a long series.

10    We can do one thing, though. We can still look down on the call girl and out-and-out hooker. When we're slipping so far ourselves, we need any sense of superiority we can get.

*The Humanist*, November-December 1995, p. 41

## Comprehension Questions

   1. What is the topic of the passage?
   2. What is the central message of the passage?

3. Determine what is at issue. What is your initial personal viewpoint?

4. Distinguish among opposing viewpoints, and provide the rationale for each.

5. Think carefully about the viewpoints. Express a personal viewpoint, and give the reasons why you favor it. Does it differ from your initial personal viewpoint? Why or why not?

6. Write a few paragraphs *in support of the viewpoint that you do* not *favor.*

## Thought and Discussion Questions

1. In your view, what are the similarities and differences between a "moral prostitute" and an "out-and-out hooker"?

2. If you were a celebrity, would you be a prostitute or a virgin? Why?

3. Would you agree to do a commercial for a product that you did not like as much as a competing one or a product that you never really used at all? Why or why not?

4. What is the tone of the writer's comments on Jesus? What point is he trying to make?

5. List any questions that came to mind while you were reading this selection, and be prepared to discuss possible answers to them.

## 3

## Drug Ads Lure Patients into Jargon-Strewn Territory

JANE E. BRODY

1    How many of these words do you understand? *Hepatic microsomal enzyme induction, altered lacrimation, menorrhagia, hyperkinesia, hypoesthesia* and *angioneurotic edema.* If your doctor prescribed a drug and warned you about such side effects, would you want to take it? Yet, these are among the scores of possible adverse reactions listed in tiny print in a many-thousand-word "brief summary" on the back side of a consumer magazine advertisement for a popular prescription drug. The front of the advertisement depicts an obviously pleased woman peering at a blue sky and suggests that you "ask your doctor for a trial of once-a-day Claritin," a nonsedating antihistamine that can relieve the symptoms of seasonal nasal allergies.

2    Once upon a time, consumers found out about prescription drugs mainly from their doctors and occasionally from friends or relatives who used them. Now, thanks to an easing of regulations from the Food and Drug Administration, scores of drugs that were once promoted only to doctors are now being promoted directly to consumers in magazines and newspapers and on television and radio. This year the pharmaceutical industry is expected to spend well over $1 billion to try to persuade you to ask your doctor about a prescription drug.

3    The tactic has its benefits and risks, its champions and detractors. Before asking your doctor to prescribe a drug you saw advertised for your allergies, arthritis, asthma, atherosclerosis or whatever might ail you, it pays to heed what the experts are saying about these advertisements and how wise consumers should respond to them.

## HOW CONSUMERS RESPOND

4    In a recent national telephone survey of 1,013 adults sponsored by the National Consumers League, a nonprofit organization based in Washington, 80 percent of those queried said that they had seen or heard prescription drug advertising, and a majority said that it provided useful information about a drug or the disease it was designed to treat. Nearly half said they had talked to their doctors about a drug they saw advertised, and a quarter said they had consulted a doctor about the disease mentioned in an advertisement.

5    About 23 percent—half those who asked about an advertised drug—said their doctors had prescribed it, but in 12 percent of cases, the doctors said the drug was not appropriate. Perhaps most significant to the patients involved, 29 percent said they were helped by the discussion prompted by asking their doctors about an advertised drug.

6    As for the "brief summary" that lists indication and usage, contraindications, warnings, precautions and adverse reactions, nearly a third of those surveyed said they had read almost all of it and a quarter said they looked at some of it.

7    "This is quite surprising," remarked Brett Kay, the league's program associate for health policy. "People tell you things that they think you want to know. The fact is you can barely see and understand the brief summary on most ads because the print is so small and the information is so technical. It's written for doctors, not for consumers."

8    Nancy Ostrove, chief of marketing practices and communications for the Food and Drug Administration, said an increasing number of drug advertisers are now using more consumer-friendly language in the brief summary.

9    In Mr. Kay's view, the brief summary should be less detailed and convey useful information in language a lay person can understand, and the print has to be large enough to be legible without a magnifying glass. He added that a drug advertisement should not imply uses beyond what the drug is approved for, and should provide sufficient information on the drug's effectiveness, dosages, safety and potential risks.

## BENEFITS AND RISKS

10    Those who defend direct drug advertising say it can improve health care by alerting patients to medical problems that warrant medical attention, and by alerting people to the availability of new or existing drugs for a problem they thought was untreatable. Based on the results of a national telephone survey of 1,200 adults, *Prevention* magazine concluded that direct-to-consumer drug advertising can be "an extremely effective means of promoting both the public health and prescription medicines."

11    Indeed, sales of advertised drugs have risen significantly, and many patients have said that in response to such advertisements, they sought medical care for symptoms they had not previously realized could be readily treated effectively.

12    For example, advertising of cholesterol-lowering drugs called statins may help save lives by bringing patients into treatment. At least four major studies have shown that statins can reduce cardiac deaths by 24 percent to 42 percent, but only about a third of the 13 million Americans with heart disease symptoms are now taking them, and an additional 16 million with no symptoms but with significantly elevated cholesterol levels are not being treated.

13    But some experts say that in a society already overmedicated, prescription drug advertisements can only compound the problem of patients' demanding prescriptions when other measures, like diet and exercise, should be tried first.

14    Another complaint involves the time it may take doctors to tell patients why an advertised drug is unsuitable for them. Patients may end up disappointed or even distrustful of their doctors. Yet, doctors are more likely to know of drug alternatives that may be safer, cheaper or more effective.

15    Some patients may become overly enthusiastic about a drug in response to a fanciful advertisement, like the one for an AIDS drug that depicts people equipped with sporting gear admiring the view from a mountaintop. Prescription drugs advertised in a 30-second television commercial can only hint at the true benefits and risks, referring patients to a Web site, a toll-free number, a print advertisement or their doctors or pharmacists for further information.

**CAVEAT EMPTOR**

16    To help assure that consumers get appropriate medical care, Dr. Gene Reeder of the University of South Carolina's College of Pharmacy offers this advice:

- Talk first to your pharmacist about a drug that interests you. The pharmacist is likely to be easier to reach than your doctor and know more about the drug and its possible interactions with other medicines.
- Do not insist on a particular drug, no matter how suitable it may sound.
- Make sure that whoever prescribes any drug knows your full medical history and is aware of the other drugs and over-the-counter supplements you take.
- Be sure you fully understand the nature of the drug and its possible side effects. Don't be swayed by glossy advertising. Remember, a drug is not a box of cereal or a candy bar; its potential risks and benefits are far greater.

*The New York Times,* December 15, 1998, p. F7

## Comprehension Questions

1. What is the topic of the passage?
2. What is the central message of the passage?
3. Determine what is at issue. What is your initial personal viewpoint?
4. Distinguish among opposing viewpoints, and provide the rationale for each.
5. Think carefully about the viewpoints. Express a personal viewpoint, and give the reasons why you favor it. Does it differ from your initial personal viewpoint? Why or why not?
6. Write a few paragraphs *in support of the viewpoint that you do* not *favor.*

## Thought and Discussion Questions

1. How would you determine if a pill in a magazine advertisement is really "the only one that helps your skin look better too"?
2. Under what circumstances, if any, would you insist that your doctor prescribe a drug that you read about in an advertisement? Why or why not?

3. What is the connection between advertising and the writer's statement that "a drug is not a box of cereal or a candy bar" (paragraph 16)?

4. Do you think the information presented is mostly fact, mostly opinion, or a combination of both? Why? Cite specific examples.

5. List any questions that came to mind while you were reading this selection, and be prepared to discuss possible answers to them.

# 4

## All Shook Up

JEANNIE RALSTON

1   Eileen Plazek has a drinking habit: Every morning without fail, she whips up a frothy concoction—a cup of water, two scoops of 40-30-30 Balance drink mix, and some ice cubes—in her blender. Plazek, a sales representative who lives in Sacramento, California, says that the protein in the drink gives her the energy to survive until noon. "I knew I needed protein," she says, reporting that her chiropractor prescribed the 40-30-30 ratio of carbohydrates, protein, and fat, respectively. "If I made a regular breakfast, I would have to cook, and that takes time. I'm not a morning person, so I like ready-made food. There's no greasy frying pan to clean up. I can't do without shakes now."

2   People used to be too busy to cook meals; now they're too busy to eat them. As a result, they're turning to the slew of nutrient-packed shakes that have flooded the market. There are weight-loss shakes, energy shakes, and bodybuilding shakes. They come in a can or in a powder form that requires a spin through the blender with water, milk, or juice. And there are now chains of stores that make shakes for their customers (at these places the drinks are usually called smoothies, perhaps to avoid association with those fattening shakes sold at Dairy Queen). As more people seek sustenance through a straw, sales have boomed. Last year grocery stores moved $226 million worth of shakes, a four-fold increase over 1993.

3   There are nutritional differences among the canned shakes. Bodybuilding shakes have a little more protein, weight-loss shakes are a tad lower in fat, and energy shakes have a few more carbohydrates. The counter-bought smoothies, which contain fresh fruit, yogurt, and supplements, are usually more substantial than the others. All are touted as self-contained nourishment that requires no thought and no time—Nutrition for Dummies, essentially. But though these concoctions provide a significant percentage of the recommended daily allowances for dozens of nutrients, experts aren't sold on the benefits of the adult population's regressing to infant formula.

4   The general consensus is that downing these liquid meals is better than resorting to a Coke and fries but worse than eating a salad. "Drinking a canned supplement is better than eating junk food or fat-saturated fast food," says George Blackburn, an associate professor at Harvard Medical School and director of the Center for the Study of Nutrition and Medicine at Boston's Beth Israel Deaconess Medical Center. "But in the long run, a can a day won't keep the doctor away."

5    The chief criticism of these shakes is that people miss out on a complex collection of nutrients in real food that liquids can't duplicate. Mainly, they lack adequate fiber and phytochemicals such as isoflavones, carotenoids, and other plant-derived compounds that maintain health and prevent disease. "These drinks don't contain everything you need to stay healthy," says Bonnie Liebman, director of nutrition for the Center for Science in the Public Interest in Washington, D.C. "We don't know exactly what it is in fruits and vegetables that leads to lower rates of heart disease and cancer, but whatever it is, it's probably not in a can." Even smoothies, which provide some fiber and phytochemicals, don't make the grade. "Smoothies are fine as a snack or as part of a meal but not as a complete meal," says Larry Lindner, executive editor of the *Tufts University Health & Nutrition Letter.*

6    No argument there, says Pete Paradossi, a spokesman for Boost. "We don't think people should drink every meal. We think people should eat more fruits and vegetables. We're not telling people to give up their apples and bagels, but we recognize that there's a big difference between what's ideal as far as healthy eating and what humans actually do."

## Into the Drink

| Shake | Cal. per serving | Protein grams | Fat grams | Calcium %DV* | Iron %DV* | Vitamin C %DV* |
|---|---|---|---|---|---|---|
| Boost | 240 | 10 | 4 | 30 | 20 | 100 |
| Sustacal High Protein | 240 | 15 | 6 | 20 | 20 | 20 |
| ReSource | 180 | 9 | 0 | 15 | 15 | 60 |
| Ensure | 250 | 9 | 6 | 30 | 25 | 50 |
| Nestlé Sweet Success | 200 | 10 | 2.5 | 35 | 25 | 25 |
| Ultra Slim-Fast | 220 | 10 | 3 | 40 | 15 | 35 |
| 40-30-30 Balance** | 180 | 14 | 6 | 25 | 30 | 30 |
| Met-Rx** | 250 | 37 | 2 | 100 | 45 | 60 |
| Designer Protein** | 85 | 18.5 | 1 | 9.5 | 1 | 0 |
| Jamba Powerboost | 347 | 9.4 | 1.7 | 112 | 128 | 879 |

*Percentage of daily values, according to recommended dietary allowance
**Mixed with water

7    The current crop of canned and powdered shakes grew out of the success of a drink called Ensure, which was developed in the early '70s for the older set by Ross Products Division of Abbott Laboratories, a manufacturer of infant formula. Its major competitor is Sustacal, produced by fellow baby-food maker Mead Johnson. Products such as Designer Protein and Met-Rx are distributed through health-food shops and drugstores. The smoothie craze went nationwide with a company called Jamba Juice, which in seven years has grown to 80 outlets.

8    Nutritionists complain that some of the ingredients in smoothies and other shakes may not be as effective as their manufacturers claim. For example, some producers imply that the protein in their shakes is superior to the protein found anywhere else. Some of these drinks are made from whey peptide protein. It's an adequate protein but no better than what's in a piece of meat or an egg. While the high protein levels in these shakes help mitigate swings in insulin levels and subsequent

hunger pangs, scientists say that extra protein does not build muscle more efficiently, as some producers suggest. "What builds bodies is training, not food," says Lindner. "Extra protein does not add bulk. If it did, we'd all look like Arnold Schwarzenegger." New Image Power Shakes and something called the Venice Burner at Robeks chain of juice bars contain chromium picolinate, which supposedly burns fat. It's true that chromium picolinate is key in the transfer of sugar from blood to muscles, which allows the sugar to fuel the muscles' activities. However, Lindner warns, "Interpreting that to mean that taking chromium can build muscle and decrease fat is taking a giant leap of faith. It's not proven."

9      In addition to being attractive to people who lack time, shakes also appeal to dieters who lack willpower. Someone who has trouble curbing portions may prefer to reduce temptation by avoiding food when possible. It is a universally acknowledged truth in the industry that dieters who rely on these shakes usually regain the weight lost once they resume normal eating, but the maker of Slim-Fast insists that its product can work long-term. Not surprisingly, the company touts an ongoing study indicating that by staying on Slim-Fast, 73 percent of men and 62 percent of women lost weight—and kept off more than half of it—for some three years. Smoothies, however, can be a dieter's enemy; even if they are low-fat or fat-free, honey or sweeteners are often added (a typical Jamba Juice drink has 320 to 500 calories).

10      At least the smoothies taste good—which is more than can be said about canned shakes. Not many people drink the canned varieties because they find them delicious. Elizabeth Stewart, a New York fashion stylist, downs Ensure for breakfast every morning because she has trouble keeping weight on. "I get full so fast—one cookie will do it," says Stewart, who is five feet seven and weighs 118 pounds. She packs cans of Ensure when she travels to Paris to cover the fashion shows. It's almost sacrilegious to be drinking milk in the home of croissants and foie gras, but Stewart says she's too busy to eat. "It's just laziness," she says. "I wouldn't say that they are yummy. I'd definitely rather have a real milk shake, but real milk shakes are more of a project."

11      There are certainly more appealing and satisfying ways to spend 250 calories. When Anne Dubner, a Houston dietitian, broke her jaw and had to drink liquid food for three weeks, she says she began craving real food, a phenomenon that could explain why people often gain back weight quickly after a liquid diet. "I missed chewing," she says. "I craved something crunchy. I knew I couldn't have it, which is why I wanted it."

12      When people turn to liquid lunches, they deprive themselves of the pleasures of food, with all its varied textures and smells, say nutritionists. "Why do Americans have to spurn healthy meals for something that doesn't taste very good and costs a lot?" laments Lindner. "Why do people feel food has to be punishing to be good for them?" Good question.

*Allure*, June 1998, pp. 100, 102, 109

## Comprehension Questions

1. What is the topic of the passage?
2. What is the central message of the passage?

3. Determine what is at issue. What is your initial personal viewpoint?

4. Distinguish among opposing viewpoints, and provide the rationale for each.

5. Think carefully about the viewpoints. Express a personal viewpoint, and give the reasons why you favor it. Does it differ from your initial personal viewpoint? Why or why not?

6. Write a few paragraphs *in support of the viewpoint that you do* not *favor.*

## Thought and Discussion Questions

1. In your view, what role, if any, does advertising play in the popularity of nutritional shakes? Why?

2. What does the popularity of nutritional shakes say about current attitudes and lifestyles?

3. If you were interested in losing weight, bodybuilding, or increasing your energy, which shakes from the list provided would you choose to drink for each of those purposes? Why?

4. Nutritionally speaking, would it be better for a person to have spaghetti and meatballs or a nutritional shake? Why?

5. List any questions that came to mind while you were reading this selection, and be prepared to discuss possible answers to them.

## 5

## African Ritual Pain: Genital Cutting

CELIA W. DUGGER

1   MAN, Ivory Coast—Marthe Bleu is 12 years old, a shy, pretty girl with a heart-shaped face, dressed in flip-flops and a lacy, white pinafore trimmed in pink satin. But already her body is taking on the soft, rounded shape of womanhood. And these days she wants more than anything to do what she believes stands between her and being grown up. She wants to have her genitals cut off.

2   In the lament of pubescent girls everywhere, she says that all her friends are getting ahead of her. Their parents have sent them into the woods where village women "cut what is down there," she said, gesturing to her lap.

3   After the rite, the girls are showered with gifts of money, jewelry and cloth. Their families honor them with celebrations where hundreds of relatives and friends feast on goat, cow and chicken.

4   "It is the custom, and I want to respect it," she said.

5   The tradition of female genital cutting is woven into the everyday life of the Yacouba people here, just as it is for hundreds of ethnic groups in a wide band of 28 countries across Africa. In Man, it is part of a girl's dreams of womanhood, a father's desire to show off with a big party and a family's way of proving its conformity to social convention.

6    The rising chorus of international condemnation of this age-old practice, voiced in recent years from the podiums of United Nations assemblies in Vienna, Cairo and Beijing, echoes only faintly in places like Man, a tourist town deep in the interior, surrounded by the craggy, cloud-shrouded Toura mountains.

7    On the coast, in the cosmopolitan hubbub of Abidjan, and in other parts of Africa, the debate about female genital cutting is slowly moving into the public arena. Only in the last few years have African nations even begun measuring the prevalence of genital cutting as part of national health surveys or in other research.

8    In the Ivory Coast and the Central African Republic, two out of five women have been cut. In Togo, it is one in eight. In the Sudan—the only country that already had reliable national estimates—it is 9 out of 10. In Mali, it is 93 percent.

9    "It looks like women in most countries are nearly as likely to undergo these procedures as their mothers and grandmothers," said Dara Carr, a researcher at Macro International Inc., the Maryland-based company that is assisting the countries in conducting the health surveys. "But there are some seeds of change."

10   In the Sudan, the prevalence of the practice has dropped from 96 percent to 89 percent over the course of a decade. And there has been a shift toward a less severe form of genital cutting. In Togo, a survey found that half of the mothers who had been cut wanted to spare their daughters. And while three-quarters of the women in Mali favor continuing the practice, a majority in the Central African Republic want to end it.

11   But what women want and what they have the power to accomplish are very different things. In most of the countries where tens of millions of girls and women have been cut, organizations have sprung up to combat the practice.

12   Like mosquitoes attacking an elephant, the small, ill-financed groups are struggling within societies where men rule women's lives, and old people, including old women, rule the young.

13   There are, for example, Ivoirian laws against physical violence that could be used to stop the cutting, said Idrissa Fofana, a high-ranking official in the Justice Ministry.

14   But the Government has no interest in imposing them on unwilling families, antagonizing village chiefs and family elders who are pillars of society and guardians of tradition.

15   "If there was a complaint from parents that their child had been excised against their wishes, the Justice Ministry could pursue the case," Mr. Fofana said. "But if there is no complaint, we cannot disturb the peace of the family and the village."

16   Like most Yacouba girls in Man, Marthe Bleu is an eager initiate. But even if she resisted, her father, Jean-Baptiste Bleu, a trim, genial, neatly dressed waiter at a local hotel, would insist on her cutting.

17   "If your daughter has not been excised, the father is not allowed to speak at village meetings," he said. "No man in the village will marry her. It is an obligation. We have done it, we do it and we will continue to do it."

18   "She has no choice. I decide. Her viewpoint is not important."

19   The Bleus have not yet chosen who will cut Marthe, but not far from their home, through a maze of dirt pathways, lives Madeleine Douan, 47, one of the local excisers.

20   The tall, sinewy woman refused to show the ceremonial knife she uses, but brought out other accouterment of her calling: a long strand of metal bells and

cloth sacks filled with bottle caps. While she cuts a group of 10 to 15 girls on the ground of the forest, other women shake the noisemakers, covering the cries of pain. Mrs. Douan herself sings traditional songs.

21    She introduced several of the girls she had recently cut. Natalie Sahi, 15, sat on the side of her thigh outside Mrs. Douan's windowless mud hut to avoid putting direct pressure on the wound. "I wanted it to happen," she said. "It's natural."

22    Patricia Vehgolou, 13, her hair neatly braided in corn rows, buried her face in her hands and would only giggle when asked if the cutting hurt. Mrs. Douan explained that the girls must swear before leaving the forest that they will not share the secrets of the rite with the uninitiated.

23    The purpose of the cutting, Mrs. Douan said, is to help insure a woman's fidelity to her husband and her family. "It's a tradition from antiquity," she said. A woman's role in life is to care for her children, keep house and cook. If she has not been cut, Mrs. Douan said, a woman might think instead about her own sexual pleasure.

## THE ORIGINS: PRIDE, TRADITION AND IGNORED RISKS

24    It is not known when, where or why the practice of female genital cutting originated. Scholars believe that it started in Egypt or the Horn of Africa more than 2,000 years ago, before the advent of Christianity or Islam. It then spread west across the continent, all the way to the Atlantic Ocean, with the migration of dominant tribes and civilizations.

25    The practice knows no class or religious boundaries. Most prevalent among Muslims, it is also performed by Christians and followers of traditional African religions. The practice is more widespread among the illiterate, but it is also common among the educated.

26    The nature of the cutting, the reasons for it and the age at which it is done vary greatly by region and ethnic group.

27    The practice involves amputating some or all of the external genitalia—the clitoris, the small genital lips and the large ones—diminishing a woman's ability to experience sexual pleasure. It can also cause serious health problems, including hemorrhaging and infection.

28    Typically, the cutting is done by traditional village women without anything to dull the pain. But sometimes, when midwives or nurses are brought in to do the job, they apply a local anesthetic.

29    Many believe that cutting helps insure a girl's virginity before marriage and fidelity afterward by reducing sex to a marital obligation. Often, people follow the custom simply because it has always been done.

30    "Children are born and the parents do it," said Awa Kone, a Malian washerwoman in Abidjan, who plans to take her baby daughter, Kadia, to an exciser in the near future.

31    In the Horn of Africa—Djibouti, Somalia, the Sudan and parts of Ethiopia—the most severe and harmful form of cutting, infibulation, is practiced.

32    In this procedure, the clitoris and some or all of the small genital lips are cut away. Then an incision is made in the large lips so the raw surfaces can be stitched together, covering the urethra and most of the vagina. Only a small opening, as tiny as a matchstick or as large as a small fingertip, is left to pass urine and menstrual

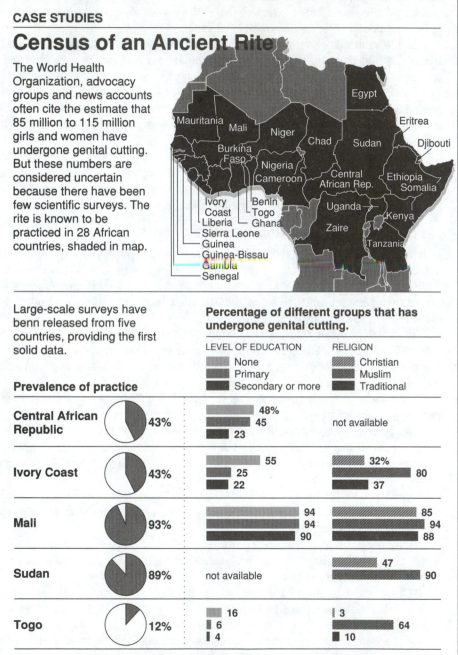

CASE STUDIES

# Census of an Ancient Rite

The World Health Organization, advocacy groups and news accounts often cite the estimate that 85 million to 115 million girls and women have undergone genital cutting. But these numbers are considered uncertain because there have been few scientific surveys. The rite is known to be practiced in 28 African countries, shaded in map.

Large-scale surveys have benn released from five countries, providing the first solid data.

**Prevalence of practice**

**Percentage of different groups that has undergone genital cutting.**

| LEVEL OF EDUCATION | RELIGION |
|---|---|
| None | Christian |
| Primary | Muslim |
| Secondary or more | Traditional |

**Central African Republic** — 43%
- None: 48%
- Primary: 45
- Secondary or more: 23
- not available

**Ivory Coast** — 43%
- None: 55
- Primary: 25
- Secondary or more: 22
- Christian: 32%
- Muslim: 80
- Traditional: 37

**Mali** — 93%
- None: 94
- Primary: 94
- Secondary or more: 90
- Christian: 85
- Muslim: 94
- Traditional: 88

**Sudan** — 89%
- not available
- Christian: 47
- Muslim: 90

**Togo** — 12%
- None: 16
- Primary: 6
- Secondary or more: 4
- Christian: 3
- Muslim: 64
- Traditional: 10

*Sources: Demographic and Health Surveys, Marco Intl. Inc., Calverton, Md. Years of reports: Sudan, 1989-90; Ivory Coast, 1994; Central African Republic, 1994-95; Mali, preliminary report, 1995-96. Togo source: Demographic Research Unit, University of Benin, Lomé, Togo, June 1996.*

The New York Times

blood, said Nahid Toubia, a Sudanese surgeon who is an associate professor at Columbia University.

33      Infibulation comes with its own set of rationales. Some men say the artificial tightness heightens their sexual enjoyment. The smoothness of the scar is found esthetically beautiful. And the stitching itself forms a chastity belt of flesh.

34      There is a common thread to all forms of cutting. Economic realities underlie the practice. Women typically have no way to survive without a husband. Parents insist on the rite so their daughters are marriageable.

35      "People do know the health risks," said Ellen Gruenbaum, a medical anthropologist at California State University, San Bernardino. "They have seen people get sick. On rare occasions, a girl might die. But you will not change people's minds by preaching to them or telling them they're primitive. They undertake the risks for reasons important to them."

36      After the cutting, more pain lies ahead. Women who have endured the more extreme forms of the practice have particularly agonizing and complicated deliveries. The scarring narrows the vaginal opening and makes the flesh inelastic, doctors and midwives say. The pressure of a baby's emerging head often causes grave tearing of the vagina.

37      Women who bear a child in their villages without a doctor to widen the vagina surgically sometimes arrive torn and bleeding at the Maternal Health Center in Man. On occasion, the tearing goes up into the urethra and bladder, down into the anus, as well as side to side. The women must then be sent to a hospital in Abidjan for surgery.

38      Clautilde Yenon, a midwife at the health center, tried to think of a way to convey the excruciating damage. Finally, she had an idea. She picked up a sheet of paper and ripped it into jagged pieces.

*The New York Times,* October 5, 1996, pp. 1, 6

## Comprehension Questions

1. What is the topic of the passage?
2. What is the central message of the passage?
3. Determine what is at issue. What is your initial personal viewpoint?
4. Distinguish among opposing viewpoints, and provide the rationale for each.
5. Think carefully about the viewpoints. Express a personal viewpoint, and give the reasons why you favor it. Does it differ from your initial personal viewpoint? Why or why not?
6. Write a few paragraphs *in support of the viewpoint that you do* not *favor.*

## Thought and Discussion Questions

1. Genital cutting is sometimes referred to as the "rite of anguish." How do you interpret that phrase?

2. What effect, if any, does level of education and religion have on the practice?

3. In your view, are the statistics presented in the passage reliable? Why or why not?

4. Will genital cutting be as prevalent in Africa 50 years from now? Why or why not?

5. List any questions that came to mind while you were reading this selection, and be prepared to discuss possible answers to them.

## LOOKING BACK

With two of your classmates, come up with a list of the most important points you learned from this chapter, and determine how they can be put to use in other classes. Be prepared to discuss both the list and the uses.

## THINK AGAIN!

Evaluate your survival skills by taking the following "self-discovery test." Be prepared to discuss your responses in class.

## Rate Your Survival Skills

LAURA BILLINGS

Most of us have mastered everyday safety basics: Always wear a seat belt. Don't let strangers into your home. Look both ways before you cross the street. But what if you were faced with a more immediate threat to your health and your life? Say a thug demands your car keys. Or a riptide carries you out to sea. Or the earth suddenly shakes beneath you. Would you know what to do—and what not to do? We've picked several high-pressure, panic-inducing situations and asked how you'd react in each case. See how many times you select the best strategy, or the worst.

1. The rain is coming down in sheets on the curvy country road ahead. You lose control of your car and steer yourself right off the pavement and into a river. How do you get out alive?
   a. Get out of the car any way you can.
   b. Stay in the car until help arrives—river currents are too dangerous for the average swimmer.
   c. Wait until the car sinks to the bottom and water pressure equalizes before you open the door to swim out.

2. On a hike, you stumble upon a mother bear and her cubs. She doesn't seem happy. What now?
   a. Run and climb up the nearest tree.

   b. Stand your ground and don't move.

   c. Charge at the bear and wave your arms to scare her and the cubs away.

3. It's been a record snowfall, and you're trapped on the side of the road. The radio says that even the tow trucks are spinning their wheels in the snow and ice, so you:
   a. hike off to find a service station.
   b. put the car in neutral and push until your tires find some traction.
   c. huddle up for warmth inside the car, turn on your dome light and check occasionally to make sure that your tailpipe isn't clogged.

4. You and your surfboard are not alone—a shark is in the neighborhood. Any way to reduce the chance that you'll end up as its afternoon snack?
   a. Leave the board and swim to shore.
   b. Pull your arms and legs on top of the board and remain still.
   c. Float face up in the water, with your limbs at your side—a shark won't attack if you look dead.

5. You hiked solo up a mountainside and are feeling very Maria Von Trapp. But now it's getting dark, and you don't remember how to get back down. You:
   a. find your way out by following flowing water downhill.
   b. build a fire and wait for rescue.
   c. spend the night retracing your tracks—you might have a hard time finding them the next day.

6. On your way out of a fast-food drive-through, a young thug asks you for your money and your car. He and his gun seem very insistent, so you:
   a. hand over your car keys and your wallet and step away from the car.
   b. lock the doors, floor the accelerator and peel out of there.
   c. scream "Help!" to attract the attention of passersby.

7. You wake up in the middle of the night to the sound of a fire alarm and the smell of smoke. Best plan:
   a. Hang a sheet from your window and jump out if the fire comes too close.
   b. Gather up important belongings and race for the door as fast as you can.
   c. Crawl to the door, check the conditions on the other side and proceed if it's safe. If not, retreat and wait for rescue.

8. You're in a Los Angeles parking lot when the Big One finally hits. You:
   a. run to your car and hop in.
   b. stop where you are, crouch into a squat and cover your head.
   c. rush to the doorway of a building, where it's structurally sound; you don't want to be in a wide-open space.

9. It's a Saturday night and you're all by yourself, tossing grapes in the air and catching them in your mouth when, suddenly, one goes down the wrong way. It's getting hard to breathe. How do you save yourself?
   a. Try sticking your fingers in your throat to pull out the offending fruit.
   b. Give yourself the Heimlich maneuver with your fists wrapped together in a ball.
   c. Throw yourself over the top of a high-backed chair with enough force to expel the grape.

10. You and three coworkers are in the office elevator when it gets stuck between floors. The lights dim, the alarm goes off and everyone is starting to panic. How to deal?

   a. Help each other climb out of the ceiling vent and up the cable to the nearest elevator landing.

   b. Take shallow breaths until help arrives—air flow may be limited.

   c. Hit the emergency button, use the elevator phone to call building security or 911, and wait for rescue.

11. You wake at night and hear a prowler. The safest strategy:

   a. Get out of the house and call 911 from a pay phone or neighbor's place.

   b. Grab your baseball bat and stand behind the door, ready to surprise him when he enters.

   c. Call the police, barricade your bedroom door and hide.

12. A rattlesnake clamped its fangs into your leg, then slithered away. Now what?

   a. Use a sharp knife or rock to cut into the site of the bite and suck the venom out, making sure not to swallow it.

   b. Wrap a tourniquet above the bite.

   c. Immobilize the leg and get medical attention immediately.

13. You planned on a dip, but a riptide has carried you far from shore. How do you stay afloat?

   a. Turn straight toward the beach and paddle as hard as you can.

   b. Swim parallel to shore, or at a 45-degree angle to it, until the wave action starts carrying you back to land.

   c. Wave while you're riding the rip out to the calmer waters behind the waves and hope a lifeguard sees you.

*Mademoiselle,* March 1998, pp. 126–127

## MASTERY TEST 8

A.  Answer the question.

1.  Advertisements require critical reading and critical thinking because they
    a.  affect our purchasing decisions
    b.  affect our political decisions
    c.  affect our philosophical decisions
    d.  influence our thinking
    e.  all of the above

B.  Read and think critically about each advertisement. Then answer the questions that follow it.

2.  How does it try to catch the interest of readers?

   _____

   _____

   _____

3.  To whom is it designed to appeal?

   _____

   _____

4.  What is it trying to persuade readers to buy, do, or think?

   _____

   _____

5.  What benefit to readers is it stressing?

    _____

    _____

6.  How convincing is it?

    _____

    _____

    _____

    _____

7.  How does it try to catch the interest of readers?

    _____

    _____

    _____

8.  To whom is it designed to appeal?

    _____

    _____

9.  What is it trying to persuade readers to buy, do, or think?

    _____

10.  What benefit to readers is it stressing?

_____

_____

11.  How convincing is it?

_____

_____

_____

12.  How does it try to catch the interest of readers?

_____

_____

_____

13. To whom is it designed to appeal?

    _____

    _____

14. What is it trying to persuade readers to buy, do, or think?

    _____

    _____

15. What benefit to readers is it stressing?

    _____

    _____

16. How convincing is it?

    _____

    _____

    _____

17. How does it try to catch the interest of readers?

    _____

    _____

    _____

18. To whom is it designed to appeal?

    _____

    _____

19. What is it trying to persuade readers to buy, do, or think?

_____

_____

20. What benefit to readers is it stressing?

_____

_____

21. How convincing is it?

_____

_____

_____

_____

**A Myth Unfit to Print**

**Alar was Not a "Scare"— It was a Threat to Kids**

The newspaper of record is ignoring the record.

The *Times'* Jane Brody has swallowed a myth manufactured by the chemical industry—that Alar in apples was no threat to kids.

Her recent column listed the Alar episode of almost 10 years ago as an "unfounded health scare."

But she omitted the most important fact—the government banned Alar from food in 1991, two years after the furor over the chemical. EPA declared "that long-term exposure to Alar poses unacceptable risks to public health" after further tests showed Alar's breakdown products caused cancer. The Bush EPA's scientific review board found it to be a "probable human carcinogen." Food scare?

Ms. Brody erroneously reported that "subsequent tests by the National Cancer Institute and the Environmental Protection Agency failed to show that Alar caused cancer." No wonder. She relied solely on a report from the American Council on Science and Health, which the *Times* previously described as a group "that often supports industry positions on regulating chemicals," and *Consumer Reports* has branded a "public interest pretender." Among the Council's chemical industry funders is Uniroyal, Alar's manufacturer.

Ms. Brody made no effort to balance her opinion. Dr. David Rall, former Director of the National Institute of Environmental Health Sciences, calls the notion that Alar was an unfounded scare "a triumph of publicity over science." Dr. Philip Landrigan, who directed the National Academy of Science study on pesticides and children, praised the Natural Resources Defense Council as "absolutely on the right track when they excoriated the regulatory agencies for having allowed a toxic material such as alar to stay on the market for 25 years . . ."

A national magazine recently reported that science coverage at *The New York Times* is at times biased in favor of industry. The pattern is disturbing—erroneous reports that dioxin is no health threat, there's no evidence sperm counts are falling, or that alar was a "scare" (a charge first made in a front page *Times* story). We call upon this great newspaper to correct the record. Industry has spent millions creating these myths—we're all in trouble if *The New York Times* buys these rotten apples.

**NATIONAL ENVIRONMENTAL TRUST**

1200 18th Street N.W.
5th Floor
Washington, D.C. 20036

www.envirotrust.com

22. How does it try to catch the interest of readers?

_____

_____

_____

23. To whom is it designed to appeal?

    _____

    _____

24. What is it trying to persuade readers to buy, do, or think?

    _____

    _____

25. What benefit to readers is it stressing?

    _____

    _____

26. How convincing is it?

    _____

    _____

    _____

# For the person who has everything
## (including lead and chlorine).

*Some of the best water on Earth. That's the gift you give
with the Brita® Water Filtration Pitcher. Tap water tastes wonderful.
And you don't have to worry about lead, chlorine or sediment.
So the person who has everything will get one really useful thing.*

**▦BRITA®**

Bed, Bath, and Beyond • The Bon Marche • Richs-Lazarus-Goldsmiths • Elder-Beerman • Carson Pirie Scott • Linens 'n Things
Fortunoff • Burdines • Sears • Sterns • Macy's • Dillard's • Lechters • Bon Ton • Kaufmann's • Crowley's • Mervyn's • Younker's

Brita removes 99% of lead. Substances removed may not be in all water.
©1998 The Brita Products Company.

27.    How does it try to catch the interest of readers?

_____

_____

_____

28. To whom is it designed to appeal?

_____

_____

29. What is it trying to persuade readers to buy, do, or think?

_____

_____

30. What benefit to readers is it stressing?

_____

_____

31. How convincing is it?

_____

_____

_____

# "I wish I could take a special trip. . ."

When a child with a life-threatening illness has a wish,
we do everything in our power to make it come true.
Since 1983, Make-A-Wish Foundation of Metro New York has
fulfilled thousands of wishes for special children just like Jason.

With your support, we will grant wishes
as long as there are children who need a special memory to cherish.

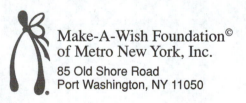

Make-A-Wish Foundation©
of Metro New York, Inc.

85 Old Shore Road
Port Washington, NY 11050

For more information regarding qualifying children, making a contribution
or volunteer opportunities, please call (212) 505-WISH.

32. How does it try to catch the interest of readers?

_____

_____

_____

33. To whom is it designed to appeal?

_____

_____

34. What is it trying to persuade readers to buy, do, or think?

_____

_____

35. What benefit to readers is it stressing?

_____

_____

36. How convincing is it?

_____

_____

_____

## "KILLER BEES ARE COMING! DON'T RISK LEAVING THE HOUSE."

– *Darryl Peck,*
*CEO of Outpost.com, the website designed for people who want computer products, but don't want to be stung by killer bees.*

Killer bees recently made headlines when a Texas man was stung over 1,000 times. I thought about this one day and realized that I wouldn't want to be stung over 1,000 times. That's why I created Outpost.com. Now when our customers order hardware, software or peripherals by midnight, they'll be delivered the next morning. So they never have to step outside their homes–placing them in grave danger!

In 1957, 26 colonies of African killer bees escaped

*Africa is a great place to visit, as long as you're not being stung to death by bees.*

from a research apiary near Brazil. In 1990, they made their way to Texas. Recently, there have been reports of swarms in Los Angeles. (I used to love visiting Los Angeles.) When the colony is on the move, it seeks a new nest site. A small hole leading to a hollow space is what the swarm looks for. An opening 1/8 inch in diameter is large enough to provide an entrance. That's why we tell our manufacturers not to make products with openings bigger than 1/8 of an inch. Trust me, you don't want a computer delivered with a bunch of angry killer bees inside it. No, sir.

> "Some of you might be thinking: 'But I have to leave the house at some point.' Let me tell you something: That's exactly what the bees want you to think."
> – Darryl Peck

*"My doctor says if I buy computer products on the internet from the safety of my own home, there is virtually no chance of being stung repeatedly by a swarm of killer bees."*

So what can we do about this terrifying development? The killer bee looks almost exactly like its docile American cousin. It's tough to tell them apart. But if you notice a large swarm of bees stinging you over and over and over, that's a sign it could be killer bees.

There are some precautions you can take. To avoid attracting killer bees, wear light, not dark, clothing. Also, if you see a colony of angry bees, do not pick up the hive and start violently shaking it. But, in my opinion, the best thing to do is just stay home. Why risk it?

At Outpost.com we've got over 140,000 computer products to help keep you busy. I just wish we could've helped that man in Texas–the one who was stung over 1,000 times. I wouldn't want to be stung over 1,000 times.

*Ask Darryl*

Q: Darryl, what if when my order is delivered some killer bees sneak in when I open the door?

A: Before you open the door, ask the delivery man if he sees any bees. If he says, "Yes," ask him if they look like killer bees.

**The computer products you want. Without the bee stings.** **Outpost.com**™

AOL keyword: Outpost
©1998 Cyberian Outpost, Inc.

37. How does it try to catch the interest of readers?

_____

_____

_____

38. To whom is it designed to appeal?

_____

_____

39. What is it trying to persuade readers to buy, do, or think?

_____

_____

40. What benefit to readers is it stressing?

_____

_____

41. How convincing is it?

_____

_____

_____

42. In the space provided below, create a convincing advertisement that catches the interest of readers, appeals to a certain audience and, by stressing the benefits to readers, tries to persuade them to buy, do, or think something.

## PLAYING HOLMES AND WATSON

With your partner, answer the questions that follow. *After you have discussed your answers and conclusions with the rest of the class*, your instructor will distribute the last part of the short story so that you can determine if you are ready to compete with the "real" Sherlock Holmes and Dr. Watson:

1. Why did Holmes look through the window into the tutor's room?
2. Why did Holmes draw in his notebook, break his pencil, and borrow a pencil and knife from two of the students?
3. Why did Holmes want to know Miles McLaren's exact height?
4. *After thinking critically about this case, who do you believe is the culprit? Why did you and your partner come to that conclusion?*
5. Once you and your partner have read the last part of the short story and know the identity of the guilty party, write a different ending to the mystery using the same clues.

## HOLMES AND WATSON TO THE RESCUE ONE LAST TIME

Read and think very carefully about the following passage. Now that the two of you are successful critical thinkers and accomplished detectives, what would you advise the poor merchant's daughter to do? Be prepared to discuss your solution to her predicament with your classmates.

Many years ago when a person who owed money could be thrown into jail, a merchant in London had the misfortune to owe a huge sum to a money-lender. The money-lender, who was old and ugly, fancied the merchant's beautiful teenage daughter. He proposed a bargain. He said he would cancel the merchant's debt if he could have the girl instead.

Both the merchant and his daughter were horrified at the proposal. So the cunning money-lender proposed that they let Providence decide the matter. He told them that he would put a black pebble and a white pebble into an empty money-bag and then the girl would have to pick out one of the pebbles. If she chose the black pebble she would become his wife and her father's debt would be cancelled. If she chose the white pebble she would stay with her father and the debt would still be cancelled. But if she refused to pick out a pebble her father would be thrown into jail and she would starve.

Reluctantly the merchant agreed. They were standing on a pebble-strewn path in the merchant's garden as they talked and the money-lender stooped down to pick up the two pebbles. As he picked up the pebbles the girl, sharp-eyed with fright, noticed that he picked up two black pebbles and put them into the money-bag. He then asked the girl to pick out the pebble that was to decide her fate and that of her father.

Edward de Bono, *Newthink*, p. 11

For additional readings, exercises, and Internet activities, visit our Web site at:

**http://longman.awl.com/englishpages**

If you need a user name and password, see your instructor.

**Take a Road Trip to** Wall Street! Be sure to visit the Graphics and Visual Aids module in your Reading Road Trip CD-ROM for multimedia tutorials, exercises, and tests.

# Glossary

**aids to understanding** elements that make a book easier to use

**antonyms** words that have opposite meanings

**appendix** section of a book containing supplementary information

**asking questions and finding answers** engaging in *critical thinking*

**bias** lack of impartiality or objectivity

**bibliography** list of works consulted while researching a book or an article

**caption** explanation of a *graphic aid*

**cause and effect** *pattern of organization* based on explaining why something happened

**central message** the *main idea* of a piece of writing longer than one paragraph

**clear purpose** the specific objective of *critical thinking*, such as an explanation, solution, or decision

**comparison and contrast** *pattern of organization* for presenting *details* by pointing out similarities and differences

**contemporary issues** current topics of interest and debate

**context** the surrounding words in a sentence that make the specific meaning of a word clear

**credits** list of sources of material appearing in a book but not original to it

**critical reading** a very high-level of written material requiring interpretation and evaluation skills that enable the reader to separate important information, use inference to come to logical conclusions, distinguish between facts and opinions, and determine a writer's purpose and tone

**critical thinking** a very careful and thoughtful way of dealing with events, issues, problems, decisions, or situations.

**details** bits of information that flesh out the *main idea* of a paragraph

**fact** a piece of knowledge that can be confirmed as accurate in a reliable and unbiased manner

**flexible thinking** considering various possibilities before coming to a conclusion

**glossary** list of relevant terms and their definitions, arranged alphabetically

**graphic aids** illustrative *aids to understanding* such as charts, graphs, maps, pictures, and tables

**index** list of cross-references, arranged alphabetically by topic

**inference** an "educated guess" based on knowledge, experience, and circumstantial evidence or clues

**informed opinion** the *opinion* of an expert who is well versed in the relevant *facts*

**irony** the use of words to mean their opposite for humorous or sarcastic effect

**learning aids** see *aids to understanding*

**logical conclusions** determinations based on rational consideration of all the *facts*

**main idea**   a sentence (stated or not) that summarizes the sense of an entire paragraph

**major details**   bits of information that explain the *main idea* of a paragraph

**minor details**   bits of information that make *major details* more specific

**mood**   see *tone*

**notes**   footnotes collected at the end of a chapter or a book

**opinion**   a personal judgment

**opposing viewpoints**   conflicting *opinions* regarding the same issue

**organization**   arranging items or tasks so as to increase efficiency or productivity

**overviewing**   *skimming* a book to find out what it is about and how it can be of use

**patterns of organization**   arrangements of *facts* to clarify *details* and *main ideas*

**preface**   introductory chapter in a book

**prejudice**   viewpoint adopted without consideration of all the *facts* or other possible viewpoints

**previewing**   *skimming* to familiarize oneself with the material

**problem**   any question or matter involving doubt, uncertainty, or difficulty

**purpose**   reason for writing

**random thinking**   thinking with no clear purpose in mind

**rationale**   specific reason or reasons supporting an *opinion*

**reference sources**   works recommended for further reading on a given subject

**research**   process of gathering information to increase knowledge of a topic

**simple listing of facts**   lists of *details* used as a *pattern of organization*

**skimming**   glancing over a text quickly

**solution**   means by which we rid ourselves of problems

**suggested readings**   see *reference sources*

**synonyms**   words that have the same meaning

**table of contents**   list of the parts, chapters, and subheadings of a book

**time and effort**   essential requirements of *critical thinking*

**time sequence**   *pattern of organization* in which events are recounted chronologically

**title**   formal name given to a book, article, chapter, *graphic aid*, or other book element

**title page**   page indicating title, author, publisher, and edition of a book

**tone**   a writer's attitude or feeling toward the *topic* being written about

**topic**   the subject of a paragraph

**topic sentence**   a sentence in a paragraph stating the *main idea* of that paragraph

**transition words**   words used to introduce *patterns of organization*

**unstated main idea**   a statement not appearing in a paragraph that summarizes the *main idea* of that paragraph

# CREDITS

**Pages 5, 17, 19, 25, 41-42** From F. Kurt Cylke, *The Environment*, copyright © 1993 by HarperCollins College Publishers. Reprinted by permission of the publisher.

**Pages 5, 6, 8, 13, 17, 22, 41, 80** R. Leroy Miller, *Economics Today*, Ninth Edition, copyright © 1997 by Addison Wesley Longman Inc.. Reprinted by permission of Addison Wesley Longman.

**Pages 5, 9, 10, 15, 21, 24, 27, 38, 43-44, 81-82, 258** From Carol Tavris & Carole Wade, *Psychology in Perspective*, Second Edition, copyright © 1997 by Addison-Wesley Educational Publishers, Inc. (Longman). Reprinted with permission of the publisher.

**Pages 6, 28-29** From Richard Sweeney, *Out of Place: Homelessness in America*, copyright © 1993 by HarperCollins College Publishers.

**Pages 8, 16, 92-93** From Janell L. Carroll and Paul Root Wolpe, *Sexuality and Gender in Society*, copyright © 1996 by HarperCollins College Publishers.

**Pages 8, 12, 14-15, 20-21, 39, 138, 277-278** From Neil A. Campbell, Lawrence G. Mitchell, and Jane Be. Reece, *Biology*, Second Edition, copyright © 1997 by Addison-Wesley Educational Publishers, Inc. (Longman). Reprinted with permission of the publisher.

**Pages 8, 9, 10, 24, 32** From George Zgourides, *Human Sexuality*, copyright © 1996 by HarperCollins College Publishers. Reprinted with permission of the publisher.

**Pages 9, 11, 12, 17, 20, 23, 26, 43** From Gary B. Nash and Julie Roy Jeffrey, *The American People*, Fourth Edition, copyright © 1998 by Addison-Wesley Educational Publishers, Inc. (Longman). Reprinted with permission of the publisher.

**Pages 9, 13, 16, 19-20** From James D. Wright and Joel A. Devine, *Drugs As a Social Problem*, copyright © 1994 by HarperCollins College Publishers.

**Pages 9, 12, 55-72, 81, 82-83, 90-92, 95-96, 149-150, 190** From Alex Thio, *Sociology: A Brief Introduction*, Third Edition, copyright © 1997 by Addison-Wesley Educational Publishers, Inc. (Longman). Reprinted with permission of the publisher.

**Pages 12-13, 15** From Kay Johnston Starks and Eleanor S. Morrison, *Growing Up Sexual*, Second Edition, copyright © 1996 by HarperCollins College Publishers.

**Pages 14, 138** Marvin L. Bittinger and David J. Ellenbogen, *Elementary Algebra: Concepts and Applications*, Fifth Edition, copyright © 1998 by Addison Wesley Longman Inc. Reprinted by permission of Addison Wesley Longman.

**Page 15** From B. Eugene Griessman, *Diversity*, Copyright © 1993 by HarperCollins College Publishers. Reprinted with permission of the publisher.

**Pages 16, 25, 29-30, 31-32, 44, 48, 77-78, 244, 329, 339-340** From Anthony F. Grasha, *Practical Applications of Psychology*, Fourth Edition, copyright © 1995 by HarperCollins College Publishers. Reprinted with permission of the publisher.

**Pages 17, 26, 39, 42, 45, 246, 270** From John A. Garraty, *A Short History of the American Nation*, Seventh Edition, copyright © 1997 by Addison-Wesley Educational Publishers, Inc. (Longman). Reprinted with permission of the publisher.

**Pages 25, 79-80, 83-84** From Robert Leo Smith and Thomas M.Smith, *Elements of Ecology*, Fourth Edition, copyright © 1998 by Addison-Wesley Educational Publishers, Inc. (Longman). Reprinted with permission of the publisher.

**Pages 32-33** "Are Car Phones Too Dangerous," from *Glamour* (September 1997), p. 232. Reprinted by permission.

**Pages 33-35** From "Close Your Eyes, Hold Your Nose, It's Dinner Time" by Eric Asimov. Copyright © 1997 by the New York Times Co. Reprinted by permission.

**Pages 38, 42-43** From Richard P. Applebaum and William J. Chambliss, *Sociology*, Second Edition, copyright © 1997 by Addison-Wesley Educational Publishers, Inc. (Longman), pp. 18-19. Reprinted with permission of the publisher.

# INDEX

Activities, 7–10, 14–18, 24–27, 31–35, 54, 74–75, 78–92, 110–120, 122–137, 145–159, 171–172, 178–210, 230, 232–243, 255–267, 279–296, 298–305, 329–354
Addresses, Web, 121–122
Advertisements, 256
    and critical thinking, 321, 327, 329
    evaluating, 322–329
Aids to understanding, 52–53, 73–74
Angry tone, 295
Answers
    about advertisements, 321–329
    for critical reading, 75–78
    for critical thinking, 114–115
Antonyms, and meaning, 6
Appendixes, 53
Articles, 28
Audiences, appealing to, 322–323, 325
Authors, professional affiliations of, 122

Benefits, stressed by advertisements, 325–326
Biases, 121–122, 254–255, 257
Bibliographies, 53, 68–69, 122
Body language, 293
Boldface, use of, 74, 76
Breaking down problems, 173–174, 177

Captions, 74
Cause/effect, 18, 22–23
Central messages, 28–31, 76, 78, 141–142
Chapter headings, 52–53, 73–74, 76–77
Chapter length, 73
Chapters, 28, 52
    critical reading of, 75–78
    parts of, 73–74
Checking back on problems, 176, 178
Choosing possible solutions, 175–178
Clear purpose, 112
Clues, and inferences, 226, 229–230
Colons, 5
Combinations
    of facts/opinions, 256

of patterns, 22
of purposes, 283
of tones, 293
Commas, 5
Commercials, 256. *See also* Advertisements
Comparison/contrast, 18, 21–22, 29
Conclusions
    inferences as, 226–227
    logical, 136–137, 227–230, 232
Contemporary issues
    defined, 139–140
    determining, 141–142
    distinguishing opposing viewpoints, 142–143
    expressing personal viewpoints, 143–145
    facts/opinions used for, 256–257
    inferences used for, 231–232
Contents, tables of, 52–53, 57–61
Context, 4–7, 76, 141
Contrast/comparison, 18, 21–22, 29
Convincing advertisements, 327–329
Copyright, 52, 56
Credits, 53, 70
Critical reading
    defined, 75–76
    and inferences, 225–226, 232
    of textbook chapters, 75–78
Critical thinking
    and advertisements, 321, 327, 329
    benefits of, 109
    characteristics of, 109–110
    clear purpose, 112
    and contemporary issues, 139–145
    defined, 108–109
    flexibility, 110
    and inferences, 230–231
    logical conclusions, 136–137
    organization, 114
    and problem solving, 172
    questions/answers, 114–115
    research, 120–122
    time/effort, 114

Dashes, 5
Decision making, 108–110, 110, 112–114, 120–121, 136, 175, 327
Definitions
    of problems, 173, 176–177
    of words, 4–7, 53, 66–67, 74, 76, 141
Details
    arrangements of, 18–23
    major/minor, 11–14, 19–23, 30–31, 78
Developmental skills, 4

"Educated guesses," 227
Effect/cause, 18, 22–23
Effort/time, 114
Entertainment, as purpose, 282–283
Essays, 28
Examples, 278
    details as, 11, 19, 22, 78
    and meaning, 7
Exercises, in textbooks, 74
Experience, and inferences, 226, 228–229
Experts, 254

Facts
    in combination with opinions, 256
    defined, 254–255
    distinguished from opinions, 252–254
    and purpose, 277, 280
    simple listing of, 18–20
    and tone, 294
    used for contemporary issues, 256–257
    used for problem solving, 254, 256–257
Flexibility, 110, 178

General sense of sentence, and meaning, 7
Glossaries, 53, 66–67
Goals, 52, 73, 173
Graphic aids, 74

Headings, 28, 30, 52–53, 73–74, 76–77. *See also* Titles
Highlighting, 76
"Holmes and Watson" activities, 100, 216, 372
Humorous tone, 294–295

Ideas. *See* Main ideas
Identifying problems, 173, 176–177
Indexes, 53, 71–72
Inferences
    and clues, 226, 229–230

defined, 226–227
    and experience, 226, 228–229
    and knowledge, 226–228
    used for contemporary issues, 231–232
    used for problem solving, 231–232
Information
    in advertising, 321

    and facts/opinions, 254–257
    and inferences, 226–230
    for problem solving, 173–174, 177
    as purpose, 277–279
    research for, 120–122
    and tone, 293–294
Informed opinions, 255–256
Interest of readers, catching, 322
Internet
    for additional activities, 49, 105, 167, 220, 248, 273, 317, 373
    for reasearch, 120–122
Interviews, 120
Introductory paragraphs, 73
Ironic events, 296–297
Ironic messages, 296–297
Ironic tone, 296–297
Irony, 296–297
Issues. *See* Contemporary issues
Italics, use of, 74, 78

Knowledge, and inferences, 226–228

Learning aids, 52–53, 73–74
Libraries, research at, 120
Listings of facts, 18–20
Logical conclusions, 136–137, 227–230, 232
Longer selections, central messages of, 28–31

Main ideas, 11–14, 18–23, 28, 76
Main purpose, 283
Main tone, 293
Major chapter headings, 74, 76
Major details, 11–14, 19–23, 30–31, 78
Mastery tests, 38–49, 94–104, 160–167, 211–220, 245–247, 269–273, 307–317, 357–371
Matter-of-fact tone, 294
Meanings. *See* Definitions
Messages
    central, 28–31, 76, 78, 141–142
    topics as, 11–14

Minor chapter headings, 74, 76
Minor details, 11–14, 19, 78
Mood. *See* Tone

Name indexes, 53, 71
Notes, 53

Objectives, 52, 73
Objectivity, 254, 283, 294
Observation, personal, 254
Opinions
    in combination with facts, 256
    defined, 255–256
    distinguished from facts, 252–254
    and purpose, 280
    used for contemporary issues, 256–257
    used for problem solving, 254, 256–257
Opposing viewpoints, 139, 142–143
Organization
    in critical thinking, 114
    patterns of, 18–23, 28–30, 76, 78
Outlines, 52, 74
Overviewing, 52–53, 73, 76

Paragraphs
    of chapters, 73–74
    main ideas in, 11–14, 28
    major/minor details in, 11–14
    organization in, 18–23
Parentheses, 5–6
Patterns of organization, 18–23, 28–30, 76, 78
Personal observation, 254
Personal opinions, 254–255
Personal problem solving, 172–176
Personal viewpoints, 139, 143–145
Persuasion
    in advertising, 321, 323–325
    as purpose, 280–281
Possible solutions, 174–178
Prefaces, 53, 62–65
Prejudices, 121–122, 254–255
Previewing, 73–74, 76
Previews, 52, 74
Problem solving
    application for typical problems, 176–178
    approaches, 172
    defined, 170–171
    and critical thinking, 172
    facts/opinions used for, 254, 256–257
    inferences used for, 231–232

    method for personal problems, 172–176
Problems
    breaking down, 173–174, 177
    checking back on, 176, 178
    choosing possible solutions, 175–178
    defined, 170–171
    identifying, 173, 176–177
    weighing possible solutions, 174–175, 177
Propaganda, 256
Punctuation, and meaning, 5–6
Purpose
    of advertisements, 321
    clear, 112
    combination, 283
    defined, 276–277
    to entertain, 282–283
    to inform, 277–279
    to persuade, 280–281

Questions
    about advertisements, 321–329
    in chapters, 74
    for contemporary issues, 141–142
    for critical reading, 75–78, 232
    for critical thinking, 114–115, 231–232
Quotation marks, 6

Random thinking, 108–109
Rationales, 142–144
Reading, critical. *See* Critical reading
"Reading between the lines," 293
Reference sources, 53, 68–69, 122
Reliability, 254, 276, 283
Reports, 120
Research, 120–122

Sad tone, 296
Secondary issues, 141–142
Sense of sentences, and meaning, 7
Sentences
    sense of, and meaning, 7
    topic, 11–14, 78
Simple listings of facts, 18–20
Skimming, 52, 73, 77
Solutions, 171, 174–178
Sources
    of facts, 254–255
    reference, 53, 68–69, 122
    research, 120–122
Subject indexes, 53, 72

Subjects. *See* Topics
Suggested readings, 53, 68–69
Summary paragraphs, 73–74
Synonyms, and meaning, 6

Tables of contents, 52–53, 57–61
Target groups, 322–323, 325
Textbook chapters, 28, 52
    critical reading of, 75–78
    parts of, 73–74
Textbooks
    parts of, 52–53, 55–72
    purpose to inform, 277
Thinking, critical. *See* Critical thinking
Time/effort, 114
Time, and problem solving, 175
Time sequences, 18, 20–21, 30
Title pages, 52, 55
Titles, 11, 28, 30, 73–74. *See also* Headings
Tone
    angry, 295
    combination, 293
    defined, 293–294
    humorous, 294–295
    ironic, 296–297

    matter-of-fact, 294
    sad, 296
Topic sentences, 11–14, 78
Topics
    of chapters, 73–74, 76, 78
    of longer selections, 28–31
    of paragraphs, 11–14
Transition words, 18–23

Underlining, 76–77
Understanding, aids to, 52–53, 73–74
Unstated main ideas, 13–14, 28

Viewpoints, 31, 283
    opposing, 139, 142–143
    personal, 139, 143–145
Vocabulary lists, 52, 74
Voice, tone of, 293

Web addresses, 121–122
Weighing possible solutions, 174–175, 177
Words
    definitions of, 4–7, 53, 66–67, 74, 76, 141
    transition, 18–23